SAMS Teach Yourself

COBOL

in 24 Hours

Thane Hubbell

SAMS 800 E. 96th Street, Indianapolis, Indiana, 46240 USA

Sams Teach Yourself COBOL in 24 Hours
Copyright © 1999 by Sams Publishing

International Standard Book Number: 0-672-31453-3

Library of Congress Catalog Card Number: 98-87215

04   9   8

Printed in the United States of America

FIRST PRINTING—December 1998

Trademarks

Warning and Disclaimer

EXECUTIVE EDITOR
Tracy Dunkelberger

ACQUISITIONS EDITOR
Holly Allender

DEVELOPMENT EDITOR
Fran Hatton

TECHNICAL EDITORS
Jack Voltz
Howard E. Hinman

MANAGING EDITOR
Jodi Jensen

PROJECT EDITOR
Heather Talbot

COPY EDITOR
June Waldman

INDEXER
Tina Trettin

PROOFREADER
Cindy Fields

SOFTWARE DEVELOPMENT SPECIALIST
John Warriner

TEAM COORDINATOR
Michelle Newcomb

BOOK DESIGNER
Gary Adair

COVER DESIGNER
Aren Howell

LAYOUT TECHNICIANS
Ayanna Lacey
Heather Hiatt Miller

Contents at a Glance

Introduction   1

PART I COBOL PROGRAM BASICS   5

Hour 1   Getting Started   7
Hour 2   Writing Your First Program in COBOL   21
Hour 3   Different Data Types   39
Hour 4   Basic User Interface   61
Hour 5   Procedure Division   81
Hour 6   Manipulating Data   95
Hour 7   Manipulating String Data   111
Hour 8   Conditional Statements   125
Hour 9   The Evaluate Statement   141
Hour 10   Processing Loops   155
Hour 11   Advanced Perform Statements   171
Hour 12   Tables   187

PART II FILE HANDLING   207

Hour 13   Sequential Files   209
Hour 14   Indexed Files   231
Hour 15   Reading Indexed File Records   249
Hour 16   Updating Indexed File Records   269
Hour 17   Sorting   285

PART III BUSINESS PROCESSING   303

Hour 18   Master File Updating   305
Hour 19   Reporting   327
Hour 20   Advanced Reporting   343

PART IV MISCELLANEOUS FUNCTIONS   365

    Hour 21   Date Manipulation   367

    Hour 22   Other Intrinsic Functions   389

PART V ADVANCED TOPICS   407

    Hour 23   The Call Interface   409

    Hour 24   The Graphical User Interface   427

APPENDIX A   QUIZ AND EXERCISE QUESTIONS AND ANSWERS   SEE CD-ROM

    INDEX   451

Contents

INTRODUCTION **1**

Who Should Read This Book 1

Special Elements of This Book 1

Q&A and Workshop 2

Conventions Used in This Book 3

PART 1 COBOL PROGRAM BASICS **5**

HOUR 1 GETTING STARTED **7**

COBOL Purpose and History 7

    Business Data Processing 8

    COBOL: The Language of Business...9

The Origin of COBOL 10

    Grace Hopper...10

The COBOL Standard 11

Installing the Compiler 12

    Required Hardware and Software 13

    Using the Examples in This Book..13

    How to Install the Fujitsu Compiler 13

    Validating the Install 15

Summary 19

Q&A 19

Workshop 20

HOUR 2 WRITING YOUR FIRST PROGRAM IN COBOL **21**

COBOL Program Layout 21

    Identification Division 23

    Environment Division 24

    Data Division...26

    Procedure Division 27

Creating a Simple COBOL Program 28

Compiling and Linking..33

    When It Won't Compile 36

    Debugging Your Program 37

Summary 38

Q&A 38

Workshop 38

HOUR 3 DIFFERENT DATA TYPES   **39**

The Picture Clause 40
  The Meaning of the Different Level Numbers 40
Numeric Fields 41
  Decimal Values 43
  Handling the Sign 43
  The Usage Clause...44
Alphanumeric Fields..46
Literals 47
Numeric Edited Fields 48
Alphanumeric Edited Fields 51
Group and Elementary Level Items 52
Using Data Types in a Program 55
Summary...59
Q&A 59
Workshop 59

HOUR 4 BASIC USER INTERFACE   **61**

Interfacing with the User 61
  Batch Versus Interactive Processing 62
The Screen Section..62
  Elements of the Screen Section 63
  Special-Names Paragraph 70
Using the Screen Section in a Program 72
Summary...79
Q&A 79
Workshop 79

HOUR 5 PROCEDURE DIVISION   **81**

Procedure Division Organization 81
  Paragraphs 82
  Sections 82
Arithmetic Statements..83
  The Add Statement 83
  The Subtract Statement 86
  The Multiply Statement 87
  The Divide Statement 88
  The Compute Statement 89
Simple Data Manipulation 90
  The Move Statement 90
Summary...93
Q&A 93
Workshop 94

HOUR 6 MANIPULATING DATA **95**

The `Accept` Statement 96

    Accepting from the User 96

    Accepting Data from the System 97

The `Initialize` Statement 98

The `Inspect` Statement 100

Reference Modification 103

Using What You Have Learned in a Program..104

Summary 108

Q&A 108

Workshop 109

HOUR 7 MANIPULATING STRING DATA **111**

The `String` Statement...112

    `String` Delimiters 114

The `Unstring` Statement 118

    `Unstring` Delimiters 118

Summary 122

Q&A 122

Workshop 123

HOUR 8 CONDITIONAL STATEMENTS **125**

Conditional Statements in COBOL 126

    The `If` Statement...126

    The `Else` Clause 131

    Using Complex Conditions 132

    Nesting `If` Statements 135

88 Levels and the `Set` Statement 136

    Using 88 Levels in an `If` Statement 137

Summary 139

Q&A 139

Workshop 140

HOUR 9 THE EVALUATE STATEMENT **141**

When to Use `Evaluate` 141

Simple `Evaluate` Statements 143

More Complex `Evaluate` Usage...147

Summary 153

Q&A 154

Workshop 154

HOUR 10 PROCESSING LOOPS   **155**

The Basic Perform Statement 156

Sections and Paragraphs..157

Creating Processing Loops Using Perform 159

Use of Go To 163

Summary 169

Q&A 169

Workshop 170

HOUR 11 ADVANCED PERFORM STATEMENTS   **171**

Perform with Varying 172

Testing Before or After 173

The Use of the Inline Perform 174

Nesting Perform Statements 177

The Inline If Statement and Perform..178

Using the Debugger 181

Summary 183

Q&A 184

Workshop 185

HOUR 12 TABLES   **187**

Defining a Table 187

Basic Table Handling 189

Populating a Table in Working-Storage...189

The Redefines Clause 189

The Search Statement..195

Multidimensional Tables..200

Variable-Length Tables 203

Summary 204

Q&A 205

Workshop 206

PART II FILE HANDLING   **207**

HOUR 13 SEQUENTIAL FILES   **209**

Connecting Your Program to a File 211

The Select Statement 211

The File Description 213

Opening the File 214

Closing the File...215

Writing to the File..215
Reading from the File...220
Updating the File 225
Variable-Length Records 228
Summary 229
Q&A 229
Workshop 230

HOUR 14 INDEXED FILES   **231**

Defining the Indexed File..233
The Select Statement for Indexed Files...................................233
Creating an Indexed File from a Sequential File 235
Creating Indexed File Records from User Input...........................239
Other Methods of Handling File Errors 244
Summary 247
Q&A 247
Workshop 248

HOUR 15 READING INDEXED FILE RECORDS   **249**

Various Access Methods 250
Sequential Access 250
Random Access 256
Dynamic Access 258
Summary 266
Q&A 267
Workshop 267

HOUR 16 UPDATING INDEXED FILE RECORDS   **269**

Opening for I-O 270
Writing Records 270
Rewriting Records 271
Deleting Records...274
Relative Files..275
Summary 282
Q&A 283
Workshop 284

HOUR 17 SORTING   **285**

Sorting a File..286
The Using and Giving Clauses 287
Manipulating Data During the Sort 292
The Input Procedure 292
The Output Procedure 296

Summary 300
Q&A 300
Workshop 301

PART III BUSINESS PROCESSING   **303**

HOUR 18 MASTER FILE UPDATING   **305**

Programming for Transaction Entry 306
Data Validation 310
Updating a Master File 313
    Updating a `Sequential` Master File 314
    Updating an `Indexed` Master File 320
Summary 325
Q&A 326
Workshop 326

HOUR 19 REPORTING   **327**

Creating Reports 328
    Designing Your Report Layout 328
    The `Write` Statement and Reports 330
    Programming for Page Breaks 331
Summary 340
Q&A 340
Workshop 341

HOUR 20 ADVANCED REPORTING   **343**

Reporting with Control Breaks..344
    Determining the Number and Hierarchy of Control Breaks.........344
    Subtotaling...345
    Walking Through a Program with Control Breaks 346
Summary 363
Q&A 363
Workshop 364

PART IV MISCELLANEOUS FUNCTIONS   **365**

HOUR 21 DATE MANIPULATION   **367**

Determining the Current System Date 368
    The `Current-Date` Intrinsic Function 369
Days Between Dates...371
Determining the Day of the Week for a Particular Date 374
Validating Dates 376
Other Kinds of Dates 382

Fun with Dates 383

Summary 386

Q&A 387

Workshop 387

HOUR 22 OTHER INTRINSIC FUNCTIONS **389**

Mathematical Functions 390

Statistical Functions 393

Financial Functions..395

String Functions 397

Miscellaneous Functions..403

Summary 404

Q&A 405

Workshop 405

PART V ADVANCED TOPICS **407**

HOUR 23 THE CALL INTERFACE **409**

Calling Other Programs 410

Simple Program Calling 410

Passing Data Between Programs 416

The Linkage Section 418

The Procedure Division of the Called Program 418

Call By Reference and By Content 420

Dynamic Versus Static Calls 421

Using Copybooks 424

Summary 425

Q&A 426

Workshop 426

HOUR 24 THE GRAPHICAL USER INTERFACE **427**

Different Methods of Achieving the Graphical User Interface 428

Using sp2 to Create a Graphical User Interface 429

Designing Your Panel 429

Modifying the Generated Program 437

The Future of COBOL 449

Summary 450

APPENDIX A QUIZ EXERCISE QUESTIONS AND ANSWERS **SEE CD-ROM**

INDEX **451**

Dedication

For my wife Darlene, for her patience, understanding, and love.

Acknowledgments

Writing a book is not unlike the team effort involved in developing a complex software system. The people at Sams Publishing are consummate professionals. Their input, support, encouragement, and guidance have been invaluable. I want to especially recognize Holly Allender, Sean Dixon, Fran Hatton, and Heather Talbot.

In the COBOL community, several individuals deserve special recognition. Bob Wolfe is the individual who first piqued my interest in a book opportunity. His contacts landed me a spot on the *COBOL: Unleashed* team, which in turn led to this work.

I had the utmost privilege of historical perspective from an individual who was *there* and involved when COBOL began. Warren G. Simmons's insight and advice proved invaluable to the completion of this book.

Another individual who deserves mention is Don Nelson, current COBOL standards committee member. Don was heavily involved in the 1985 COBOL standard, and helped me greatly in areas concerning why things are the way they are, and what really *is* part of the present standard. For COBOL syntax, I relied on Don's excellent book, *COBOL85 for Programmers*.

The chapter on date manipulation was particularly interesting to write. I want to thank Judson McClendon for his assistance and advice on those issues, and on COBOL coding style in general.

Todd Yancy of Fujitsu Software Corporation assisted in securing the compiler for use with this book. The Fujitsu COBOL compiler is a strong, stable, and accurate compiler. Todd and Fujitsu have been instrumental in trying to bring the price of COBOL compilers within the reach of the average individual programmer.

Last, but certainly not least, I want to thank my very special partner, friend, and mate—my wife, Darlene. She supported me throughout this all-consuming process. She gave up much of her time with me to allow me the time to write this book. Her contribution is personal, and lovingly appreciated.

Lest I forget from whence this talent springs, I must thank God for granting me the gift of this talent for programming, and the ability to convey it in some small measure to the reader.

About the Author

THANE HUBBELL has been programming in COBOL for 15 years. He started in computer operations and rapidly moved into programming. He has worked on a variety of platforms, from the PC up to the large MVS mainframe systems. Along the way, he has had the opportunity to develop new systems ranging in size from small, isolated programs to large, interactive, enterprise-driving systems.

He has designed and written applications ranging from a full CICS security and menuing system in COBOL to a VSAM database inquiry and reporting tool. Thane is a pilot and one of his more interesting projects was a system to translate FAA-formatted Aviation weather reports into English.

Thane makes his home in Texas and is married to a wonderful woman, Darlene, who kindly tolerates the spare time he spends programming on his computer after work. Occasionally he will even take on a custom programming project for her.

Thane can be reached via email at cobol24@softwaresimple.com, and frequents the comp.lang.cobol Internet newsgroup.

Tell Us What You Think!

As the reader of this book, *you* are our most important critic and commentator. We value your opinion and want to know what we're doing right, what we could do better, what areas you'd like to see us publish in, and any other words of wisdom you're willing to pass our way.

As an associate publisher with Sams Publishing, I welcome your comments. You can email or write me directly to let me know what you did or didn't like about this book—as well as what we can do to make our books stronger.

Please note that I cannot help you with technical problems related to the topic of this book, and that due to the high volume of mail I receive, I might not be able to reply to every message.

When you write, please be sure to include this book's title and author as well as your name and phone or fax number. I will carefully review your comments and share them with the author and editors who worked on the book.

Email: `feedback@samspublishing.com`
Mail: Mike Stephens
        Executive Editor
        Sams Publishing
        800 E. 96th Street
        Indianapolis, IN 46240 USA

Introduction

Written in a clear, easy to follow format, this book was designed to help you learn COBOL as quickly as possible.

The numerous real-world examples and exercises in this book will help you to understand computer programming, and COBOL in particular. This book provides a complete grounding in the COBOL language. After completing this book, you should be able to write useful and meaningful computer programs using COBOL.

Who Should Read This Book

The lessons in this book assume no previous computer programming experience. The lessons can be used as an introduction to COBOL specifically, and computer programming in general. Even experienced COBOL programmers, who want to find out the latest techniques available in the current COBOL standard, will find this book valuable.

Special Elements of This Book

This book contains the following special elements that make the presentation clearer and easier to understand:

- New Term Boxes
- Notes
- Tips
- Cautions

 New terms and definitions are explained in New Term boxes. These are introduced throughout the lessons as required by the material being covered.

Interesting information relating to the discussion is presented in these notes.

Tips and interesting shortcuts are represented in this manner, for easy recognition. Tips can help make your coding easier and more accurate.

Common pitfalls and misconceptions are presented as cautions. When a caution appears, you can be assured that the potential problems discussed occur in the real world of COBOL programming.

Throughout the lessons, full and partial examples from actual programs are listed. When a complete program is included in the text, it will be signified with a listing heading. This serves to offset the full program listings from the text. You will often find explanations of the programs embedded in the listings. The listing itself will appear in an easy to identify, monospace font. A simple listing example follows:

LISTING INTRODUCTION.1   HELLO WORLD

```
000001 @OPTIONS MAIN
000002 Identification Division.
000003 Program-Id.  Hello.
000004 Environment Division.
000005 Configuration Section.
000006 Source-Computer.  IBM-PC.
000007 Object-Computer.  IBM-PC.
000008 Data Division.
000009 Procedure Division.
000010 Hello-Start.
000011    Display "Hello World".
000012    Stop Run.
```

The lines in the program are numbered so that I can refer to them later in the text, explaining the different elements of the program. The goal is to prevent the code from being unwieldy for the user—that's you!

Q&A and Workshop

Following each chapter, you'll find a "Q & A" section, where issues relating to the material covered in the lesson are discussed. Selected areas are reinforced and explanations are expanded.

In the *Sams Teach Yourself in 24 Hours* series, usually after the Q&A section, you will find a quiz and a programming exercise. However, to conserve pages, in *Sams Teach Yourself COBOL in 24 Hours*, we have opted to move this information to the CD-ROM accompanying the book. This information is not just extraneous stuff we're adding to beef up the CD. Answering the quiz questions correctly assures you that the material covered has been completely understood. The programming exercises build on the concepts covered in the chapter and require you to make that small, but essential extra leap in understanding to solve the problem. Some are simple modifications of programs discussed within the chapter, whereas others are completely new programs that need to be created. For optimum retention and understanding, I urge you to work through the quiz questions and exercise section as you finish an hour.

Conventions Used in This Book

This book uses special typefaces to help you differentiate between text used to explain the concepts, and the elements of the COBOL language. Anytime a reserved COBOL word is used, or a data item is encountered, it will appear in a special `monospace` font.

The CD-ROM that comes with the book contains the Fujitsu compiler and the third-party GUI screen design tool, COBOL sp2 from Flexus International. In addition, the source code for all the examples and exercises is included. To aid you in understanding the examples, each is accompanied by a Lotus Screencam™ movie, which can be found in the \CAMS directory of the CD-ROM.

Thane Hubbell
Bryan, Texas
December 1998

PART I
COBOL Program Basics

Hour

1 Getting Started
2 Writing Your First Program in COBOL
3 Different Data Types
4 Basic User Interface
5 Procedure Division
6 Manipulating Data
7 Manipulating String Data
8 Conditional Statements
9 The Evaluate Statement
10 Processing Loops
11 Advanced Perform Statements
12 Tables

HOUR 1

Getting Started

Welcome to *Sams Teach Yourself COBOL in 24 Hours*. In the first hour, you learn about the following:

- The history and purpose of COBOL
- The special requirements of business data processing
- The mother of modern information technology and COBOL in particular
- Installing and using your compiler

COBOL Purpose and History

NEW TERM   *COBOL* stands for Common Business Oriented Language. It is one of the oldest high-level computer programming languages. The purpose of a programming language is to communicate instructions to the computer. Each type of *central processing unit*, or CPU, understands a particular set of instructions. Because these instructions appear cryptic and confusing to humans, the early pioneers of the computer industry developed programming languages. These languages, which add a layer of comprehension for the programmer and analyst, are translated into the native instructions of the computer's processor, otherwise known as *machine language*. The process of translating the original program, or *source code*, into machine language is called *compilation*. The compiler program translates (or compiles) the source code, that is, code with instructions that humans can understand, into machine language.

> A *high-level* language is one that must be converted or translated into machine language. The closer a language is to machine language, the lower its level. Languages in which each statement in the source language corresponds to only one or two machine language instructions are very low-level languages. When source statements are converted, or compiled, into many machine language statements, as is the case with COBOL, the programming language is considered a high-level language.

COBOL is essentially a recipe for making a program. You list the ingredients, determine the amounts and proportions for the mixture, and describe the order and method of their assembly. You could mix the batter for a cake, including all the proper ingredients in all the proper proportions, but until it is baked, it can't be served. The compiler program is what takes your program recipe and prepares it for the computer's consumption.

Business Data Processing

Business data processing began long before computers entered the picture. In the interest of efficiency, businesses found ways to handle the large volume of information necessary to successfully manage their operation. Computers were initially considered the tools of scientists and engineers. However, business rapidly recognized the value of computers in automating tedious and repetitive tasks that were necessary for the success of commerce.

The computing needs of business are unique and are different from those in the scientific or engineering fields. Programming languages geared toward solving complex engineering or mathematical formulas were ill suited to business processing. Early scientific computations centered on solving complex mathematical formulas. The computer could make these calculations with much more speed and accuracy. In contrast, business typically does not need to solve complex mathematical formulas. Business processing centers more on large amounts of transactional data and is geared more toward financial accuracy.

Businesses typically collected transactional data and applied those transactions manually to books or ledgers. Entire divisions of large companies were dedicated to bookkeeping. Reports were carefully prepared for management to analyze. Creating and analyzing these reports was a time-consuming process, and in many cases businesses were harmed because they were unable to react to events in a timely manner.

The advent of the computer changed all that. Business readily accepted the computer into its daily operation. Business now demands fast and reliable results. These results help businesses stay competitive and viable.

COBOL: The Language of Business

COBOL is ideally suited to business processing. Business processing involves data collection, validation, updating, and reporting. The types of data processed are frequently numbers and amounts. No other computer language is as well equipped to excel at this type of processing.

COBOL was designed to be an easy-to-understand and self-documenting language. It intentionally mirrors common English. As a COBOL programmer, I can testify to the fact that nearly anyone can look at a section of a COBOL program and see exactly what is happening. I have had people look over my shoulder as I examine a program and understand exactly what is occurring and why.

Although COBOL is the language of business, its use has grown over time to include many other areas. Any organization that follows common business practices can take advantage of the strengths of the COBOL language. Governments are a prime example. They operate very much like businesses, and their needs are often satisfied by the use of COBOL as the primary computer programming language.

Contrary to popular media description, COBOL is far from a dead language. If COBOL is dead, someone forgot to tell the computer programs that hold businesses together! COBOL is the dominant computer language for business processing applications. Even in areas in which COBOL was once considered inappropriate, it has made tremendous inroads. Client/server development is relying more and more upon COBOL.

Client/server processing has become the watchword of the day. In a nutshell, it involves a central server, usually holding a repository of information that is accessed by clients that attach to this server. Large mainframes and COBOL programs have historically carried out these processes. Many businesses have tried to replace these systems with client/server processes, only to find the reliability and performance to be lacking. Consequently, large mainframes frequently become the server in client/server processing, with the root business logic written in COBOL remaining intact. COBOL is used today for both the client side and the server side of client/server processes.

At the root of COBOL is a very simple set of instructions. Like any good game, the rules are simple, but using those rules in combination can make for a very fun and challenging adventure.

This book uses real-world business examples to illustrate and teach programming techniques. The sample business I have chosen is a small consignment or antique store. No matter what the source of your interest in learning COBOL, these examples will help you to understand the language and make learning fun.

The Origin of COBOL

The first specification for COBOL was developed in 1959 by the Conference on Data Systems Language, or CODASYL. Its goal was to define a common business computer programming language, and COBOL was the result. The design of the language was heavily influenced by the only business programming language in use at the time, FLOW-MATIC. FLOW-MATIC was the brainchild of a very interesting and colorful individual, whose influence on data processing and the use of computers in modern life is often and frequently understated. That person is Admiral Grace Murray Hopper.

Grace Hopper

Admiral Grace Murray Hopper (1906–1992) is generally considered to be the mother of business computing and COBOL. Her early insights and ideas have echoed down through the years and still affect the entire information technology industry. Admiral Hopper was a strong advocate for the use of computers in business. She was the first to advocate sharing common libraries of programming code. Throughout her life, she stressed efficiency in programming, desiring that programmers not waste even a microsecond of time. She actively participated in demonstrations of COBOL, showing how the language lent itself to machine independence. COBOL was the first cross-platform, compatible language and remains one of the few programming languages that can easily be rehosted to other platforms.

 Rehosting is changing a program to run on a different platform. For example, you might take a COBOL program written for a mainframe computer and recompile it, making any necessary changes, and then run it on a personal computer. This type of change is an example of rehosting.

Grace began her work in computers as a research fellow at Harvard University from 1946 to 1949 in the computing laboratory. While there she developed the first compiler, a program that converted mnemonics into machine language, called A-0. Grace was convinced that computers could be a great boon to business and, to that end, started working with the UNIVAC series of computers at a company that later became Sperry. She firmly believed that computers should be programmed in English, but was admonished that computers did not understand English. She made sure that they could.

Her first English-like computer language was FLOW-MATIC, which understood 20 English words. The language was geared toward activities such as payroll processing and automated billing. It took several years for her approach to be accepted, and in 1952, she published her first compiler paper.

Grace participated in the early CODASYL meetings that defined the standard for COBOL. She stayed on the committee as one of its two technical advisors. She remained a strong COBOL advocate. After entering the U.S. Navy, she was instrumental in the Department of Defense move to make COBOL its first required programming language. Her work with the Navy on standardization remains one of her most important legacies. She developed tests to validate the different COBOL compilers. Her work led directly to the formation of different international and national standards for programming languages.

Along with her work on computer programming languages and data processing in general, Admiral Hopper is credited with coining the term *computer bug*. When a computer problem was traced to a moth stuck in one of the electronic relays, Hopper taped the offender in her logbook next to the entry "bug."

A famous quote that is widely used in computer circles is attributed to her: "It's always easier to ask forgiveness than it is to get permission."

The COBOL Standard

In 1968 the American National Standards Institute (ANSI), in an attempt to eliminate the growing incompatibility between different COBOL compilers, developed a common standard for the language. This version was called ANS COBOL. Programs written to this standard will continue to compile 30 years later. Although the language today has many more features and enhancements, many programs written in the 1960s are still in use. In the last year, I have maintained programs that were originally written in 1972.

The COBOL standard was revised in 1974, adding many new features. This version received wide acceptance and was the basis for IBM's VS COBOL. In 1985 the language was again revised, further enhancing and enriching COBOL. Several very powerful features were added to aid in the development of structured programs.

> This book generally follows the structured programming approach.
> *Structured programs* have small, organized sections of processing. Each area
> performs only a single function. Structured programming avoids the GO TO
> statement, which branches, or jumps, to another place in the program with-
> out returning; structured programs proceed in an organized and orderly
> fashion and do not jump from place to place with little rhyme or reason.
> Structured programming uses a top-down design approach. Each major
> function is made up of smaller functions, each of which is also made up of
> smaller functions, and so on until the problem is broken down to individual
> programming statements. Structured programs are easy to maintain and
> debug.

NEW TERM In 1989 a special modification to the 1985 standard was issued. This modification introduced an item called intrinsic functions. *Intrinsic functions* formalized
some of the features most desired by COBOL programmers, including many that relate
to the next century. Prior to the 1989 extensions, COBOL did not have a formally
defined method for determining the current four-digit year. The Current Date intrinsic
function solved that problem in 1989, a full 11 years before problems processing two-
digit years would occur, in the year 2000.

The 1985 standard, with the 1989 extensions, is the current standard for COBOL. The
ANSI committee is currently considering the next standard, which will include object
orientation. Several compiler vendors are beginning to support features that are in the
next standard.

This book conforms to the current COBOL standard with one exception. In an effort to
standardize the user interface portion of COBOL, because none was defined in the ANSI
standard, a committee named X/OPEN defined a language extension called the Screen
Section. A form of the Screen Section is included in the pending COBOL standard.
Most compiler vendors already support the Screen Section, and the examples and
exercises in this book should work with those compilers.

Installing the Compiler

The accompanying CD-ROM contains a Windows-based COBOL compiler. Fujitsu
COBOL has been kind enough to provide its free COBOL starter kit for your use with
this book. This compiler has everything you need to learn COBOL and to compile and
run the exercises and examples. Although the examples work with other COBOL compilers, many elements related to writing programs are closely linked to the development

tools used. It is beyond the scope of this book to cover all of the many available COBOL compilers. All examples and exercises are geared toward the Fujitsu COBOL development environment.

Required Hardware and Software

The following hardware and software are required to run the Fujitsu COBOL compiler:

- 486 or better processor
- VGA graphics display monitor
- 25MHz CPU or better (recommended)
- Mouse or other pointing device
- 5MB RAM
- 48MB of available hard disk space for basic configuration; more to install the on-disk documentation and utilities
- CD-ROM drive

Using the Examples in This Book

All the examples, exercises, and quiz answers are included on the CD-ROM and can be used with the Fujitsu development environment, also on the CD-ROM. If you are using a different compiler, you will have to familiarize yourself with the requirements for that development environment and compiler.

How to Install the Fujitsu Compiler

Take the time now to install and test the Fujitsu COBOL 3.0 Starter Set compiler. You will use the development environment and compiler very shortly. These steps guide you through the installation process.

1. Insert the CD-ROM into your CD-ROM drive.
2. Click the Start button.
3. Choose Run.
4. Choose Browse.
5. Select the down arrow next to Look In.
6. Choose your CD-ROM drive.
7. Double-click the COBOL32 folder.
8. Choose SETUP.EXE and click the Open button.
9. Click OK.

10. When the required serial number entry appears, type in **99-03811-10092**, making sure to include the dashes. The first portion of the number is provided for you, and it must remain on the screen. Do not overtype this number; only complete it with the number above. The full number entered should be 103-2001-1699-03811-10092.

    Next, you are prompted to select the different options for the install. I suggest using the default options. However, if you are interested in installing other features and tools, feel free to do so. The instructions associated with these are presented during the install. These additional options require significantly more disk space.

11. Follow the onscreen instructions, choosing the default values for all selections.

12. After the setup process is complete, restart your computer.

The following instructions install the 16-bit Windows 3.1 version of the Fujitsu compiler, also included on the accompanying CD-ROM.

1. Insert the CD-ROM into your CD-ROM drive.

2. From Program Manager, click File, and then click Run.

3. At the command line, type **d:\COBOL16\SETUP.EXE**.

   Replace the **d:** with the drive letter of your CD-ROM drive.

4. Click OK to begin the installation process.

5. Click Next to acknowledge the copyright.

6. Click Yes to accept the license agreement.

7. Complete the serial number displayed so that the entire number reads as follows:
   103-2001-1699-03811-10092

8. Click Next.

9. Accept the default selections as provided by the install program and click Next.

   The next portion of the installation process selects the location for the install and copies the programs to your computer.

10. Accept the default installation location and click Next.

11. The default action on the next screen is to copy all the books to your hard drive. If you do not want to do so, and you want to save disk space, click the View Books from CD check box. You may then deselect the COBOL 85 Books and the PowerCOBOL Books check boxes. *Do not* deselect the PowerCOBOL 16-bit check box. Click Next.

12. Accept the default program folder by clicking Next.

13. Click Next once more to accept the install options. The program files will now be installed on your computer.

14. After the files are installed, you will be prompted to register the software. You may complete the registration or cancel that process.

    A long delay occurs between completing the registration and the installation of the Common Ground viewer. Your computer has not locked up, and the program will eventually proceed with the installation. This delay is upward of 2 minutes and is related to the launching of the secondary installation of the Common Ground viewer.

    In addition to the Common Ground viewer, you may elect to view the documents in Adobe™ Acrobat format. These viewers are included on the CD in the SOFT-COPY folder.

15. Continue with the installation of the Common Ground viewer, following the prompts.

16. After the Common Ground installation is complete, click the Return to Windows button; the installation of the rest of the system will complete.

17. Click OK to acknowledge the changes made to your AUTOEXEC.BAT file, adding the compiler to your path.

18. Click Finish to complete the installation.

Validating the Install

To make sure the compiler will run on your computer, you need to try to compile a program. The Fujitsu compiler comes with many examples and samples. Perform the following steps to compile and run one of the sample programs. Hour 2, " Writing Your First Program in COBOL," discusses the purpose for each of these steps. Performing them here ensures that the compiler software has installed properly.

1. Click the Start button.
2. Highlight Programs.
3. Highlight Fujitsu COBOL 3.0.
4. Click Programming Staff.
5. Click the Tools menu option.
6. Click WINCOB[Compile].
7. Click the Browse button.
8. The current folder will be the PCOBOL32 folder. Double-click the SAMPLES folder.
9. Double-click the SAMPLE1 folder.

At this point, some necessary compiler options must be set. The purpose for these options is covered in detail in the appropriate hours. To ensure that you can compile the sample programs and exercises, simply follow these instructions:

1. Single-click the SAMPLE1.COB item and then click Open.
2. Click the Options button.
3. Click the Add button.
4. Scroll down the window until you see Main. Single-click Main and then click the Add button.
5. The Compiler Option window appears. Click the Compile Program as Main Program radio button and then click the OK button.
6. Close the Compiler Options window by clicking the X in the upper-right corner.
7. Click the OK button.
8. Click the Compile button. A countdown clock appears during the compilation process.
9. When the compile is complete, an Editor window displays the results of the compiler diagnostics. The message should be the following:

    STATISTICS: HIGHEST SEVERITY CODE=I, PROGRAM UNIT=1.

10. Close the Editor window by clicking on the top X in the upper-right corner.
11. Close the WINCOB window by clicking the X in the upper-right corner.

Compiling the program is the first step applied against a source program to get it ready to run. The second step is to link the program. Linking is covered in more detail in Hour 2.

1. Click Tools again and select WINLINK[Link].
2. Click the Browse button.
3. A Browse Files window shows a single .OBJ file. Select that file and click Open.
4. Click the Add button.
5. Click the Link button.
6. When the link is finished, close the Link window by clicking the X in the upper-right corner.
7. Close the WINLINK window by clicking the X in the upper-right corner of the window.

After successfully compiling and linking the program, it is time to run the program. The Fujitsu Programming Staff development environment provides a shortcut for running the programs you have recently compiled and linked.

1. Select the Tools option again.

2. Select the WINEXEC[Execute] option.

3. Click the Browse button.

4. Choose SAMPLE1 and click Open.

5. Click the Execute button.

6. When the Runtime Environment Setup window appears, click OK.

7. This sample program accepts a single lowercase letter and displays a word that starts with that letter. For this test, type the letter **a** and press Enter.

8. The word *apple* appears and a message box tells you that the Console window is closed. Click OK. Your screen should now appear as illustrated in Figure 1.1.

9. Close the WINEXEC window by clicking the X in the upper-right corner.

10. Close the Programming Staff window by clicking the X in the upper-right corner.

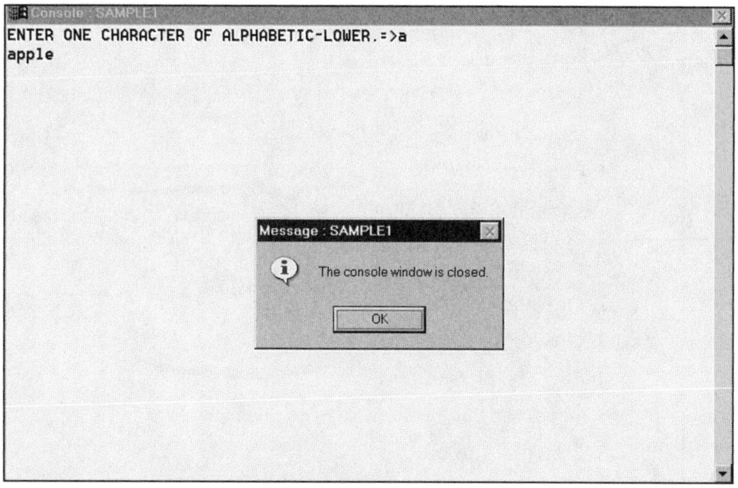

FIGURE 1.1

Results of running the Sample1 program.

If you are using Windows 3.1 and have installed the 16-bit version of the Fujitsu COBOL compiler, follow these instructions to compile and link the sample program:

1. Open the Fujitsu COBOL Family V2 program group by double-clicking the icon.

2. Start Programming Staff 16 by double-clicking the icon.

3. Click the Utilities menu option.

4. Click WINCOB.

5. Select Browse and double-click the SAMPLES folder.

6. Double-click the SAMPLE1 folder.

7. Click SAMPLE1.COB and then click OK to accept your selection.

At this point, some necessary compiler options must be set. The purpose for these options is covered in the correct context in later hours. To ensure that you can compile the sample programs and exercises, simply follow these instructions:

1. Click the Options menu item.

2. Click the Add button.

3. Scroll down to the word Main. Select it and then click the Add button.

4. Toggle on the Compile Program as Main Program option by clicking the radio button.

5. Click OK.

6. Click Exit.

7. Click OK in the Compiler Options window.

8. Click the Compile button to compile the program. A countdown clock appears during the compilation process.

9. When the compile is complete, an Editor window appears with the results of the compiler diagnostics. The message should be the following:

   STATISTICS: HIGHEST SEVERITY CODE=I, PROGRAM UNIT=1.

10. Close this window by double-clicking the upper-left corner of the window.

11. Close the WINCOB window by selecting the Exit menu option.

    Compiling the program is the first step applied against a source program to get it ready to run. The second step is to link the program. Linking is covered in more detail in Hour 2.

12. Click the Utilities menu option.

13. Choose WINLINK.

14. Click the Browse button.

15. Select the Sample1.obj file and click OK.

16. Click the Add button.

17. Click the Build button to link the program.

18. After the program is linked, a message box displays the following message: `Linking files has ended.` Click OK.

19. Close the WINLINK window by selecting the Exit menu option.

After successfully compiling and linking the program, it is time to run the program. The Fujitsu Programming Staff development environment provides a shortcut for running the programs you have recently compiled and linked.

1. Click the Utilities menu option again.

2. Click WINEXEC.

3. Click the Browse button, select Sample1.EXE, and then click OK.

4. Click the Execute button to run the program.

5. When the Runtime Environment Setup:SAMPLE1 window appears, click Run.

6. Type the letter **a** and press Enter.

7. Your screen should display the word *apple,* and a message box states The con-sole window is closed. The screen should look a lot like Figure 1.1. (Because you are using Windows 3.1, the look of the window border and the message box icon will be slightly different from the figure's.)

8. Click OK to close the window. You may exit the WINEXEC utility by selecting the Exit menu option.

If all the steps completed successfully, you have installed the compiler and it can be used for all the exercises and examples in this book.

Summary

In this hour, you learned the following:

- COBOL is one of the earliest programming languages.
- COBOL is an English-like programming language, designed to satisfy the computing needs of business.
- The early design of COBOL, and business programming in general, was greatly influenced by Admiral Grace Hopper.
- Grace Hopper discovered the earliest computer bug, an actual insect in a computer.

Q&A

Q Why is COBOL such an accepted language?

A COBOL is an English-based language that is self-documenting and easy to understand. COBOL is the first language mandated for use by the U.S. Department of Defense. A version of COBOL exists for virtually every computing platform, and programs written for one computer are easy to convert to run on other computers.

Q Is COBOL easy to learn?

A Yes. COBOL is a fairly simple language. The commands and features that make up the language are in English and are easy to use and comprehend.

Q What is structured programming, and why is it important?

A Structured programming is a reverse building-block approach. The first element is a wall, which is made up of rows. Each row is made up of individual bricks, and each brick is made up of mud being poured into a mold and hardened by heat. In structured programming, the programmer breaks a large problem—building a wall, for example—into the next smallest task, which in this analogy is laying the bricks. This task is further broken down into making the bricks. In structured programming, each task performs one and only one function. The program follows one orderly path; it doesn't jump around from within one task, out to an unrelated task, and back. In contrast, a nonstructured program might jump to one place; then, depending on a condition, do something else; and then go in a different direction. This type of program is extremely hard to follow and debug. It's like following a piece of spaghetti through a dish, trying not to disturb the other strands of pasta. That's why nonstructured programs are sometimes referred to as "spaghetti code."

Workshop

To help reinforce your understanding of the material presented in this hour, refer to the section "Quiz and Exercise Questions and Answers" that can be found on the CD. This section contains quiz questions and exercises for you to complete, as well as the corresponding answers.

HOUR 2

Writing Your First Program in COBOL

In Hour 1, "Getting Started," you learned about the history of COBOL. You also installed and tested the compiler. In this hour, you learn the basic layout of a COBOL program and write your first program. This hour covers the following basics:

- The divisions of a COBOL program
- How to key a simple program into the editor
- Compiling, linking, and running your program
- What to do when the program won't compile

COBOL Program Layout

The layout, or format, of a COBOL program follows certain simple rules, which originated long ago when programs were punched onto 80-column punch cards. With COBOL, columns 1–6 are reserved for line numbering. Line numbers are not mandatory, nor do they have to be in sequence.

However, you can imagine how important these line numbers were if someone accidentally dropped a deck of program cards on the floor!

Column 7 is the continuation or indicator area. When a line is to be continued from a previous line, a dash – in column 7 indicates the continued line. Column 7 can also contain either an asterisk (*) to indicate a comment line or a slash (/) to cause a page eject, or new page, when printing a listing of the program.

NEW TERM   A *comment line* contains any comments the programmer wants to put into the program. Commenting a program is important for many reasons. It helps other programmers, or even you, figure out what you are trying to accomplish with the programming statements, or code, that you have written. In addition to a - or *, most compilers support Debugging mode. In this mode, a D in column 7 means that the line is to be included only when the program is compiled in Debugging mode. When Debugging mode is not selected, these lines are treated as comment lines. The compiler ignores any other character that appears in column 7.

> *Code*, *line*, and *programming statement* are different names that mean the same thing. The actual programs you write in the COBOL language are considered *source code*. In other words, they are the main source that you wrote. Your programs must be translated for the computer, which is why they are called *code*. Writing a program is also referred to as *coding*. A programmer's job is to code a program.

Columns 8–11 are considered Area A. Area A contains Division, Section, and Paragraph headings. If other statements appear in Area A, the program may or may not compile, depending on your compiler. Having the Paragraph and Section headings appear in Area A creates a more readable program. The statements under these headings appear to be indented. Throughout the lessons, you will see this convention in action.

Area B extends from column 12 through column 72. Some COBOL compilers ignore this right margin. To be safe, you should limit your code to column 72. The main body of your program appears in Area B.

Many modern compilers allow free-form coding. Free-format source, where the column numbers no longer matter, is being considered in the next COBOL standard, and many compiler vendors have implemented this option. However, a number of them have not. If you have source code that is free format, ignoring the limits of Area A and Area B, and you try to move this source to another compiler, the code might not compile. The safest practice is to follow the current standard and keep your code in Area B within columns 12–72.

Columns 73–80 are for program identification. When programs were on punch cards, the program name would typically appear here. This book ignores these columns.

In Hour 1, I compared a COBOL program to a recipe. COBOL programs are broken into four divisions. Like a recipe, the first sections contain the ingredients and the last section, the preparation instructions. Each division is further broken into paragraphs. Each division is explained further in the sections that follow. The four divisions of a COBOL program are

- Identification Division
- Environment Division
- Data Division
- Procedure Division

The only required division is the Identification Division; the others are optional. If you don't have anything to put under them, you may omit them. However, I suggest that you at least include the division headers, just in case you need to add something later.

Identification Division

The Identification Division identifies the program to the compiler. In the current defined standard for the COBOL language, the Identification Division consists of one paragraph: the Program-Id. The Program-Id contains the name of the program. This name is very important, as it controls the ultimate name of the program during execution. Any references the operating system makes to the program depend on this name. In Hour 23, "The Call Interface," you learn about COBOL programs calling and being called by other programs. The Program-Id is the name that is used when COBOL programs are called. When looking at older COBOL programs, you might see other paragraphs under the Identification Division. Although these paragraphs are accepted by the current COBOL standard, they are slated for removal in the next. The Identification Division is coded as follows:

```
000001 Identification Division.
000002 Program-Id.   NameOfProgram.
```

> Line numbers are indeed optional. In this book, however, they are included in all examples for later reference in the text.

> The names of the divisions, paragraphs, and statements in COBOL are not case sensitive. NameOfProgram is exactly the same as NAMEOFPROGRAM and nameofprogram. Note that each line, or sentence, in the code ends with a period.
>
> Prior to the 1985 COBOL standard, COBOL was case sensitive. All COBOL had to be coded with uppercase letters. If you look at older COBOL programs, you are likely to observe this type of coding.

Environment Division

The Environment Division contains information relating to the computer on which the program will run. The Environment Division consists of sections and paragraphs under those sections. The sections in the Environment Division are

- Configuration Section
- Input-Output Section

The Configuration Section contains three paragraphs. The first paragraph concerns the type of computer on which the program is being compiled, that is, the Source-Computer. The compiler vendor for the environment in which you are running defines the name of the computer. The programs in this book use IBM-PC. The Source-Computer Paragraph has one clause, and it is optional. This clause is the With Debugging Mode clause. Including this clause activates the lines of code with a D in the indicator column (column 7) the next time the program is compiled. The word With is optional on the With Debugging Mode clause.

The Object-Computer Paragraph describes the computer on which the program is designed to run. Rarely will you be compiling on one computer type and running on another. Again, use IBM-PC for the Object-Computer Paragraph. Only one clause to the

Object-Computer Paragraph is relevant in normal programming, and that is the Program Collating Sequence is clause. The Program Collating Sequence is clause describes the order of the characters for the program. When this clause is omitted, the collating sequence defaults to the collating sequence native for the computer on which the program runs. The programs in this book do not need to code the Program Collating Sequence is clause.

> Collating sequence is very important. Even when you use the native collating sequence of the computer, you need to understand it. Another way to think of collating sequence is as a sort sequence, or alphabetic sequence. You know that ABCDEFGHIJKLMNOPQRSTUVXYZ is the proper sequence of alphabetic letters. You know that E is greater than A, and the Z is the highest letter of all. This order describes the alphabet's collating sequence. The character set used by personal computers is ASCII. Each character is assigned a number in ASCII. The ASCII code for the letter A is 65, and the code for the letter E is 69. Therefore, the letter A comes before the letter E in the ASCII collating sequence. The native alphabet and collating sequence is ASCII. For other computers, the alphabet is different. In some cases, programmers working on multiple computers with different alphabets might want to use the native alphabet, but collate on a specific machine's alphabet. That is the purpose of the collating sequence is clause. In typical COBOL programming, the clause is rarely used.

The Special-Names Paragraph can contain numerous clauses. For the most part, this flexibility enables you to program for specific items that are provided either by the compiler being used or by the computer on which the program runs. The command line from the execution of the program is one of the items that Fujitsu COBOL lets you retrieve via a special name. Controlling the cursor position and determining which function keys are pressed are tasks that are accomplished using Special-Names. These tasks are discussed in more detail in Hour 4, "Basic User Interface," and Hour 6, "Manipulating Data."

Two useful clauses are Currency-Sign is and Decimal-point is Comma. They do exactly what they appear they do. With the Currency-Sign is clause, you can specify the symbol to be used for currency, and with the Decimal-point is Comma clause, you can use a comma instead of the decimal point to indicate decimal positions. A typical Configuration Section follows.

```
000001 Identification Division.
000002 Program-Id.  NameOfProgram.
000003 Environment Division.
000004 Configuration Section.
000005 Source-Computer.  IBM-PC With Debugging Mode.
000006 Object-Computer.  IBM-PC.
```

```
000007 Special-Names.
000008     Currency-sign is $.
```

Notice the With Debugging Mode clause on the Source-Computer line (line 0005). This clause activates any lines in the program that have a D in column 7. When With Debugging Mode is specified, the compiler uses these marked lines as if they were regular source code entries. Its use here is just to show you how it is turned on. This book does not contain any programs that use Debugging mode.

The Input-Output Section contains two paragraphs: File-Control and I-O Control. File-Control describes the use of data files in the COBOL program and is covered in depth throughout Part 2, "File Handling," and Part 3, "Business Processing." I-O Control describes the behavior and internal handling of some of the input and output with the associated files. The I-O Control is not often used.

An example of a typical COBOL program Input-Output Section follows.

```
000001 Identification Division.
000002 Program-Id.   NameOfProgram.
000003 Environment Division.
000004 Configuration Section.
000005 Source-Computer.   IBM-PC.
000006 Object-Computer.   IBM-PC.
000007 Input-Output Section.
000008 File-Control.
000009     Select Input-File assign to "IN.DAT".
```

Data Division

The Data Division describes the data used by the program. The data can come from input sources such as disk files or from intermediate data fields and working areas in storage. The Data Division is broken into the following sections:

- File Section
- Working-Storage Section
- Linkage Section
- Communications Section
- Report Section
- Screen Section

Each section has fairly detailed entries and is discussed in depth in the appropriate hours, with the exception of the Communications Section and the Report Section. The Report Section is used by a module of COBOL that is optional in the COBOL standard, called Report Writer. The Report Writer is not included in many COBOL implementations and is not included in this book. The Communications Section is used by another optional module, the Communications Facility, and it too is included here only in the interest of presenting a complete picture. Its usage is not discussed.

The File Section describes the files being used by the COBOL program. The entries under the File Section include file descriptions for regular input files, and sort descriptions for sort work files. Sort work files are temporary files used by the sort process within a COBOL program. Sorting is discussed in depth in Hour 17, "Sorting." One of COBOL's strengths is that it describes the contents of each file in great detail.

The Working-Storage Section describes data areas to be used by the program during its processing. Like the File Section, data areas are described in great detail. All data items referenced by the program are declared in one of the sections of the Data Division.

The Linkage Section passes data between programs.

The Screen Section describes a screen full of input, output, and update data for the user interface. In this book, the Screen Section communicates directly with the users of the programs. Each item is carefully and explicitly defined.

Following is a sample of a typical Data Division in a COBOL program:

```
000001 Identification Division.
000002 Program-Id.  NameOfProgram.
000003 Environment Division.
000004 Configuration Section.
000005 Source-Computer.  IBM-PC.
000006 Object-Computer.  IBM-PC.
000007 Input-Output Section.
000008 File-Control.
000009     Select Input-File assign to "IN.DAT".
000010 Data Division.
000011 File Section.
000012 FD  Input-file.
000013 01  Input-Record   Pic X(100).
000014 Working-Storage Section.
000015 01  Work-Field Pic X(20).
```

Procedure Division

The Procedure Division is where the program's processing occurs. In the Procedure Division, you tell the program how to assemble and use the ingredients you specified in the other divisions. The Procedure Division is made up of Sections and Paragraphs. Sections may be omitted if they are not required. For the most part, you will have no need to program any Sections in your Procedure Division. However, if you do, please remember that each `Section` entry must be followed by a `Paragraph` name. The use of `Paragraphs` and `Sections` is discussed in detail in Hour 5.

The `Procedure Division` must contain at least one `Paragraph`. The `Paragraph` name begins in `Area A` starting in column 8. With COBOL, all data, paragraph, and section names may be up to 30 characters long. You may use any convention you desire. Most COBOL programmers use the convention of separating words within names by dashes. For example: `Read-The-File`, could be a paragraph name, as could `ReadTheFile`. The dashed separated words are easier to read and understand.

Programming statements, or sentences, that appear under paragraph headings begin in `Area B`. Most of this book discusses areas of the `Procedure Division`.

Creating a Simple COBOL Program

Now is the time to put all these pieces together and write your first COBOL program. What would a programming book be without a Hello World program? This first program displays "Hello World" on the screen and then ends; it uses the `Display` statement.

The `Display` statement outputs data to an output device. Normally, this device is a CRT (monitor) or printer. The `Display` statement may use the `Upon` phrase to specify the device on which the display is to occur. If the `Upon` phrase is omitted, the default device, as defined by the specific compiler, is used. On IBM mainframes, this device is the printer. With the Fujitsu compiler, it is the `console`, which is your monitor. The name specified in the `Upon` phrase can also be a device name specified in the `Special-Names` clause. An example of the `Display` statement is

```
000100 Display "Hello World" Upon Console.
```

Console is the main operator console. For programming on a PC, it is the regular PC's display. Console is a COBOL reserved word. Any word that makes up the COBOL programming language, or is used for a special extension or enhancement to the language, is considered a reserved word. A reserved word cannot be used as a variable or data item name in your COBOL program. A list of reserved words is available in Appendix A of the Fujitsu COBOL language reference that is on the CD-ROM.

In addition to the Display statement, you need some way to tell the program to end. This is done with a Stop Run statement. The Stop Run behaves just as it sounds. When it is encountered, the program stops running. If you fail to code a Stop Run statement, most compilers insert it for you. However, it is good practice to always code the Stop Run statement where you want your program to stop.

> If you are using a compiler other than the Fujitsu COBOL compiler that comes on the CD-ROM, you will need to familiarize yourself with the methods for editing, compiling, and linking your programs with that compiler. Compiler directives may be different when using other compilers, and the procedures for compiling, linking, and running your programs will probably be different.

2

NEW TERM Before you start the editor and enter the lines of code for the program, you need to understand one more item. In addition to regular COBOL statements, the compiler may have to deal with compiler directives. Different COBOL compilers understand different compiler directives. *Compiler directives* tell the compiler how to behave when compiling this particular program. They can be used to make the process of compiling and linking your program much easier. When you compile your program, you have to tell the provided Fujitsu compiler whether your program is a Main program or a sub-program. For most of the examples and exercises in this book, the programs are Main programs. You indicate to the compiler that your program is a Main program by entering @OPTIONS MAIN on the first line of the program, before the Identification Division.

You should create a new folder on your computer to hold your source code. There are two easy ways to create this folder. I suggest you call it \TYCOBOL, which is the name used in this book.

One method to create the folder follows.

1. Click the Start button.
2. Select Programs.
3. Click the MS-DOS prompt icon.
4. At the prompt, type **MD\TYCOBOL** and press Enter.

Another method:

1. Double-click the My Computer icon.
2. Double-click the drive where you want to create the folder.
3. Click the File menu.

4. Select New.

5. Click Folder.

6. The cursor will on the new folder name. Change that name to **TYCOBOL** and press Enter.

7. Close the open windows.

The following procedure is used to create the TYCOBOL folder under Windows 3.1.

1. Open the Main program group by double-clicking its icon.

2. Open File Manager by double-clicking its icon.

3. Select the File menu option.

4. Choose the Create Directory option.

5. For the Name, type **\TYCOBOL**

   The \ is very important. If you forget it, the TYCOBOL directory is not created under your root directory and may be hard to find.

6. Click the OK button to create the directory.

7. Close File Manager by double-clicking the upper-left corner of the File Manager window.

Start the Fujitsu COBOL development environment, Programming Staff.

1. Click the Start button.

2. Select Programs.

3. Select Fujitsu Cobol 3.0.

4. Click Programming Staff.

Use the following steps under Windows 3.1 to start the Programming Staff development environment.

1. Open the Fujitsu COBOL Family V2 group by double-clicking its icon.

2. Double-click the Programming Staff 16 to start Programming Staff.

Now you need to create your new program.

1. Select the File menu.

2. Click New.

3. When the Editor window appears, again select the File menu.

4. Click New.

5. When the New dialog box appears, use the selection box to change the extension to COB and click the OK button.

The window shown in Figure 2.1 should now be displayed.

FIGURE 2.1

The new Editor window.

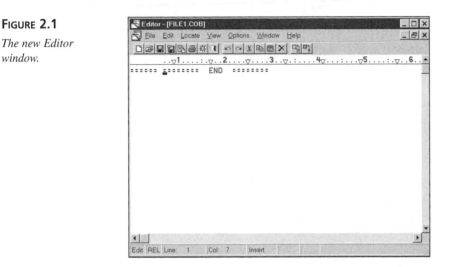

Notice that the cursor is in column 7 of the first line. Fujitsu inserts a space between column 6 and column 7 to separate the line numbers from your programming code. The space does not take up a character position. Before you enter any lines of code, you should change some of the editor settings. Normally, the editor numbers the lines in increments of 100. This convention is from the days when programs were on cards and programmers left a gap in the numbers so that cards could be inserted later without having to renumber the entire deck. The compiler reports errors by their relative line number, so to make finding these errors in your source easier, you should use the Relative line-numbering option. In addition, the compiler will color COBOL reserved words for you. This feature will help you tremendously as you start out programming in COBOL. However, by default, the compiler colors only words that are in all uppercase characters. You should change that option by deselecting the Match Case of Keyword check box. To do so, as well to change the line numbering to Relative, perform the following steps:

1. Select the View menu option.

2. Click Display Format.

3. Select the Relative radio button next to Line Number Type.

4. Deselect the Match Case of Keyword check box, making sure it is not checked.

5. Click the Save Setting check box.

6. Press the OK button.

> If you are using the 16-bit version of the compiler, for Windows 3.1, you will not have the options for Match Case and coloring the source code. Simply change the Relative radio button, select the Save Setting check box, and click OK.

You are ready to start entering your program. Start by typing in the necessary compiler option **@OPTIONS MAIN**. Make sure that you start in Area A, and that the phrase @OPTIONS MAIN is all in upper case. Do not terminate the line with a period. Line numbers are inserted automatically. Press the Enter key to advance to the next line. Next, type in the Identification Division. Be sure to start at the beginning of Area A (column 8).

On the next line, type the Program-Id Paragraph, again making sure to start in Area A. Immediately after Program-Id, on the same line type the name of your program. Call this one Hello. If you are typing the names correctly, Identification Division and Program-Id will be blue and the rest of the text will be black.

Next, type in the Environment Division and Configuration Section lines. You need to tell the compiler what type of computer will do the compiling and running. Don't forget to end each line with a period. Next type in the Source-Computer and Object-Computer Paragraphs. After each of these, on the same line, type **IBM-PC**. Be sure to put a period between Source-Computer and IBM-PC.

This program doesn't need anything further in the Environment Division. Next, enter the Data Division. Again, this program does not need anything under the Data Division, so go ahead and enter the Procedure Division.

The Procedure Division is where you tell the program what you want it to do. Every program must have at least one paragraph under the Procedure Division. Title the paragraph Hello-Start. Begin the paragraph title in Area A and make sure to end the title with a period.

The next step is to enter an actual statement telling the program what to do. Start the statement in Area B (column 12). Type **Display "Hello World".**, making sure to enclose the words *Hello World* in quotation marks.

The Fujitsu editor will help you find Areas A and B. At the bottom of the Editing window, the editor displays the line and column number. Remember that Area A begins in column 8 and Area B begins in column 12. (This feature is not available in the 16-bit Windows 3.1 version.)

Finally, on the next line, in Area B, enter the Stop Run statement telling the program to stop execution.

Save your program into the \TYCOBOL directory by selecting the File menu and the Save As option. Change the filename to **Hello.Cob**. Use the down arrow next to the Save In box to find and select the \TYCOBOL folder; then click the Save button.

Your program should appear exactly as illustrated in Figure 2.2. Compare your program with the figure and correct any obvious differences.

FIGURE 2.2

The Hello.Cob program.

Compiling and Linking

It's time to compile your program, but before you do, you need to understand the compile process. The compiler is a program that analyzes your source code, which is the program you just entered, performing several functions. The compiler checks your program for syntax errors. A syntax error occurs when the statement entered does not follow the defined rules for the language. The compiler checks for required elements, such as the Identification Division and Program-Id. It checks to make sure that all of your

Division headings, Sections, and Paragraphs start in the proper columns. It checks for dependencies, areas where you must define something before you can reference it later. Some basic logic errors are also checked. For example, if you define a file to your program, but never open it, the compiler issues a warning. If your program analyzes correctly, the compiler creates an *object module* by translating your source code into machine code. The object module contains all the instructions necessary for the computer to run your program. However, the machine addresses for these instructions are not yet assigned—that is the job of the linkage editor or linker.

To compile your program, follow these steps:

1. Click the X in the upper-right corner of the editor window to close the window. (In Windows 3.1, double-click the upper-left corner.)
2. Choose the Tools menu option. (In Windows 3.1, choose Utilities.)
3. Click the WINCOB[Compile] menu item.
4. Click the Browse button.
5. Change the Look In to the \TYCOBOL folder. (In Windows 3.1, change to Directories.)
6. Select Hello.cob and click Open. (In Windows 3.1, click OK.)
7. Click the Compile button. A countdown clock appears.

If your compilation was not successful, the countdown clock changes momentarily to an exclamation point. If successful, the countdown clock counts down to 1 and then shows the word End. After the compile, an Edit window with the compile results is displayed. If the compile is successful, the window should say:

STATISTICS: HIGHEST SEVERITY CODE=I, PROGRAM UNIT=1

If it says anything else, skip down to the section "When It Won't Compile."

After your program is compiled, it must be linked. The link edit process assigns the actual internal addressing to the compiler-generated object. In addition, the linker adds any supporting machine code necessary to run your program.

> Do not attempt to link your program if the compile was not successful; there will be no object file to link.

Follow these steps to link your program:

1. Close the edit window by clicking the top-right X. (For Windows 3.1, double-click in the upper-left corner.)

2. Close the WINCOB dialog box by clicking the top-right X. (For Windows 3.1, choose the Exit menu option.)

3. Choose the Tools menu option. (For Windows 3.1, choose Utilities.)

4. Select the WINLINK[Link] menu selection.

5. Click the Browse button.

6. Select the Hello.Obj file and click the Open button. (For Windows 3.1, click OK.)

7. Click the Add button. `C:\TYCOBOL\HELLO.EXE` appears in the Target field.

8. Click the Link button. (For Windows 3.1, click the Build button.)

9. When the link finishes, close the window.

10. Close the WINLINK window.

Now you are ready to run your first COBOL program! Follow these steps:

1. Choose the Tools menu option again. (For Windows 3.1, choose Utilities.)

2. Select the WINEXEC[Execute] menu item.

3. Click the Browse button.

4. Select Hello (some settings cause Hello.Exe to show) and click Open. (For Windows 3.1, click OK.)

5. Click the Execute button.

6. When the Runtime Environment Setup appears, click OK. (For Windows 3.1, select Run.)

7. Your program will run and display `"Hello World"`! A message tells you that the Console window is closed. Click OK, and the display window closes. Close the WINEXEC window.

Your screen should look like Figure 2.3.

FIGURE 2.3

The output from the Hello program.

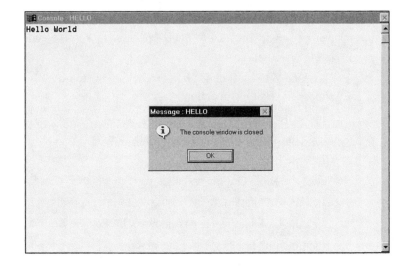

It might appear that you have to run your programs from within the development system. That is not the case. The WINEXEC tool is there for convenience. You could also run the program by using the Start button, selecting Run, and then entering **\TYCOBOL\Hello.Exe**.

When It Won't Compile

If your program does not compile, you will have to determine the reason by using the compiler diagnostic messages that are displayed. Don't let a large number of compiler error messages discourage you. Sometimes even a single error early on can cascade down through the program. For example, if you don't capitalize @OPTIONS MAIN, you will see the following errors:

```
** DIAGNOSTIC MESSAGE ** (NOPRGMID)
C:\TYCOBOL\hello.cob 0: JMN1102I-S  IDENTIFICATION DIVISION HEADER IS
MISSING. HEADER ASSUMED TO BE CODED.
C:\TYCOBOL\hello.cob 1: JMN1000I-S  CHARACTER EXCLUDED FROM COBOL
CHARACTER SET IS USED. THAT CHARACTER IS IGNORED.
C:\TYCOBOL\hello.cob 1: JMN1005I-W  CHARACTER STRING 'OPTIONS' MUST
START IN AREA B. ASSUMED TO START IN AREA B.
C:\TYCOBOL\hello.cob 1: JMN1356I-W  INVALID WORD 'OPTIONS' IS SPECIFIED
IN IDENTIFICATION DIVISION. IGNORED UNTIL NEXT PARAGRAPH OR DIVISION.
C:\TYCOBOL\hello.cob 2: JMN1104I-S  PROGRAM-ID PARAGRAPH IS MISSING.
PROGRAM-NAME GENERATED BY SYSTEM.
C:\TYCOBOL\hello.cob 5: JMN1113I-S  CONFIGURATION SECTION CANNOT BE
SPECIFIED IN INTERNAL PROGRAM.
C:\TYCOBOL\hello.cob 6: JMN1113I-S  CONFIGURATION SECTION CANNOT BE
```

```
SPECIFIED IN INTERNAL PROGRAM.
C:\TYCOBOL\hello.cob 7: JMN1113I-S  CONFIGURATION SECTION CANNOT BE
SPECIFIED IN INTERNAL PROGRAM.
C:\TYCOBOL\hello.cob 12: JMN1044I-S  PROGRAM CONTAINED WITHIN PROGRAM
'NOPRGMID' MUST END WITH END PROGRAM HEADER. END PROGRAM HEADER ASSUMED.
STATISTICS: HIGHEST SEVERITY CODE=S, PROGRAM UNIT=1
```

The reason for so many errors is that the compiler expects either valid compiler options or the Identification Division to appear on the first line of the program. The numbers immediately after the name of the file are the line numbers where the compiler found errors. After these are some error message numbers and information that is specific to the compiler being used. If you use a different compiler, you might see different error messages.

> If you place the cursor on the first line that is in error, in the first column, and press F11, the editor loads your program and sets the cursor on the first line in error.

In this small program, only a limited number of things could go wrong. Check to see whether you put dashes between the words where they are required; for example, Program-Id. Make sure you haven't inadvertently mistaken column 7 for Area A (column 8). Check to make sure you included the necessary division headers. Make sure you enclosed **Hello World** in quotation marks. Make sure that the word *Display* began in Area B. Make sure that you included a period after the divisions, sections, and paragraph headings. Make sure you have a period after your Stop Run statement.

Correct your problems, comparing your program to Figure 2.2 if necessary, and compile it again. Once you get a clean compile, link the program and run it! Don't be the least bit upset; fixing these problems is all part of being a COBOL programmer!

> When correcting your errors and recompiling your program, make sure to close all Edit windows before compiling the program again. The compiler will not be allowed to open the program or create the error message file properly if an old one is still open on your desktop.

Debugging Your Program

Sometimes your programs don't behave the way you think they should. A "broken" program usually has a bug in it. A *bug* is something wrong with the program's logic. The only bug that could really appear in the first program is if "Hello World" does not display when you run the program. Perhaps you forgot to put in the Display statement.

Perhaps, instead of displaying "Hello World," the program displayed "Hello Wrld." Both of these are examples of bugs. When a bug appears, you need to edit your program and correct the bug. After fixing your source code, you can't just run the program again and expect to have the change in effect. If you change anything in your source code, you have to recompile and relink your program. Hour 11, "Advanced `Perform` Statements," discusses more advanced debugging procedures.

Summary

In this hour, you learned the following:

- The general layout of a COBOL program, including the different divisions and the purpose of each
- What a compiler is and how it works
- How to use the editor
- How to compile, link, and run a program
- How to correct problems in your programs if they won't compile or run properly

Q&A

Q How many divisions make up a COBOL program, and what are they called?

A A COBOL program has four divisions: `Identification`, `Environment`, `Data`, and `Procedure`.

Q What is the minimum item that the `Procedure Division` must contain?

A At least one paragraph heading.

Q What is the purpose of the compiler?

A The compiler checks your program for COBOL language syntax errors, missing or extra items, and basic logic errors. If everything passes the edit, then the compiler creates the basic machine code that is linked, using the link edit program, or linker, to create your actually running program.

Q Do all programs work correctly the first time?

A Of course not! According to an old programmers' superstition, any program that compiles without errors the first time must have a bug! The compiler is designed to catch these coding errors and allow you to fix them.

Workshop

To help reinforce your understanding of the material presented in this hour, refer to the section "Quiz and Exercise Questions and Answers" that can be found on the CD. This section contains quiz questions and exercises for you to complete, as well as the corresponding answers.

HOUR 3

Different Data Types

Before you can write meaningful programs, you must be able to manipulate data. In this hour, you learn about many different types of data and how to declare them in a COBOL program. This hour covers the following topics:

- The `Picture` clause
- Level numbers in COBOL
- Numeric and alphanumeric fields
- Defining initial values for data items
- Editing fields for an attractive presentation

One of the strengths of COBOL is its explicit definition of various types of data. In COBOL (as well as other programming languages), data areas are referred to as fields. A *field* is a unique and specific piece of data, for example, an address or telephone number. In programming, when you define an area to contain this data, the area is called a field. Another term used to reference a field is *data item*.

The Picture Clause

In COBOL you must define a field before you can reference it in the program, using an element called the Picture clause. The word is particularly descriptive of what happens in COBOL. The Picture clause paints a picture of how a field looks by defining every detail and characteristic of the field. The Picture clause is abbreviated PIC.

The Meaning of the Different Level Numbers

NEW TERM When a field is defined in the Data Division, a level number precedes the field. These level numbers separate fields into groups. The higher level is called a *Group Level*, and the level where the field's Picture clause is coded is called the *Elementary Level*. A Group Level item contains all the fields under it with higher level numbers.

```
01  Data-Field.
    02  Data-Item-1     Pic X(1).
    03  Data-Item-2     Pic X(1).
```

In the preceding example, Data-Field is a Group Level item. It has the lowest level number. Data-Item-1 and Data-Item-2 are elementary items because they contain the Picture clauses, which define the items.

> Group Level items are discussed in more detail later this hour in the "Group and Elementary Level Items" section.

Several level numbers have specific meanings in COBOL. Table 3.1 explains when each level is used.

TABLE 3.1 COBOL LEVELS AND THEIR USES

Level	Description
01-49	May be used to describe data items.
01	May be used to describe a single field or the start of a group of fields. Level 01 is the only level number that may be used to either begin a group or describe an independent field.
02-49	Must appear only under a higher Group Level. These level numbers may describe further groups or individual fields under a group.
66	Reserved for the Renames clause. The Renames clause is rarely used and is not covered in any detail in this book. The level is included here for reference.

Level	Description
77	Reserved for individual elementary items that are not part of a group. In practice, a level 77 item is the same as a level 01 that describes an elementary item.
88	Used for condition names. Level 88 is described in detail in Hour 8, "Conditional Statements."

The level numbers and the Picture clause are very closely related. After you examine the Picture clause, you'll have an opportunity to review the meaning of the level numbers and how to put them together in a meaningful fashion.

> The different level numbers can be coded without their leading digits. In COBOL, 01 levels are the same as 1 levels. However, I have never seen a program that did not use the leading digits. They facilitate code alignment and make the program easier to read.

Numeric Fields

COBOL supports three types of data fields: numeric, alphanumeric, and literal. This section considers numeric fields, which are simply fields containing numbers. Numeric fields are defined in the Data Division as Pic 9 items.

The 9 in the Picture clause defines a field as numeric. In COBOL a numeric field can be up to 18 digits long. When you code a Picture clause, you use a 9 to represent every numeric position of your field. If your field is two digits long, you code Pic 99. If your field is three digits long, you code Pic 999. Very large fields can get confusing, so COBOL allows you to abbreviate by putting the number of digits within parentheses. For example, Pic 99999 could be coded as Pic 9(5).

The following code might be in the Working-Storage Section of the Data Division of your program.

```
000023 01  Quantity-On-Hand          Pic 9(3).
000024 01  Quantity-On-Order         Pic 9(2).
000025 01  Quantity-Sold-To-Date     Pic 9(12).
```

Line 23 describes a numeric item that can be from 0 to 999 in value. Line 24, Quantity-On-Order, can contain from 0 to 99, and line 25, Quantity-Sold-To-Date, can contain from 0 to 999,999,999,999.

When you use these fields in the Working-Storage Section, you can initialize them with particular values. These values are set when the program starts. To use this technique, simply add a `Value` clause immediately following the `Picture` clause and before the period. For example, to initialize your `Quantity-On-Hand` to 20, your `Quantity-On-Order` to 15, and your `Quantity-Sold-To-Date` to 5021, you would code the following:

```
000023 01  Quantity-On-Hand        Pic 9(3)  Value 20.
000024 01  Quantity-On-Order       Pic 9(2)  Value 15
000025 01  Quantity-Sold-To-Date   Pic 9(12) Value 5021.
```

You should always provide an initial value for numeric data items. Most compilers do not place any special value in numeric data items, and if you use them for computations later in the program, they may contain invalid data.

When assigning a value to a numeric field, you need not worry about specifying the leading digits. The computer correctly positions the data in the numeric fields. For example, `Value 20` and `Value 020` yield exactly the same result.

Numeric fields are right-justified. That is, values proceed from the right side of the field to the left. Therefore, if you have a value of `1000` in a field with a `Picture` definition of three positions, the actual value the field will contain when run is `000`. Most compilers warn you of this condition.

The formatting of the various lines of field definitions is almost entirely up to you. What you see in the examples is the most common method, but you can line up the clauses any way you desire. Nicely formatted source code is relatively easy to read, and I suggest that you be as consistent as possible. In reality, the `Value` clause does not have to follow the `Picture` clause, and even can precede it. Remember to terminate each line of field definition with a period. The field name must always be the first item after the level number. Remember that field names are limited to 30 characters. Try to make the names as descriptive as possible; doing so makes your program that much easier to read and maintain.

Decimal Values

NEW TERM When working with numbers, especially in business, you often need to work with decimal values. In COBOL specifying the decimal point's position is extremely easy. In the `Picture` clause, a v represents the decimal point. The symbolic v is called an *implied decimal position*. The decimal point does not take up any additional storage space.

```
000026 01  Cost-of-each-item    Pic 9(5)v9(2) value 10.00.
000027 01  Average-cost         Pic 9(3)v9(4) value 10.0000.
000028 01  Overall-dollars      Pic 9(7)      value 10.
```

Line 26 represents a number that contains two decimal positions. The numbers can range in value from 0 to 99999.99. Line 27 represents a number that contains four decimal positions. Line 28 represents a number that has no decimal positions. All three examples, however, take up exactly the same amount of internal storage and, by using the `Value` clause, have the same values. Notice how the v splits the `Picture` clause, and the 9 must be repeated followed by the number of positions desired.

Remember that the maximum size of a numeric data item in COBOL is 18 digits. Regardless of where you place the decimal point, the field must not exceed 18 digits.

Handling the Sign

Under many circumstances, you may want to handle numbers that are both positive and negative, or *signed numbers*. You specify a signed numeric field by placing an S immediately after the `Picture` clause and before the 9s that represent the positions of the numbers.

```
000029 01  Net-Profit    Pic S9(5)v9(2) Value -10.00.
```

Like the decimal point, unless explicitly stated otherwise, the sign does not take up any storage positions. Notice how the negative value is represented in the `Value` clause. Different versions of COBOL on different types of computers store the sign with different internal representations. For the most part, the COBOL programmer need not be concerned with this issue. However, if the data is to be shared among different computers or different programming languages, the programmer might want to make the sign of the number a separate character, thus eliminating any problems with differences in internal representation. To do so, add the `Sign Separate` clause to the definition of the field. With this clause, you must specify the position of the sign in relation to the rest of the number. Both positive and negative signs are represented—the positive with a + character and the negative with a -.

When `Sign` `Separate` is used, the sign takes up a position of storage.

```
000030 01  Monthly-Net-Profit        Pic s9(5)v9(2) Sign is Leading
000031                                Separate Character.
000032 01  Quarterly-Net-Profit      Pic s9(5)v9(2) Sign Trailing Separate.
```

In line 30, the sign leads the data value; a positive number is represented by a leading + sign, and a negative with a leading -, for example, +00010.00 and -00010.00.

Line 32 shows an example with the sign trailing. Notice the omission of the words `Is` and `Character`. Many COBOL statements may be abbreviated in this fashion.

The `Usage` Clause

The `Usage` clause tells the computer how to represent numbers internally. You can realize performance gains in your programs by representing numbers in a way that allows the computer to use numbers without translating them into a more usable (to the computer!) format.

The default usage, when none is specified, is `Usage` `Display`. `Usage` `Display` works just like it sounds. The numbers are represented in the same format as a normal display of numbers. All the examples so far have utilized `Usage` `Display`. Each position of a number takes up a character, or byte, of storage.

```
000033 01  Yearly-Net-Profit      Pic s9(5)v9(2) Value Zeros.
000034 01  Yearly-Gross-Profit    Pic s9(5)v9(2) Value Zeros Sign Leading
000035                             Separate.
```

Line 33 takes 7 bytes of storage: 5 bytes for the leading digits and 2 bytes for the decimal positions. Notice that the sign and the implied decimal do not take up any extra storage positions. By contrast, line 34 takes 8 bytes of storage. The extra byte is used because the definition specifies that the sign is a separate character.

In addition to improving performance efficiency, `Usage` clauses can save storage space.

> Compiler vendors determine the actual internal representation associated with `Usage` clause values. The most common representations and uses are discussed here.

The values of the various `Usage` clauses are

- `Computational`
- `Comp`
- `Display`

- Binary
- Index
- Packed-Decimal

Computational and Comp are the same thing. In addition to Comp, most compiler vendors provide Comp-1, Comp-2, Comp-3, and so on as values of the Usage clause. Each value represents a different internal storage method for numeric data. The actual storage space used and how each is represented vary with different computers and COBOL compilers. Usage Index passes the value of an index item to other programs or stores an index item in a file. This clause is seldom used, and often discouraged, as different computers represent index values differently. Index values are discussed in more detail in Hour 12, "Tables."

Packed-Decimal and Binary may or may not be supported by the different compiler vendors, depending on the target computer's capability to handle these data types.

For example, Packed-Decimal is a way to "pack" numeric values into a smaller area. Each byte of data is made up of two sets of half-bytes, or nibbles. A number can be represented in a single nibble of data. Packed-Decimal reserves the last nibble of the data area representing a number for the sign. Each number position in Packed-Decimal usage takes one nibble.

Table 3.2 shows the internal byte, or character representation, of two Packed-Decimal defined numbers. The first is positive, and the second is negative. Notice how the sign is stored as a C in the last half-byte if the number is positive and as a D if the number is negative. Also, note that five digits are being stored in 3 bytes. If the number had six or seven digits, it would take 4 bytes.

TABLE 3.2   INTERNAL REPRESENTATION OF PACKED DECIMAL

Picture Clause	Internal Representation	Byte 1,	Byte 2,	Byte 3
Pic S9(5) Packed-Decimal Value 12345.		12	34	5C
Pic S9(5) Packed-Decimal Value −12345.		12	34	5D

Comp fields are also packed in a method similar to Packed-Decimal but with slightly different rules. Comp fields take up space in 2-byte increments. A single-digit number, Pic 9 Comp, takes 2 bytes. The sign is stored in the left-most bit of the storage area.

> *Byte* is another word for a single character of data. A byte is made up of 8 bits. Each bit has a value of either 1 or 0. A *nibble* is half a byte. When representing these byte values to humans, the computer uses hexadecimal notation. The binary 1s and 0s are converted into their single-digit base 16 equivalent. These numbers range from 0-9 and then go to A-F.

The beginning programmer needs to understand that there is a difference between these representations and needs to know how to determine exactly how much space each number is using. Your compiler's manual has a section on the internal representation of `Usage` clauses. Each vendor may differ in its representation and the amount of space used by the different `Usage` types.

Alphanumeric Fields

Alphanumeric fields can contain information other than numbers. An alphanumeric field could contain any data, including numbers. However, when an alphanumeric field does contain numeric data, it cannot be used as a number. In COBOL, alphanumeric fields are indicated in the `Picture` clause as X items.

```
000034 01  Customer-Name      Pic X(30).
```

Line 34 defines an item called `Customer-Name` that contains 30 characters. Just as with numeric items and the associated placeholder of 9, the X in the `Picture` clause of an alphanumeric item corresponds to one position of the field.

`Value` clauses may be applied to alphanumeric items. Values assigned to alphanumeric items are enclosed within quotation marks.

```
000035 01  Customer-Name      Pic X(30) Value "John Jones".
```

Line 35 assigns the value `John Jones` to the field titled `Customer-Name`.

You need not specify the trailing spaces when assigning a value to an alphanumeric data item because COBOL automatically fills the remaining characters of the field with spaces.

> You should remember that, unlike numeric fields where the numbers of the `Value` clause are correctly positioned in the field, alphanumeric items are left-justified. That is, they start from the left-most position in the field and proceed to the right. If your field is shorter than your value clause, the right-most characters will be truncated.

> If you have an alphanumeric field in which you want to repeat a value, for instance, `"*"`, you can code the field as either `Pic X(20) Value All "*"` or `Pic X(20) Value "********************"`.

Literals

Literals are items that are specified explicitly by their values. You have already seen literals in action. Any of the `Value` clause items specified earlier are considered literals. The `"Hello World"` in your first COBOL program was a literal. Alphanumeric literals are enclosed within quotation marks, whereas numeric literals are not.

The following are some examples of numeric literals:

- 1
- 76
- -12.73

The following are some examples of alphanumeric literals:

- `"Uncle"`
- `"Aunt"`
- `"Computer"`

COBOL provides some special-use literals to make programming easier. The values of these literals are exactly as they sound:

- `Spaces`. `Spaces` are blank characters and are part of the alphabetic portion of the character set used by the computer. `Space` may be used instead of `Spaces`.

- `Zeros`. `Zeros` specifies a numeric literal of the value zero. When used with an alphanumeric field, all characters in that field are changed to a zero. `Zeroes` or `Zero` may be substituted for `Zeros`.

- `Quote`. The `Quote` literal specifies a quotation mark. Most compilers will accept `""""`, to indicate a single quotation mark, but this provided literal is much clearer. `Quotes` may be substituted for `Quote`.

- `Low-Value`. `Low-Value` is the lowest value of a storage item in the computer's collating sequence. It is valid only with alphanumeric fields. When compared to any other field, `Low-Value` is always less. The internal representation of `Low-Value` in most computers is that of all bits in a byte set to zero. `Low-Value` is *not* equal to either zeros or spaces. `Low-Values` may be substituted for `Low-Value`.

- `High-Value`. In contrast to `Low-Value`, `High-Value` is the highest value in the computer's collating sequence. It is valid only with alphanumeric fields. When compared to any other field, `High-Value` is always greater. The internal representation of `High-Value` in most computers is that of all bits in a byte set to one. `High-Value` is not equal to either the letter `Z` or the number `9` unless those characters are the highest characters in the computer's collating sequence. `High-Values` may be substituted for `High-Value`.

Literals are used throughout the COBOL language. In this book, you will see numerous examples of their use.

Numeric Edited Fields

When the computer uses numeric fields internally, their representation does not much matter to the programmer. However, when these numbers are reported to the user in output from the program, their appearance becomes very important. COBOL provides some very powerful tools for editing numeric fields for either printing or display.

Numbers that are edited are much easier to read than numbers that aren't. For example, `123999873.32` is not as easy to read as `123,999,873.32`. With computers, if you don't edit the numbers, a large numeric field might appear to the user as `0000000019.99`. In COBOL you can edit this field to appear as `19.99`.

When a number is moved to a numeric edited field, the computer treats that number as an alphanumeric field. You cannot reference the numeric edited field as a number within your program except as the object of a `move` or `compute` statement (as discussed in Hour 5, "`Procedure Division`"). Numbers moved to numeric edited items remain right justified. This feature is particularly useful because columns of numbers should remain aligned on a printed report.

Table 3.3 shows the difference between edited and unedited numbers.

TABLE 3.3 EDITED AND UNEDITED NUMBERS

Edited Numbers	Unedited Numbers
123,456.78	00012345678
1,000.00	000100000
12.99	000001299

Table 3.4 shows how much easier aligned numbers are to read in a column compared to nonaligned numbers.

TABLE 3.4 ALIGNED AND NONALIGNED NUMBERS

Aligned Numbers	Nonaligned Numbers
123,456.78	123,456.78
1,000.00	1,000.00
12.99	12.99

Several `Picture` clause values can be used to edit a number.

.	Inserts a decimal point at the position of the implied decimal point
Z	Indicates zero suppression
*	Indicates zero suppression and replaces the zero with an *
- or +	Indicates negative or positive sign
CR or DB	Indicates credit or debit balances
$	Indicates the currency symbol
B	Indicates a blank fill character
/	Inserts a slash character in the representation of a numeric field
0	Inserts a zero character
,	Inserts a comma character

The `.` `Picture` item shows the decimal point in a numeric field. When coded, the `.` takes the place of the implied decimal point in a numeric field.

The `Z` `Picture` item indicates zero suppression of digits. When a `Z` is used and the number in that position is a zero, a blank or space is placed in the field instead. Once the first nonzero value is encountered, no further `Z` characters are replaced with blanks.

```
000036 01  Edited-Number      Pic ZZZZZ.
000037 01  Edited-Number-Also Pic Z(5).
```

Lines 36 and 37 have the same representation. Like the X and 9 items of the `Picture` clause, the `Z` item may be repeated by using the parenthetical notation for the number of positions to occupy with the `Z`.

For example, if a numeric field contained `000010.01` and it was moved to a field defined as `Pic ZZZZZZ.ZZ`, the actual value in the field would be `"    10.01"`. Note the four leading spaces and the fact that the 0s after the initial 1 are not replaced with spaces. Instead of coding `ZZZZZZ.ZZ`, you could code `Z(6).ZZ`.

The * performs a similar zero suppression. The only difference is that instead of replacing the zeros with spaces, they are replaced with *. An item with a numeric value of 10.00 and a picture of *(5).** would have a value of ***10.00.

The – item indicates the position of the sign. If the number is negative, then the – appears. If the number is positive, the – is not displayed and a space appears instead. You may use multiple – characters in a single picture clause. This notation will both zero suppress and place the – sign in the right-most position that contains a – sign. Consider the following:

```
000038 01  Edited-Number        Pic -9(5).
000039 01  Edited-Number-Also    Pic ----9.
000040 01  Edited-Number-Too     Pic -(4)9.
000041 01  Edited-Number-Again  Pic 9(5)-.
```

If the number 10 were placed in these fields, line 38 would appear as " 00010". Note the leading space. Line 39 would appear as "   10".

If negative 10 were in these fields, line 38 would appear as "-00010" and line 39 as "   -10". Line 40 depicts exactly the same representation as line 39. Line 41 shows the sign trailing the field. If the field contained a negative 10, it would appear as "00010-".

The + item works similarly to the – item. The + displays a – sign if the field is negative and a + sign if the field is positive.

The CR and DB items are related. Each takes two positions and must be specified either at the beginning or at end of the data item. In either case, if the number is negative, the CR or DB appears. If the number is positive, the CR or DB does not appear. This feature is especially useful for credit or debit balances. If a person owes a negative amount, he or she has a credit, or CR. A transaction is applied to that account might be a negative number and show as a debit, or DB.

Table 3.5 illustrates some examples of debit and credit usage.

TABLE 3.5   CREDIT AND DEBIT EDITED FIELDS

Value	Edited Field	Appearance
12345.00	Pic 9(5).99DB	12345.00
12345.00-	Pic 9(5).99DB	12345.00DB
12345.00	Pic 9(5).99CR	12345.00
12345.00-	Pic 9(5).99CR	12345.00CR

The $ Picture item indicates currency. Like the Z, *, and -, the $ performs zero suppression. You may repeat the character at the start of a field to "float" the dollar sign along with the numbers, or you may code a single $ and have it fixed in position.

```
000042 01  Dollar-Field     Pic $$$$.99.
000043 01  Dollar-Field-Too Pic $9999.99.
```

If each of these fields contained 10.00, the first would appear as " $10.00" and the second as "$0010.00". The $ sign appears by default, but if your country uses a different symbol for its currency, you may use the Special-Names paragraph to change the character that appears. The $ is still used to indicate that currency in your picture clause.

> When using the $, realize that the field is always displayed with at least one leading $. Consequently, if you define a field as $$$.00 and move 100 into the field, the 1 does not display and the field appears as $00.00.

The B (blank), / (slash), comma (,), and 0 characters all behave in the same manner. They are insertion characters (see Table 3.6) and appear in your numeric field exactly where coded. They are not replacing values in your numeric field, but are instead inserting characters.

TABLE 3.6 INSERTION CHARACTERS IN NUMERIC FIELDS

Numeric Value	Picture	Appearance
12311999	99/99/9999	12/31/1999
123456	999,999	123,456
1234	999900	123400
4095551212	9(3)B9(3)B9(4)	409 555 1212

Alphanumeric Edited Fields

It is also often useful to apply edit patterns to alphanumeric fields. COBOL provides several edit patterns to make that job easy.

- B to insert a blank character
- / to insert a slash
- 0 to insert a zero

Just as in the numeric data fields, the B, /, and 0 insert these characters wherever they are encountered. See Table 3.7.

TABLE 3.7 INSERTION CHARACTERS IN ALPHANUMERIC FIELDS

Alphanumeric Value	Picture	Appearance
MMDDYYYY	XX/XX/XXXX	MM/DD/YYYY
ABCDEFG	XBXBXBXBXBXBX	A B C D E F G
ABCDEF	X0X0X0X0X0X	A0B0C0D0E0F

Group and Elementary Level Items

These levels are basically two methods of referencing items that are defined in the `Data Division`. You may reference either an Elementary or Group level item. Group Level items have subordinate Elementary Level items. Any item that has items with subordinate level numbers under it is a Group Level item. The compiler treats Group Level items as alphanumeric variables. Any item with a final definition, with no further subordinate items, is an Elementary Item.

```
000044 01  Numeric-Fields.
000045     03  Field-1          Pic 9(5).
000046     03  Field-2          Pic 9(5).
```

In this example, line 44 represents the Group Level item. It is made up of two elementary items: `Field-1` and `Field-2`. Either the Group Level item or the elementary items may have a `Value` clause, but not both. The rules for the `Value` clause at the Group Level are the same as those for alphanumeric items.

Using the `Value` clause at the Group Level is strongly discouraged. It is an easy way to get nonnumeric data into numeric data fields that appear under the Group Level. No examples or exercises in this book assign a value to a Group Level item.

Notice that subordinate items have higher level numbers. Consider this example:

```
000047 01  Numeric-Fields.
000048     03  Amount-Fields.
000049         05  Amount-1     Pic 9(5)v99.
000050         05  Amount-2     Pic 9(5)v99.
000051     03  Quantity-Fields.
000052         05  Quantity-1   Pic 9(5).
000053         05  Quantity-2   Pic 9(5).
```

Line 47 is a group field composed of four elementary items. Lines 48 and 51 are also group fields: They are made up of two elementary fields each.

> In the preceding example, the level numbers are aligned and indented. This common practice is highly recommended. The compiler is perfectly capable of figuring out the levels based solely on the level numbers; however, the programmer would have trouble reading the program if all the level numbers started in the same column.

Listing 3.1 demonstrates the use of Group and Elementary Levels.

LISTING 3.1 DEMONSTRATE GROUP AND ELEMENTARY LEVELS

3

```
000001 @OPTIONS MAIN
000002 Identification Division.
000003 Program-Id.  Chapt03a.
000004 Environment Division.
000005 Configuration Section.
000006 Source-Computer.   IBM-PC.
000007 Object-Computer.   IBM-PC.
000008 Data Division.
000009 Working-Storage Section.
000010 01  Hello-Text.
000011     03  Part-One Pic X(6) Value "Hello ".
000012     03  Part-two Pic X(5) Value "World".
000013 Procedure Division.
000014 Chapt03a-Start.
000015     Display Part-One.
000016     Display Part-Two.
000017     Display Hello-Text.
000018     Stop Run.
```

In Listing 3.1, when the elementary item Part-One is displayed, the word "Hello " appears. When the elementary item Part-Two is displayed, the word "World" appears. But when the Group Level item, Hello-Text is displayed, you see the entire group, "Hello World", displayed.

Level numbers 02-49 must define elements under a Group Level. Each can be its own subgroup level if it has further subordinate elementary items under it. You may skip any level numbers you desire, so long as each subordinate item starts with a higher level number than the group that contains it.

FIGURE 3.1

*The output from
Listing 3.1.*

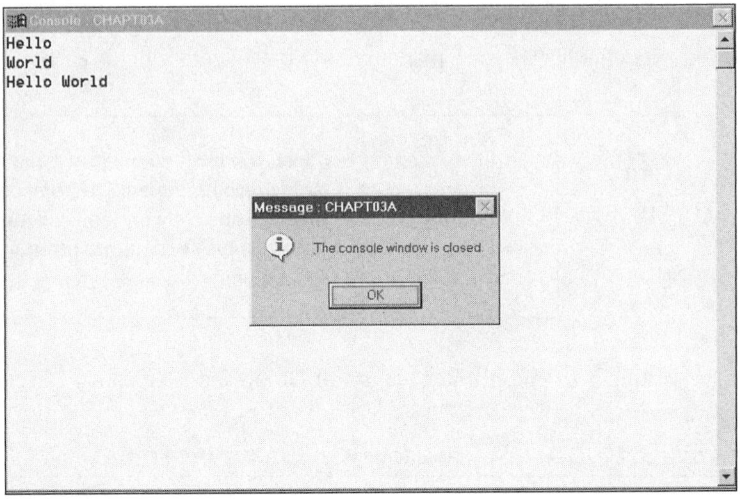

```
Console : CHAPT03A                                                    X
Hello
World
Hello World

                        Message : CHAPT03A            X
                         (i)    The console window is closed.

                                    OK
```

Level 01 is unique among the first 49 level numbers in that it can start a group definition
or it may be an elementary item on its own. The first examples earlier in this hour used
level number 01 as an elementary item.

Level 77 items are the same as level 01 elementary items. Level 77 items must be elementary items, may not be part of a group, and may not define a group. They must stand
alone.

When you need to define a data item, but you do not need to directly reference it, or
when you need to just reserve some space for future expansion, COBOL allows you to
use the reserved word Filler. Filler is essentially what it sounds like. It is an area that
is defined and takes up space, but has no associated data name. If you wanted to define a
Group Level item that contained a first and last name separated by a space, you could
use a Filler item.

```
000020 01  Full-Name.
000021     03  First-Name        Pic X(20).
000022     03  Filler            Pic X Value Spaces.
000023     03  Last-Name         Pic X(30).
```

Note that you may assign a value to a Filler item, just as with any other elementary
item.

> When defining a Filler item, the word Filler is optional. However, I
> suggest that you code the word whenever you define Filler area. I find
> programs that omit the word very hard to read.

Using Data Types in a Program

The next program uses some of the data types described in this lesson. To use these items, you must first define them in the Working-Storage Section of the Data Division.

Working-Storage is an area defined in your COBOL program for use by your program, only while your program is running. Any data that you want to reference internally in your program that does not come from an outside source, such as a file, is defined in Working-Storage.

> Fields defined in Working-Storage can be as organized or disorganized as you allow them to be. However, programming is easier if you place like fields into groups. Having similarly used fields scattered about Working-Storage makes the program harder to maintain later.

Edited fields may have a Value clause associated with them. However, these are rarely used. Edited fields are treated as alphanumeric items, and thus your Value clause must consist of an alphanumeric item. If your value does not match the pattern of the edit, the program will still use the "invalid" Value clause contents.

The edit patterns defined for an edited numeric or alphanumeric data item are applied when data is moved into the fields with a Move statement. The Move statement is discussed in detail later in the book. This session uses simple Move statements.

The Move statement causes the first data item to be moved into the second data item.

```
000050      Move Field-1 To Field-2.
```

In this example, the contents of Field-1 are moved into Field-2. If Field-2 is an edited data item, then the edit pattern specified in your picture clause is applied.

Open the Fujitsu COBOL editor, following the same steps outlined in Hour 2, "Writing Your First Program in COBOL." Enter the following program shown in Listing 3.2.

LISTING 3.2 DEMONSTRATE EDITED FIELDS

```
000001 @OPTIONS MAIN
000002 Identification Division.
000003 Program-Id.  Chapt03b.
000004 Environment Division.
```

continues

LISTING 3.2 CONTINUED

```
000005 Configuration Section.
000006 Source-Computer.  IBM-PC.
000007 Object-Computer.  IBM-PC.
000008 Data Division.
000009 Working-Storage Section.
000010 01  Group-Level-Item.
000011     05  Elementary-Numeric        Pic 9(7)        Value 12345.
000012     05  Elementary-Numeric-Dec    Pic 9(5)v99     Value 123.45.
000013     05  Elementary-Numeric-Sign   Pic S9(5)v99    Value -123.45.
000014 01  Edited-Group-Item.
000015     05  Elementary-Zero-Sup       Pic Z(6)9.
000016     05  Elementary-Aster-Sup      Pic ******9.
000017     05  Elementary-Edited         Pic Z,Z(3),Z(3).
000018     05  Elementary-Edited-Dec     Pic Z,Z(3),Z(3).99.
000019 01  Group-Alphanumeric-Item.
000020     05  Elementary-Alphanum       Pic X(20)
000021         Value "ABCDEFGHIJKLMNOPQRST".
000022     05  Elementary-Alphanum-A     Pic X(6)
000023         Value "UVWXYZ".
000024 01  Group-Alphanumeric-Edited.
000025     05  Edited-Alphanumeric       Pic X(3)/X(3)/X(3).
000026 Procedure Division.
000027 Chapt03b-Start.
000028     Move Elementary-Numeric      to Elementary-Zero-Sup.
000029     Move Elementary-Numeric      to Elementary-Edited.
000030     Move Elementary-Numeric      to Elementary-Aster-Sup.
000031     Move Elementary-Numeric-Dec to Elementary-Edited-Dec.
000032     Move Elementary-Alphanum     to Edited-Alphanumeric.
000033     Display "1 Group Alphanumeric="     Group-Alphanumeric-Item.
000034     Display "2 Elementary Alpha="       Elementary-Alphanum.
000035     Display "3 Elementary Alpha A="     Elementary-Alphanum-A.
000036     Display "4 Edited Alphanumeric="    Edited-Alphanumeric.
000037     Display "5 Group Level Item="       Group Level-Item.   group
000038     Display "6 Elementary Numeric="     Elementary-Numeric.
000039     Display "7 Elementary Numeric Dec=" Elementary-Numeric-Dec.
000040     Display "8 Elementary Numeric Sign=" Elementary-Numeric-Sign.
000041     Display "9 Elementary Zero Sup="    Elementary-Zero-Sup.
000042     Display "10 Elementary Aster Sup="  Elementary-Aster-Sup.
000043     Display "11 Elementary Edited="     Elementary-Edited.
000044     Display "12 Elementary Edited Dec=" Elementary-Edited-Dec.
000045     Stop Run.
```

Notice the spacing to align the data names. This type of source formatting is entirely up to you. In this example, the data items are aligned to make the source easier to read. The number of spaces between the display literal and the data item does not affect the actual display. Although at least one space must separate items, the compiler ignores any other spaces.

Each `Display` statement in this example actually displays two items. The first is an identifying alphanumeric literal, and the second is the data item.

Save the program as **CHAPT03B.COB** in your TYCOBOL folder. You might have to reselect that folder. The name is very important. Make sure that the `Program-Id` is CHAPT03B. After saving the program, close the editor and then compile and link the program as you did in Hour 2. If you have any compiler error messages, remember that you can position the cursor at the start of the line in error and press F11 to position the editor on the actual source line in error. When you get a clean compile and link, run the program.

When `The console window is closed` message appears, move it down and to the right so you can examine the output of your program.

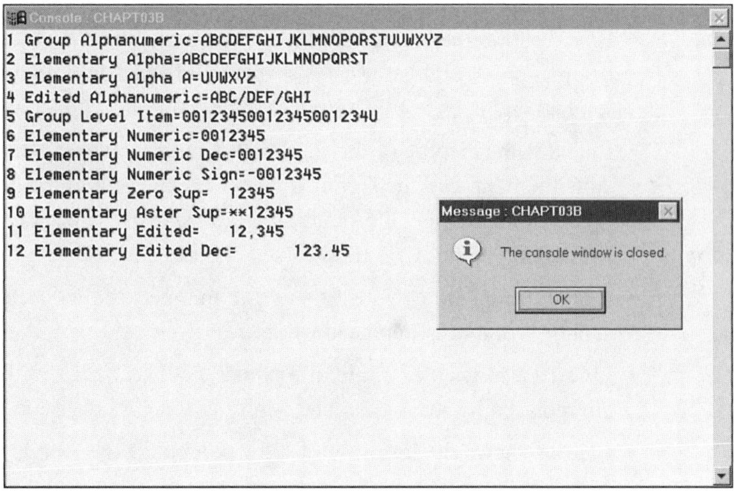

FIGURE 3.2

Output from Listing 3.2.

```
Console : CHAPT03B                                                          ×
1 Group Alphanumeric=ABCDEFGHIJKLMNOPQRSTUUWXYZ
2 Elementary Alpha=ABCDEFGHIJKLMNOPQRST
3 Elementary Alpha A=UUWXYZ
4 Edited Alphanumeric=ABC/DEF/GHI
5 Group Level Item=0012345001234500123450
6 Elementary Numeric=0012345
7 Elementary Numeric Dec=0012345
8 Elementary Numeric Sign=-0012345
9 Elementary Zero Sup=  12345
10 Elementary Aster Sup=**12345
11 Elementary Edited=   12,345
12 Elementary Edited Dec=      123.45
```

```
Message : CHAPT03B                 ×
  (i)    The console window is closed.
              [    OK    ]
```

Refer to your output and take note of the following:

- Line 1 shows the entire alphanumeric group item `Group-Alphanumeric-Item` made up of the two elementary items `Elementary-Alphanum` and `Elementary-Alphanum-A`. As you can see from the display, the Group Level is treated as a single alphanumeric variable.

- Lines 2 and 3 show the individual elementary items that make up the alphanumeric group: `Elementary-Alphanum` and `Elementary-Alphanum-A`.

- Line 4 demonstrates the insertion of the / characters by the edit pattern. Note that the / does not replace any letters in `Elementary-Alphanum`. Also, notice that the entire elementary item that was moved to the edit pattern is not displayed. The move operation stopped when the field you were moving to, also known as the receiving field, was full.

- Line 5 is perhaps the most interesting. Notice how all the numbers appear on one line. The group item is made up entirely of numeric elementary items. No decimal points appear because the decimal position is *implied* by the v. Another interesting observation is that the last character is a U. The computer stores the negative sign within the same byte as the last number in the numeric item, and when this strange value is translated into a display character, it ends up being a U. Consequently, you should be very careful with your references to numeric items and to the groups that might contain them.

- Line 6 shows the first elementary numeric item. The leading zeros are displayed, even though they were not specified in the Value clause. The computer handles that for you.

- Line 7 shows the second elementary numeric item. This item was specified with a decimal point, and yet none is displayed. In this case, the decimal point position is implied and does not take up a storage position.

- Line 8 is the display of the field with a negative value. The Fujitsu compiler converts the item, and the sign is displayed. Other compilers may not be this forgiving. Some would display the same thing you saw in the display of the Group Level item containing the numeric fields.

- Line 9 demonstrates your first use of a numeric edited field. The leading zeros are suppressed, that is, replaced by spaces.

- Line 10 also is an example of a numeric edited field, but this time the leading zeros are replaced by the * character. Refer to your source code and see why.

- Line 11 shows the insertion of the , edit character. Although you specified other commas, those that would have appeared between leading zeros have been replaced with spaces by the compiler. This capability is a very powerful editing feature of COBOL.

- Line 12 shows the combination of zero suppression and the placement of the decimal point. If you had specified the picture clause to be Pic ZZZZZ.999, the number would have been displayed as " 123.450". The compiler automatically aligns the decimal point at the position of the implied decimal in the item being moved to the edited field.

Summary

In this hour, you learned many things that will be the foundation for your future COBOL programming.

- The meaning of the `Picture` clause
- The various types of data items: numeric and nonnumeric literals, numeric fields, alphanumeric fields, numeric edited fields, and alphanumeric edited fields
- The `Value` and `Usage` clauses
- The meaning of different level numbers
- The difference between an Elementary and a Group Level item
- How to apply powerful editing to numeric and alphanumeric fields
- How to handle signs and decimal points

Q&A

Q What is the purpose of the `Picture` clause?

A The `Picture` clause describes the type of data item to be used in a COBOL program.

Q Can Group Level items be numeric?

A No, Group Level items are always handled as alphanumeric items by the compiler.

Q What is the maximum size of a numeric item in COBOL?

A Cobol is limited to 18 digits. It does not matter on which side of the decimal point these numbers appear. The total number of digits may not exceed 18.

Q Where are data items defined in a COBOL program?

A Data items are always defined in the `Data Division`. Any item referenced by your COBOL program must either be a special variable defined by the COBOL language or declared in the `Data Division`.

Workshop

To help reinforce your understanding of the material presented in this hour, refer to the section "Quiz and Exercise Questions and Answers" that can be found on the CD. This section contains quiz questions and exercises for you to complete, as well as the corresponding answers.

Hour **4**

Basic User Interface

In Hour 3, "Different Data Types," you learned about the various types of fields available in a COBOL program and a little bit about how to use them. The data used by your COBOL programs is useful only when presented to an end user, the person for whom your program was written. To that end, some interface with the user must exist. This hour focuses on aspects of the user interface, including

- Definitions of and the differences between batch and interactive processing
- Using the keyboard and screen to interface with the user
- Using the COBOL Screen Section to interact with the user

Interfacing with the User

You cannot create a useful program unless you are able to interact with the user. Your user may be a person who runs your program, or another program or process that passes information to your program for processing.

Until recently, the COBOL language did not have a built-in method for interfacing with a human user. By using add-on tools, provided by different vendors, you may add simple or complex user interfaces to your programs. COBOL, historically used to process large volumes of business data, did not initially need a way to gather data from a human user. The invention of the desktop personal computer changed all of that.

Batch Versus Interactive Processing

Traditionally, computers processed data in large batches. The transactions were gathered together in groups, and then these files of transactions were applied to a master file. Processes with the sole function of reading input data and writing related output are called *batch processes*. Batch processes typically run without any human interaction.

Interactive processing involves a user interacting with a program, somewhat like having a conversation with the computer. This type of give and take with the user, accepting data and displaying results, is called *interactive processing*. In the early days of COBOL when the language was available only on large mainframe computers, special methods were developed to communicate between the user and the COBOL program. One of the more successful and prevalent in the IBM mainframe world is called Customer Information Control System, or CICS. CICS is still in use; it relies on a special IBM-defined syntax for the program to communicate with CICS, which communicates with the user.

The Screen Section

COBOL compilers were available with the very first PCs. Having no user interface, the different compilers made use of some vendor-specific extensions to the `Display` and `Accept` verbs.

In reference to COBOL, a *verb* and a *statement* are synonymous.

The one revision to the ANSI COBOL standard that has been completed since the invention of the PC did not address the user interface. The different makers of compilers for the PC used different methods for addressing the user interface problem. Before graphical user interfaces came on the scene, a normal text mode interface, similar to that utilized on large mainframe computers was used. However, the differences among the different compilers made it difficult to transition from one COBOL to another. This problem with the user interface is virtually the only issue that prevents COBOL from being a truly unrestricted cross-platform-compatible programming language.

COBOL was and is also in heavy use on UNIX systems. The X/Open committee concerned itself heavily with UNIX issues and worked with the different compiler vendors to develop a standard for the text mode user interface. The result of this standard is the Screen Section.

The Screen Section, not being part of the current ANSI standard, is not implemented exactly the same way among the different compiler vendors, nor do all of them use it. However, it has gained enough usage to be a part of the new COBOL standard currently under consideration.

> The Screen Section provides a more than adequate user interface for the programs in this book and for learning COBOL. Most PC compilers support some minor variation of the Screen Section. Even if you are not using the Fujitsu compiler that comes with this book, you should be able to compile and run the examples and exercises with minor modifications.

4

Elements of the Screen Section

The Screen Section appears in the Data Division, after the Working-Storage Section. A Screen Section may have several screen descriptions. A screen description has several elements. The first is the screen literal, which is where you want textual information to appear onscreen; no user entry is necessary. Another element is data you want to display, but not allow the user to change. A third element is data that you want to display and preserve. In this case, the user keys into a field on the screen, corresponding to the same screen location, but the data is stored in a different location in Working-Storage. The last element of a screen description is a field that you want to update. In an update field, an initial value is displayed for the user and is then updated.

The Screen Section works by using simple Display and Accept statements. A screen is first displayed, and then the same screen definition is accepted and the input is processed.

The first portion of the screen description is a level 01 group item. This item describes the name of the screen and any special attributes that are to be applied to the entire screen. If these are specified, they will be applied to all subordinate items in this screen. These special attributes are

- Blank Screen
- Foreground-Color

- Background-Color
- Sign
- Usage
- Auto
- Full
- Secure
- Required

The Blank Screen clause clears the screen.

The Foreground-Color and Background-Color clauses specify the colors for the display. Valid colors are described with integer values between 0 and 7. (See Table 4.1.)

TABLE 4.1   DISPLAY COLOR VALUES

Color	Numeric Value
Black	0
Blue	1
Green	2
Cyan	3
Red	4
Magenta	5
Brown	6
White	7

The behavior of the Sign clause was described in Hour 2, "Writing Your First Program in COBOL." If used at the group level of a screen description, this clause causes all numeric signed fields to store the sign as specified (Separate, Leading, or Trailing).

The behavior of the Usage clause was discussed in Hour 3. Applying the Usage at the group level of a screen description reduces the need for repetitive specification of the Usage on numeric items.

The Auto clause causes the cursor to skip to the next field onscreen when you have keyed all available data into the field where the cursor is located. Using the Auto clause makes data entry much easier for the user. When Auto is specified, if the last field onscreen is filled, the Accept will be terminated.

Using the Full clause requires the user to fill the entire field before advancing to the next field. For alphanumeric items, a character must be input into the first and last positions of the field. For numeric items, zeros or a number must be input into each position of the field. If the field is zero suppressed, only those digits not suppressed are required entries.

The `Full` clause is ignored if the `Accept` operation is terminated with a function key.

`Secure` allows the screen to accept user input, but does not display the characters that are entered. It is useful for password entry.

`Required` forces the user to enter at least one character into each input or update field in the associated screen description. Like the `Full` clause, if a function key terminates the `Accept`, the `Required` clause is ignored.

In the following example, a Group Level screen description entry requires the user to enter a value in each input field and automatically advances to the next field when each field is full. The foreground color is white, and the background color is blue. The screen is cleared when this screen description is displayed.

```
000020 Screen Section.
000021 01  My-Main-Screen
000022     Blank Screen, Auto, Required,
000023     Foreground-Color is 7,
000024     Background-Color is 1.
```

> The commas used as punctuation in the example are optional. The COBOL compiler ignores them when compiling your program. You may spread the clauses over multiple lines, terminating the level with a period.

Screen Literals

Screen literals are specified using their values and the `Line` and `Column` numbers at which they are to appear. No `Picture` clause is coded for a screen literal. A data name may follow the level number of a literal, or you may use `Filler`. If no data name is specified, `Filler` is assumed. In addition to the `Line` and `Column`, the following special clauses may be applied. The clauses that are the same as those for Group Level screen description entries follow the previously discussed rules.

- `Blank Screen`
- `Blank Line`
- `Erase`
- `Foreground-Color`
- `Background-Color`

- Blink
- Highlight
- Lowlight
- Reverse-Video
- Underline
- Bell

The `Blank Line` clause causes the line on which the elementary screen item appears to be cleared before the screen is displayed.

The `Erase` clause is followed by one of two values. `EOL` causes the erase to clear from the beginning column of the screen item to the end of the line. `EOS` causes the screen to be cleared from the beginning of the screen item to the end of the screen.

`Blink` causes the associated screen item to blink onscreen.

`Highlight` causes the associated screen item to be highlighted, or brightened, onscreen.

`Lowlight` causes the associated screen item to be dimmed. If the system does not support the dimming of an item, standard intensity is used. For a PC, this is the case.

`Reverse-Video` reverses the values of the foreground and background colors of screen items.

`Underline` causes the screen item to appear underlined on systems that support the underlined display attribute. The Fujitsu compiler on the PC supports the use of the `Underline` clause.

The `Bell` clause causes a beep or bell to sound when the screen item is displayed. It can be used to get the attention of the user.

The `Line Number` and `Column Number` clauses specify the line and column position of the first character in the screen item. The first line on the screen is `Line 1`, and the first column is `Column 1`. You may abbreviate the clause by leaving out the word `Number`, specifying only `Line` or `Column`. The following expanded example shows some screen literals. The first is an underlined heading line. The next is a name field heading that is highlighted and sounds the bell when displayed. Take special note of the subordinate level numbers.

```
000020 Screen Section.
000021 01  My-Main-Screen
000022     Blank Screen, Auto, Required,
000023     Foreground-Color is 7,
000024     Background-Color is 1.
000025     03  Line 01 Column 27 Value "Name and Address Entry"
```

```
000026          Underline.
000027     03   Line 3 Column 5 Value "Last Name " Highlight Bell.
```

Using From

An output item is described using From on an elementary level of a Screen Section screen description entry. From utilizes an item described in the Data Division and places it on the display in the position specified and using the attributes specified. The following special clauses may be specified with an output, input, or update item. Clauses that have already been discussed follow the previously covered rules.

- Auto
- Required
- Secure
- Full
- Blank Line
- Blank Screen
- Erase
- Foreground-Color
- Background-Color
- Highlight
- Lowlight
- Underline
- Blink
- Bell
- Sign
- Usage
- Picture
- Justified
- Blank When Zero

The newly introduced items are Picture, Justified, and Blank When Zero. The Picture clause can be any valid Picture clause. This clause can be extremely useful. You can specify an edit pattern for field display while having a very different Usage specified for the field.

Blank When Zero is used for numeric or numeric edited item to cause the screen to display the field as spaces if the value of the item referenced is zero.

The Justified clause (abbreviated Just) has only one possible value, and that is Justified Right. This clause positions an alphanumeric field into the screen item that may be smaller or larger. Normally when an alphanumeric item is moved, if it is larger than the destination field, the right-most characters are lost. By specifying Justified Right, if a smaller item is referenced, the characters to the left are truncated. If the item being referenced is smaller, then the left-most positions are filled with spaces.

Listing 4.1 is an example of a Screen Section using From to display two output fields. The first is a numeric edited field in which the screen displays spaces if the field is zero. The second is a small alphanumeric item. The third is the same alphanumeric item with Justified Right specified, as an illustration of its behavior.

LISTING 4.1   DEMONSTRATE SCREEN SECTION WITH JUSTIFIED RIGHT

```
000001 @OPTIONS MAIN
000002 Identification Division.
000003 Program-Id.   Chapt04a.
000004 Environment Division.
000005 Configuration Section.
000006 Source-Computer.   IBM-PC.
000007 Object-Computer.   IBM-PC.
000008 Data Division.
000009 Working-Storage Section.
000010 01   Dollar-Amount        Pic 9(5)v99 Value 12.99.
000011 01   Item-Description     Pic X(10) Value "Gold Coins".
000012 Screen Section.
000013 01   Main-Screen
000014      Blank Screen, Auto, Required,
000015      Foreground-Color is 7,
000016      Background-Color is 1.
000017      03   Line 1 Column 35 Value "Item Entry".
000018      03   Line 3 Column 5  Value "Item Value " Highlight Bell.
000019      03   Line 3 Column 16 Pic $$,$$$.99 From Dollar-Amount.
000020      03   Line 5 Column 5  Value "Item Description" Highlight.
000021      03   Line 5 Column 22 Pic x(10) From Item-Description.
000022      03   Line 6 Column 4  Value "Short Description" Highlight.
000023      03   Line 6 Column 22 Pic x(5) From Item-Description.
000024                                        Justified Right.
000025 Procedure Division.
000026 Chapt04a-Start.
000027      Display Main-Screen.
000028      Stop Run.
```

The output of this Screen Section shows the edit pattern applied to the numeric field. It also shows the action of the Justified Right clause. Notice how with the Short Description, only the word Coins is displayed, even though the From clause specifies the same data item in both lines 5 and lines 6 of the display.

FIGURE 4.1

Example of a Screen
Section.

 When displaying or accepting a screen description, if no Line and Column
numbers are specified in the Display or Accept statements, then the Line
and Column numbers specified for the elementary items in the Screen
Section are used. However, if Line and Column numbers are specified on
the Display statement, then that Line and Column are the offset for the
screen definition. For example, if an item was defined in a screen description
to reside at Line 2 and Column 10 and the display of the screen description was at Line 5 and Column 15, the item would appear at Line 6,
Column 24.

Using To

Specifying To on a screen description elementary item creates an input field. The same
special clauses that are used with From are available with To. When using To, the contents of the field are not shown on the screen when the screen description is displayed.
As data is keyed into the field, it appears onscreen. However, the next time the screen
description is displayed, it does not appear. Input is accepted into the data items referenced in the screen description by use of an Accept statement.

```
000055     Accept Main-Screen.
```

> Take special care when using Justified Right with an input field. As
> your data is keyed into the input field, it will be left-justified, and will *not*
> be positioned in the field as you might expect when using Justified
> Right. Justified Right is only used to position the field in the display.
> When the screen description is accepted, the field, exactly as the user keyed
> it, will reside in the target field. I suggest that Justified Right clause be
> used sparingly, if at all.

To and From can be used together for the same screen description elementary item. Doing
so causes one item from the Data Division to be displayed while accepting data into a
different data item. This approach can be used to preserve the original display field.

```
000032    03  Line 6 Column 22 Pic x(5) From Item-Description
000033                                    To   New-Item-Description.
```

Using Using

When Using is specified, an update item is created. An update item displays and accepts
input into the same data area. Any changes are shown when the screen description is next
displayed. An update item may have the same special clauses as input and output items.
Using allows you to use a single data item for display and update by the user.

Special-Names Paragraph

When using the Screen Section, you sometimes have to capture and set the cursor location. In addition, specific function keys can be activated that may be detected by your
program. If no function keys are activated, the only key that can terminate the Accept of
a screen description is the Enter key.

To capture the cursor and the function keys, you need to make entries in the
Special-Names paragraph of the Configuration Section. These entries relate the actual
cursor position and function key status to Working-Storage data items that you can reference in the program. The two special names you will assign are Cursor and Crt Status.

Cursor is the position of the cursor. When you make the Special-Names entry, you are
specifying a data item that contains the row and column of the position of the cursor.
When a screen definition is displayed, the cursor appears at the field, with the starting
position closest to, but not less than, the row and column specified in the cursor field.
The field referenced by the Cursor special name must be either four or six characters
long. If four characters, the first two are the row and the last two are the column of the
cursor position. If the field is six characters long, then the first three correspond to the
row and the last three to the column.

```
000005 Configuration Section.
000006 Special-Names.
000007     Cursor is Cursor-Position.
000008 Source-Computer.  IBM-PC.
000009 Object-Computer.  IBM-PC.
000010 Data Division.
000011 Working-Storage Section.
000012 01  Cursor-Position.
000013     03  Cursor-Row    Pic 9(2) value 1.
000014     03  Cursor-Column Pic 9(2) value 1.
```

Line 6 starts the Special-Names paragraph. Only the last item in the paragraph should be followed by a period. The Special-Names entry, Cursor, for example, starts in Area B (column 12).

Some compilers differ in the area of the specifications for the Cursor Special-Names entry. The cursor position field for the VMS COBOL compiler DEC/Alpha systems may be either four or five positions long. If four positions, the first two positions are the row and the last two the column. If five positions long, the last three are the column number. If you are not using the Fujitsu compiler, see the language reference provided with your compiler to determine the proper values for the Cursor Special-Names entry.

The other Special-Names entry associated with the Screen Section is Crt Status.

The field assigned to the Crt Status special name is three characters long. The first two positions provide codes that correspond to the reason for the termination of the Accept. The system uses the third position for internal housekeeping and should not be referenced.

It is useful to define this status value as a Group Level item with three subordinate elementary items corresponding to the three individual return characters.

```
000013 01  Keyboard-Status.
000014     03  Accept-Status  Pic 9.
000015     03  Function-Key   Pic X.
000016     03  System-Use     Pic X.
```

The first character, Accept-Status, contains a 0 if the Accept is terminated normally, either by the Enter key being pressed or by the last field in the screen definition being filled when the Auto clause is specified. In this case, the second character, Accept-Status, contains either a 0 or a 1. A value of 0 means that the user terminated the Accept by pressing Enter. A value of 1 means that the user filled the last field of the screen and the Accept was terminated because the Auto clause was specified.

Accept-Status has a value of 1 or 2 if the accept statement is terminated by the press of a function key. In this case, the second field contains a coded value corresponding to the function key that is pressed. A value of 1 in the Accept-Status field indicates that a default function key terminated the Accept, whereas a value of 2 indicates a user-defined function key.

> The size and meaning of the Crt Status data item depend on the COBOL compiler. If you are not using the Fujitsu compiler, check your documentation for the appropriate size and meanings for the different values.

```
000005 Configuration Section.
000006 Special-Names.
000007     Crt Status is Keyboard-Status
000008     Cursor is Cursor-Position.
000009 Source-Computer.  IBM-PC.
000010 Object-Computer.  IBM-PC.
000011 Data Division.
000012 Working-Storage Section.
000013 01   Keyboard-Status.
000014      03  Accept-Status Pic 9.
000015      03  Function-Key  Pic X.
000016      03  System-Use    Pic X.
000017 01   Cursor-Position.
000018      03  Cursor-Row    Pic 9(2) Value 1.
000019      03  Cursor-Column Pic 9(2) Value 1.
```

> Notice the single period after the statements in the Special-Names paragraph. If you need to specify any other items in the Special-Names paragraph, remember to use a single period after the last item only.
> Additionally, some compilers are sensitive to the order of items listed in the Configuration Section. If you have trouble compiling the program under a different compiler, try placing the Special-Names paragraph after the Source-Computer and Object-Computer paragraphs.

Using the Screen Section in a Program

The simple data entry screen in the following example gathers information about the different sellers in a consignment store. Before designing any screens, you need to consider the requirements. What kind of data is to be collected? How is it to be displayed? What do you want the screen to look like? The program displays a screen and then waits for the user to enter the data. Some default values are provided so that the user does not need to key everything.

First, decide which items you need to track and the size you want to assign to them. Be very careful to make the fields large enough without being wasteful. COBOL programmers are always mindful of future maintenance needs in their programs. Create yours with that in mind, and if you or other programmers have to modify the program, the task will be easy.

The program tracks the following items for each tenant, using the specified field types and lengths. The default value to assign is also listed.

- Last Name—Alphanumeric 25 characters
- First Name—Alphanumeric 15 characters
- Middle Name—Alphanumeric 10 characters
- Address Line 1—Alphanumeric 50 characters
- Address Line 2—Alphanumeric 50 characters
- City—Alphanumeric 40 characters
- State or Country—Alphanumeric 20 characters
- Postal Code—Alphanumeric 15 characters
- Home Telephone—Alphanumeric 20 characters
- Work Telephone—Alphanumeric 20 characters
- Other Telephone—Alphanumeric 20 characters
- Start Date—Numeric eight digits, formatted MM/DD/YYYY
- Last Rent Paid Date—Numeric eight digits, formatted MM/DD/YYYY
- Next Rent Due Date — Numeric eight digits, formatted MM/DD/YYYY
- Rent Amount — Numeric six digits, two decimal positions, default $50.00
- Consignment Percentage — Numeric three digits, default 40

Take special notice of the extra space in the Postal Code and Telephone Number fields. Also, notice that the dates are eight digits long, even though with the slashes they fill 10 display positions.

The required fields are First Name, Last Name, Home Telephone, Start Date, Rent Amount, and Consignment Percentage. Try to format the screen clearly and neatly, using literals to title the various fields. Make the entry fields reverse video to differentiate them from the screen literals.

4

The screen requires a title describing its purpose and a fancy store name. Use Darlene's Treasures. Listing 4.2 is one way to code the Screen Section.

Key the following program into the editor and name it **Chapt04C.Cob**.

LISTING 4.2   SCREEN SECTION DEMONSTRATION

```
000001 @OPTIONS MAIN
000002 Identification Division.
000003 Program-Id.  Chapt04c.
000004* Data entry Screen
000005 Environment Division.
000006 Configuration Section.
000007 Special-Names.
000008        Crt Status is Keyboard-Status
000009        Cursor is Cursor-Position.
000010 Source-Computer.  IBM-PC.
000011 Object-Computer.  IBM-PC.
000012 Data Division.
000013 Working-Storage Section.
000014 01  Keyboard-Status.
000015     03  Accept-Status Pic 9.
000016     03  Function-key  Pic X.
000017     03  System-Use    Pic X.
000018 01  Cursor-Position.
000019     03  Cursor-Row    Pic 9(2) Value 1.
000020     03  Cursor-Column Pic 9(2) Value 1.
000021 01  Screen-Items.
000022     03  Last-Name            Pic X(25)   Value Spaces.
000023     03  First-Name           Pic X(15)   Value Spaces.
000024     03  Middle-Name          Pic X(10)   Value Spaces.
000025     03  Address-Line-1       Pic X(50)   Value Spaces.
000026     03  Address-Line-2       Pic X(50)   Value Spaces.
000027     03  City                 Pic X(40)   Value Spaces.
000028     03  State-or-Country     Pic X(20)   Value Spaces.
000029     03  Postal-Code          Pic X(15)   Value Spaces.
000030     03  Home-Phone           Pic X(20)   Value Spaces.
000031     03  Work-Phone           Pic X(20)   Value Spaces.
000032     03  Other-Phone          Pic X(20)   Value Spaces.
000033     03  Start-Date           Pic 9(8)    Value Zeros.
000034     03  Last-Rent-Paid-Date  Pic 9(8)    Value Zeros.
000035     03  Next-Rent-Due-Date   Pic 9(8)    Value Zeros.
000036     03  Rent-Amount          Pic 9(4)V99 Value 50.00.
000037     03  Consignment-Percent  Pic 9(3)    Value 40.
000038 Screen Section.
000039 01  Data-Entry-Screen
000040     Blank Screen, Auto
000041     Foreground-Color is 7,
000042     Background-Color is 1.
```

```
000043        03   Line 01 Column 30 Value "Darlene's Treasures"
000044             Highlight Foreground-Color 4 Background-Color 1.
000045        03   Line 03 Column 30 Value "Tenant Entry Program"
000046             Highlight.
000047*
000048        03   Line 5 Column 01  Value "Name, Last: ".
000049        03   Line 5 Column 13  Pic X(25) Using Last-Name
000050             Reverse-Video Required.
000051        03   Line 5 Column 39  Value "First: ".
000052        03   Line 5 Column 46  Pic X(15) Using First-Name
000053             Reverse-Video Required.
000054        03   Line 5 Column 62  Value "Middle: ".
000055        03   Line 5 Column 70  Pic X(10) Using Middle-Name
000056             Reverse-Video.
000057*
000058        03   Line 6 Column 01 Value "Address 1: ".
000059        03   Line 6 Column 15 Pic X(50) Using Address-Line-1
000060             Reverse-Video.
000061*
000062        03   Line 7 Column 01 Value "Address 2: ".
000063        03   Line 7 Column 15 Pic X(50) Using Address-Line-2
000064             Reverse-Video.
000065*
000066        03   Line 8 Column 01 Value "City: ".
000067        03   Line 8 Column 15 Pic X(40) Using City
000068             Reverse-Video.
000069*
000070        03   Line 9 Column 01 Value "Country/State: ".
000071        03   Line 9 Column 15 Pic X(20) Using State-Or-Country
000072             Reverse-Video.
000073        03   Line 9 Column 36 Value "Postal Code: ".
000074        03   Line 9 Column 50 Pic X(15) Using Postal-Code
000075             Reverse-Video.
000076*
000077        03   Line 11 Column 01 Value "Phone/Home: ".
000078        03   Line 11 Column 13 Pic X(20) Using Home-Phone
000079             Reverse-Video.
000080        03   Line 11 Column 34 Value "Work: ".
000081        03   Line 11 Column 41 Pic X(20) Using Work-Phone
000082             Reverse-Video.
000083*
000084        03   Line 12 Column 06 Value "Other: ".
000085        03   Line 12 Column 13 Pic X(20) Using Other-phone
000086             Reverse-Video.
000087*
000088        03   Line 14 Column 01 Value "Start Date: ".
000089        03   Line 14 Column 13 Pic 99/99/9999 Using Start-Date
000090             Reverse-Video.
000091        03   Line 14 Column 24 Value "Last Paid Date: ".
```

continues

LISTING 4.2 CONTINUED

```
000092       03  Line 14 Column 40 Pic 99/99/9999 Using Last-Rent-Paid-Date
000093           Reverse-Video.
000094       03  Line 14 Column 50 Value "Next Rent Due on: ".
000095       03  Line 14 Column 68 Pic 99/99/9999 Using Next-Rent-Due-Date
000096           Reverse-Video.
000097       03  Line 15 Column 01 Value "Rent Amount: ".
000098       03  Line 15 Column 14 Pic Z,ZZZ.99 Using Rent-Amount.
000099       03  Line 16 Column 01 Value "Consignment Percent: "
000100           Reverse-Video.
000101       03  Line 16 Column 22 Pic ZZ9 Using Consignment-Percent
000102           Reverse Video.
000103 Procedure Division.
000104 Chapt04c-Start.
000105       display Data-Entry-Screen.
000106       accept Data-Entry-Screen.
000107       Stop Run.
```

Notice the comment lines (indicated by an * in column 7) that separate the code and make the program more readable. COBOL also tolerates plain blank lines. The fields are grouped so that the text literal appears in the screen definition before its associated field. Look at the Value clauses in use and the special screen colors. Pay special attention to the way that the subordinate data items override the attributes of the higher levels. If most of a screen is to be one color, you can code that color at the major Group Level and then override that color for individual fields at the subgroup level or even at the Elementary item Level.

When you key this program and compile it, you are liable to have typographical errors. Now is a good time to get used to correcting these errors from the compile listing. Remember that you can position the cursor on the first character of an error line and press F11 to jump to the editor screen, where you are automatically positioned at the source line that is in error. Although your compile listing may seem to disappear at this point, it hasn't. You can make your change, realizing that an error, such as a missing period on one line, can cause errors to be reported on other lines that, in fact, are correct. After making the change, you can save the program and then exit the editor to return to the compile listing, or you can minimize the edit window to see the compile listing. Another method is to click on the Window menu and select the program file you're working on. Positioning the cursor on the next error and pressing F11 repositions the cursor in the source edit window. Maximizing the edit window then displays the line in error. Alternatively, you can choose to tile the two windows.

When you save your program for the first time, make sure to specify the entire name of the program file, including the .COB file extension. If you fail to do so, you may not see your program when you try to reopen it. If that happens, rename the file to have the .COB file extension.

FIGURE 4.2

Chapt04c screen image.

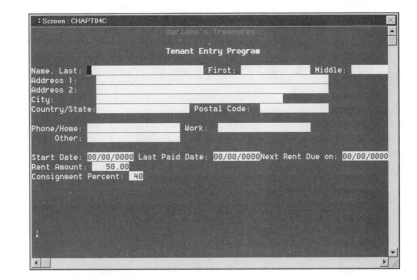

A better, less verbose way to code the preceding Screen Section is to organize fields with the same display characteristics under a single group. This way, elements such as Reverse-Video don't need to be coded for each elementary item. The following example shows another way to code this Screen Section.

```
000038 Screen Section.
000039 01  Data-Entry-Screen
000040     Blank Screen, Auto
000041     Foreground-Color is 7,
000042     Background-Color is 1.
000043*
000044     03  Screen-Literal-Group.
000045         05  Line 01 Column 30 Value "Darlene's Treasures"
000046             Highlight Foreground-Color 4 Background-Color 1.
000047         05  Line 03 Column 30 Value "Tenant Entry Program"
000048             Highlight.
000049         05  Line 5  Column 01  Value "Name, Last: ".
000050         05  Line 5  Column 39  Value "First: ".
000051         05  Line 5  Column 62  Value "Middle: ".
000052         05  Line 6  Column 01  Value "Address 1: ".
000053         05  Line 7  Column 01  Value "Address 2: ".
000054         05  Line 8  Column 01  Value "City: ".
```

```
000055          05  Line 9  Column 01   Value "Country/State: ".
000056          05  Line 9  Column 36   Value "Postal Code: ".
000057          05  Line 11 Column 01   Value "Phone/Home: ".
000058          05  Line 11 Column 34   Value "Work: ".
000059          05  Line 12 Column 06   Value "Other: ".
000060          05  Line 14 Column 01   Value "Start Date: ".
000061          05  Line 14 Column 24   Value "Last Paid Date: ".
000062          05  Line 14 Column 50   Value "Next Rent Due on: ".
000063          05  Line 15 Column 01   Value "Rent Amount:".
000064          05  Line 16 Column 01   Value "Consignment Percent: ".
000065     03   Required-Reverse-Group Reverse-Video Required.
000066          05  Line 5 Column 13  Pic X(25) Using Last-Name.
000067          05  Line 5 Column 46  Pic X(15) Using First-Name.
000068*
000069     03   Reverse-Video-Group Reverse-Video.
000070          05  Line 5  Column 70 Pic X(10) Using Middle-Name.
000071          05  Line 6  Column 15 Pic X(50) Using Address-Line-1.
000072          05  Line 7  Column 15 Pic X(50) Using Address-Line-2.
000073          05  Line 8  Column 15 Pic X(40) Using City.
000074          05  Line 9  Column 15 Pic X(20) Using State-Or-Country.
000075          05  Line 9  Column 50 Pic X(15) Using Postal-Code.
000076          05  Line 11 Column 13 Pic X(20) Using Home-Phone.
000077          05  Line 11 Column 41 Pic X(20) Using Work-Phone.
000078          05  Line 12 Column 13 Pic X(20) Using Other-phone.
000079          05  Line 14 Column 13 Pic 99/99/9999 Using Start-Date.
000080          05  Line 14 Column 40 Pic 99/99/9999
000081              Using Last-Rent-Paid-Date.
000082          05  Line 14 Column 68 Pic 99/99/9999
000083              Using Next-Rent-Due-Date.
000084          05  Line 15 Column 14 Pic Z,ZZZ.99 Using Rent-Amount.
000085          05  Line 16 Column 22 Pic ZZ9 Using Consignment-Percent.
```

Run the program and experiment with it. Notice that you cannot leave the Last Name field by tabbing or by pressing the Enter key until you key some data. You must enter some data because Last Name is a required field. However, the Enter key does work after some data is keyed into the Last Name field, although First Name is also a required field. The Required attribute is in effect only while the cursor is on a field that is required. Once the requirement is satisfied for that field, Enter or Tab will work.

Also, note that only numbers may be entered in the date fields. Try to key in some letters and see what happens. You may key the slashes or omit them as you desire; the fields are always formatted with the slashes in the proper positions.

Summary

In this hour, you learned

- About the Screen Section and its development
- How to create a screen definition
- How to apply an edit pattern to a field used in a screen definition
- How to use input, output, and update fields
- How to use Special-Names entries to get and control the cursor position and detect function keys
- Efficient ways of coding a screen definition

Q&A

Q **What are the different elements of the Screen Section?**

A A Screen Section is made up of one or more screen definitions. A screen definition consists of screen literals and input, output, and update fields.

Q **What is the difference between using Using and defining a screen element with both From and To fields?**

A Specifying Using causes a field to be displayed and then updated when the user keys data into the field. Specifying From and To causes data to be displayed from one field but accepted into another.

Q **How can the position of the cursor be determined?**

A As you write more complex programs, you will need to know which field the cursor was on last and how to position it there. When using a Screen Section, you use the Special-Names paragraph of the Configuration Section to specify a field in Working-Storage for tracking the cursor position.

Q **Can more than one screen definition be present in a program?**

A Yes. You can specify multiple screen definitions in a Screen Section. Start each new definition with a new level 01 group.

Workshop

To help reinforce your understanding of the material presented in this hour, refer to the section "Quiz and Exercise Questions and Answers" that can be found on the CD. This section contains quiz questions and exercises for you to complete, as well as the corresponding answers.

HOUR 5

Procedure Division

In Hour 4, "Basic User Interface," you learned about the different types of data declared within a COBOL program. In this hour, you learn how to use that data in your programs. The main thrust of any programming language is the manipulation of the input data. This lesson covers the mathematical and basic data manipulation statements used in COBOL, such as

- The `Procedure Division`, where the statements are coded
- Arithmetic statements such as `Add`, `Subtract`, `Multiply`, `Divide`, and `Compute`
- Simple data manipulation using the `Move` statement

Procedure Division Organization

The `Procedure Division` is where everything happens. The `Procedure Division` contains all of your procedural code. It is like the mixing instructions in the recipe analogy used earlier. The prior divisions in the program listed the ingredients, and the `Procedure Division` is where they are all combined to create a programming masterpiece.

Keeping the `Procedure Division` organized and structured is paramount to creating a functioning, efficient, and useful program. Very few real COBOL rules govern the flow of logic within the `Procedure Division`. The flow that the program follows is from the top of the `Procedure Division` down. The `Procedure Division` must contain at least one paragraph, and a paragraph or section name must be the first statement in the division.

Paragraphs

Remember that COBOL was designed to be as English-like as possible. This similarity is the source of the term *paragraph*. Like a good essay, each programming paragraph should have only one topic.

Paragraphs begin with a name, which starts in `Area A` (column 8), may be up to 30 characters long, and ends with a period. Under a paragraph, you should have at least one sentence or statement. Groups of programming statements in COBOL are referred to as *sentences*. The diagnostic messages issued by the compiler refer to your `Procedure Division` code as sentences.

COBOL statements tell the computer what to do. They start in `Area B` (column 12). Each statement *may* end with a period, but the end punctuation is not an absolute requirement. However, each paragraph must have at least one period. Misplaced periods cause COBOL programmers no end of headaches. If your programs are structured, you don't need more than one period per paragraph.

> To enforce the one-period-per-paragraph approach, I suggest that you place the period in column 12 on a single line at the end of the paragraph. The remaining examples in this book follow this convention.

Sections

Sections are optional in the COBOL language. A `Section` in the `Procedure Division` is made up of paragraphs. The COBOL standard states that when a section is coded, the next statement must be a paragraph title. Most compilers, but not all, ignore this standard and allow sections to be coded without paragraph titles immediately following.

Sections can be used to group paragraphs. A `Section` is titled in the same manner as a paragraph except the name is followed by the word `Section`. Sections and their use are discussed again in Hour 10, "Processing Loops."

Arithmetic Statements

COBOL has a full complement of mathematical functions. These can be used for the simplest of calculations or for complex, intricate formulas. The five basic arithmetic statements are Add, Subtract, Multiply, Divide, and Compute. You can combine these statements to accomplish virtually any arithmetic function you desire.

The Add Statement

The Add statement has three basic formats: You may add a data item or numeric literal to an existing data item, you may add any combination of numeric data items and numeric literals together and store the result in a separate data item, or you may add a group of elementary items to another group of elementary items.

The first format of the Add statement is the most basic:

```
000078     Add Data-Item-1 To Data-item-2.
```

The computer adds all the numbers or data items on the left of the To and stores the result in a temporary internal area. The computer then adds that temporary variable to every elementary item it finds to the right of the To and stores the result in the corresponding field (to the right of the To). Numeric data items or numeric literals may appear to the left of the To, but only data items may appear to the right. For example, if the value of Data-Item-1 is 5 and the value of Data-Item-2 is 6, the computer adds the 5 in Data-Item-1 to the 6 in Data-Item-2 and stores the result in Data-Item-2, which will then be equal to 11.

Consider this example:

```
000079     Add 1 2 3 To Data-Item-2.
```

The computer adds 1, 2, and 3 together to get 6 and then adds the 6 to the value in Data-Item-2. If Data-Item-2 contains 4, after the add is performed, it will contain 10.

Here's another example. Assume that Data-Item-1 contains 10 and Data-Item-2 contains 20:

```
000080     Add 5 To Data-Item-1 Data-Item-2.
```

After the Add is complete, Data-Item-1 will contain 15 and Data-Item-2 will contain 25.

You may also add multiple data items to multiple data items. For this example, Data-Item-1 contains 5 and Data-Item-2 contains 10:

```
000081     Add 10 Data-Item-1 To Data-Item-1 Data-Item-2.
```

5

Can you determine the values in Data-Item-1 and Data-Item-2 after the Add is complete? Remember that the items to the left of the To are first added together and then that result is added to the values in the data items to the right of the To. Data-Item-1 will contain 20, and Data-Item-2 will contain 25.

There are some other issues to consider when adding. What happens if you are adding values with differing decimal positions? For example, you could add an item with three decimal positions to an item with two. In the examples shown thus far, the extra decimal position would be dropped. If 10.126 is added to 10.00, the result is 20.12. This outcome may not always be desirable. Rounding may be applied to your Add statement by coding the word Rounded after the data items to the right of the To.

```
000082     Add 10.126 to Data-Item-1 Rounded.
```

If Data-Item-1 had a value of 10.00, the result of the addition would be 20.13. COBOL rounds up, or "half adjusts." Any value of 5 or above is rounded up.

Another problem that can occur with addition happens when the value of the field you are adding into exceeds the size of the field you have defined for the item. For example, suppose you define a field as Pic 99. If it starts with a value of 60 and you add 45 to it, the new value should be 105, but because the field is defined as two positions, the high-order digit (1) is lost. The field would end up having a value of 5 because numbers are processed and stored from right to left. If the numeric field overflows, the left-most positions are lost.

You can detect this condition when performing an Add operation by coding On Size Error. When you use this clause, the statements you place after the condition are executed. You may also code a Not On Size Error clause. If your Add statement has multiple data items, the field that caused the size error is not changed, but the other fields are.

The Add statement will be complete when the compiler encounters a period, an End-Add, or a new programming statement that is not part of a size error clause. You are encouraged to use the End-Add explicit scope terminator portion of the Add statement whenever you use the Size Error or Not On Size Error clauses.

NEW TERM   End-Add is the explicit scope terminator for the Add statement. An *explicit scope terminator* is a phrase used to terminate a COBOL statement. Many COBOL statements allow the use of the explicit scope terminator. Each terminator begins with the word End followed by a dash and the name of the statement being terminated. Statements that allow explicit scope terminators are pointed out in the relevant discussions.

The following example adds one number to another and displays the completion status of the Add statement.

```
000088      Add Data-Item-1 to Data-Item-2
000089          On Size Error
000090              Display "Field Overflowed on Add"
000091          Not On Size Error
000092              Display "The Field did not Overflow"
000093      End-Add
```

Notice how the Add statement is coded across multiple lines. If you place a period within the Add statement, the compiler will issue an error message when you compile the program. In addition to the Add statement, nearly any other valid COBOL mathematical statement may be coded in the Size Error and Not On Size Error phrases.

The second format of the Add statement allows you to add a list of data items or literals and store the result in another data item. In contrast to the first format, the Add operation does not change the values of the items being added. You may place the optional word To between data items if you desire, but it is not necessary.

```
000093      Add 1, 2, 3, 4, Data-Item-1 To Data-Item-2 Giving Data-Item-3
000094      Add 1, 2, 3, 4, Data-Item-1, Data-Item-2 Giving Data-Item-3
```

The results of lines 93 and 94 are the same. Assuming Data-Item-1 contains 10 and Data-Item-2 contains 5, Data-Item-3 will contain 25 when the Add operation is complete. A temporary variable holds the intermediate results, and that value is moved into the data item specified after Giving. The result of the Add statement in this format may be either a numeric data item or a numeric edited data item. The Rounded and Size Error phrases are available when using this format of the Add statement.

The commas in lines 93 and 94 make the statements easier to read. COBOL allows you to punctuate your code with commas for readability but ignores the commas when compiling.

If you need to store the result of the Add statement in multiple data items, you may specify more than one Giving data item. For example: Add 1, 2, 3, 4 Data-Item-2 Giving Data-Item-3, Data-Item-4.

The third format of the Add statement is perhaps the most interesting. If you define two groups of elementary numeric items, you can add the values of each of the members in one group to each of the members in the second group. Consider this portion of code:

```
000020 Working-Storage Section.
000021 01  Field-Group-1.
```

5

```
000022      03  FG-First      Pic 9(2) Value 1.
000023      03  FG-Second     Pic 9(2) Value 2.
000024      03  FG-Third      Pic 9(2) Value 3.
000025 01  Field-Group-2.
000026      03  FG-First      Pic 9(2) Value 10.
000027      03  FG-Second     Pic 9(2) Value 20.
000028      03  FG-Third      Pic 9(2) Value 30.
000029 Procedure Division.
000030 Required-Paragraph.
000031      Add corresponding Field-Group-1 To Field-Group-2
000032      Stop Run
000033          .
```

The Add Corresponding causes FG-First to be added to FG-First in the second group, then FG-Second to FG-Second of the second group, and so on. The results of the operation are that FG-First of Field-Group-2 contains 11, FG-Second of Field-Group-2 contains 22, and FG-Third of Field-Group-2 contains 33.

How can this be? How can two elementary items have the same name? In COBOL, elementary items *can* have the same name if the items are under different groups. (Under the same group level, the elementary items must all have unique names.) If you need to reference the elementary items in your program, you have to specify the elementary item name and the group to which it belongs. For example, to display FG-Third in the second group, you would code Display FG-Third Of Field-Group-2.

If you do not specify a group for the field, the compiler issues an error, reminding you to do so, as it cannot figure out which field you mean. Because of this extra required coding, I recommend that you keep your data item names unique except when you are using the Corresponding phrase. Corresponding is also available with statements other than Add.

When a data name is used in multiple locations in the Data Division, it must be *qualified*. To qualify a data name, use the word Of (or In) and specify the group under which the item is declared.

The Rounded and On Size Error phrases are available with this format of the Add statement.

The Subtract Statement

The syntax and rules for the Subtract statement are virtually identical to those for the Add. The differences are that (1) From is used instead of To and (2) that with the first format all data items to the left of the From are added in a temporary variable and then subtracted from the data items on the right side of the From. The Rounded and Size Error phrases are available with the Subtract statement as is the End-Subtract explicit scope terminator.

For this example, assume that Data-Item-1 contains 20 and that Data-Item-2 contains 30.

000100   Subtract Data-item-1 From Data-item-1 Data-Item-2.

After this subtraction is complete, Data-Item-1 will contain 0 and Data-Item-2 will contain 10.

> When doing subtraction, keep the sign in mind. If your data item is not a signed field, the sign will be lost. For example, if Data-Item-2 is defined as Pic S99 and contains 10 and 20 is subtracted from it, the value of the field will be −10. However, if Data-Item-2 is defined as Pic 99 and 20 is subtracted, the result will be 10. The sign is lost. Coding for Size Error does not capture this condition. Only digit overflow is captured by Size Error.

In the following example, Data-Item-1 contains 1, and Data-Item-2 contains 10.

000101   Subtract 1, Data-Item-1 From Data-Item-2 Giving Data-Item-3.

When this subtraction is complete, Data-Item-1 and Data-Item-2 will still contain their original values. The value of Data-Item-3 will be 8.

The Multiply Statement

The syntax of the Multiply statement is similar to that of Add and Subtract. Instead of To and From, the Multiply statement uses By.

000102   Multiply Data-Item-1 By Data-Item-2.

The result of the multiplication is stored in the data items to the right of the By—Data-Item-2 in this example.

Only one data item may appear to the left of the By in a Multiply statement; however, multiple data items may appear to the right. The item to the left of the By is multiplied in turn by each item on the right, and the result is stored in each data item on the right. In the next example, Data-Item-1 contains 4 and Data-Item-2 contains 5.

000103   Multiply 4 By Data-Item-1, Data-Item-2.

The results of this statement are 16 in Data-Item-1 and 20 in Data-Item-2.

The second format for the Multiply statement utilizes the Giving phrase. The two operands on either side of the By are multiplied and the result is stored in the data items after the Giving phrase.

5

```
000104      Multiply 4 By 5 Giving Data-Item-1, Data-Item-2.
```

Data-Item-1 and Data-Item-2 will both contain 20 after the multiplication is complete. The Rounded and Size Error phrases are available with the Multiply statement, as is the End-Multiply explicit scope terminator.

```
000105      Multiply Data-Item-1 By Data-Item-2 Giving Data-Item-3 Rounded
000106          On Size Error Display "Multiplication Error"
000107          Not On Size Error Display "No Multiplication Error"
000108      End-Multiply
```

If multiple fields follow Giving, only the fields that have a Size Error remain unchanged.

There is no Multiply Corresponding statement.

The Divide Statement

The Divide statement has five formats. As in grade school, division can be tricky! Examine these formats one at a time and look at the examples. Be certain you understand each format before proceeding to the next. All formats of the Divide statement allow for the use of the Rounded and On Size Error phrases, in addition to the End-Divide explicit scope terminator.

The first format is the simplest:

```
000109      Divide Data-Item-1 Into Data-Item-2.
```

In this example, assume that Data-Item-1 is 2 and Data-Item-2 is 10. Data-Item-1 is divided into Data-Item-2, and the result stored in Data-Item-2. In other words, 10 is divided by 2, and the 5 that results is stored in Data-Item-2. Multiple data items may appear to the right of the Into, and each is divided by Data-Item-1 in turn. When On Size Error is coded, items that cause a Size Error are not changed.

The second format uses the Giving phrase. Like the first format, the data item on the right of the Into is divided by the data item on the left of the Into, but the result is stored in a third data item. Multiple data items may be specified after the word Giving.

```
000110      Divide 5 Into Data-Item-1 Giving Data-Item-2.
```

If Data-Item-1 contains 10, then the result of the division is 2, which is stored in Data-Item-2. When using Giving, the contents of the two operands are not changed.

The third format is very similar to the second. However, instead of using the word Into, the word By is used and the functions of the two operands in the Divide are reversed. You are free to use the syntax and method you most easily understand.

```
000111      Divide Data-Item-1 By 5 Giving Data-Item-2.
```

The results of the Divide statement in the example line 111 are exactly the same as those of the example given as line 110.

The fourth format provides for the capturing of a remainder from the Divide statement. In this format, only one field can follow the Giving.

```
000112      Divide 3 Into Data-Item-1 Giving Data-Item-2 Remainder
000113                     Data-item-3.
```

If Data-Item-1 is 10, the result of this division will be a 3 in Data-Item-2 and the remainder 1 in Data-Item-000113.

The final format for the Divide statement is similar to the fourth. However, By is used instead of Into, and the order of the operands is reversed.

```
000112      Divide Data-Item-1 By 3 Giving Data-Item-2 Remainder
000113                     Data-Item-3.
```

The results of this division are exactly the same as the previous example.

> You must be very careful when performing division to avoid dividing by zero. The results are undefined, and most systems cause the program to end abnormally if such a division is attempted.

The Compute Statement

The Compute statement provides a method of performing a complex calculation in more of an algebraic or mathematical format. Rounding is available with the Compute, as are the On Size Error phrase and the End-Compute explicit scope terminator.

Any valid mathematical expression can be used in a Compute statement. For example:

```
000118      Compute Data-Item-1 Rounded = (Data-Item-2 * 15)
0000119            + (Data-Item-2 * 7).
```

Multiplication is handled with the *, and division with the /.

Exponents are coded using two asterisks followed by the power. For example, to find out what 36 squared is, you would code:

```
000118      Compute Data-Item-1 = 36**2.
```

When using `Compute`, be mindful of intermediate results. Different compilers store the intermediate results of `Compute` statements in different size
fields. This disparity is especially evident when using division within the
`Compute` statement. If you code `Compute Data-Item-1 = (1 / 3) * 3`
and `Data-Item-1` is defined as a `Pic 9` item, the result will not be 1 as you
might expect, but instead will be 0. That is because the compiler stores the
result of the division 1/3 in an intermediate one-digit field, the same as your
destination field. When the division is performed, the results are less than 1,
so 0 is stored in the intermediate value. When the intermediate field is multiplied by 3, the result is still 0. Even declaring the value of your destination
field with several decimal positions is not sufficient to cure the problem. To
help prevent this occurrence, code the division portion of any `Compute`
statement alone and last. Coding `Compute Data-Item-1 = (3 * 1) /
3` yields the correct result of 1.

Simple Data Manipulation

By using the arithmetic functions of COBOL, you are already manipulating some data.
Manipulating data is the main thing that programs do. Input is processed, and results are
produced. Mathematical statements cause the contents of data items to be changed.
Another very frequently used method of manipulating data is to move it from one field to
another. Advanced data manipulation is covered in Hour 6, "Manipulating Data."

The Move Statement

The `Move` statement moves data from one field to another. The simplest version of the
statement is as follows:

```
000119     Move Data-Item-1 To Data-Item-2.
```

This `Move` transfers the data in `Data-Item-1` to `Data-Item-2`. The field to the left of the
`To` is the sending field, and the field or fields to the right of the `To` are the receiving
fields. The receiving field may not be a literal, but the sending field may be. How the
`Move` actually occurs depends on the types of fields defined.

The simplest `Move` is from alphanumeric item to alphanumeric item. When this `Move` is
performed, the individual characters of the sending field are moved one at a time, from
left to right, into the receiving field. If the sending field is longer than the receiving field,
then the extra characters are not moved. The result is said to be "truncated."

```
000120     Move "ABCDE" To Field-4.
```

If `Field-4` is defined as `Pic X(4)`, then the result of this `Move` is `"ABCD"` in `Field-4`. As you can see, you may move literals or data items.

If the receiving alphanumeric field is longer than the sending field, the extra trailing characters are filled with spaces.

```
000121    Move "AB" To Field-4.
```

Assume that before the `Move` operation `Field-4` contains `"WXYZ"`. After the `Move`, `Field-4` will contain `"AB  "`.

You may specify more than one receiving field with the `Move` statement. When you do so, the sending field is first moved to a temporary area, and then that temporary area is moved to the individual receiving fields.

```
000122    Move Field-1 To Field-2, Field-3, Field-4.
```

In this example, the contents of `Field-1` are placed into `Field-2`, `Field-3`, and `Field-4`.

Another type of `Move` is numeric item to numeric item. When this `Move` occurs, the characters (numeric digits) are moved from the right-most position to the left. That means that if the receiving field is shorter than the sending field, the digits to the left-most side of the number will be lost. If the receiving field is longer than the sending field, then the left-most digits will be padded with zeros. Truncation of digits can occur both on the right and left side of the decimal point. Consider the moves and results shown in Table 5.1.

TABLE 5.1 TRUNCATION EXAMPLES

Number	Picture Clause	Result
123.45	99.99	23.45
123.456	999.99	123.45
123.456	9.9	3.4

Numeric literals or elementary items may be moved to numeric edited items (see Table 5.2). In this case, the edit pattern is applied to the result. Additionally, these numeric edited items may be moved either to alphanumeric data items or to numeric data items. When moved to an alphanumeric data item, the sending numeric edited item is treated as an alphanumeric item and the data is moved from the left to the right. When a numeric edited item is moved to a numeric item, the rules for a numeric-item-to-numeric-item `Move` are observed.

TABLE 5.2 NUMERIC EDITED MOVE EXAMPLES

Edited Number	Numeric Result	Alphanumeric
123,999.99	000123999.99	123,999.99
12.99	000000012.99	12.99

Alphanumeric data items can be moved to numeric items, but that practice is strongly discouraged. You cannot be sure what value the computer will interpret the number to have! On some computers, the operation will cause the program to end abnormally. Additionally, numeric items may be moved to alphanumeric data fields. When this Move is performed, the decimal point and sign are ignored. Moving a field with a value of –12345.67 to an alphanumeric field results in a field containing 01234567. Some compilers issue a warning message about this type of Move.

Alphanumeric literals or elementary items may also be moved to edited alphanumeric data items. In this case, the edit pattern is applied. Data is moved from left to right, and any "left over" characters are truncated.

When group items are moved to alphanumeric edited or numeric edited fields, the fields are moved from left to right *and no edit pattern is applied*. For example, if a receiving field is defined as Pic XX/XX/XX and the sending field is a Group Level item having the value of "ABCDEFG", the value of the receiving field after the move will be "ABCDEFG ", not "AB/CD/EF" as you might expect. If the elementary item under that group item is moved, the edit pattern is applied.

In addition to the Move statement from a sending field to one or more receiving fields, another format of the Move uses the Corresponding phrase. Move Corresponding moves fields with the same name under one group into fields with the same name under another group.

```
000050 Working-Storage Section.
000051 01   Group-1.
000052      03   Field-1          Pic X(5).
000053      03   Field-2          Pic X(6).
000054      03   Field-3          Pic X(6).
000055 01   Group-2.
000056      03   Field-1          Pic X(6).
000057      03   Field-2          Pic X(6).
```

```
000058    03  Field-3          Pic X(6).
000059 Procedure Division.
000060 Start-Paragraph.
000061    Move Corresponding Group-1 To Group-2
000062    Stop Run
000063        .
```

In the preceding example, the contents of Field-1, Field-2, and Field-3 of Group-1 are moved, one at a time, into Field-1, Field-2, and Field-3 of Group-2.

Summary

In this hour, you learned the following:

- That the Procedure Division is made up of paragraphs, which can be organized into sections.

- How to use Add, Subtract, Multiply, and Divide to manipulate numeric data items.

- How to use the Compute statement and how to avoid any pitfalls associated with intermediate results.

- How to move data from one field to another.

- That when the receiving field is alphanumeric, moves proceed from left to right, and when the receiving field is numeric, moves are from right to left.

- That group items and alphanumeric items are moved in the same manner with one exception: When group items are moved to edited fields, no edit patterns are applied.

5

Q&A

Q Can the Procedure Division be coded without paragraphs?

A No. The Procedure Division must have at least one paragraph title.

Q Can the Add statement be used to add a single value into multiple fields?

A Yes. You simply list the items you want to add the value to on the right side of the To in the Add statement.

Q Can the Compute statement accept complex formulas with multiple levels of parentheses?

A Yes. Any valid arithmetic expression may be coded; however, use caution when performing division. It is best to code any required division operations at the end of the Compute statement.

Q What happens if a numeric field is moved into an alphanumeric field?

A The decimal position is lost as well as the sign. The field is moved from the left to the right into the alphanumeric field.

Workshop

To help reinforce your understanding of the material presented in this hour, refer to the section "Quiz and Exercise Questions and Answers" that can be found on the CD. This section contains quiz questions and exercises for you to complete, as well as the corresponding answers.

HOUR 6

Manipulating Data

You have now learned some simple data manipulation statements. You can do some basic math and move fields around. You have learned some basic features to allow you to interface with the user. Now it is time to cover some more advanced statements used to work with data fields.

In its role at fulfilling the needs of business, COBOL works with myriad data. It must handle the mathematics of business and be able to process textual data. Textual data consists of items such as names, addresses, and telephone numbers. Textual data can also contain descriptions of other important data, such as medical procedures. COBOL comes with a suite of very powerful tools to handle and manipulate this type of data. In this hour you learn about

- The Accept statement
- The Initialize statement
- The Inspect statement
- Reference modification

The Accept Statement

Some uses of the Accept statement, in the area of communicating with the user, have already been covered. In addition, you can use the Accept statement for more than just retrieving user input. You may accept data either from the user or from the operating system. You have already seen the method for accepting input from a screen definition.

Accepting from the User

When interfacing with the user, the Accept statement moves data from a specific device into a data field. In the absence of a specifically coded device, the default device for the Accept is used. For example:

```
000033    Accept Some-Field.
```

This Accept statement moves data from the default device, normally the console or current user terminal, into the data item Some-Field.

The different items that can be accepted using the Accept statement vary from compiler to compiler. Different computers have different devices and different requirements.

One of the interesting uses of the Accept with the Fujitsu compiler is to allow the programmer to retrieve command-line arguments. These are the items passed to the program on the command line. For example, if your program is CHAPT06A.EXE and you type **CHAPT06A MyName**, the command-line argument is MyName. Here is an example of how Fujitsu allows you to use the Accept statement to retrieve the command-line argument.

```
000001 @OPTIONS MAIN
000002 Identification Division.
000003 Program-Id.  Chapt06a.
000004* Command Line Argument
000005 Environment Division.
000006 Configuration Section.
000007 Source-Computer.  IBM-PC.
000008 Object-Computer.  IBM-PC.
000009 Special-Names.
000010     Argument-Value Is Command-line.
000011 Data Division.
000012 Working-Storage Section.
000013 01  Command-Line-Argument Pic X(80).
000014 Procedure Division.
000015 Chapt06a-Start.
000016     Accept Command-Line-Argument From Command-Line
000017     Display "Command Line: " Command-Line-Argument
000018     Stop Run
000019     .
```

Take special notice of the Special-Names paragraph. The name Argument-Value is a Fujitsu provided special name. Using this method of assigning a value in the Special-Names paragraph sets up most of the special items that may be accepted.

Enter and compile this program. When you run it, add an argument after the Chapt06a.exe on the command line. Notice that if you add more than one word, only the first is displayed. You may code multiple Accept statements to retrieve all the command-line arguments. In addition, Fujitsu provides a special name, Argument-Number, that can be used to determine the number of command-line arguments.

Accepting Data from the System

A number of very useful, predefined Accept variables are part of the COBOL standard. These relate to retrieving the system date, time, and day of the week. Two date formats are supported. One is the Gregorian date, and the second is the Julian date. The Gregorian date is the type of date you are used to seeing; its numbers correspond to the month, day, and year. The Julian date is made up of the year and the number of the days in the year to the present date. For example, January 1 is day 1. December 31, during a year that is not a leap year, is day 365. If the year is a leap year, December 31 is day 366.

The following examples show the syntax for these Accept statements.

```
000045     Accept Date-Field  From Date.
000046     Accept Day-Field   From Day.
000047     Accept Week-Day    From Day-Of-Week.
000048     Accept Time-Of-Day From Time.
```

The field that Date is accepted into must be a six-digit numeric data field. The format of the input is YYMMDD, where YY is the current two-digit year, MM is the current month where 01 is January and 12 is December, and DD is the day of the month.

The field that Day is accepted into must be a five-digit numeric data field. The format of the input is YYDDD, where is the current two-digit year and DDD is the current Julian day.

6

When working with the current date, try to avoid using the Accept statement with Date and Day. The reason is that only a two-digit year is returned. To get the current full four-digit year, use the intrinsic function Current Date, which is discussed in detail in Hour 21, "Date Manipulation."

The field that Day-Of-Week is accepted into must be a single-digit numeric field. If the field contains 1, the current weekday is Monday, 2 is Tuesday, and so on.

The field that Time is accepted into must be an eight-digit numeric field. The format of the time is HHMMSShh, where HH corresponds to the hour in military time format, for example: 01 is 1 a.m., 13 is 1 p.m. MM corresponds to the minutes, SS corresponds to the seconds, and hh to the hundredths of seconds.

The Initialize Statement

As you write programs, you may want to reset the values of your fields. If you are accumulating totals for a report, after you print a total you may want to clear your detail fields. After retrieving a screen from the user, you may want to clear the screen of all user-entered values. Writing individual Move statements to erase the values in the fields can be a cumbersome exercise.

The Initialize statement is a very powerful statement for setting the initial values of your data fields. It can be a very fast and easy way to set the value for a data item or series of data items.

> Exercise caution when using the Initialize statement against items in Working Storage to which you have assigned a value with the value clause. Initialize sets their value as appropriate for the type of field and does not set their content to that specified in the value clause.

For example, the following group is defined in the Working-Storage Section of your program.

```
000040 01  Working-Variables.
000041     03  Numeric-Variables.
000042         05  First-Numeric-Variable        Pic 9(5).
000043         05  Second-Numeric-Variable       Pic 9(5).
000044     03  Alphanumeric-Variables.
000045         05  First-Alphanumeric-Variable   Pic X(20) value all "*".
000046         05  Second-Alphanumeric-Variable  Pic X(20).
```

First, notice line 45. The field contains 20 * characters. The other fields can have any value that your program has moved into the fields. If you wish to reset all these fields, there are a couple of choices.

You may move spaces to the Working-Variables field. However, this Move places invalid data into the numeric fields. Another solution is to code multiple Move statements to move zeros to the numeric fields and spaces to the alphanumeric fields. In that case, you must explicitly move something to each field name. A better option is to code an `Initialize` statement.

```
000101     Initialize Working-Variables.
```

When the `Initialize` is performed, each field in the group, at its elementary level, is either set to zeros or spaces, depending on the type of field. Numeric and numeric edited fields are set to zeros, and alphanumeric fields are set to spaces, just as if a `Move` statement had been performed with each field as the receiving field.

The `Initialize` verb can also target specific field types within a group. If you have a group defined, do not want to group like field types together, and only want to initialize the numeric fields in the group, you can still use `Initialize` if you just add the `Replacing` clause.

```
000102     Initialize Working-Variables Replacing Numeric Data By Zeros.
```

The `Replacing` clause allows you to specify the type of field, within a group, on which the `Initialize` is to operate. In this example, only the numeric elementary fields defined within the `Working-Variables` group are set to zero. You may specify `Alphanumeric`, `Alphanumeric-Edited`, `Numeric`, or `Numeric-Edited` after the word `Replacing`.

Another powerful feature is the ability to use `Initialize` to set fields of various types to unique values other than spaces and zeros. If you want to change `First-Alphanumeric-Variable` to contain all asterisks again, you can code as follows:

```
000103     Initialize First-Alphanumeric-Variable
000104     Replacing Alphanumeric Data By "********************"
```

An alternative to coding all the asterisks, and potentially miscounting, is to use `All  "*"` or the `Move` statement with the `All` clause. For example:

```
000105     Initialize First-Alphanumeric-Variable
000106     Replacing Alphanumeric Data By All "*"
```

or

```
000107     Move All "*" To First-Alphanumeric-Variable
```

Notice that the `Initialize` is not restricted for use against Group Level items, although in this instance, a simple `Move` will accomplish the same thing. If, however, you wanted all alphanumeric fields within a group to contain the asterisks, then `Initialize` makes more sense.

6

> When using `Initialize` with `Replacing`, remember that the field or literal you specify after the word `By` is *not* repeated within the object of the `Initialize`. For example, if you code `Initialize First-Alphanumeric-Variable to "*"`, the result will be `"*"` and not `"********************"` as you might expect.

You are not restricted to literals in the `Replacing` phrase. You may also `Initialize` a field with the contents of another field.

```
000102     Initialize Working-Variables Replacing Numeric Data By Field-1.
```

In this example, every numeric field defined under the group `Working-Variables` is initialized to the current value of `Field-1`.

The `Inspect` Statement

One of the more versatile and powerful COBOL data manipulation verbs is the `Inspect` statement. `Inspect` can be used for anything from testing a field for specific contents to converting those contents to other values. The `Inspect` statement may be coded in several formats.

The first usage allows you to count the occurrences of a particular character or characters within a field. For example, to determine whether a data item contains a comma, you can use the `Inspect` statement to count the commas in the field.

```
000103     Inspect Data-item tallying Work-Counter For All ",".
```

After this statement is executed, `Work-Counter` contains the number of commas in `Data-Item`. For example, if `Data-Item` contains `"Hubbell, Darlene"`, `Work-Counter`'s value is 1.

What if you want to count all of the times that the letter b occurs in the last name? You need to stop counting when the , is encountered. The `Inspect` statement makes this very easy by allowing you to add the phrase, `Before Initial`.

```
000104     Inspect Data-item Tallying Work-Counter For All "b" Before
000105            Initial ",".
```

In this example, the result stored in `Work-Counter` is 2. In addition to allowing you to code the `Before Initial` clause, `Inspect` also supports the `After Initial` clause. You can use `After Initial` to count the occurrence of a character or characters after the comma.

Instead of counting all occurrences of a single character, you may want to determine the number of leading characters.

Leading characters precede any other character in a field. For example, if a field contains "****ABC", it contains four leading asterisks. If you want to determine the number of leading characters in a field, you might code as follows:

```
000105     Inspect Data-Item Tallying Work-Counter For Leading "*".
```

This format of Inspect also determines the number of total characters in a field that meet specific conditions. You can determine the number of characters that occur before or after a comma, for example. Using the earlier example, you can use Inspect to determine the length of the last name.

```
000106     Inspect Data-Item Tallying Work-Counter For Characters Before
000107             Initial ",".
```

If you want to count the number of characters after the comma, you may change the Before Initial to After Initial.

> The word Initial is optional. You may omit it when coding the Before or After phrases.

A second format of the Inspect statement allows you to replace characters in a field with other characters. This tool is very powerful for editing data fields into specific formats. For example, if you have a date field that was entered with "/" characters separating the values and you needed to replace the "/" with a "-", you can use the Inspect statement. Assume your date field contains "01/04/1999".

```
000107     Inspect Data-item Replacing All "/" By "-".
```

You may replace literals or data items with either literals or data items. The statement is very flexible. The following example uses the Inspect statement to format a telephone number for display.

LISTING 6.1   TELEPHONE NUMBER FORMAT

```
000001 @OPTIONS MAIN
000002 Identification Division.
000003 Program-Id.   Chapt06b.
000004* Telephone Number Format
000005 Environment Division.
000006 Configuration Section.
000007 Source-Computer.   IBM-PC.
000008 Object-Computer.   IBM-PC.
000009 Data Division.
```

continues

LISTING 6.1   CONTINUED

```
000010 Working-Storage Section.
000011 01  Phone-Number.
000012     03  Area-code      Pic XXX    Value "409".
000013     03  Prefix-Num     Pic XXX    Value "555".
000014     03  Last-Four      Pic X(4)   Value "1212".
000015 01  Formatted-Number     Pic X(14) Value "(XXX) YYY-ZZZZ".
000016 01  Formatted-Alternate Pic X(14) Value "(XXX) XXX-XXXX".
000017
000018 Procedure Division.
000019 Start-Of-Program.
000020     Inspect Formatted-Number
000021        Replacing All "XXX"  By Area-Code
000022                   All "YYY"  By Prefix-Num
000023                   All "ZZZZ" By Last-Four
000024     Display Formatted-Number
000025     Inspect Formatted-Alternate
000026        Replacing First "XXX"  By Area-Code
000027                  First "XXX"  By Prefix-Num
000028                  First "XXXX" By Last-Four
000029     Display Formatted-Alternate
000030     Stop Run
000031        .
```

Notice that multiple replacing statements may appear within an Inspect statement, and they are processed in order. The first Inspect in line 21 replaces all occurrences of the text. The second Inspect statement replaces only the first occurrence of the text: in the example, "XXX" was used repeatedly, and a single Replacing would have changed all three sets of "XXX" to the area code.

The Leading phrase may be used instead of All if you need to change only the leading characters to something else.

The Characters phrase is also valid in this format of the Inspect statement. It can be used to change every character in a field to another character. You can use Inspect to change all characters in a field to "*" characters.

```
000035     Inspect Data-Field Replacing Characters By "*".
```

This statement replaces every character in a field, regardless of the length of the field, with asterisks.

The third format of the Inspect statement allows you to count characters using Tallying and to replace characters using Replace. This format can be useful to count the number of characters or occurrences you have changed.

```
000036     Inspect Data-Field Tallying Character-Count For All Spaces
000037        After "-" Replacing All Spaces After "-" by "X".
```

The preceding example converts all spaces that appear after a "-" in a field with the letter X. The Character-Count field contains the number of spaces that were changed to the letter X.

The final format of the Inspect statement allows you to convert characters from one value to another. Although similar to Replacing, the Converting allows you to specify a string of single characters (data item or literal) that will be converted to the values specified in a second string. This can be used to convert a name, or portion of a name, from lowercase to uppercase letters. For example, to change "Hubbell, Darlene" to "HUBBELL, DARLENE", code the following:

```
000038      Inspect Data-Field Converting "abcdefghijklmnopqrstuvwxyz" To
000039                              "ABCDEFGHIJKLMNOPWRSTUVWXYZ".
```

Every time a character in the string of values on the left of the To is encountered, it is changed to the matching character on the right of the To. If you want to convert only the last name from the example and leave the first name alone, code the following:

```
000038      Inspect Data-Field Converting "abcdefghijklmnopqrstuvwxyz" To
000039                              "ABCDEFGHIJKLMNOPWRSTUVWXYZ"
000040                      Before initial ",".
```

Do you remember playing code games as a kid? Remember the simple substitution codes? The letters of the alphabet were rearranged to make a code. If you knew which letters of the alphabet corresponded to the letters in the code, you could solve the puzzle. The Inspect statement with Converting works in a similar fashion, performing a single substitution for each character.

In addition to being able to restrict the conversion by specifying the Before Initial phrase, you may also specify After Initial.

Reference Modification

Reference modification is a method provided to reference a portion of a data item. Reference modification allows you to use a portion of a field as if it were its own elementary item. You may use reference modification on alphanumeric fields or on numeric fields that are Usage Display. The way you specify reference modification in your program is to place a starting position and length in parenthesis separated by a colon, after your data item.

```
000041      Display Data-Item (1:4).
```

If the Data-Item field contains "Inventory", this Display statement displays "Inve". The first number denotes the starting position, and the one after the colon specifies the

6

length. You may use reference modification with virtually any COBOL statement that references a data item.

The numbers used to define the starting position and length may be in the form of numeric literals as in the example, data items, or arithmetic expressions. If an arithmetic expression is used, the values must be positive. The length item after the colon may be omitted. If it is omitted, then the remaining characters to the end of the data item are used.

```
000042     Display Data-Item (5:).
```

Using the same Data-Item value as the previous example, this example displays "ntory".

Reference modification is a very powerful feature. It can be used for many things. However, it can also be abused. Don't use reference modification to further divide a data item when it can be more clearly defined as a group item made up of elementary items. For example, if a data item consists of last and first name, define a group:

```
01  Full-Name.
    03  Last-Name     Pic X(30).
    03  First-Name    Pic X(20).
```

If you want to display the last name, code the following:

```
Display Last-Name.
```

Don't use reference modification. Display Full-Name (1:30) is not nearly as clear.

Using What You Have Learned in a Program

It is time to put these pieces together and accomplish a programming task. For this example, you develop a program that accepts a full name, with the first name separated from the last by a comma, and an email address. The first and last names are split into separate fields, and the email address is converted to lowercase. The results are then displayed.

Open the Fujitsu Editor and create a new file in your TYCOBOL folder. Code the normal COBOL statements required to identify the program.

```
000001 @OPTIONS MAIN
000002 Identification Division.
000003 Program-Id.  Chapt06c.
000004* Name and E-mail Edit
```

```
000005 Environment Division.
000006 Configuration Section.
000007 Source-Computer.   IBM-PC.
000008 Object-Computer.   IBM-PC.
```

Notice the use of the comment in line 4 to identify the purpose of the program. Now code the `Data Division` and the `Working-Storage Section`. You need fields to hold the input and to display the output. You also need two numeric fields to contain some numbers that are used in your program.

```
000009 Data Division.
000010 Working-Storage Section.
000011 01  Screen-Items.
000012     03  Name-Entry          Pic X(40) Value Spaces.
000013     03  E-mail              Pic X(30) Value Spaces.
000014     03  Last-Name           Pic X(30) Value Spaces.
000015     03  First-Name          Pic X(30) Value Spaces.
000016 01  Work-Number             Pic 99 Value Zeros.
000017 01  Work-Number-1           Pic 99 Value Zeros.
```

Take special note of the fact that initial values were assigned to these fields. Otherwise, the initial display of the screen items might contain junk characters. Also, note that only one field is defined for `E-mail`. Because you are not splitting the `E-mail` field into two fields, like the name, you need only the one field.

Next, code the `Screen Section` for displaying and accepting the entered values.

```
000018 Screen Section.
000019 01  Name-Entry-Screen
000020     Blank Screen, Auto
000021     Foreground-Color Is 7,
000022     Background-Color Is 1.
000023*
000024     03  Screen-Literal-Group.
000025         05  Line 01 Column 30 Value "Name and E-mail Entry"
000026             Highlight Foreground-Color 4 Background-Color 1.
000027         05  Line 05 Column 05 Value "  Name: ".
000028         05  Line 06 Column 05 Value "E-mail: ".
000029         05  Line 08 Column 05 Value "  Last: ".
000030         05  Line 09 Column 05 Value " First: ".
000031     03  Reverse-Video-Group Reverse-Video.
000032         05  Line 05 Column 13 Pic X(40) Using Name-Entry.
000033         05  Line 06 Column 13 Pic X(30) Using E-mail.
000034         05  Line 08 Column 13 Pic X(30) From  Last-Name.
000035         05  Line 09 Column 13 Pic X(30) From  First-Name.
```

In the screen definition, note the use of the `Using` phrase for the `Name-Entry` and `E-mail` but the `From` phrase for `Last-Name` and `First-Name`. Because you will be splitting the name entered into these two fields, you don't want the user to enter any data into those fields.

6

The `Procedure Division` is coded next, up to the point of displaying and accepting the screen.

```
000036 Procedure Division.
000037 Chapt06c-Start.
000038     Display Name-Entry-Screen
000039     Accept  Name-Entry-Screen
```

The next step is to determine how many characters in the `Name-Entry` field appear before the comma. Then you can move those characters to the new `Last-Name` field. Notice the use of the comment in the following code, used to explain what you are trying to do.

```
000040* Split the first and last name out into separate fields
000041     Inspect Name-Entry Tallying Work-Number
000042          For Characters Before ","
000043     Move Name-Entry (1:Work-Number) To Last-Name
```

The `Inspect` statement in lines 41 and 42 counts the number of characters that appear before the comma. This number is stored in the `Work-Number` field. Line 43 uses reference modification to move this portion of the `Name-Entry` field into the `Last-Name`. Reference modification causes the characters starting in position 1 and extending for a length of the value of `Work-Number` to be moved into the `Last-Name` field.

The first part is done; now you need to move the last name into the `Last-Name` field. To do that, you need to make sure that the position you start working on in the `Name-Entry` field is the first position after the comma. To do that, add 2 to `Work-Number` because the value of `Work-Number` is the number of characters in the field that appear before the comma.

```
Add 2 to Work-Number
```

The user may have entered the name with a space after the comma, multiple spaces after the comma, or no spaces. You want the `First-Name` field to start in the left-most position, also called *left-justified*, so you need to exclude any leading spaces in the first name portion of the input field.

```
000044* You need to exclude the leading spaces, after the comma
000045     Inspect Name-Entry (Work-Number:)
000046          Tallying Work-Number-1 For Leading Spaces
000047     Move Name-Entry (Work-Number + Work-Number-1:) To First-Name
```

The `Inspect` statement in line 45 uses reference modification on the `Name-Entry` input field to count the number of spaces that appear after the comma but before any other character. Note in the reference modification that only the : is coded, not a length. This format causes the `Inspect` to start at the position defined in `Work-Number` and end at the end of the field.

When you know the number of spaces, you can then move the portion of Name-Entry that is the first name into the First-Name field. You do so by using reference modification. Within the reference modification, the starting position is determined by a numeric expression. This expression is the sum of Work-Number, which is now equal to the first position after the comma, and Work-Number-1, which contains the number of spaces that appear after the comma. This step positions the starting point for the move on the first nonblank character that appears after the comma in the input field.

Now that the first and last names are moved, it's time to convert the email address to lowercase. This step is accomplished with a simple Inspect statement.

```
000048*Change the e-mail address to all lower case letters.
000049     Inspect E-mail Converting "ABCDEFGHIJKLMNOPQRSTUVWXYZ"
000050                To           "abcdefghijklmnopqrstuvwxyz"
```

Finally, you need to display the results of the program for the user and then end the program. The screen display output from this program is shown in Figure 6.1.

```
000346* Show the results
000347     Display Name-Entry-Screen
000348     Stop Run
000349     .
```

FIGURE 6.1

Output from Chapt06C.

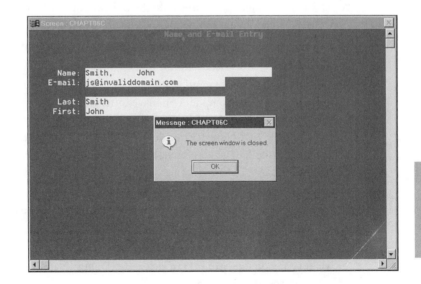

Summary

In this hour, you learned the following:

- How to use the Accept statement to get the date and time from the computer
- How to use the Accept statement to find the parameters the user entered on the command line
- How to use the Initialize statement to reset the values in various fields
- How to use the Inspect statement to count characters in a field
- How to use the Inspect statement to convert data in a field from one value to another
- How to use reference modification to address a portion of a data field
- How to combine these elements in a program to perform a useful function

Q&A

Q Why do you need to be careful when accepting the date from the system in an Accept statement?

A The Accept statement returns only the last two digits of the current year. Another COBOL function that returns the entire year is discussed in Hour 21.

Q Are the special names that accept data from the command line the same for all COBOL compilers?

A No. Although most are similar, the environments, or computers and operating systems, on which the compilers run have different requirements. The COBOL standard allows implementers some leeway in defining the interface to these special areas of their environment. You should review your compiler documentation, specifically the language reference, to determine which special names are available for your use.

Q Will the Initialize statement reset a data item to contain the value that was specified as a value in the picture clause definition of the data item?

A No. The Initialize statement, by default, sets alphanumeric data fields to spaces and numeric data fields to zeros. However, you can specify which values to use when you code the Initialize statement. Doing so allows you to place specific values in specific field types.

Q Can inspect count the number of times that more than a single character appears in a data item? For example the combination "JR"?

A Yes. The Inspect statement is not limited to looking at only a single character. You may code an Inspect statement as follows: Inspect Data-Item Tallying Numeric-Work For All "JR".

Q Can reference modification be used on numeric data fields as well as on alphanumeric data fields?

A Yes. However, the numeric data field must be defined as Usage Display, which is the default usage. If you have specified any other usage, such as COMP-3 or Binary, then reference modification may not be used.

Q Can reference modification be used on Group Level items as well as elementary items?

A Yes. Reference modification treats Group Level items as alphanumeric items.

Workshop

To help reinforce your understanding of the material presented in this hour, refer to the section "Quiz and Exercise Questions and Answers" that can be found on the CD. This section contains quiz questions and exercises for you to complete, as well as the corresponding answers.

6

HOUR 7

Manipulating String Data

In Hour 6, "Manipulating Data," you learned some basic methods for manipulating data. However, programming often requires more-complex data manipulation, especially when working with character strings. In this hour, you learn about manipulating character strings. The following topics are covered:

- The definition of a string
- The String statement
- Using delimiters with the String statement
- The Unstring statement
- Using delimiters with the Unstring statement

A *string* is a set of characters. It can be described as being all the characters in any particular field. The field, or data item, can also be referred to as a *string*. Working with strings is a common task in all kinds of computer programming. In your programming, you may need to disassemble a field, or string, of data. On the other hand, you might be required to create a string of data for some special use. For example, you might have a file that has first and last names in separate fields, and you want to print the combined name on an address label.

Some database and spreadsheet systems generate a delimited text file. You may want to read one of these files and separate the values in the individual delimited records into different fields. In other cases, you might want to create a comma- or comma-quote–delimited file to import into one of these systems.

A *delimiter* is a field-separation character. When data fields are strung together by these different systems, the compiler needs some way to distinguish the individual fields that make up the string. Many systems create what is termed a *CSV file,* which is a file made up of strings where the individual fields are separated by a comma. *CSV* stands for "comma-separated value." Some systems further separate fields by placing quotation marks around the alphanumeric fields. This practice is the origin of the term *comma-quote–delimited file*. The comma separates the individual fields, and this separation character is known as a delimiter.

The String functions in COBOL are very robust. The two basic statements for manipulating a string of data are String and Unstring. String combines data into a single string. Unstring separates a string of data into individual fields.

The String Statement

When you need to merge, or string, multiple data fields into a single field, you should use the String statement. The simplest form of the String statement uses one or more input fields and moves them consecutively into an output field, sometimes referred to as the *target field*.

```
000032   String "ABC" "123" Delimited By Size Into Output-Field.
```

This String statement results in the value "ABC123" being stored in Output-Field. The Delimited By Size clause indicates that the entire input field is to be used in the String operation.

There are some important rules to remember when using the String statement.

- The target field cannot be reference modified. That is, you may not String Into Output-Field (3:5).

- Numeric fields must be Usage Display data items.

- You may string into Group Level items. I discourage this practice, however, because it is too easy to get invalid data into subordinate numeric data fields.

- The target field is not cleared, or padded with spaces, as in a Move statement. Use caution to ensure that your target field is properly initialized.

If the target of your String operation is too small to contain the characters that are being strung into it, an overflow condition occurs. You may capture this occurrence by coding the On Overflow clause. After this clause, you may place any logic that you desire to execute when an output field overflow occurs. You can also code a corresponding clause—Not On Overflow—to execute any time an overflow condition does not occur.

An overflow condition does not exist if your String statement fails to fill the target field.

Examine the following snippet of code:

```
000025 Working-Storage Section.
000026 01  Data-Field    Pic X(20).
000027 01  Field-1       Pic X(12)   Value "Total".
000028 01  Field-2       Pic X(12)   Value "Price".
000029 Procedure Division.
000030 Start-String-Example.
000031     String Field-1 Delimited By Size
000032            Field-2 Delimited By Size
000033              Into Data-Field
000034     On Overflow
000035            Display "String Overflow"
000036     End-String
000037     Stop Run
000038        .
```

This code contains several notable items. First, the Delimited By clause is repeated on each field that is being strung into the output field. You may list as many fields as you desire before any Delimited clause. The next Delimited clause encountered applies to all prior fields after the preceding Delimited clause. Second, an explicit scope terminator is associated with the String statement. I suggest you use End-String any time you code an On Overflow or Not On Overflow clause and any time the String statement is very long or complex. The End-String makes your code easier to understand.

Notice also that this String always triggers the overflow condition. The reason is that the two fields being strung together are each 12 characters, and the target field is only 20. Because 24 characters cannot fit into 20 positions, the overflow always occurs. In COBOL the actual values of the fields used in the String statement have no bearing on the results when Delimited By Size is used. It is not the size of the data within the field that matters, but the field size itself.

7

String Delimiters

Why would anyone code a `String` statement where the target field cannot hold the full size of the source fields? Look at a real-world example. Assume that you have two fields defined: one for a person's first name and one for his or her last name. You want to print an address label with the full name, and your label is only wide enough for 30 characters. The fields in which you are storing first and last name are 25 characters each. The potential exists for a complete name to exceed the target field, especially when the single space separating the names is added. When you print your label and the name is cut off, or truncated, because it is too long, you want to print only the last name on the label. This way you avoid any insulting renditions of the person's name. To accomplish this task, you need to use a delimiter other than `Size` in your `String` statement.

You may delimit, or stop, the operation of the `String` statement using any value you desire. When the value indicated is encountered, the string operation stops and the delimiter itself is not included in the target field. For the task specified here, you use the space character to terminate the `String` for the first and last names.

When working with real-world data, you cannot be sure that the first and last names contain single words. It is essential to remember that when a character delimiter is specified, the `String` operation is terminated the first time that character is encountered. Therefore, if you delimit by space and the field contains "Bobby Sue", only "Bobby" makes it to the target field. Hour 22, "Other `Intrinsic` Functions," covers an efficient way to handle this situation.

Key Listing 7.1 into the editor.

LISTING 7.1   STRING EXAMPLE

```
000001 @OPTIONS MAIN
000002 Identification Division.
000003 Program-Id.  Chapt07a.
000004* String Example
000005 Environment Division.
000006 Configuration Section.
000007 Source-Computer.  IBM-PC.
000008 Object-Computer.  IBM-PC.
000009 Data Division.
000010 Working-Storage Section.
000011 01  First-Name   Pic X(25)   Value Spaces.
000012 01  Last-Name    Pic X(25)   Value Spaces.
```

```
000013 01  Combined-Name Pic X(30)    Value Spaces.
000014 Procedure Division.
000015 Chapt07a-Start.
000016     Move "First" To First-Name
000017     Move "Last"  To Last-Name
000018     String First-Name Delimited By Space
000019            " "          Delimited By Size
000020            Last-Name  Delimited By Space
000021        Into
000022            Combined-Name
000023        On Overflow
000024            Move Last-name To Combined-Name
000025     End-String
000026     Display "1 " Combined-Name
000027     Move "A" to First-Name
000028     Move "B" to Last-Name
000029     String First-Name Delimited By Space
000030            " "          Delimited By Size
000031            Last-Name  Delimited By Space
000032        Into
000033            Combined-Name
000034        On Overflow
000035            Move Last-name To Combined-Name
000036     End-String
000037     Display "2 " Combined-Name
000038     Move Spaces To Combined-Name
000039     Move "ReallyLongFirstName" To First-Name
000040     Move "ReallyLongLastName"  To Last-Name
000041     String First-Name Delimited By Space
000042            " "          Delimited By Size
000043            Last-Name  Delimited By Space
000044        Into
000045            Combined-Name
000046        On Overflow
000047            Move Last-name To Combined-Name
000048     End-String
000049     Display "3 " Combined-Name
000050     Stop Run
000051        .
```

A single alphanumeric literal, space, has been added to the String statements to separate
the two names. For this example, the two input fields, First-Name and Last-Name, are
strung into the target field until a space is encountered. Compile and run the program.
Your output should look like Figure 7.1.

7

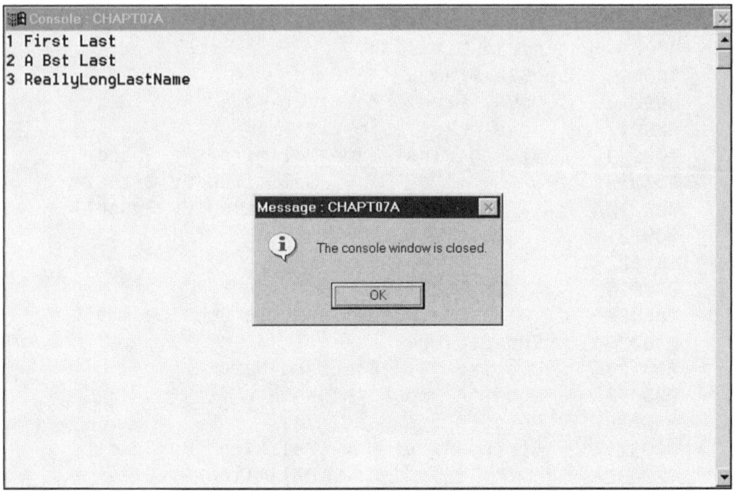

FIGURE 7.1

Output from Listing 7.1.

Line 1 of the display is what you might expect. However, line 2 looks strange because the target field, Combined-Name, was not cleared between the String statements. Line 3 contains only the Last-Name because the overflow condition occurred and the Move statement coded for that condition was executed.

The delimiters used by the String statement need not be single characters only. Delimiters can be any character or string of characters. Delimiters do not have to be literals, but can instead be data items. Table 7.1 illustrates the results of stringing different data items using various delimiters.

TABLE 7.1 RESULTS OF STRING OPERATIONS WITH VARIOUS DELIMITERS

Strings	Delimiter	Result
David Jr. Mike Jr.	Jr	David Mike
John Sr. Mike Jr.	Jr	John Sr.Mike
David123 Mark123	123	DavidMark

Notice in the second example, when in the first field the delimiter is not encountered, the entire field contents are moved. Notice also that all characters including and after the delimiter are omitted.

Occasionally, you may want to String fields into a target field starting from other than the first position. The obvious answer might be to use reference modification on the target field, but COBOL prohibits that practice. However, there is another way to accomplish this task.

You may add a Pointer clause to the String statement. The Pointer indicates the starting position in the target field for the String operation. When the String operation is complete, this Pointer is updated to contain the next position in the target field. The Pointer must be a numeric variable of sufficient size to hold the number of character positions in the target field. If the field is 100 characters long, a pointer variable with a Picture of 9(2) is too small. The pointer variable must always have a value greater than zero.

When using the String statement with the Pointer clause, you must be certain that you have initialized the field with the desired value.

Assume that Target-Field is defined with a value of "TEST FIELD", and you want to change the word "FIELD" to "FILES", using the String statement. You can define a numeric field named String-Pointer, set its value to 6, and then issue the following COBOL statement:

```
000040      String "FILES" Delimited By Size
000041              Into Target-Field
000042              With Pointer String-Pointer
000043      End-String
```

After this string operation, the value of String-Pointer is 11.

One common use for the Pointer clause is to format data that requires special edit patterns. Sometimes these edit patterns can change based on the number of positions or values of the specific data items. For example, a telephone number might be formatted (999) 999-9999, or just 999-9999 if the area code is not provided. The Pointer clause on the String statement can hold the starting position for the seven-digit number portion of the telephone number. If the area code exists and is strung first, the value of the pointer will be 6; otherwise, it will be 1. When the rest of the telephone number is strung into the target field, the number will be properly positioned.

7

The `Unstring` Statement

Sometimes, instead of creating a new string, you need to separate an existing string into separate fields. You might receive data in a file that contains a first name, middle initial, and last name. You need to separate these into separate data fields. To handle this task, COBOL provides a statement called `Unstring`.

`Unstring` Delimiters

`Unstring`, in its simplest form, merely splits a field into parts based on a delimiter. Like the `String` statement, the delimiter may be a single character, a nonnumeric variable, or a nonnumeric literal. The target field or fields of an `Unstring` statement are not initialized before the the `Unstring` statement moves values into them. You must use caution to ensure that the target fields are properly initialized.

`Unstring` uses a single source field and one or more target fields. The source field may not be reference modified. `Unstring` examines the source field character by character, moving the data into the first target field. When the specified delimiter is encountered, the `Unstring` process begins to fill the next target field. If you have a data item that contains a name, for example, `"John Joe Jones"`, that you want to split into separate fields, code the following `Unstring` statement:

```
000044      Unstring Source-Field Delimited By Space
000045              Into Target-1, Target-2, Target-3
000046      End-Unstring
```

> `Unstring` supports the use of the `End-Unstring` explicit scope terminator.
> I suggest that you use `End-Unstring` whenever your `String` statement
> uses any optional clauses or extends over several lines.

What would happen if your source field contained `"John   Joe Jones"`, where several spaces separate the fields you want to unstring? If you use the code example in lines 44-46, you will end up with `Target-1` containing `"John"`, `Target-2` containing `"Joe"`, and `Target-3` containing spaces. The `Unstring` considers only the first space it encounters to be a delimiter. To handle the possible repetition of delimiters, insert the word `All` before the delimiter. The following `Unstring` statement properly handles the input field example:

```
000047      Unstring Source-Field Delimited By All Space
000048              Into Target-1, Target-2, Target-3
000049      End-Unstring
```

When you use Unstring, you may use multiple delimiters. Your source field might contain "Jones, Joe John", and you might want to separate this into three different fields. If you were restricted to only a single delimiter, you would have to issue two Unstring statements to handle this input. However, Unstring allows you to use multiple delimiters:

```
000050     Unstring Source-Field Delimited By All Space Or
000051                                   All ","
000052          Into Target-1, Target-2, Target-3
000053     End-Unstring
```

In this example, if either a space or a comma is encountered, the Unstring proceeds to the next target field.

In addition, the Unstring statement enables you to count the number of target fields that it actually changes. For example, you can determine whether the source field has two names or three by coding the Tallying In clause. When you use this clause, the numeric variable that is specified after Tallying In is incremented by the number of target fields changed.

> When using Tallying In, you must make sure to reset to zero the numeric data item being used before each Unstring statement. The tally is incremented by the Unstring statement, but is not set to zero at the start.

```
000050     Move Zeros To Numeric-Counter
000051     Unstring Source-Field Delimited By All Space Or
000052                                   All ","
000053          Into Target-1, Target-2, Target-3
000054          Tallying In Numeric-Counter
000055     End-Unstring
```

In this example, if the source field contains "David Jones", the field Numeric-Counter has a value of 2 after the Unstring operation.

It might be desirable to know the total number of characters from the source field that were moved into the different target fields. You can capture this information by coding the Count In clause. Delimiters that are encountered are not included in the count. Count In references a numeric data item.

7

> When using the `Count In` clause and a delimiter other than spaces, the result might not be what you expect. If you are not using spaces as a delimiter, any spaces encountered are added to the character count that is stored in the associated `Count In` data item.

```
000050        Move Zeros To Numeric-Counter
000051        Move Zeros To Character-Counter
000052        Unstring Source-Field Delimited By All Space Or
000053                                           All ","
000054               Into Target-1, Target-2, Target-3
000055               Count In Character-Counter
000056               Tallying In Numeric-Counter
000057        End-Unstring
```

If the source field has a value of `"Expect A Miracle"`, the value in `Numeric-Counter` is `14` after the `Unstring` is executed; the space character between the words is the delimiter and is not added to the data item specified by `Count In`.

If any of the target fields are too small to contain the data from the `Unstring` operation, an overflow condition occurs. As with the `String` statement, you can capture this occurrence by coding the `On Overflow` clause. However, the `On Overflow` clause does not capture which target field overflowed.

The last delimiter encountered can be captured by using the `Delimiter In` clause. When this clause is used, the last delimiter is stored in the associated data item. If the end of the source field is encountered, the stored delimiter is spaces if alphanumeric or zeros if numeric.

The `Pointer` clause can indicate the starting position in the source field where you desire the `Unstring` operation to begin. The data item associated with the `Pointer` clause must be numeric and have a value greater than zero. You should be sure the field is properly initialized before the next `Unstring` statement. Listing 7.2 combines many of the features discussed so far. This example accepts a simple mathematical expression and dissects it, displaying the components of the expression. The program requires two `Unstring` statements.

LISTING 7.2 UNSTRING EXAMPLE

```
000001 @OPTIONS MAIN
000002 Identification Division.
000003 Program-Id.  Chapt07x.
000004* Unstring Example
000005 Environment Division.
```

```
000006 Configuration Section.
000007 Source-Computer.  IBM-PC.
000008 Object-Computer.  IBM-PC.
000009 Data Division.
000010 Working-Storage Section.
000011 01  Expression-In    Pic X(10)    Value Spaces.
000012 01  First-Term       Pic X(5)     Value Spaces.
000013 01  Second-Term      Pic X(5)     Value Spaces.
000014 01  Operation        Pic X        Value Spaces.
000015 01  Unstring-Pointer Pic 9(2)     Value Zeros.
000016 Screen Section.
000017 01  Main-Screen Blank Screen.
000018     03  Line 01 Column 01 Value "Enter Expression:".
000019     03  Line 01 Column 19 Pic X(10) Using Expression-In.
000020     03  Line 03 Column 01 Value "First Term ".
000021     03  Line 04 Column 01 Value "Second Term ".
000022     03  Line 05 Column 01 Value "Operation ".
000023     03  Line 03 Column 13 Pic X(5) From First-Term.
000024     03  Line 04 Column 13 Pic X(5) From Second-Term.
000025     03  Line 05 Column 13 Pic X    From Operation.
000026 Procedure Division.
000027 Chapt07x-Start.
000028     Display Main-Screen
000029     Accept Main-Screen
000030     Unstring Expression-In
000031       Delimited By "+" or "-" or "*" or "/"
000032       Into First-Term
000033       Delimiter In Operation
000034       Count In Unstring-Pointer
000035     End-Unstring
000036     Add 2 To Unstring-Pointer
000037     Unstring Expression-In
000038       Delimited By "="
000039       Into Second-Term
000040       Pointer Unstring-Pointer
000041     End-Unstring
000042     Display Main-Screen ·          Accept Main-Screen
000043     Stop Run
000044       .
```

It is entirely permissible, and often desirable, to use Unstring to strip off only a single portion of a source field. The preceding program uses this technique to capture the delimiter. The delimiter, which is the mathematical symbol of the expression entered, is stored in the Operation field. The first term of the expression is stored in the First-Term field. The length of the first term is stored in the Unstring-Pointer field.

The next step is to position the pointer for the start of the next Unstring. The pointer needs to be positioned at the first character after the delimiter. If the first term had three characters before the delimiter, the value of String-Pointer is 3. Then 2 is added to achieve the start position for the next Unstring, which is 5. The delimiter is in the fourth position, and the first character of the second term is in the fifth.

Enter, compile, and run the program. Experiment with it. Enter various expressions and examine the results. Try things like "17-6=", and "A*123=".

Summary

In this hour, you learned the following:

- You can use the String and Unstring statements to manipulate data fields.
- You can use delimiters to determine the action of the statements.
- With the String statement, Delimited By Size causes the entire source field to be moved into the target field.
- The Pointer clause can position the String statement at various points in the target field.
- Unstring can strip characters from a source field into one or more target fields.

Q&A

Q When using the String statement, is the target field cleared before the String operation is performed?

A No, so that you can execute multiple string operations into a single target. The Pointer clause allows you to position the next character in the target field.

Q Can I string more than two fields together in a single String statement?

A Yes. You can list the different fields you want to use in a single String statement.

Q What if I want to use a different delimiter for each field?

A You can list the different delimiters with each field you are unstringing. If all the fields use the same delimiter, you only need to specify the Delimited By clause once, after all the fields are listed.

Q Must the delimiters always be single characters? Can I use something like "SEPARATOR" as a delimiter?

A Delimiters can be of any size that can be contained in the source field. The word "SEPARATOR" can be used as a delimiter.

Q **How do I find out how many fields are found when I unstring a field? I don't know how many to expect.**

A You can determine the number of target fields used by an Unstring operation by specifying the Tallying In clause on your Unstring statement. The tally field is incremented by the number of fields changed. Be careful that you initialize the tally field each time it is used, as the Unstring statement does not automatically do this for you.

Q **I already used Unstring to operate on part of a field. I want to Unstring some more data, but I don't want to start over at the beginning of the field. I know that reference modification is not allowed. What should I do?**

A You may use the Pointer clause of the Unstring statement to indicate a data field containing the position of the next character that should be included in the Unstring operation.

Workshop

To help reinforce your understanding of the material presented in this hour, refer to the section "Quiz and Exercise Questions and Answers" that can be found on the CD. This section contains quiz questions and exercises for you to complete, as well as the corresponding answers.

7

Hour **8**

Conditional Statements

Computer programs can perform tasks that range from very simple to very complex. More complicated tasks require making choices. Under some circumstances, you might want the program to perform one function; but under other circumstances, you might desire a different function. Conditional statements perform the act of choosing the appropriate function. A *conditional* is the statement or question asked in order to make a choice. It is somewhat like a question you might ask yourself, for example, "If I have enough money, can I buy an ice cream sundae?" In this hour, you learn about the various types of conditional statements available in COBOL, such as

- The If statement.
- Various conditions that can be tested using If.
- The Else clause
- Evaluating complex conditions
- 88 levels and how they relate to conditions.

Conditional Statements in COBOL

Conditional statements control the flow of a program. For the most part, the examples that have been examined thus far involved statements that were always executed. With conditional statements, you can decide which statements to execute under different conditions. For example, if the user can enter multiple types of transactions, you need the program to decide the appropriate action to take based on the type of transaction. A debit transaction cannot be processed the same way as a credit transaction. Conditional statements are coded to tell the program what to do when various conditions are encountered.

You have already seen some conditional statements in action. The `Size Error` phrase that can be coded with mathematical statements is one example. When a `Size Error` occurs, the statements coded with the `Size Error` phrase are executed. The `Size Error` is the condition under which the statements are executed. It is similar to stating, "Do the add operation; then if there is a size error, do something special."

The `If` Statement

The `If` statement is the most fundamental of the COBOL conditional statements. With the `If` statement, you tell the program to make a simple choice. If the condition stated is true, then do what is specified. It is in stating these conditions that an infinite variety of possibilities is found. COBOL allows you much freedom in the coding of conditional statements. They can be as simple or complex as you allow them to be. These conditional statements are at the heart of computer programming.

When you code an `If` statement and the condition tested is true, every statement after the `If` is executed until an `End-If`, `Else`, or period is encountered. (`Else` is discussed in the next section; for now concentrate on the different conditions.)

The `If` statement can be used to test the relationship between two or more data items. When two data items are compared, one of three things can be determined:

- The data items are equal.
- The first data item is greater in value than the second.
- The second data item is greater in value than the first.

When writing your conditional statement, you are asking if one or more of these three conditions is true. If the condition is true, then the `If` statement is considered to be true.

8

As I look over my programming career, I find that two courses I took in school contributed most to my success. One is typing. The second, and more important, is a course I took in symbolic logic. I cannot overstress the value of such a course to the computer programmer. If your local community college offers such a course, and you are serious about computer programming in any language, take this course.

The simplest condition is the test for equality. This test can be coded in two ways. You may use the = sign, or you may spell out Is Equal To. The words, Is and To are optional. Table 8.1 shows a few examples of tests for equality and whether or not they are true.

TABLE 8.1 TESTING THE EQUALITY CONDITION

Condition	True or False
"A" = "B"	False
"A" Is Equal To "B"	False
"A" Equal "B"	False
1 = 10	False
"A " = "A"	True
1.0 = 1	True
10 = "Ten"	False

To properly understand equality, you need to understand how the different data items are compared. Different types of data items are compared differently.

Alphanumeric data items and literals are compared from left to right, character by character. Trailing spaces in an alphanumeric data item do not affect the comparison. "A" is the same as "A   ". The compiler pads the shorter field with trailing spaces to make the fields of equal length for the comparison.

Numeric fields are compared based on their values. If a field defined as having one decimal position is compared to a field having three and the numeric values are equal, the condition is true.

Numeric items may be compared with numeric expressions. That is, you may perform tests that compare 1 and (3-2). The expressions are evaluated before the comparison is made.

When numeric and alphanumeric items are compared, the comparison proceeds as if it were an alphanumeric compare.

Numeric edited items are treated as alphanumeric items for the purpose of comparisons.

The If statement tests the truth of these conditions. If the test is true, then the statements following the If are executed. If the test is false, the statements are not executed. Consider some examples. For clarity, these use numeric variables and expressions for comparison.

```
000027    If 1 = 12
000028        Display "Condition True"
000029    End-If
```

This condition is false, because 1 is not equal to 12. The Display statement is not executed. The End-If is an explicit scope terminator that terminates the If statement. Flow through the program continues immediately following this End-If.

> An If statement may also be terminated with a period. The preceding example could have been coded: If 1 = 12, Display "Condition True". However, for the structured programming style used in these lessons, only one period per paragraph is used. The End-If signifies the end of the statements to be executed if the condition being tested is true.

More than one statement may be executed after an If statement's condition is determined to be true.

```
000030    If Data-Item-1 = Data-Item-2
000031        Display "The Data Items are The Same"
000032        Unstring Data-Item-1
000033            Delimited By Space
000034            Into Unstring-Field-1
000035                Unstring-Field-2
000036        End-Unstring
000037    End-If
```

In this example, if the values of Data-Item-1 and Data-Item-2 are true, then two COBOL statements are executed. The first displays a literal, and the second performs an Unstring operation. Neither of the statements is executed if the condition is false, that is, if Data-Item-1 and Data-Item-2 are not equal. However, if the condition is true, *both* statements are executed.

In addition to testing for equality, you may test for inequality. There are two ways to express the condition. You may code Not Equal or Not =. The condition is tested, and if true, that is, the data items compared are not the same, then the statements following the If are executed.

> The If statement may be coded with the word Then. Using Then does nothing special as far as evaluating the If statement, but it can clarify the If logic, making it a bit easier to understand. For example, you could code: If 1 = 12 Then … This method is often easier to follow at first. After you are more comfortable with the If statement, you may find that the word Then is simply extra typing.

The next condition type is a test to compare the value of two data items to determine whether the first item is less than the second. Less than is pretty easy to understand when discussing numbers. It is obvious that 1 is less than 10. What can be confusing is alphanumeric data items in conditions. Can you see why "Four" is less than "One"?

The testing of relative values of alphanumeric data items is controlled by the collating sequence of the computer's character set. A character set is simply the group of characters that the computer understands. For the PC, this character set is called the ASCII character set. This character set consists of 256 characters. Each character has a ranking within that set. The character with the lowest ranking is less than one with a higher ranking in any condition.

> The characters might not compare the way you might expect. Within the alphabet, "A" is less than "Z", and "0" is less than "9". However, a lowercase "a" is *greater* than an uppercase "Z". The characters "A" and "a" are separate and have different values within the ASCII collating sequence. You must use caution when comparing alphanumeric variables to ensure that you understand the potential results of your comparisons.

When two alphanumeric items are compared in a less-than condition, each character in each item is compared one at a time. The comparison proceeds from left to right. When the first character that determines the condition is either true or false is encountered, the comparison is terminated. When comparing "APPLE" and "ORANGE", only a single character in each needs be compared to determine which is greater. When "ZZZZZT" and "ZZZZZP" are tested, seven characters must be compared before it is decided that "ZZZZZZP" is less than "ZZZZZZT".

The less-than comparison may be coded as either < or Less Than. For example:

```
000038      If Data-A Is Less Than Data-B
000039          Display "A less than B"
000040      End-If
```

is exactly the same as

```
000038      If Data-A < Data-B
000039          Display "A less than B"
000040      End-If
```

The Is in the first example is optional. The condition is true only if Data-A is less than Data-B. If Data-A and Data-B are the same, or equal, the condition is not true. The opposite of Less Than is *not* Greater Than. Greater Than leaves out the potential for the items to compare equally. The opposite condition of Less Than is Greater Than Or Equal To. If you want to test whether Data-A is not less than Data-B, code the following:

```
000041      If Data-A Not < Data-B
000042          Display "A not less than B"
000043      End-If
```

In this case, if the values of Data-A and Data-B are the same, the condition is true. In other words, if the values of Data-A and Data-B are the same, then the value of Data-A is certainly not less than the value of Data-B!

The next condition is a test for whether the first variable is greater than the second. This test can be coded with > or Greater Than. If the two items being compared are equal, then the condition is false. The opposite condition may be tested by coding Not in front of the > symbol.

The Less Than and Greater Than conditions can be combined with the Equal. The combination is coded as <= or Less Than Or Equal, and conversely, >= or Greater Than Or Equal. For the <= condition, the condition is true if the first data item is either less than the second or the same as the second. These conditions are sometimes confusing. Here are some examples of If statements that use these conditions.

```
000044      If Data-A Not > Data-B
000045          Display "A < B"
000046      End-If
000047      If Data-B >= Data-A
000048          Display "B >= A"
000049      End-If
```

These two If statements are different ways of coding exactly the same thing. Plug in various values for Data-A and Data-B and see that both conditions are true when the same values for Data-A and Data-B are inserted. Using >= and <= is a way to avoid using the

Not, which some people find confusing.

Literals may be used in conditions. For example, you can test whether Data-A is Greater Than Spaces.

In addition to comparing the values of data items, a condition can test the class of an item. This test determines whether the item is Numeric, Alphabetic, Alphabetic-Lowercase, Alphabetic-Uppercase, or some other special condition as provided for in the Special-Names paragraph by the compiler. You may specify Class in the Special-Names paragraph and create a new class based on a range of values. For example:

```
000008 Special-Names.
000009     Class ABC is "A" thru "C"
000010                Space.
```

This Special-Names paragraph defines a new class named ABC, which consists of the letters A, B, and C and the space. You may test a field to determine whether it consists of these values by coding:

```
000100     If Test-Field ABC
000101         Display "Test-Field is of Class ABC"
000102     End-If
```

If you have an alphanumeric data field that you need to move to a Usage Display numeric data item, you should test the field first to see whether it is numeric. Moving nonnumeric data into a numeric field can cause erroneous results or a program crash. This test may be coded as

```
000050     If Data-A Is Numeric
000051         Move Data-A To Number-A
000052     End-If
```

The word Is in the expression is optional.

The Else Clause

When coding your If statements, you may wish to do one thing if the condition is true but something else if the condition is false. This option is available to you by using the Else clause. When you code an If statement and use an Else clause, when the condition being tested is false, the statements after the Else are executed until an End-If or period is encountered.

```
000053     If Data-A < Data-B
000054         Display "A < B"
000055     Else
000056         Display "A not < B"
000057     End-If
```

Remember that the statements that are executed when the condition tested is true stop when the `Else` is encountered. If the condition is true, the statements after the `Else` are not executed. Terminating the `If` statement with the `End-If` explicit scope terminator or period is very important. You may find that many lines of your program are not being executed because they fall under an `Else` statement inside an `If` that was not properly terminated.

As with the `If`, multiple statements may be executed after the `Else`.

Using Complex Conditions

`If` statements can test complex conditions. A complex condition is like a series of conditions combined into a single condition. Complex conditions are created by using `And`, `Or`, and `Not`.

When `And` is used, all conditions linked by the `And` must be true for the entire condition to be true. It is the true or false state of the entire condition that the `If` statement is testing. Consider an example:

```
000058      If Data-A = Data-B And Data-C = Data-D
000059          Display "Condition True"
000060      End-If
```

In this example, the display only occurs if the values of `Data-A` and `Data-B` are the same *and* if the values of `Data-C` and `Data-D` are the same. For example, if `Data-A` has a value of 3, `Data-B` has a value of 3, `Data-C` has a value of 5, and `Data-D` has a value of 5, then the entire condition is true.

You may use parentheses to isolate your conditions when using complex conditions. Parentheses help to clarify the individual conditions that make up your complex conditions. The preceding example could have been more clearly coded as If (Data-A = Data-B) And (Data-C = Data-D).

When `Or` is used, only a single one of the conditions being tested need be true for the entire complex condition to be true.

```
000058      If Data-A = Data-B Or Data-C = Data-D
000059          Display "Condition True"
000060      End-If
```

In this case, if either `Data-A` = `Data-B` *or* `Data-C` = `Data-D` is true, then the entire condition is true and the `Display` statement is executed.

The word Not can be used to negate a condition. That is, for a condition preceded by Not to be true, the condition must be false. When using Not, it is useful to enclose the condition that is being negated in parentheses. Some examples can help to make this clear.

```
000061    If Not (Data-A = Data-B)
000062        Display "Condition True"
000063    End-If
```

This condition first tests Data-A and Data-B for equality. If that condition is false, then the entire condition is true. It is exactly the same thing as stating If Data-A not = Data-B. The Not phrase can be very useful but also baffling. Using Not is very similar to using Else, except the statements normally coded under the Else are coded after the If statement instead. In the next example, the two If statements perform the same function.

```
000064    If Data-A = Data-B
000065        Display "A = B"
000066    Else
000067        Display "A not = B"
000068    End-If
000069    If Not (Data-A = Data-B)
000070        Display "A not = B"
000071    Else
000072        Display "A = B"
000073    End-If
```

Using Not basically reverses the statements that are executed after the If and Else. If you want to avoid using Not, you can always code If statements with the Else clause. The only problem with this approach is what to do when you only have statements to execute under the Else clause. For this problem, COBOL provides the Continue statement.

Continue performs no activity and can be used as a nonoperational statement. It can be coded when the COBOL syntax requires a statement to be present, but you have nothing you want to do, as in this example:

```
000074    If Data-A = Data-B
000075        Continue
000076    Else
000077        Display "A not = B"
000078    End-If
```

Complex conditions can be abbreviated, but you should be careful. The abbreviated version may be hard to grasp logically. The two If statements in the next example are the same. The second one is an abbreviated version of the first:

```
000079    If Data-A = Data-B Or Data-A = Data-C Or Data-A = Data-D
000080        Display "Condition is True"
000081    End-If
```

```
000082      If Data-A = Data-B Or Data-C Or Data-D
000083          Display "Condition is True"
000084      End-If
```

The condition is abbreviated by removing the repeated data item.

Examine a variation on one of the examples previously discussed. In an earlier example, you were formatting a telephone number in the format (999) 999-9999. If the telephone number does not include the area code, you want to leave it off. Listing 8.1 is a small program that shows the use of an If statement to determine the proper formatting logic for the telephone number.

LISTING 8.1   INTELLIGENT TELEPHONE NUMBER FORMAT

```
000000 @OPTIONS MAIN
000001 Identification Division.
000002 Program-Id.  Chapt08a.
000003* Intelligent Telephone Number Format
000004 Environment Division.
000005 Configuration Section.
000006 Source-Computer.  IBM-PC.
000007 Object-Computer.  IBM-PC.
000008 Data Division.
000009 Working-Storage Section.
000010 01  Phone-Number        pic 9(10) Value Zeros.
000011 01  Formatted-Number     Pic X(14) Value "(XXX) XXX-XXXX".
000012 01  Formatted-Alternate Pic X(8)  Value "XXX-XXXX".
000013 01  The-Edited-Number   Pic X(14) Value Spaces.
000014 Screen Section.
000015 01  Phone-Entry Blank Screen.
000016     03  Line 01 Column 01 Value " Enter Phone Number: ".
000017     03  Line 01 Column 22 Pic Z(10) Using Phone-Number.
000018     03  Line 03 Column 01 Value "Edited Phone Number: ".
000019     03  Line 03 Column 22 Pic X(14) From The-Edited-Number.
000020 Procedure Division.
000021 Chapt08a-Start.
000022     Display Phone-Entry
000023     Accept  Phone-Entry
000024     If Phone-Number > 9999999
000025* Number large enough to contain area code
000026         Inspect Formatted-Number
000027           Replacing First "XXX"  By Phone-Number (1:3)
000028                     First "XXX"  By Phone-Number (4:3)
000029                     First "XXXX" By Phone-Number ·(7:4)
000030         Move Formatted-Number To The-Edited-Number
000031     Else
000032* Number not large enough to contain an area code
000033         Inspect Formatted-Alternate
000034           Replacing First "XXX"  By Phone-Number (4:3)
```

```
000035                    First "XXXX" By Phone-Number (7:4)
000036           Move Formatted-Alternate To The-Edited-Number
000037        End-If
000038        Display Phone-Entry
000039        Stop Run
000040           .
```

8

This program has several interesting features. First, note that the If, Else, and End-If are aligned to make the code easier to follow. Notice also the use of reference modification in the Inspect statements. A numeric data item accepts the telephone number so that the value can be tested to see whether the number was keyed with an area code. Additionally, using a numeric data field causes the number to be right-justified. This technique allows you to know where the specific portions of the telephone number are so that you may use reference modification. The If statement is used with an Else clause to determine which of the Inspect and Move statements to execute.

Key the program into the editor. Then compile, link, and run the program. Experiment with inputting different telephone numbers, and view the results.

Nesting If Statements

NEW TERM   If statements may be nested. That is, after the condition, or the Else, another If statement can occur. One case in which nesting might be useful is when a variable could have three possible values that you need to test.

```
000085     If Data-Item-1 = "A"
000086         Display "Apple"
000087     Else
000088         If Data-Item-1 = "B"
000089             Display "Berry"
000090         Else
000091             Display "Chocolate"
000092         End-if
000093     End-if
```

After the Else associated with the test for "A", there is another condition, testing for "B". You can nest If statements up to the limit of the compiler. Different compilers allow a different number of levels of nesting.

> When coding nested If statements, it is a good idea to always make use of the End-If explicit scope terminator. Your source code will be easier to follow if you align your If, Else, and associated End-If statements. Hour 9, "The Evaluate Statement," and later hours describe alternatives to deeply nesting If statements.

88 Levels and the Set Statement

NEW TERM In the `Data Division`, you may define a special level numbered item called a condition name. This condition name can be tested as a condition. Condition names may be associated with any elementary data item including a `Filler` data item. Another commonly used term to describe these condition names is *flag*. In your program, if you want to perform a special operation, you might set a flag. For example, after reading the last item from a file, you might set a flag to indicate that the entire file has been read. Later in the program, you can test that flag to determine when to stop processing.

Condition names are defined by coding an 88 level with the condition name and the value or values that cause the condition to be true.

```
000020 01  Flag-Variable      Pic X.
000021      88  Flag-On   Value "1".
```

The condition `Flag-On` is true when `Flag-Variable` has a value of 1. You may code as many 88 levels under a data item as you want. Additionally, an 88 level may specify a range of values or even multiple ranges. If the data item that the condition name is coded for is equal to any of the values, then the condition is true.

```
000022 01  Data-Flags.
000023      03  Filler          Pic X(3) Value Spaces.
000024          88  Test-One    Value "ONE" "one" "One".
000025          88  Test-Two    Value "TWO" "two" "Two".
000026      03  Filler          Pic X Value Spaces.
000027          88  A-Thru-Z    Value "A" Thru "Z".
000028          88  0-Thru-9    Value "0" Thru "9".
000029      03  Number-Flag     Pic 9.
000030          88  Low-Number  Value 0 Thru 4.
```

`Test-One` is true when the value of the three-character `Filler` is equal to one of the three values defined. The condition `A-Thru-Z` is true when the `Filler` item has a value of any letter between "A" and "Z".

Because you cannot move a value directly into a `Filler` item, you might be curious as to how the condition can become true. Consider this example:

```
000031 01  Filler Pic X.
000032      88  Letter-A     Value "A".
```

You cannot move a value into the `Filler` or into the condition name `Letter-A`. However, with COBOL you can use the `Set` verb to set a condition name to a true state. When you code the statement, `Set Letter-A To True`, an A is moved into the `Filler` item and the condition is true. Using `Set` is a good way to control the state of conditions.

Presently in COBOL, there is no way to "unset" a condition, or to set a condition to false. In the preceding example, when an A gets into the Filler item, there is no way to get it out. When using conditions with Filler items, you should always allow for a second 88 level item that has a different state. For example, in the preceding example you could code another 88 level with a condition name of Space-Item, and then using the Set statement, set that condition true.

```
000031 01   Filler Pic X.
000032      88  Letter-A    Value "A".
000033      88  Space-Item  Value Space.
```

When Space-Item becomes true, a space is moved into the Filler. If you have conditions that you need to set and reset in your program, you should assign a variable name instead of using Filler so that you may either use Initialize, or move a value directly into the field.

Using 88 Levels in an If Statement

Condition names, or 88 level items, may be used with an If statement. If the condition name is true, then the statements after the If are executed. To illustrate, look at Listing 8.2. This program unstrings a name entry into three fields. Then, depending on the number of names entered, the code moves the data field to the appropriate name for display.

LISTING 8.2   INTELLIGENT NAME SEPARATION

```
000001 @OPTIONS MAIN
000002 Identification Division.
000003 Program-Id.  Chapt08b.
000004* Intelligent Name Separation
000005 Environment Division.
000006 Configuration Section.
000007 Source-Computer.  IBM-PC.
000008 Object-Computer.  IBM-PC.
000009 Data Division.
000010 Working-Storage Section.
000011 01   Name-Entered        Pic X(50) Value Spaces.
000012 01   First-Name          Pic X(30) Value Spaces.
000013 01   Middle-Name         Pic X(30) Value Spaces.
000014 01   Last-Name           Pic X(30) Value Spaces.
000015 01   Unstring-Fields               Value Spaces.
000016      03  First-Field     Pic X(30).
000017      03  Second-Field    Pic X(30).
000018      03  Third-Field     Pic X(30).
000019 01   Number-Of-Fields    Pic 9     Value Zeros.
000020      88  Last-Name-Only            Value 1.
```

continues

LISTING 8.2   CONTINUED

```
000021      88  First-And-Last        Value 2.
000022      88  First-Last-Middle     Value 3.
000023 Screen Section.
000024 01  Name-Entry Blank Screen.
000025      03  Line 01 Column 01 Value "Enter Name: ".
000026      03  Line 01 Column 13 Pic X(50) Using Name-Entered.
000027      03  Line 03 Column 01 Value " First: ".
000028      03  Line 03 Column 09 Pic X(30) From First-Name.
000029      03  Line 04 Column 01 Value "Middle: ".
000030      03  Line 04 Column 09 Pic X(30) From Middle-Name.
000031      03  Line 05 Column 01 Value "  Last: ".
000032      03  Line 05 Column 09 Pic X(30) From Last-Name.
000033 Procedure Division.
000034 Chapt08b-Start.
000035      Display Name-Entry
000036      Accept  Name-Entry
000037* Unstring into possible 3 fields, allow for multiple spaces
000038* between names
000039      Unstring Name-Entered Delimited By All Space
000040          Into First-Field, Second-Field, Third-Field
000041          Tallying In Number-Of-Fields
000042      End-Unstring
000043* Now, move as appropriate.
000044      If Last-Name-Only
000045          Move First-Field  To Last-Name
000046      End-If
000047      If First-And-Last
000048          Move First-Field  To First-Name
000049          Move Second-Field To Last-Name
000050      End-If
000051      If First-Last-Middle
000052          Move First-Field  To First-Name
000053          Move Second-Field To Middle-Name
000054          Move Third-Field  To Last-Name
000055      End-If
000056      Display Name-Entry
000057      Stop Run
000058      .
```

Number-Of-Fields is the field that contains the number of fields that are changed when
the Unstring statement is executed. Under that field, three conditions are defined. Then
three If statements follow the Unstring. Notice how much easier the statements are to
understand when the conditions are spelled out with condition names. The If statements
can be coded as If Number-Of-Fields = 1 and so on, but that is not nearly so clear.

Summary

In this hour, you learned the following:

- Conditions can be tested to cause the COBOL program to execute different instructions under different circumstances.
- You can test two data items for equality or to determine which of the two is greater.
- The collating sequence controls how alphanumeric data items are compared.
- You can use And, Or, and Not to create complex conditional statements.
- The If statement can test these various conditions.
- Else can execute different statements if a condition is not true.
- The Continue statement can be used when a statement is required, but you want the program to perform no action.
- If statements can be nested.
- Condition names can be defined in the Data Division and then tested in your program.

Q&A

Q What is the purpose of the If statement?

A The If statement allows the programmer to test for certain conditions and to perform different statements based on the results of those tests.

Q When creating a complex condition using Or, what determines whether the entire condition is true?

A When using an Or, if one of the conditions coded is true, then the entire complex condition is true. You may code a string of Or conditions, and if any one of them is true, then the entire condition is true.

Q Can I use And and Or in the same condition?

A Yes. You can code something like, If A = 1 and B = 1 or C = 1. However, this syntax is hard to understand. It is better to code this condition as follows: If (A = 1 And B = 1) Or C = 1. When this statement is tested, the condition is true if A and B are both 1, or if C is 1 regardless of the values in A and B.

Q Can I code an If statement under another If statement?

A Yes. These statements are called nested If statements.

Q How do I make a condition name defined with an 88 level true?

A You can do so in two ways. Either you can move the appropriate value into the elementary item with which the condition name is associated, or you can use the Set statement to set the condition to the true state.

Workshop

To help reinforce your understanding of the material presented in this hour, refer to the section "Quiz and Exercise Questions and Answers" that can be found on the CD. This section contains quiz questions and exercises for you to complete, as well as the corresponding answers.

HOUR 9

The **Evaluate** Statement

In computer programs, it is often necessary to determine which action to take based on a complex set of conditions. You may end up coding a significant number of If statements to handle these decisions. As you nest the If statements deeper and deeper, the code can become very confusing. If you have to come back later and change the program, you may find yourself spending a lot of time just trying to figure out what you were attempting to do with all those If statements.

COBOL comes equipped with a very versatile statement as an alternative to using complex, highly nested If statements. This statement is the Evaluate statement.

When to Use **Evaluate**

After analyzing the decisions you need to make in your program, you will probably find that some conditions are very simple and can be handled with a single If statement. Others will be more complex. Evaluate is ideal for circumstances in which you want to execute different statements based on the value of a single data item. When more than two values are possible, you may find yourself coding multiple If statements or creating highly nested If structures.

You can use Evaluate to simplify the coding and to help keep your code clear and concise. Imagine that some of the consignment dealers in your antique store pay you a percentage of their sales. The percentage may vary from dealer to dealer, but you have instituted four commission plans. The first plan pays you 10% of every sale. The second pays you 20%, the third pays you 25%, and the final plan pays you nothing. For each sale, you must determine the plan being used and pay yourself the proper commission. Using If statements is one way to write the necessary code:

```
000040     If Commission-Plan = "A"
000041        Move 10 To Commission-Percent
000042     Else
000043        If Commission-Plan = "B"
000044           Move 20 To Commission-Percent
000045        Else
000046           If Commission-Plan = "C"
000047              Move 25 To Commission-Percent
000048           Else
000049              Move Zero To Commission-Percent
000050           End-If
000051        End-If
000052     End-If
```

Another option is to code individual If statements for each commission plan, but that approach makes the last plan harder to test:

```
000053     If Commission-Plan = "A"
000054        Move 10 To Commission-Percent
000055     End-If
000056     If Commission-Plan = "B"
000057        Move 20 To Commission-Percent
000058     End-If
000059     If Commission-Plan = "C"
000060        Move 25 To Commission-Percent
000061     End-If
000062     If Commission-Plan Not = "A" And
000063        Commission-Plan Not = "B" And
000064        Commission-Plan Not = "C"
000065        Move Zeros To Commission-Percent
000066     End-If
```

The Evaluate statement makes this situation much easier to write and understand:

```
000067     Evaluate Commission-Plan
000068        When "A"
000069           Move 10    To Commission-Percent
000070        When "B"
000071           Move 20    To Commission-Percent
```

```
000072          When "C"
000073              Move 25    To Commission-Percent
000074          When Other
000075              Move Zero  To Commission-Percent
000076        End-Evaluate
```

The Evaluate statement has only one basic format, but that format has many variations. The preceding code illustrates the simplest format, but conditions that are more complex can benefit from the use of the Evaluate statement as well.

Simple Evaluate Statements

The code that immediately follows the word Evaluate defines what you are testing, or evaluating. You may evaluate an expression, a literal, or a data item, for a true condition, or for a false condition.

The code that follows the word When within the Evaluate statement does two things. First, it defines the circumstances under which the statements that follow are to be executed. Second, the statements after the When are those that are executed when the circumstances described by the evaluation of code after the word Evaluate, in conjunction with the code after the When, are evaluated against each other.

The text that follows the word Evaluate is defined as the selection subject. The text that follows the word When is defined as the selection object. As the Evaluate statement is executed, each selection object is evaluated against each selection subject. When the result of this evaluation is true, the statements after the When are executed. The evaluations occur in the order of the coded When items. After a subject and object are evaluated to be true, the statements after the When are executed and the processing of the Evaluate statement ends. Statements after the selection object are executed until the next selection object (When), End-Evaluate, or period, is encountered.

> A common mistake in using the Evaluate statement is to assume that once the statements coded after one When are executed, the other When statements continue to be evaluated. That is not so. After a When selection object is evaluated with the selection subject and the evaluation is determined to be true, no further selection objects are evaluated.

The extreme versatility of the Evaluate statement can lead to some confusion. Examine this example of two different ways to code an Evaluate that do the same thing. When the condition Data-Item-A = Data-Item-B is true, one thing is to be displayed, but when it's not true, different text is to be displayed.

```
000061      Evaluate Data-Item-A = Data-Item-B
000062         When True
000063            Display "Items are Equal"
000064         When False
000065            Display "Items are not equal"
000066      End-Evaluate
000067      Evaluate True
000068         When Data-Item-A = Data-Item-B
000069            Display "Items are Equal"
000070         When Data-Item-A not = Data-Item-B
000071            Display "Items are not equal"
000072      End-Evaluate
```

Note the use of the explicit scope terminator, End-Evaluate. I recommend that you always use this feature of the statement. The first of these statements uses the condition Data-Item-A = Data-Item-B as its subject. When such a condition is used as a selection subject, the only selection objects that make sense are True and False. This statement is equivalent to coding an If statement with an Else clause.

The second Evaluate uses True as its selection subject. The condition to be tested is then coded as a selection object. The second selection object is the opposite condition. The output of these two statements is the same.

Evaluate also offers a catchall selection object that is coded after the other selection objects. The statements that follow are always executed when no other selection objects are evaluated to be true with the selection subject. This is the selection object Other. In the preceding example, the second Evaluate could have used this selection object as follows:

```
000067      Evaluate True
000068         When Data-Item-A = Data-Item-B
000069            Display "Items are Equal"
000070         When Other
000071            Display "Items are not equal"
000072      End-Evaluate
```

Other examples might be helpful in understanding how the Evaluate statement works. If you have a numeric data item and you want to perform different actions based on its value, using the Evaluate statement is an excellent choice. For example, you might pay a different commission based on the price of an item. The more expensive items in your store might pay a higher commission percentage.

```
000160      Evaluate Sale-Price
000161         When 1000 Thru 10000
000162            Move 50 To Commission-Percent
000163         When 500 Thru 1000
000164            Move 25 To Commission-Percent
000165         When 250 Thru 500
000166            Move 10 To Commission-Percent
```

```
000167        When Other
000168            Move  5 To Commission-Percent
000169        End-Evaluate
```

There are several important considerations in how this Evaluate is coded. First, notice the order of the selection objects. If the sale price is $1,000, it seems as if the second selection object should be executed. It is not. The reason is that the first selection object is true for a sale price of $1,000, so the commission is moved, and no further selection objects are evaluated. Next, consider the size of the sale price field. The high range of $10,000 is chosen because the field is hypothetically defined as Pic 9(4)v99. If the field were larger, you would need a larger value in the first Thru. If the sale price field had a larger definition and a sale price greater than $10,000 is encountered, the commission would be paid at 5%. The logic flow within this Evaluate falls into the Other selection object.

Another method of coding this Evaluate statement follows. This method makes use of the True selection subject.

```
000160        Evaluate True
000161          When Sale-Price >= 1000
000162            Move 50 To Commission-Percent
000163          When Sale-Price >= 500
000164            Move 25 To Commission-Percent
000165          When Sale-Price >= 250
000166            Move 10 To Commission-Percent
000167          When Other
000168            Move  5 To Commission-Percent
000169        End-Evaluate
```

In this second example, the order of the selection objects is very important. For example, if the >= 500 is coded first, the $1,000 items fall under that condition. Remember that the selection objects are evaluated against the selection subject one at a time, from the top of the Evaluate down.

More than one statement may be executed as part of the When. You might want to move the commission percentage to a display field and Compute the actual commission.

```
000170        Evaluate True
000171          When Sale-Price >= 1000
000172            Move 50 To Commission-Percent
000173            Compute Commission Rounded = Sale-Price * .5
000174          When Sale-Price >= 500
000175            Move 25 To Commission-Percent
000176            Compute Commission Rounded = Sale-Price * .25
000177          When Sale-Price >= 250
000178            Move 10 To Commission-Percent
000179            Compute Commission Rounded = Sale-Price * .1
000180          When Other
000181            Move  5 To Commission-Percent
```

```
000182            Compute Commission Rounded = Sale-Price * .05
000183       End-Evaluate
```

This statement is the same as the prior example, with only the added computation.

Another situation in which you can use Evaluate is in separating names into groups based on the first letter of the last name. You might want to divide a mailing into three groups. Assume that you want last names starting with A through F in one group, G through N in the second, and the remaining letters in the third group.

```
000184       Evaluate Last-Name (1:1)
000185          When "A" Thru "F"
000186             Move 1 To Group-Id
000187          When "G" Thru "N"
000188             Move 2 To Group-Id
000189          When Other
000190             Move 3 To Group-Id
000191       End-Evaluate
```

The use of the Other selection object is very important in this case. If the third selection object were coded as When "O" Thru "Z" instead and the first character of the name happened to contain invalid data, such as a number or a space, then no group would be assigned.

What about the circumstance when a range will not do? What if you wanted to group the last names based on the first letters, but not in consecutive groups? Perhaps the last names starting with vowels belong in one group, then those starting with B through J in the second, and the remaining names in the third group.

You may stack selection objects. If no statements follow the selection object, it is treated as part of the next selection object. Therefore, if any selection object evaluates with the selection subject to be true, the statements after the final stacked selection object are executed.

```
000192       Evaluate Last-Name (1:1)
000193          When "A"
000194          When "E"
000195          When "I"
000196          When "O"
000197          When "U"
000198             Move 1 To Group-Id
000199          When "B" Thru "J"
000200             Move 2 To Group-Id
000201          When Other
000202             Move 3 To Group-ID
000203       End-Evaluate
```

In this example, any last name that starts with A, E, I, O, or U will be assigned a group of 1.

More Complex Evaluate Usage

Like If statements, you may nest Evaluate statements. Subsequent Evaluate statements may be coded in the statements that appear after the selection objects. Consider the previous example in which the names were grouped based on the first letter of the last name. You might further subdivide the names based on the first letter of the first name. Consider this example, which divides the names into nine groups.

```
000204      Evaluate Last-Name (1:1)
000205         When "A" Thru "F"
000206            Evaluate First-Name (1:1)
000207               When "A" Thru "F"
000208                  Move 1 To Group-Id
000209               When "G" Thru "N"
000210                  Move 2 To Group-Id
000211               When Other
000212                  Move 3 To Group-Id
000213            End-Evaluate
000214         When "G" Thru "N"
000215            Evaluate First-Name (1:1)
000216               When "A" Thru "F"
000217                  Move 4 To Group-Id
000218               When "G" Thru "N"
000219                  Move 5 To Group-Id
000220               When Other
000221                  Move 6 To Group-Id
000222            End-Evaluate
000223         When Other
000224            Evaluate First-Name (1:1)
000225               When "A" Thru "F"
000226                  Move 7 To Group-Id
000227               When "G" Thru "N"
000228                  Move 8 To Group-Id
000229               When Other
000230                  Move 9 To Group-Id
000231            End-Evaluate
000232      End-Evaluate
```

The Evaluate statement can create complex decision-making structures. More than one selection subject may be used. If multiple selection subjects are used, the same number of items must be specified on the selection object (When) lines of the Evaluate statement.

This type of structure gives the Evaluate tremendous power. Multiple selection subjects and objects are separated with the word Also. Another possible value that can be checked as a selection object is Any. Any means that the evaluation evaluates to be true no matter what the value of the selection object. Consider another solution to coding the previous example.

9

```
000233      Evaluate Last-Name (1:1) Also First-Name (1:1)
000234         When "A" Thru "F" Also "A" Thru "F"
000235            Move 1 To Group-Id
000236         When "A" Thru "F" Also "G" Thru "N"
000237            Move 2 To Group-Id
000238         When "A" Thru "F" Also Any
000239            Move 3 To Group-Id
000240         When "G" Thru "N" Also "A" Thru "F"
000241            Move 4 To Group-Id
000242         When "G" Thru "N" Also "G" Thru "N"
000243            Move 5 To Group-Id
000244         When "G" Thru "N" Also Any
000245            Move 6 To Group-Id
000246         When Any Also "A" Thru "F"
000247            Move 7 To Group-Id
000248         When Any Also "G" Thru "N"
000249            Move 8 To Group-Id
000250         When Other
000251            Move 9 To Group-Id
000252      End-Evaluate
```

When creating complex Evaluate statements using multiple selection subjects, remember that Other is a catchall. You cannot code Other with any
other selection object. Instead of using Other for an individual item when
Also is used, the word Any is provided.

Try to follow the tests that are given in this example. For each selection object, both subjects must be evaluated with the selection objects. If all the different conditions evaluate
to true, then the statements after the selection object line are executed.

Notice that the Other selection object is different from the other selection objects. In the
other selection objects, the number of objects matches the number of selection subjects
coded after the Evaluate statement.

Consider another example. In this example, a commission is calculated based on the
price of the item sold. However, if the commission is less than $1, the commission is
made $1 unless the sale amount is less than $1, in which case the commission is 75% of
the total sale price. Under certain circumstances, the commission is limited to a maximum value.

These rules might seem complex, but this situation is typical in programming. The following Evaluate statement handles these conditions.

These are the rules:

- Items $1,000 and over earn a commission of 50%.
- Items $500 and over, but less than $1,000, earn a commission of 25%.
- Items $250 and over, but less than $500, earn a commission of 10%.
- Items less than $250 earn a commission of 5%.
- If the commission is less than $1, it is adjusted up to $1 unless the sale price is less than $1, in which case the commission is 75% of the sale price.
- For the items with the 50% commission, the maximum commission is $750.
- For the items with the 25% commission, the maximum commission is $150.
- For the items with the 10% commission, the maximum commission is $30.
- For the items with the 5% commission, there is no maximum commission.

First, try to find some conditions that can be isolated. The first is which of the four regular percentages to test for. Next, you need to know whether the commission is too high. The minimum $1 commission can occur only with the 5% rate plan, so a separate selection subject is not required. Instead, code an If statement under the appropriate selection object.

```
000160     Evaluate True Also True
000161        When Sale-Price >= 1000 Also Sale-Price * .5 > 750.00
000162           Move 750.00 To Commission-Amount
000163        When Sale-Price >= 1000 Also Any
000164           Compute Commission-Amount = Sale-Price * .5
000165        When Sale-Price >= 500  Also Sale-Price * .25 > 150.00
000166           Move 150.00 To Commission-Amount
000167        When Sale-Price >= 500  Also Any
000168           Compute Commission-Amount = Sale-Price * .25
000169        When Sale-Price >= 250  Also Sale-Price * .10 > 30.00
000170           Move 30.00 To Commission-Amount
000171        When Sale-Price >= 250  Also Any
000172           Compute Commission-Amount = Sale-Price * .10
000173        When Other
000174           Compute Commission-Amount = Sale-Price * .05
000175           If Commission-Amount < 1.00
000176              Move 1.00 To Commission-Amount
000177           End-If
000178           If Commission-Amount > Sale-Price
000179              Compute Commission-Amount = Sale-Price * .75
000180           End-If
000181     End-Evaluate
```

The complex business rules for this example boil down to a straightforward and easy-to-follow Evaluate statement. Note how the test for each of the first three commission plans is repeated in the Evaluate. This approach allows the maximum to be checked in the first portion of the selection object, and the rest of the values to fall through the second selection object for each rate.

The two If statements under the Other selection object handle the problem of the minimum commission. The first makes sure that the minimum is applied, and the second makes sure that the commission does not exceed the sale price of the item. Note also how the mathematical expressions and condition tests are used. The Evaluate statement is checking two conditions for truth. The content of those conditions can easily be another condition or arithmetic statement.

One more example demonstrates how an Evaluate statement can simplify coding. Your store divides merchandise into categories. You have agreements with your vendors to put some items, but not all, within certain categories on sale during certain times of the year. The percentage off depends on that time of year. Some sale items are on sale at all times. The categories are

- ANTI - Antiques
- CRAF - Crafts
- HOLI - Holiday Items
- JEWL - Jewelry
- MISC - Miscellaneous
- XMAS - Christmas Items

Other categories do not have special time frames for their sales. They are discounted year-round if marked as sale items. The rules for the discount are

- Item must be a sale item.
- During January, February, and March, antiques, jewelry, and miscellaneous sale items are discounted 50%.
- During January, February, and March, Christmas and craft items are discounted 75%. All other sale items receive a 10% discount.
- During April, May, and June, Christmas and craft items are discounted 50%.
- During April, May, and June, antiques, jewelry, and miscellaneous sale items are discounted 25%. All other sale items receive a 10% discount.
- During July, August, and September, all items are discounted at 25%.
- During October, November, and December, antiques are discounted 50%, and all other items receive a 10% discount.

First, examine the code necessary to use nested If logic. Check this code carefully and follow it through different possible conditions. The columns are aligned for easier reading.

```
000160    If Sale-Item
000161        If Month-Of-Sale = 01 Or 02 Or 03
000162            If Category-Of-Sale = "ANTI" Or "JEWL" Or "MISC"
000163                Move 50 To Discount-Percent
000164                Compute Sale-Price = Full-Price * .5
000165            Else
000166                If Category-Of-Sale = "XMAS" Or "CRAF"
000167                    Move 75 To Discount-Percent
000168                    Compute Sale-Price = Full-Price * .25
000169                Else
000170                    Move 10 To Discount-Percent
000171                    Compute Sale-Price = Full-Price * .90
000172                End-If
000173            End-If
000174        Else
000175            If Month-Of-Sale = 04 Or 05 Or 06
000176                If Category-Of-Sale = "XMAS" Or "CRAF"
000177                    Move 50 To Discount-Percent
000178                    Compute Sale-Price = Full-Price * .5
000179                Else
000180                    If Category-Of-Sale = "ANTI" Or "JEWL" Or "MISC"
000181                        Move 25 To Discount-Percent
000182                        Compute Sale-Price = Full-Price * .75
000183                    Else
000184                        Move 10 To Discount-Percent
000185                        Compute Sale-Price = Full-Price * .90
000186                    End-If
000187                End-If
000188            Else
000189                If Month-Of-Sale = 07 Or 08 Or 09
000190                    Move 25 To Discount-Percent
000191                    Compute Sale-Price = Full-Price *  .75
000192                Else
000193                    If Category-Of-Sale = "ANTI"
000194                        Move 50 To Discount-Percent
000195                        Compute Sale-Price = Full-Price * .5
000196                    Else
000197                        Move 10 To Discount-Percent
000198                        Compute Sale-Price = Full-Price * .9
000199                    End-If
000200                End-If
000201            End-If
000202        End-If
000203    Else
000204        Move Full-Price To Sale-Price
000205    End-If
```

9

As you can see, this code accomplishes the task but is hard to read and follow. What if you had to add another condition later? What would you code to add a new set of months and a new discount type? Maintaining this program would be difficult.

Now examine the same problem solved with the Evaluate statement:

```
000208      Evaluate Sale-Item Also Month-Of-Sale Also Category-Of-Sale
000209          When True Also 1 Thru 3 Also "ANTI"
000210          When True Also 1 Thru 3 Also "JEWL"
000211          When True Also 1 Thru 3 Also "MISC"
000212              Move 50 To Discount-Percent
000213              Compute Sale-Price = Full-Price * .5
000214          When True Also 1 Thru 3 Also "XMAS"
000215          When True Also 1 Thru 3 Also "CRAF"
000216              Move 75 To Discount-Percent
000217              Compute Sale-Price = Full-Price * .25
000218          When True Also 1 Thru 3 Also Any
000219              Move 10 To Discount-Percent
000220              Compute Sale-Price = Full-Price * .9
000221          When True Also 4 Thru 6 Also "XMAS"
000222          When True Also 4 Thru 6 Also "CRAF"
000223              Move 50 To discount-Percent
000224              Compute Sale-Price = Full-Price * .5
000225          When True Also 4 Thru 6 Also "ANTI"
000226          When True Also 4 Thru 6 Also "JEWL"
000227          When True Also 4 Thru 6 Also "MISC"
000228              Move 25 To Discount-Percent
000229              Compute Sale-Price = Full-Price * .75
000230          When True Also 4 Thru 6 Also Any
000231              Move 10 To Discount-Percent
000232              Compute Sale-Price = Full-Price * .90
000233          When True Also 6 Thru 9 Also Any
000234              Move 25 To Discount-Percent
000235              Compute Sale-Price = Full-Price * .75
000236          When True Also 10 Thru 12 Also "ANTI"
000237              Move 50 To Discount-Percent
000238              Compute Sale-Price = Full-Price * .5
000239          When True Also 10 Thru 12 Also Any
000240              Move 10 To Discount-Percent
000241              Compute Sale-Price = Full-Price * .9
000242          When Other
000243              Move Full-Price To Sale-Price
000244      End-Evaluate
```

The Evaluate statement coded here is much easier to follow than the earlier example but accomplishes the same task. It would be much easier to add a new set of months or a new category. In addition to those benefits, you can easily see where you have redundant code: 50%, 25%, and 10% discounts are applied in several places. You can easily reposition your When lines and reduce the code further.

```
000249        Evaluate Sale-Item Also Month-Of-Sale Also Category-Of-Sale
000250           When True Also 1 Thru 3 Also "ANTI"
000251           When True Also 1 Thru 3 Also "JEWL"
000252           When True Also 1 Thru 3 Also "MISC"
000253           When True Also 4 Thru 6 Also "XMAS"
000254           When True Also 4 Thru 6 Also "CRAF"
000255           When True Also 10 Thru 12 Also "ANTI"
000256              Move 50 To Discount-Percent
000257              Compute Sale-Price = Full-Price * .5
000258           When True Also 1 Thru 3 Also "XMAS"
000259           When True Also 1 Thru 3 Also "CRAF"
000260              Move 75 To Discount-Percent
000261              Compute Sale-Price = Full-Price * .25
000262           When True Also 4 Thru 6 Also "ANTI"
000263           When True Also 4 Thru 6 Also "JEWL"
000264           When True Also 4 Thru 6 Also "MISC"
000265           When True Also 6 Thru 9 Also Any
000266              Move 25 To Discount-Percent
000267              Compute Sale-Price = Full-Price * .75
000268           When True Also 1 Thru 3 Also Any
000269           When True Also 4 Thru 6 Also Any
000270           When True Also 10 Thru 12 Also Any
000271              Move 10 To Discount-Percent
000272              Compute Sale-Price = Full-Price * .9
000273           When Other
000274              Move Full-Price To Sale-Price
000275        End-Evaluate
```

As you can see, the complex set of rules required to figure out the discounted price has become a fairly simple Evaluate statement.

When you rearrange your selection objects (When lines) within an Evaluate statement, you must watch for Any clauses because they will always be evaluated to true. The Any items must appear after all prior selection objects have been tested. In the preceding example, notice where the 10% discount selection objects were moved.

Summary

In this hour, you learned the following:

- The Evaluate statement can simplify and clarify the conditional logic of your program.
- The code immediately following the word Evaluate is the selection subject.
- The code following the When is the selection object.

- Only one set of statements is executed from within an `Evaluate`. After a selection object is evaluated with a selection subject and found true, the subsequent statements are executed. After that, processing of the `Evaluate` statement ends.

- Selection objects may be stacked so that if any one of them evaluates to true, the programming statements after the last stacked object are executed.

- `Evaluate` statements may be nested.

- Complex `Evaluate` statements may be used like decision tables for solving complex conditions. The word `Also` adds multiple selection subjects and selection objects.

- `Evaluate` statements, because of their simplicity and easy-to-read format, should be used instead of complex nested `If` statements.

Q&A

Q What is one condition in which an `Evaluate` statement is a better choice than an `If` statement?

A When a data item is being tested for more than two possible values. For example, a `State` field could cause different actions in your program for every state. The nested `If` to handle this condition would be very deep and complex. `Evaluate` is a better choice.

Q If I want to execute some statements for more than one evaluated condition, do I have to code the statements over and over?

A No. You may stack your selection objects, and when any one of them is true, the statements after the last stacked object are executed.

Q Can I test several data items for different values in a single `Evaluate` statement?

A Yes. You have to make sure that the number of selection objects on each `When` line matches the number of selection subjects on the `Evaluate` line. The `Other` selection object is the only line in which this rule does not apply.

Q Can I nest `Evaluate` statements?

A Yes. Under a selection object, you may code another `Evaluate` statement.

Workshop

To help reinforce your understanding of the material presented in this hour, refer to the section "Quiz and Exercise Questions and Answers" that can be found on the CD. This section contains quiz questions and exercises for you to complete, as well as the corresponding answers.

HOUR 10

Processing Loops

The utility of computer programs is derived from their capability to perform repetitive tasks accurately and quickly. To do so, a programmer codes a processing loop. A *processing loop* is simply something in your program that happens over and over. The word *loop* comes from what it looks like in a flowchart. The flow of your program keeps looping repeatedly until some specified condition is reached. In this hour, you learn the basic steps you need to create processing loops in COBOL. The following topics are discussed:

- The `Perform` statement
- COBOL `Sections` and `Paragraphs`
- Program flow in the `Procedure Division`
- The use of `Go To` in structured programming design

Figure 10.1 shows a simple processing loop. You can follow the arrows for the direction of flow through the program. The diamond is a decision box. If the answer to the question it asks is yes, the loop is finished and the program stops. However, if the answer is no, then the loop is not finished and the program repeats the *computing process*.

A typical computer program will start, perform some function or functions until a specified condition is encountered, then stop.

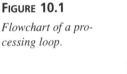

The Basic Perform Statement

One way to create a processing loop with COBOL is to use a Perform statement. The Perform statement executes the code you specify after the Perform and then returns in your program to the point immediately after the Perform statement.

The simplest format of the Perform statement allows you to Perform a Section or Paragraph within the Procedure Division of your program.

```
000020 Procedure Division.
000021 Start-Of-Program.
000022     Perform Paragraph-1
000023     Display "Return From Paragraph 1"
000024     Stop Run
000025     .
000026 Paragraph-1.
000027     Display "Paragraph 1"
000028     Display "End of Paragraph 1"
000029     .
```

The Procedure Division from this example Displays "Paragraph 1" and then "End of Paragraph 1" followed by "Return from Paragraph 1". The Perform statement jumps to Paragraph-1, executes the statements in the Paragraph, and then jumps back to the point in the program immediately following the Perform.

Sections and Paragraphs

Remember that in COBOL you can divide the Procedure Division into Sections, using Section headings. The examples thus far have not used Sections. The COBOL standard states that a Paragraph title should follow any Section headings. Most compilers ignore this rule and allow you to insert programming statements immediately following Section headings. These lessons are coded according to the standard and use Paragraph titles after Section headings.

A Section can have many Paragraphs. When you Perform a Section, all the Paragraphs in the Section are performed from the top down. At the start of the next Section, the program returns to the next line after the Perform of that Section. This practice is not often used and is not recommended. It is not obvious when you read the Perform statement that multiple Paragraphs are going to be executed.

10

If a Paragraph in a Section is performed, then the program returns to the statement immediately after the Perform when the next Paragraph or Section is encountered. The example from Listing 10.1 should clarify this sequence of events.

LISTING 10.1 PERFORM EXAMPLE

```
000001 @OPTIONS MAIN
000002 Identification Division.
000003 Program-Id.  Chapt10a.
000004* Perform Example
000005 Environment Division.
000006 Configuration Section.
000007 Source-Computer.  IBM-PC.
000008 Object-Computer.  IBM-PC.
000009 Data Division.
000010 Working-Storage Section.
000011 Procedure Division.
000012 Chapt10a-Section Section.
000013 Chapt10a-Start.
000014     Perform First-Section
000015     Perform Para-2
000016     Stop Run
000017     .
000018 First-Section Section.
000019 Para-1.
000020     Display "Para 1"
000021     .
000022 Para-2.
000023     Display "Para 2"
000024     .
000025 Para-3.
000026     Display "Para 3"
000027     .
```

As you can see from the output as shown in Figure 10.2, the first Perform causes each statement in the entire Section to be executed. The second Perform executes only the statement under Para-2.

FIGURE **10.2**

Output from Listing 10.1

```
Console : CHAPT10A                                                    ☒
Para  1
Para  2
Para  3
Para  2



                    Message : CHAPT10A              ☒

                      ⓘ    The console window is closed.


                             ┌──────────┐
                             │    OK    │
                             └──────────┘
```

Aside from performing a Section or a Paragraph, you may Perform a range of Paragraphs. To do so, state the starting Paragraph, the word Thru (or Through), and the last Paragraph to be executed. Each Paragraph between the two Paragraph titles specified is executed, and all statements under the last Paragraph are executed. For example, to execute Para-1 and Para-2 in the example, you may code the following:

```
000063      Perform Para-1 Thru Para-2
```

The program Displays "Para-1" followed by "Para-2".

> The Perform with the Thru clause has been widely used for years. However, the advances in the COBOL language that were included in the 1985 standard have made its use unnecessary. As you will see in the next section, the Perform with Thru is often used when a Go To is used to control the processing loop. No exercises in this book require the use of Perform with Thru. I am presenting it because I am sure that if you do pursue a career in COBOL, you will see it in use, and you should understand it.

When using Perform with the Thru clause, many programmers code a dummy Paragraph after the end of the Paragraph. The dummy Paragraph contains only the

word Exit. Exit does nothing and is coded only because each Paragraph has to contain
at least one statement.

```
000060      Perform Para-1 Thru Para-1-Exit
000061      Stop Run
000062         .
000063 Para-1.
000064      Display "Para 1"
000065         .
000066 Para-1-Exit.
000067      Exit.
```

This example performs both Para-1 and Para-1-Exit, but it looks as though only
Para-1 is being performed because Para-1-Exit has no processing statements. It is
important to remember that when Thru is used with a Perform, all statements in the Thru
Paragraph are performed.

Creating Processing Loops Using Perform

You are probably asking yourself how Perform relates to processing loops. If Perform
executes a Paragraph only once, how can it be used to create a loop?

With Perform, you can Perform a Paragraph multiple times. For example, if you want to
count to 10, you can Perform a counting Paragraph 10 times.

```
000078      Move Zeros To Num-Counter
000079      Perform Count-By-1 10 Times
000080      Stop Run
000081         .
000082 Count-By-1.
000083      Add 1 To Num-Counter
000084      Display Num-Counter
000085         .
```

This Procedure Division code Performs the Count-By-1 Paragraph 10 times. The program does not return to the statement after the Perform until the Perform is executed 10
times.

> The Stop Run that is coded after the Perform is very important. If you did
> not have it, the flow of the program would fall through the Count-By-1
> Paragraph and execute it yet again.

The number of times a Perform is to be executed can be specified by a numeric data
item or a numeric literal.

In addition to performing a `Paragraph` a certain number of times, you can base a `Perform` on a conditional test. You do this by using `Until`. With `Until` you tell the program to `Perform` the `Paragraph`, testing for your condition before every execution of the `Paragraph`, `Until` the condition is true. All statements under the `Paragraph` are executed. The test for your condition occurs before the `Paragraph` is next executed. If your condition is true, the `Paragraph` is not executed.

The program in Listing 10.2 uses `Perform` with `Until` to control the processing. This program is a modification of the program used in Hour 6, "Manipulating Data," to split up the name and change the email address to lowercase. Listing 10.2 continues to `Accept` new input `Until` the user presses the F1 key.

LISTING 10.2   NAME AND EMAIL EDIT PROCESSING LOOP

```
000001 @OPTIONS MAIN
000002 Identification Division.
000003 Program-Id.  Chapt10c.
000004* Name And E-Mail Edit - Processing Loop.
000005 Environment Division.
000006 Configuration Section.
000007 Special-Names.
000008      Crt Status Is Keyboard-Status.
000009 Source-Computer.  IBM-PC.
000010 Object-Computer.  IBM-PC.
000011 Data Division.
000012 Working-Storage Section.
000013 01  Keyboard-Status.
000014     03  Accept-Status Pic 9.
000015     03  Function-Key  Pic X.
000016         88 F1-Pressed Value X"01".
000017     03  System-Use    Pic X.
000018 01  Screen-Items.
000019     03  Name-Entry              Pic X(40) Value Spaces.
000020     03  E-Mail                  Pic X(30) Value Spaces.
000021     03  Output-Fields.
000022         05  Last-Name           Pic X(30) Value Spaces.
000023         05  First-Name          Pic X(30) Value Spaces.
000024         05  Error-Message       Pic X(60) Value Spaces.
000025 01  Work-Numbers.
000026     03  Work-Number             Pic 99 Value Zeros.
000027     03  Work-Number-1           Pic 99 Value Zeros.
000028     03  Work-Number-2           Pic 99 Value Zeros.
000029 Screen Section.
000030 01  Name-Entry-Screen
000031     Blank Screen, Auto
000032     Foreground-Color Is 7,
000033     Background-Color Is 1.
000034*
```

```
000035     03   Screen-Literal-Group.
000036          05   Line 01 Column 30 Value "Name and E-mail Entry"
000037               Highlight Foreground-Color 4 Background-Color 1.
000038          05   Line 05 Column 05 Value "  Name: ".
000039          05   Line 06 Column 05 Value "E-mail: ".
000040          05   Line 08 Column 05 Value "  Last: ".
000041          05   Line 09 Column 05 Value " First: ".
000042          05   Line 22 Column 05 Value "Press F1 to Exit".
000043     03   Reverse-Video-Group Reverse-Video.
000044          05   Line 05 Column 13 Pic X(40) Using Name-Entry.
000045          05   Line 06 Column 13 Pic X(30) Using E-Mail.
000046          05   Line 08 Column 13 Pic X(30) From  Last-Name.
000047          05   Line 09 Column 13 Pic X(30) From  First-Name.
000048          05   Line 20 Column 01 Pic X(60)
000049               Highlight From Error-Message.
000050 Procedure Division.
000051 Chapt10c-Start.
000052     Perform Display-And-Accept-Screen Until F1-Pressed
000053     Stop Run
000054     .
000055 Display-And-Accept-Screen.
000056     Display Name-Entry-Screen
000057     Accept  Name-Entry-Screen
000058* Reset The Working Fields
000059     Initialize Output-Fields
000060               Work-Numbers
000061* Make Sure There Is A Comma In The Name
000062     Inspect Name-Entry Tallying Work-Number-2 For All ","
000063* Only Try To Split If There Is One
000064     If Work-Number-2 > Zeros
000065         Perform Process-The-Data
000066     Else
000067         Move "Name must contain a comma" To Error-Message
000068     End-If
000069     .
000070 Process-The-Data.
000071* Split The First And Last Name Out Into Separate Fields
000072     Inspect Name-Entry Tallying Work-Number
000073               For Characters Before ","
000074     Move Name-Entry (1:work-Number) To Last-Name
000075     Add 2 To Work-Number
000076* We Need To Exclude The Leading Spaces, After The Comma
000077     Inspect Name-Entry (Work-Number:)
000078               Tallying Work-Number-1 For Leading Spaces
000079     Move Name-Entry (Work-Number + Work-Number-1:) To First-Name
000080* Change The E-Mail Address To All Lower Case Letters.
000081     Inspect E-Mail Converting "ABCDEFGHIJKLMNOPQRSTUVWXYZ"
000082               To          "abcdefghijklmnopqrstuvwxyz"
000083     .
```

10

The first item to examine in this program is the addition of the Special-Names
Paragraph. As you learned in Hour 4, "Basic User Interface," in relation to the Screen
Section, the Special-Names Paragraph captures the function key pressed by the user. A
conditional (88 level) item corresponds to the value in the field when F1 is pressed.

An error message line has been added to the screen. This message appears if the user
does not enter a comma in the name field. A new numeric data item was added in which
to accumulate the number of commas in the Name-Entry, using the Inspect statement. If
no commas occur, an error message is displayed and the input fields are not processed.

The working fields are initialized between every execution of the logic to split the name.
You don't need the headache of having any leftover values in these fields. The initializa-
tion of these fields is simplified by grouping them and using an Initialize statement
against the two groups.

Notice the use of the Perform with Until. This Perform continues to be executed Until
the F1 key is pressed. The second Perform is coded as part of an If statement. You may
code a Perform anywhere you would normally code any other COBOL statement.

Take note of the general program structure. This style of coding is called structured programming. The program uses what is sometimes referred to as a top-down design. Top-
down design takes the highest level and gradually breaks down each function into smaller and smaller parts until you have simple programming statements.

The main Paragraph shows the logic of the program. It is to display and accept a screen
Until the user presses F1 and then terminate. Using the 88 level for the F1 key makes
the program self-documenting. Liberal use of comments helps to clarify the action.

Within the processing Paragraph, you can easily discern what is happening in the program. There is no jumping around. The only condition that is tested is the one used to
validate the input and determine whether the field should be processed. If so, that single
Paragraph is executed. Its sole function is to process the input data.

This example uses an 88 level item to determine the termination of the performed
Paragraph. Any condition may be coded with the Perform to control the processing
loop. You must remember that the condition that is specified in the Perform statement is
tested before the Perform is executed. If the condition is true upon the first pass, your
Perform is never executed. Look at this example:

```
000086      Move "A" to Test-Item
000087      Perform Para-1 Until Test-Item = "A"
000088      Stop Run
000089         .
000090 Para-1.
000092      If Data-A + Data-B = 25
```

```
000093          Move "A" to Test-Item
000094      End-If
000095      .
```

In this example, Para-1 is never executed. (Remember that the test of the condition occurs before the Paragraph is executed.) It seems obvious when you look at the code, but once the program is compiled the computer does not really know how many times processing has passed through this Perform. The tests are always the same, whether this is the first execution or the one-millionth.

Use of Go To

COBOL, like most other programming languages, has a Go To statement. The Go To causes the program to jump to the Paragraph title or Section header specified in the Go To statement. As with Perform ... Thru, the advances in the COBOL language with the 1985 standard have eliminated any need to use Go To. However, it seems to be the "easy way out" for many programmers, and I think it is worthwhile to spend some time explaining its use and abuse.

Go To causes what is referred to as an unconditional branch. The logic of your program jumps to the point of the Go To and does not return, in contrast to the logic of a Perform. What follows is an example of a processing loop using Go To.

```
000096 Start-Of-Loop.
000097     If Data-A + Data-B not = 25
000098         Go To Start-Of-Loop
000099     End-If
000100     Stop Run
000101     .
```

This code seems simple enough. The loop continues until Data-A + Data-B is equal to 25. In its simplest form, Go To doesn't appear to be so bad; however, when mixed with more Go To statements, multiple Paragraphs, and Perform statements, your program soon becomes unreadable and hard to follow.

In order to demonstrate the differences between using Go To and Perform, consider this programming problem. You need a processing loop to Accept a screen of data. The screen has three fields: First Name, Last Name, and E-mail Address. For each field, check to see whether an entry was made. If entered, convert the first and last names to uppercase. If the email address was entered, convert it to lowercase. If the fields are blank, replace them with asterisks. Both approaches are shown in Chapt10d.Cob, as shown in Listing 10.3.

The first part of the program is the same for both approaches. The differences begin in the Procedure Division.

10

LISTING 10.3   Go To Versus Perform Logic

```
000001 @OPTIONS MAIN
000002 Identification Division.
000003 Program-Id.  Chapt10d.
000004* Go To Vs Perform Logic
000005 Environment Division.
000006 Configuration Section.
000007 Special-Names.
000008        Crt Status Is Keyboard-Status.
000009 Source-Computer.  IBM-PC.
000010 Object-Computer.  IBM-PC.
000011 Data Division.
000012 Working-Storage Section.
000013 01  Keyboard-Status.
000014     03  Accept-Status Pic 9.
000015     03  Function-key  Pic X.
000016         88 F1-Pressed Value X"01".
000017     03  System-Use    Pic X.
000018 01  Screen-Items.
000019     03  Last-Name             Pic X(20) Value Spaces.
000020     03  First-Name            Pic X(20) Value Spaces.
000021     03  E-mail                Pic X(30) Value Spaces.
000022 Screen Section.
000023 01  Entry-Screen
000024     Blank Screen, Auto
000025     Foreground-Color Is 7,
000026     Background-Color Is 1.
000027*
000028     03  Screen-Literal-Group.
000029         05  Line 01 Column 30 Value "Name and E-mail Entry"
000030             Highlight Foreground-Color 4 Background-Color 1.
000031         05  Line 06 Column 05 Value "E-mail: ".
000032         05  Line 08 Column 05 Value " Last: ".
000033         05  Line 09 Column 05 Value " First: ".
000034         05  Line 22 Column 05 Value "Press F1 to Exit".
000035     03  Reverse-Video-Group Reverse-Video.
000036         05  Line 06 Column 13 Pic X(30) Using E-mail.
000037         05  Line 08 Column 13 Pic X(20) Using Last-Name.
000038         05  Line 09 Column 13 Pic X(20) Using First-Name.
000039 Procedure Division.
000040 Chapt10d-Start.
```

For the Perform version, the main processing loop can be stated in one simple statement:

```
Perform Display-And-Accept-Screen Until F1-Pressed
```

Now the next level down in the top-down design is coded. This is the Display-And-Accept-Screen Paragraph.

```
000041 Display-And-Accept-Screen.
000042     Display Entry-Screen
000043     Accept  Entry-Screen
000044     If F1-Pressed
000045         Continue
000046     Else
000047         Perform Process-Data-Fields
000048     End-If
000049     .
```

This Paragraph displays and then accepts the entry screen. The If following the Accept checks for the F1 key. If it was pressed, the data fields are not processed; however, if it was not pressed, the data fields are processed.

The processing of the data fields is coded simply. Each field is checked to see whether it was entered. If so, the conversion is performed. If not, asterisks are placed in the field.

```
000050 Process-Data-Fields.
000051     If Last-Name > Spaces
000052         Perform Process-Last-Name
000053     Else
000054         Move "********************" To Last-Name
000055     End-If
000056     If First-Name > Spaces
000057         Perform Process-First-Name
000058     Else
000059         Move "*******************" to First-Name
000060     End-If
000061     If E-Mail > Spaces
000062         Perform Process-E-Mail
000063     Else
000064         Move "****************************" to E-Mail
000065     End-If
000066     .
```

As each field is checked, any data that was entered into the field is processed in the appropriate Paragraph.

```
000067 Process-Last-Name.
000068     Inspect Last-Name Converting "abcdefghijklmnopqrstuvwxyz"
000069                       To        "ABCDEFGHIJKLMNOPQRSTUVWXYZ"
000070     .
000071 Process-First-Name.
000072     Inspect First-Name Converting "abcdefghijklmnopqrstuvwxyz"
000073                        To         "ABCDEFGHIJKLMNOPQRSTUVWXYZ"
000074     .
000075 Process-E-Mail.
000076     Inspect E-Mail Converting "ABCDEFGHIJKLMNOPQRSTUVWXYZ"
000077                    To         "abcdefghijklmnopqrstuvwzyz"
000078     .
```

Each `Paragraph` handles conversion of each associated field. Much more could be happening in these `Paragraphs`, but this example is just for demonstration. Normally, you would not code a `Perform` with only a single statement under it.

This program is easy to follow. Each `Paragraph` performs a function and returns. The program was easy to design. Each step was broken down into smaller steps until the program was written. This method is top-down, structured programming.

One interesting feature of this style is that you can rearrange the `Paragraphs` in any order you desire. For example, you can put the `Process-E-Mail` `Paragraph` before the `Process-Last-Name` `Paragraph`, and everything will function properly. The program will never fall through a `Paragraph` name.

Now examine the code and process necessary to produce the same results using the `Go To` statement.

```
000079 Process-Screen.
000080     Display Entry-Screen
000081     Accept Entry-screen
000082     If F1-Pressed
000083        Stop Run
000084     End-If
000085     If Last-Name > Spaces
000086        Go To Process-Last-Name-Goto
000087     Else
000088        Move "********************" to Last-Name
000089     End-If
000090        .
```

Notice lines 82 and 83; the `Stop Run` statement is coded so that if the user presses the F1 key, the program stops immediately and does not continue to process. Next, the last name is checked. If it is entered, the `Go To` `Paragraph` processes the last name. If it is not entered, asterisks are moved into the field.

The logic flow of the program falls through the next `Paragraph`. The only reason for a `Paragraph` name is that after the last name is processed, a label is required as a return point so that the program can continue to process the screen.

```
000091 Check-First-Name.
000092     If First-Name > Spaces
000093        Go To Process-First-Name-Goto
000094     Else
000095        Move "********************" To First-Name
000096     End-If
000097        .
000098 Check-E-Mail.
000099     If E-Mail > Spaces
000100        Go To Process-E-Mail-Goto
```

```
000101      Else
000102         Move "*****************************" to E-mail
000103      End-If
000104      Go To Process-Screen
000105         .
```

These two `Paragraphs` determine whether the first name and email need to be processed. Again, the `Check-E-Mail Paragraph` is coded so that there is a place to return to from an earlier `Go To`.

The process `Paragraphs` are coded as follows:

```
000106 Process-Last-Name-Goto.
000107      Inspect Last-Name Converting "abcdefghijklmnopqrstuvwxyz"
000108                      To         "ABCDEFGHIJKLMNOPQRSTUVWXYZ"
000100      Go To Check-First-Name
000110         .
000111 Process-First-Name-Goto.
000112      Inspect First-Name Converting "abcdefghijklmnopqrstuvwxyz"
000113                       To          "ABCDEFGHIJKLMNOPQRSTUVWXYZ"
000114      Go To Check-E-Mail
000115         .
000116 Process-E-Mail-Goto.
000117      Inspect E-Mail Converting "ABCDEFGHIJKLMNOPQRSTUVWXYZ"
000118                   To          "abcdefghijklmnopqrstuvwzyz"
000119      Go To Process-Screen
000120         .
```

Notice in the first `Paragraph`, the logic jumps back to `Check-First-Name`. In the second, the logic jumps back to `Check-E-Mail`, and in the third it goes back to the main screen process. See how hard this logic is to follow? It is also easy to really mess up later. You have to be aware that you are falling through the `Paragraph` titles. If you forget, or don't realize it, you can corrupt the logic of the program by moving a `Paragraph` or by inserting a new `Paragraph` or `Go To`.

What if you want to add a fourth field? With the `Perform` method, you it can simply add one more `If` statement in the `Process-Data-Fields Paragraph` and then code that process `Paragraph` by itself. Contrast this approach with the modifications needed in the `Go To` example.

First, you have to change the `Process-E-Mail-Go To Paragraph` to not `Go To Process-Screen`, but instead to go back to your new `Paragraph`. Your new `Paragraph` would assume the role of going back to the `Process-Screen Paragraph`. In addition, you have to change the `Check-E-Mail Paragraph` so that it does not go back to `Process-Screen` and, instead, falls through another new `Paragraph`. This new `Paragraph` would go back to `Process-Screen`.

10

What if, for some reason, you wanted this new field to be processed first? Nearly every Paragraph would require a change. With the Perform version, all you have to do is position the new If statement in the proper place in the Process-Data-Fields Paragraph.

Listing 10.4 shows what happens when you mix Go To with Perform logic.

LISTING 10.4 PERFORM WITH GO TO EXAMPLE

```
000001 @OPTIONS MAIN
000002 Identification Division.
000003 Program-Id.  Chapt10e.
000004* Perform With Go To Example
000005 Environment Division.
000006 Configuration Section.
000007 Source-Computer.  IBM-PC.
000008 Object-Computer.  IBM-PC.
000009 Data Division.
000010 Working-Storage Section.
000011 Procedure Division.
000012 Chapt10a-Section Section.
000013 Chapt10a-Start.
000014     Perform Para-2
000015     Stop Run
000016        .
000017 First-Section Section.
000018 Para-1.
000019     Display "Para 1"
000020        .
000021 Para-2.
000022     Display "Para 2"
000023     Go To Para-1
000024        .
000025 Para-3.
000026     Display "Para 3"
000027        .
```

Try to follow the logic and see what you think this program should do. It appears as if the program will Display "Para 2", then "Para 1", and then stop. That's not what happens. The Perform of Para-2 is not going to stop until it encounters the next Paragraph title, which is Para-3. The Go To prevents this from happening. This program executes an infinite, or endless, loop. After the Go To, Para-1 is executed. Then the program falls through the Para-2 label and continues. It then hits the Go To and goes back to Para-1 yet again. If you run the program, you will see endless displays of "Para 1" and "Para 2". You can stop the program by right-clicking the toolbar on the Chapt10e program item and choosing Close.

I strongly suggest that you use the structured approach introduced by this book for your programs. Do not use Go To. Keeping your programming structured leads to programs that are easy to design, follow, and understand.

Summary

In this hour, you learned the following:

- A processing loop repeats a task until some specified condition is reached.
- The Perform statement can execute a Paragraph or Section and then return to the point in the program immediately after the Perform.
- Perform can execute a Paragraph once, a specified number of times, or until a condition is satisfied.
- By performing a Section, you can fall through multiple Paragraphs, even though this approach is not recommended.
- By using Thru, you can Perform a range of Paragraphs.
- The difference between structured and non-structured programming.
- How mixing structured and non-structured programming can lead to problems.
- Why Go To causes your programs to be non-structured and should be avoided.

Q&A

Q I don't quite understand the term *processing loop*. Can you explain it?

A A processing loop tells the computer to execute, or Perform, a process multiple times. The loop is repeated until some specified condition occurs. Think of it like a race. The cars go round and round until the checkered flag is thrown. The race track is the loop, and the checkered flag is the condition that causes the loop to end.

Q When I Perform an individual Paragraph within a Section, when does the Perform stop and return?

A The Perform terminates when the next Paragraph title, also called a label or heading, is encountered. The Perform also ends if another Section is encountered.

Q Besides grouping Paragraphs, is there another purpose for Sections? They seem unnecessary to me.

A For most of your programming, Sections are unnecessary. Some earlier versions of COBOL required Sections under certain circumstances, but modern COBOL doesn't have that restriction. Sections can also be coded with Section numbers.

They follow the word Section and cause the compiler to group like numbered Sections into overlays. Some compilers had limits to the size of a program, and you needed to divide your code into Sections that could be loaded and unloaded as memory became available. These overlays were the original purpose for defining Sections as part of the COBOL language. The behavior of Paragraphs within Sections is largely a byproduct of the actual behavior of overlays. With modern compilers, the use of overlays and Sections is no longer an issue.

Q Are you serious when you say I should avoid using Go To? Can't I just use it when it's really convenient?

A Yes, I am serious. You should not use Go To. With structured programming, Go To is entirely unnecessary. If you find yourself tempted to use it, you might want to reconsider the design of your program. Some programmers use Go To statements sparingly to jump either to the start or end of a Paragraph or Section. Even this use is unnecessary. However, if you end up programming for a living, you will probably encounter COBOL code that looks like spaghetti when you try to follow the logic because of all of the Go To usage. You need to know how to maintain that code, and trying to turn spaghetti code into structured code is not an easy task. For the most part, when you are maintaining someone else's program, you are best advised to follow the style he or she used.

Workshop

To help reinforce your understanding of the material presented in this hour, refer to the section "Quiz and Exercise Questions and Answers" that can be found on the CD. This section contains quiz questions and exercises for you to complete, as well as the corresponding answers.

Hour **11**

Advanced Perform Statements

NEW TERM In Hour 10, "Processing Loops," you learned the basic format for the Perform statement. In this hour, among other things you learn some more advanced methods of using Perform, such as

- Using inline Perform statements
- Using Perform with Varying
- Testing before and after the Perform
- Nesting Perform statements
- Compiling and linking a program for use with the interactive debug utility

Several other ways to use Perform make it a very powerful looping tool. In addition to the previously discussed methods of using Perform, you may code what is called an *inline Perform*. In this type of Perform, the lines of code that are to be performed are located immediately after the Perform verb and not elsewhere in the program. You may have a Perform adjust a numeric field up or down by a specified amount as it executes. Instead of the default behavior of testing for your condition before the Perform is executed, you can have the Perform statement make the test after the Perform.

Perform with Varying

When Varying is used with the Perform statement, a numeric data item is specified. This item will be incremented by the value specified in a second data item or literal each time the Perform is executed. The starting value of the field before the increment is also specified. If you want the count down, you can vary the data item by a negative number. When Varying is used, the test for terminating the Perform is usually, but not always, based on the data item that is being varied. This feature is used often when working with tables. (Tables are discussed in detail in Hour 12, "Tables.")

When using Varying, the field being varied is incremented after the Perform is executed. The test for the condition that terminates the Perform, specified by the Until phrase, is made before the Perform is executed.

In Listing 11.1, a field is incremented from 0 by 1 until that field is greater than 10. In this case, the computer counts from 1 to 10.

LISTING 11.1 COUNT TO 10

```
000001 @OPTIONS MAIN
000002 Identification Division.
000003 Program-Id.  Chapt11a.
000004 Environment Division.
000005 Configuration Section.
000006 Source-Computer.  IBM-PC.
000007 Object-Computer.  IBM-PC.
000008 Data Division.
000009 Working-Storage Section.
000010 01  Counter Pic 9(2) value zeros.
000011 Procedure Division.
000012 Chapt11a-Start.
000013     Perform Count-Routine Varying Counter
000014             From 1 by 1 Until Counter > 10
000015     Stop Run
000016     .
000017 Count-Routine.
000018     Display Counter
000019     .
```

When using Varying, you specify first the field you are going to adjust. The next item, after the word From, is the starting value of the variable. The number or data item that follows the word By is the amount by which you want to adjust the data value for each execution of the Perform. Any condition may appear after the word Until. When that condition is true, the Perform stops looping.

Here are some important points to remember about using Varying: First, the initial execution of the Perform is made with the item you decide to vary set at the initial value as specified with the word From. At the end of the Perform, the counter is adjusted by the amount specified after the By. The condition is tested before the Perform is executed.

What if you wanted to count by fives? In that case you would just change the number or data item after the word From in the Perform statement. If you wanted to count down instead of up, you could vary from 10 by -1. This adds a negative 1 to the counter each time, which is the same as subtracting 1, thus counting down.

```
000015     Perform Count-Routine With Test After Varying Counter
000016             From 10 by -1 Until Counter = 1
```

This code displays 10, counts down until 1 is displayed, and then stops. The value in Counter when the routine is complete is 1.

Testing Before or After

Notice that you Perform Until the counter is greater than 10. Why do you think you didn't say Until Counter = 10? The reason is that the Perform is not executed if the condition is true. If you coded the Counter = 10 condition, the Perform would not execute when the counter's value is 10 and the loop would stop after displaying 9. When using Varying this way and testing for a value, you need to remember that the counter you use will have been incremented to a value beyond that which you might expect.

COBOL provides a way around this problem. Instead of the default behavior of testing for the condition before the Perform is executed, you can code With Test After. This option causes the Perform to test the condition immediately after the Perform has been executed and before any adjustment is made by the use of Varying. This approach ensures that you can use more understandable looping parameters. It also guarantees that the Perform will be executed at least once because the condition is not tested until after the Perform has executed. Listing 11.2 revisits the code from Listing 11.1, this time coded With Test After.

LISTING 11.2 COUNT TO 10, REVISED

```
000001 @OPTIONS MAIN
000002 Identification Division.
000003 Program-Id.  Chapt11a.
```

continues

LISTING 11.2   CONTINUED

```
000004 Environment Division.
000005 Configuration Section.
000006 Source-Computer.   IBM-PC.
000007 Object-Computer.   IBM-PC.
000008 Data Division.
000009 Working-Storage Section.
000010 01  Counter Pic 9(2) value zeros.
000011 Procedure Division.
000012 Chapt11a-Start.
000013     Perform Count-Routine With Test After Varying Counter
000014           From 1 by 1 Until Counter = 10
000015     Stop Run
000016        .
000017 Count-Routine.
000018     Display Counter
000019        .
```

The With Test After is coded following the Paragraph to be performed. If you want to make sure you know which method is being used—the default test before the Perform or the Test After—you may also code With Test Before.

> These examples use numeric literals for the starting value and increment. You may also use numeric data items for each of these.

The Use of the Inline Perform

Having Perform statements that execute different Paragraphs is an excellent way to maintain a structured programming design. However, even these statements can be hard to follow. If you want to find out what is happening in a Perform, you have to jump to the portion of your source code where the Paragraph being performed is coded. Then you have to jump back to the place in your source code where the Perform statement is coded. This approach can be time-consuming and can easily lead you to lose your train of thought. COBOL allows you to have the best of both worlds. You can have a structured program, performing separate tasks, without having to search through your source every time you want to find what is happening inside a performed Paragraph. This technique uses an inline Perform.

NEW TERM   The *inline* Perform has all of the characteristics of a regular Perform with two exceptions. First, it is always terminated with the explicit scope terminator, End-Perform. Second, it has no Paragraph or Section name to be performed. The statements that are to be performed are coded between the Perform statement and the End-Perform explicit scope terminator.

The next bit of code modifies the program shown in Listing 11.2. Instead of performing the single-line Count-Routine, the following code uses an inline Perform.

```
000013     Perform  With Test After Varying Counter
000014             From 1 by 1 Until Counter = 10
000017             Display Counter
000015     End-Perform
```

How do you decide when to use an inline Perform instead of performing a Paragraph? Here are some very general guidelines. Each programmer has a different style of programming. Programming is sometimes a matter of style and sometimes a question of which method is easier for you to understand and follow.

- If only one or two statements are being executed, use an inline Perform.

- If you are using this code in only one place in the program, use an inline Perform.

- If the code can be reused and is performed from more than one place in the program, Perform a Paragraph instead. If you end up coding exactly the same statements inside two inline Performs, you should use a common Paragraph instead.

- If the Perform is heavily nested or takes up several pages of source code, you might want to break it down into individual paragraphs. Page after page of inline Perform code can be as hard or harder to follow than separated paragraphs.

The next example considers a more complex inline Perform and one of the many tasks that can be accomplished. What if you want to string two names together, but you don't want any extra space between the names? You might have a First-Name field that is 20 characters long and a Last-Name field that is 20 characters long that you want to put together in one field. You can't use the String statement, because the first name might contain embedded spaces. You really need to know the actual length of the name in the First-Name field.

One technique is to look at each character of the field until you find the end of the field. However, if embedded blanks are present, as in a name such as Daisy Mae, how do you find the end? The answer is to search from the end of the field toward the front looking for any character with a value greater than spaces. The program in Listing 11.3 accepts two names and creates one as the result. Each name may contain embedded spaces.

11

LISTING 11.3 INLINE PERFORM EXAMPLE, NAME JOIN

```
000001 @OPTIONS MAIN
000002 Identification Division.
000003 Program-Id.  Chapt11b.
000004* Inline Perform Example, name join
000005 Environment Division.
000006 Configuration Section.
000007 Source-Computer.  IBM-PC.
000008 Object-Computer.  IBM-PC.
000009 Data Division.
000010 Working-Storage Section.
000011 01  Last-Name            Pic X(20) Value Spaces.
000012 01  First-Name           Pic X(20) Value Spaces.
000013 01  Combined-Name        Pic X(40) Value Spaces.
000014 01  Name-Length          Pic 99    Value Zeros.
000015 Screen Section.
000016 01  Name-Entry Blank Screen.
000017    03  Line 01 Column 01 Value " Last Name: ".
000018    03  Line 01 Column 13 Pic X(20) Using Last-Name.
000019    03  Line 03 Column 01 Value "First Name: ".
000020    03  Line 03 Column 13 Pic X(20) Using First-Name.
000021    03  Line 05 Column 01 Value " Full Name: ".
000022    03  Line 05 Column 13 Pic X(40) From Combined-Name.
000023 Procedure Division.
000024 Chapt11b-Start.
000025    Display Name-Entry
000026    Accept  Name-Entry
000027    Perform Varying Name-Length from 20 By -1
000028        Until First-Name (Name-Length:1) > Space
000029          or Name-Length = Zeros
000030        Continue
000031    End-Perform
000032    If Name-Length = Zeros
000033       Move Last-Name to Combined-Name
000034    Else
000035       String First-Name (1:Name-Length)
000036              Space
000037              Last-Name
000038              Delimited by Size
000039              Into Combined-Name
000040    End-If
000041    Display Name-Entry
000042    Stop Run
000043       .
```

Examine the Perform statement that starts in line 27. It uses a numeric data item called Name-Length to hold the value of Varying. This code does not use Test After, because you are starting with a value of 20. If the field is full, then the Perform is not executed the first time through and 20 remains in the Length field for the next step.

Notice the complex condition for termination of the Perform. You want the Perform to stop when it finds a character that is greater than a space. The code uses reference modification to examine the field contents one character at a time. Reaching zero means that there are no characters greater than a space, and the field is empty. The Perform is not executed when the Name-Length field is zeros. This is essential, because testing the zero offset with reference modification is invalid.

When the Perform is complete, the Name-Length field contains the length of the first name that the user entered. If no first name is entered, there is no need to even try to construct a full name. The If statement in line 32 checks for this condition. If there is no first name, then the last name is just moved into the Combined-Name field. However, if there is something in the first name, the String statement in line 35 takes care of assembling the name. Only the portion of the First-Name field that is occupied by the first name the user entered is used, along with a space, and the last name.

Make a special note of the Continue statement used in the inline Perform. A statement must occur within the Perform. Because the Perform is actually accomplishing all the necessary testing and data manipulation, nothing actually happens inside the Perform. The Continue statement does nothing and is coded just to satisfy the compiler requirement that the inline Perform contain at least one statement.

Nesting Perform Statements

You already know that you can Perform another Paragraph inside a Paragraph that is being performed. These multiple Perform statements can get confusing, especially when the Paragraphs being performed are scattered throughout your source code. Inline Performs can be used inside these performed Paragraphs. Additionally, you may also nest inline Performs.

```
000050     Perform 10 Times
000051       Perform 20 Times
000052         Add 1 to Data-A
000053       End-Perform
000054     End-Perform
000055     .
```

In this example, 1 is added to Data-A 200 times. The exterior Perform in line 50, performs the Perform in line 51 ten times, and this interior Perform adds 1 to Data-A 20 times.

> When nesting Performs, it is a good idea to keep the End-Perform explicit scope terminator lined up with the Perform statement. Doing so makes the source code much more readable and easier to follow. This alignment clearly shows when a nested inline Perform ends.

11

The Inline **If** Statement and **Perform**

You can create complex processing loops using inline If statements with inline Perform statements. This technique can handle complex processing without having paragraphs in far-flung areas of your source code. As an example, Listing 11.4 combines some of the programs you have recently written. The new program Displays and Accepts a screen. It Accepts last name, first name and telephone number. You should format the number as before, using either 10 or 7 digits and using a proper edit pattern. In addition, however, you want to left-justify the user input for the names. If someone keys in names with leading spaces, you want the code to remove the spaces. All of this activity occurs in one paragraph but still maintains a structured design.

LISTING 11.4   INLINE PERFORM WITH INLINE IF EXAMPLE

```
000001 @OPTIONS MAIN,TEST
000002 Identification Division.
000003 Program-Id.  Chapt11c.
000004* Inline Perform With Inline If Example
000005 Environment Division.
000006 Configuration Section.
000007 Special-Names.
000008      Crt Status Is Keyboard-Status.
000009 Source-Computer.  IBM-PC.
000010 Object-Computer.  IBM-PC.
000011 Data Division.
000012 Working-Storage Section.
000013 01  Keyboard-Status.
000014     03  Accept-Status    Pic 9.
000015     03  Function-Key     Pic X.
000016         88 F1-Pressed    Value X"01".
000017     03  System-Use       Pic X.
000018 01  Temp-Field           Pic X(20) Value Spaces.
000019 01  Formatted-Number     Pic X(14) Value "(XXX) XXX-XXXX".
000020 01  Formatted-Alternate  Pic X(8)  Value "XXX-XXXX".
000021 01  Name-Length          Pic 99    Value Zeros.
000022 01  Counter              Pic 99    Value Zeros.
000023 01  Input-Output-Fields.
000024     03  Last-Name        Pic X(20) Value Spaces.
000025     03  First-Name       Pic X(20) Value Spaces.
000026     03  Phone-Number     Pic 9(10) Value Zeros.
000027     03  The-Edited-Number Pic X(14) Value Spaces.
000028     03  Combined-Name    Pic X(40) Value Spaces.
000029 Screen Section.
000030 01  Phone-Entry Blank Screen.
000031     03  Line 01 Column 01 Value " Enter Phone Number: ".
000032     03  Line 01 Column 22 Pic Z(10) Using Phone-Number.
000033     03  Line 02 Column 01 Value "     Enter Last Name: ".
```

```
000034      03  Line 02 Column 22 Pic X(20) Using Last-Name.
000035      03  Line 03 Column 01 Value "   Enter First Name: ".
000036      03  Line 03 Column 22 Pic X(20) Using First-Name.
000037      03  Line 05 Column 01 Value "         Full Name: ".
000038      03  Line 05 Column 22 Pic X(40) From Combined-Name.
000039      03  Line 07 Column 01 Value "Edited Phone Number: ".
000040      03  Line 07 Column 22 Pic X(14) From The-Edited-Number.
000041      03  Line 20 Column 01 Value "Press F1 to Exit".
000042 Procedure Division.
000043 Chapt11c-Start.
000044      Perform Until F1-Pressed
000045          Display Phone-Entry
000046          Accept Phone-Entry
000047* Prepare To Format The Numbers
000048          Move "(XXX) XXX-XXXX" To Formatted-Number
000049          Move "XXX-XXXX" To Formatted-Alternate
000050* Format Based On Size
000051          If Phone-Number > 9999999
000052              Inspect Formatted-Number
000053                  Replacing First "XXX"  By Phone-Number (1:3)
000054                            First "XXX"  By Phone-Number (4:3)
000055                            First "XXXX" By Phone-Number (7:4)
000056              Move Formatted-Number To The-Edited-Number
000057          Else
000058              Inspect Formatted-Alternate
000059                  Replacing First "XXX"  By Phone-Number (4:3)
000060                            First "XXXX" By Phone-Number (7:4)
000061              Move Formatted-Alternate To The-Edited-Number
000062          End-If
000063* Left Justify The First Name
000064* If It's Blank It's A Waste Of Time
000065          If First-Name > Spaces
000066              Perform Varying Counter From 1 By 1 Until
000067                          First-Name (Counter:1) > Space
000068                  Continue
000069              End-Perform
000070* Counter Contains The Starting Offset
000071              Move First-Name (Counter:) To Temp-Field
000072              Move Temp-Field To First-Name
000073          End-If
000074* Left Justify The Last Name
000075          If Last-Name > Spaces
000076              Perform Varying Counter From 1 By 1 Until
000077                          Last-Name (Counter:1) > Space
000078                  Continue
000079              End-Perform
000080              Move Last-Name (Counter:) To Temp-Field
000081              Move Temp-Field To Last-Name
000082          End-If
```

11

continues

LISTING 11.4   CONTINUED

```
000083* Now Put Them Together
000084          Perform Varying Name-Length From 20 By -1
000085              Until First-Name (Name-Length:1) > Space
000086                Or Name-Length = Zeros
000087              Continue
000088          End-Perform
000089          If Name-Length = Zeros
000090              Move Last-Name To Combined-Name
000091          Else
000092              String First-Name (1:name-Length)
000093                      Space
000094                      Last-Name
000095                      Delimited By Size
000096                      Into Combined-Name
000097          End-If
000098* Now We Repeat
000099          End-Perform
000100      Stop Run
000101          .
```

Line 44 starts the outermost Perform. All the logic inside will execute until the F1 key is pressed. After you Display and Accept the user input, you process the fields. First, the telephone number is processed in exactly the same manner as in the previous code example (Listing 11.3).

NEW TERM   The one new element of code introduced here is the *left-justification routine*. The example uses an inline Perform in line 182 to search for the first character of the input field that is greater than spaces. You don't Perform the routine at all if the field has no data in it. When you know the offset of the first character, you move the data from that position to the end of the field into a temporary variable. This temporary field now contains the left-justified name. You then move the data back to its original field. The same routine is used for the last name.

This move to the temporary field is probably unnecessary. Because COBOL moves alphanumeric data fields 1 byte at a time from left to right, you could move the field in place. Move First-Name (Counter:) to First-Name. I refer to this type of Move as a "stupid COBOL trick". It's pretty neat but also pretty dangerous. It works on every compiler I tried, but some vendor may implement the mechanics of the Move statement differently. This technique is something that is more clever than clear, and I don't recommend using it.

Using the Debugger

It might be interesting to be able to see exactly what is happening inside the program when you run this example. Most modern compilers include a tool called an *interactive debugging utility*. The debugger enables programmers to step through the program one statement at a time and examine the values of the data fields involved.

This kind of facility can be a very powerful tool when it comes to debugging your programs. As an example, try running Listing 11.4 in debugging mode with the Fujitsu compiler. If you are using a different compiler, you can look at your documentation for instructions on running a debug session.

First, you need to add a compiler option to the program. Change the options at the top of the program to read:

```
000001 @OPTIONS MAIN,TEST
```

Compile the program with these options, but don't link it. you also have to change some options on the link step.

Proceed with the link step as you normally would. Before clicking the Link button, click the Options button. On the Options window, click the Debug button. Click the OK button. Then click the Link button. After the program links, you are ready to run it in debug mode.

11

> If you are running under Windows 3.1, proceed to the link step normally. Before clicking the Build button, select the Options menu option. Select the /CO check box and click the OK button. Click the Build button and then link the program in debug mode.

Select the Tools menu option (Under Windows 3.1, you want the Utilities menu). Choose WINSVD[Debug], click File, and then click Start Debugging. In the window that appears, click the Browse button. Choose Chapt011c and then click OK. Click the OK button to start the debug session. Click OK when the Runtime Options window appears. The screen shown in Figure 11.1 should appear.

The current source line is highlighted in yellow. You can do several things in debug mode. The right mouse button is active and provides quick access to many functions. To follow the program, however, click the Step Into button. This executes the highlighted line of source. Step into each source line until the Accept statement. When you step into it, the Step Into icon should be grayed out. You need to activate the screen window so that you can enter the required data.

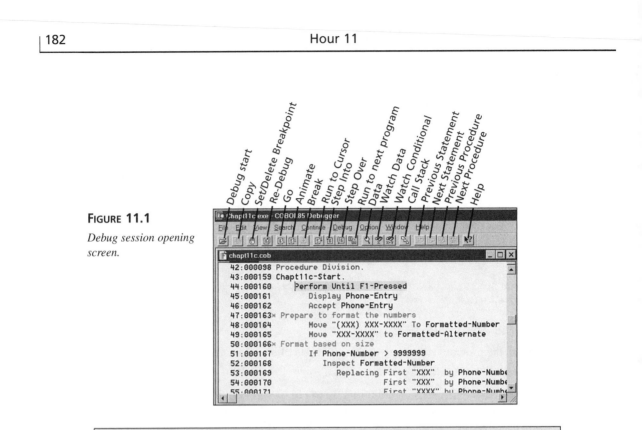

FIGURE 11.1

Debug session opening screen.

The Fujitsu debug facility under Windows 3.1 is very different from that provided for Windows NT and Windows 95/98. Follow these steps to start the debug session under Windows 3.1:

1. From Programming Staff, choose the Utilities menu option.

2. Choose the WINSVD selection.

3. When the Start Parameter screen appears, leave all the fields blank and click the OK button.

4. Select the \TYCOBOL folder from the Directories window.

5. Select the Chapt11c.exe program and click OK.

6. Click OK again on the Start Parameter screen.

7. When the Runtime Environment Setup appears, click the Run button.

8. The current source line is indicated by blue superimposed X characters over the active COBOL verb.

9. To step through the program, use the Step L button.

To activate the Screen window, click on the Screen item on the Windows taskbar. (Under Windows 3.1, use the ALT+TAB key combination to select SCREEN:CHAPT11C.) Key in the input data and space over a bit for each name so that you can see the left-justify routine in action.

As soon as you press Enter, the debug screen is displayed again. Use the Step Into button and step to the first If statement. Before it is executed, position the mouse pointer over the Phone-Number field and click the right mouse button. (Under Windows 3.1, select the Data then Data Control menu options. You have to key the name of the field you want to view in the Data input field. Then click OK to view the field contents.) From the pop-up menu, choose the Data menu option. A new window displays the length, format, and value of data field you selected. If you want to see the internal representation of the data value, you may select the Hex radio button. (Under Windows 3.1, use the Change Format button from the Data Control window.) The data value is displayed in hexadecimal notation. To modify a data value, you can key over it and then select the Modify button. Doing so will allow you to test the program action when a field contains specific data.

Close the data window. Use the Step Into button until you get to the next Perform statement. Because this Performs no statements, the active line remains the End-Perform until the test condition is satisfied.

Use the scroll bar to scroll down to the If statement at line 89. Position the mouse over this line, click the right mouse button, and choose Set Breakpoint. (Under Windows 3.1, use the Break menu option followed by the Set Breakpoint selection.) The selected line turns red. A *breakpoint* tells the debugger where to stop while executing. You don't have to step through every instruction in the program. You can now click the Go icon. (Under Windows 3.1, choose the Runto menu option and then select Run.) The debugger stops on the line you have set for a breakpoint.

Another interesting option is Animate. (Under Windows 3.1, use the Runto menu option and then select Trace.) This option enables you to watch the program step through its instructions. It stops on any statements requiring user input or on any breakpoints that have been set. When user input is accepted and Animate is enabled, you have to use the taskbar to return the focus to the debugging window. The debugging window does not automatically appear. While animating, the debugger stops on the last statement prior to a breakpoint. To step into that breakpoint, click the Breakpoint icon, which will be enabled.

Continue experimenting with the debugging session. Close the debugger when you are finished.

Summary

In this hour, you learned the following:

- How to use the Perform option Varying to set a counter, increment it by a specified amount for each execution, and stop when the specified condition is reached.
- How to use Test After to change the behavior of the condition testing in a Perform statement. Normally, your condition is tested before the statements after the Perform are executed. Using Test After guarantees at least one execution of the Perform.

11

- How to place your program statements between a Perform statement and the End-Perform explicit scope terminator, creating an inline Perform, instead of performing Paragraphs or Sections.

- How to nest Perform statements and include complex If logic, even when using the inline Perform. This approach maintains program design structure, but the statements are not scattered about your source code.

- How to compile and link a program for use with the interactive debugger. You found out how to use the debugger and to follow what is happening inside a program.

Q&A

Q When I use the Varying statement, does the data item I am incrementing have to be initialized to any particular value?

A No. The word From in the Perform statement specifies the starting value of the data item. Its value before the Perform does not matter.

Q I am confused about when I should use an inline Perform versus performing a Paragraph. Can you give me some insight?

A The decision on using an inline Perform instead of an out-of-line Perform is basically a matter of style. Some people prefer inline Performs, and some do not. The inline Perform is particularly useful for tasks like the left-justify procedure used Listing 11.4. If you have programming statements that are repeated in several inline Perform statements, you might want to change these to be distinct Paragraphs.

Q When I nest a Perform within an inline Perform, can I Perform a Paragraph, or must all the Performs be inline?

A You may Perform a Paragraph or Section. The inline Perform allows you to use any valid COBOL statements, which includes performing Paragraphs.

Q What should I watch for when using an inline Perform?

A You should never use a Go To to exit the inline Perform. In addition, you must be very careful not to terminate any statements inside the Perform, with a period. Use the End-If explicit scope terminator with every If statement you code inside the inline Perform. You should also use caution not to Perform the paragraph that contains the inline Perform, from within that inline Perform.

Q **When I try to debug my program, what should I do if the debugging screen does not appear?**

A Make sure you have compiled your program with the TEST compiler option. Then make sure you have chosen the Debug option when linking the program. (Under Windows 3.1, use the /CO option.)

Workshop

To help reinforce your understanding of the material presented in this hour, refer to the section "Quiz and Exercise Questions and Answers" that can be found on the CD. This section contains quiz questions and exercises for you to complete, as well as the corresponding answers.

11

Hour **12**

Tables

Tables are the COBOL version of an array. Tables have a variety of uses, from subtotal tracking to data validation. Table handling is an integral part of many COBOL programs. In this hour, you learn the different aspects of table handling, including

- The definition of a table
- Populating a table in `Working-Storage`
- Table searches
- Handling variable-length tables

Defining a Table

NEW TERM   A *table* is a set of different data items with identical definitions. They are defined so that the individual items in the set can be accessed via a reference, known as a *subscript*. Tables are also known as *arrays*. When a table is defined, the number of individual items, or elements, in the table is established. You can access the individual elements of the table by using the proper COBOL syntax.

A table is like a box of sequentially numbered index cards. You can locate a particular card by using its number and then counting the cards until you get to that number. The computer can perform this process faster than a person can because it can go directly to that card using the subscript value and because all the elements of the table have the same definition. The computer uses the subscript value to find the offset in the table and immediately access the element. This method is similar to what a person might do if the thickness of each card in the box of index cards is known. The number of the card sought can be determined and then, based on the thickness of the cards, the deck can be measured to immediately find the location of the card being sought. With the computer, table access is very fast.

A table is defined by using the Occurs clause in the Data Division. The Occurs clause may not be used on a level 01 or level 77 data item. In the following example, a table stores the names of the months in the year.

```
000010 01  Month-Table.
000011     03   Month-Name    Pic X(9) Occurs 12 Times.
```

The Occurs clause in line 11 specifies that this field is repeated 12 times; in other words, the table has 12 elements. The subscript associated with the first element is 1, and the subscript associated with the last is 12.

The Occurs clause may also be used at the Group Level to create an array containing several elementary items. The next example might be used to define a table containing the different state abbreviations and state names.

```
000012 01  State-Table.
000013     03   State-Abbrev-Name   Occurs 51 Times.
000014          05  State-Abbrev    Pic X(2).
000015          05  State-Name      Pic X(30).
```

Notice that the Occurs clause is specified only at the Group Level above the two associated elementary items. Therefore, the pairing of State-Abbrev and State-Name repeats 51 times. The table can be defined as follows:

```
000012 01  State-Table.
000013     03   State-Abbrev-Name.
000014          05  State-Abbrev    Pic X(2)  Occurs 51 Times.
000015          05  State-Name      Pic X(30) Occurs 51 Times.
```

Note that the Occurs clause appears only with the elementary items. In this example, if you looked at the table in memory within the computer, you would see the 50 state abbreviates listed together, followed by the 50 state descriptions. This arrangement becomes an important consideration as values are assigned to the individual table elements.

Basic Table Handling

To reference an element within a table, you need to specify the subscript. The first element of the table has a subscript value of 1. Subscripts are specified by stating the subscript, enclosed in parentheses, after the field name. For example:

```
000060    Display State-Name (24)
```

This line of code displays the 24th occurrence of State-Name.

You may use a table entry in the same way you use any other COBOL data item. You may move data into it or out if it. If it is a numeric data item, you may perform mathematical functions against the field.

Populating a Table in Working-Storage

Before a table can be of much use, values must be assigned to the table's individual elements. Consider a table that is to contain the individual month names.

```
000010 01  Month-Table.
000011     03  Month-Name    Pic X(9) Occurs 12 Times.
```

One way to get the individual month names into the table is to move them individually.

```
000061    Move "January"  To Month-Name (1)
000062    Move "February" To Month-Name (2)
```

This code is repeated for each month. The subscript references in this example are numeric literals. This need not be the case, as a numeric data item can be used instead.

After the table is loaded, the individual fields can be referenced by using the subscript.

```
000063    Display Month-Name (10)
```

This line displays October.

The Redefines Clause

NEW TERM In some cases, loading a table with individual Move statements makes sense. However, for the preceding example, in which the values in the table never need to change, a better way to initialize the table is to use a Data Division feature called the Redefines clause. In this case, the contents of the table can be defined in Working-Storage, instead of being loaded in the Procedure Division.

The Redefines allows you to specify a different Picture clause for a previously defined data item. An individual item may be the subject of multiple Redefines clauses. Examine this example:

12

```
000040 01   Data-Group.
000041      03  Numeric-Item              Pic 9(5)V99.
000042      03  Numeric-Split Redefines Numeric-Item.
000043          05  Numeric-Whole-Portion   Pic 9(5).
000044          05  Numeric-Decimal-Portion Pic 9(2).
```

The two fields, Numeric-Item and Numeric-Split, reference the same physical location in storage. The group item Numeric-Split is further defined as two individual fields: The first part makes up the whole number, and the second portion makes up the decimal position of Numeric-Item. If you move 12.99 to Numeric-Item, then Numeric-Whole-Portion contains 00012 and Numeric-Decimal-Portion contains 99.

> When using Redefines, you must make sure that the item you are redefining is the same size as the item in your Redefines clause. The compiler warns you of a size difference if the Redefines clause does not redefine a level 01 item. In contrast, level 01 items may redefine items with differing size; in this case, no compiler warning message is issued or required. Because this practice can cause problems, I suggest that you do not redefine items at the 01 level.

You can take advantage of the Redefines clause to populate the month table in Working-Storage. First, an area is defined with the different month descriptions listed in order.

```
000025 01   Month-Table-Area.
000026      03  Month-Descriptions.
000027          05  Filler              Pic X(9) Value "January".
000028          05  Filler              Pic X(9) Value "February".
000029          05  Filler              Pic X(9) Value "March".
000030          05  Filler              Pic X(9) Value "April".
000031          05  Filler              Pic X(9) Value "May".
000032          05  Filler              Pic X(9) Value "June".
000033          05  Filler              Pic X(9) Value "July".
000034          05  Filler              Pic X(9) Value "August".
000035          05  Filler              Pic X(9) Value "September".
000036          05  Filler              Pic X(9) Value "October".
000037          05  Filler              Pic X(9) Value "November".
000038          05  Filler              Pic X(9) Value "December".
```

The next step is to redefine this data area with the month table. Then the table is automatically populated, or loaded, with the appropriate data values.

```
000039      03  Month-Table Redefines Month-Descriptions.
000040          05  Month-Name          Pic X(9) Occurs 12 Times.
```

When you use redefines to establish initial values for the elements of a table, you cannot use the Initialize verb to reset the table to these values. Initialize moves spaces or zeros, as appropriate, to each element of a table, thus clearing your predefined values.

There are many ways to put tables to good use. One way to take advantage of a table involves the program you wrote (see Listing 12.1) as an answer to the exercise problem in Hour 10, "Processing Loops." This problem involved accepting a date and then reformatting the date to spell out the month, creating a nicely edited date. You probably used the Evaluate statement to find and use the correct month name. Using a table simplifies the program.

LISTING 12.1 DISPLAY THE NAME OF THE MONTH CORRESPONDING TO THE DATE

```
000001 @OPTIONS MAIN,TEST
000002 Identification Division.
000003 Program-Id.  Chapt12a.
000004 Environment Division.
000005 Configuration Section.
000006 Special-Names.
000007       Crt Status Is Keyboard-Status.
000008 Source-Computer.  IBM-PC.
000009 Object-Computer.  IBM-PC.
000010 Data Division.
000011 Working-Storage Section.
000012 01  Keyboard-Status.
000013     03  Accept-Status    Pic 9.
000014     03  Function-Key     Pic X.
000015         88 F1-Pressed    Value X"01".
000016     03  System-Use       Pic X.
000017 01  Date-Field           Pic 9(8)  Value Zeros.
000018 01  Date-Field-Split     Redefines Date-Field.
000019     03  Month-Portion    Pic 99.
000020     03  Filler           Pic X(6).
000021 01  Edited-Date-Field    Pic X(20) Value Spaces.
000022 01  Error-Flag           Pic X     Value Spaces.
000023     88  Month-Error      Value "Y".
000024 01  Error-Message        Pic X(50) Value Spaces.
000025 01  Month-Table-Area.
000026     03  Month-Descriptions.
000027         05  Filler           Pic X(9) Value "January".
000028         05  Filler           Pic X(9) Value "February".
000029         05  Filler           Pic X(9) Value "March".
000030         05  Filler           Pic X(9) Value "April".
```

continues

12

LISTING 12.1   CONTINUED

```
000031            05  Filler              Pic X(9) Value "May".
000032            05  Filler              Pic X(9) Value "June".
000033            05  Filler              Pic X(9) Value "July".
000034            05  Filler              Pic X(9) Value "August".
000035            05  Filler              Pic X(9) Value "September".
000036            05  Filler              Pic X(9) Value "October".
000037            05  Filler              Pic X(9) Value "November".
000038            05  Filler              Pic X(9) Value "December".
000039        03  Month-Table Redefines Month-Descriptions.
000040            05  Month-Name          Pic X(9) Occurs 12 Times.
000041 Screen Section.
000042 01  Date-Entry Blank Screen.
000043        03  Line 01 Column 01 Value " Enter Date: ".
000044        03  Line 01 Column 14 Pic 99/99/9999 Using Date-Field.
000045        03  Line 02 Column 01 Value "Edited Date: ".
000046        03  Line 02 Column 14 Pic X(20) From Edited-Date-Field.
000047        03  Line 05 Column 01 Pic X(50) From Error-Message.
000048        03  Line 20 Column 01 Value "Press F1 to Exit".
000049 Procedure Division.
000050 Chapt12a-Start.
000051     Perform Until F1-Pressed
000052         Display Date-Entry
000053         Accept Date-Entry
000054* Clear The Error Message For The Next Display
000055         Move Spaces To Error-Message
000056* If They Did Not Press F1 To Exit, It's Ok To Process The Input
000057         If Not F1-Pressed
000058             Perform Process-Input
000059         End-If
000060     End-Perform
000061     Stop Run
000062     .
000063 Process-Input.
000064* Reset The Error Flag.
000065     Move Spaces To Error-Flag
000066     If Month-Portion < 01 Or Month-Portion > 12
000067         Set Month-Error To True
000068         Move "Invalid Month" To Error-Message
000069     Else
000070         Move Spaces To Edited-Date-Field
000071         String Month-Name (Month-Portion) Delimited By Space
000072                 Space
000073                 Date-Field (3:2)
000074                 ","
000075                 Date-Field (5:4)
000076                 Delimited By Size
000077                 Into Edited-Date-Field
000078         End-String
000079     End-If
000080     .
```

Redefines appears in two places in the listing. The first Redefines clause, in line 18, handles the user-entered date. This clause allows numeric fields that contain only the month. This month is first checked to make sure that it is within the *bounds,* or "limits," of the table. The bounds of this table are 1 through 12. Most compilers have an option that allows you to capture a so-called boundary violation, or to not report the error if reported by default. If you reference a table element that is outside the bounds of your table, you receive a boundary violation.

> I suggest that you always write your programs to check for and eliminate any possible boundary violations. This does not mean that you have to code your programs with compares before every table element reference. Simply make sure that any invalid value that can occupy the field is not used as a table reference.

The second use of Redefines populates the table. This method requires far less code than you used in the Procedure Division method. The month is formatted using fewer instructions. Notice that the String statement uses multiple delimiters. The first is by spaces, so the end of the month name can be detected, and the rest are by size. This program produces a perfectly formatted date.

NEW TERM The preceding examples have shown the simplest use of a table. Another use for a table is as a *lookup.* You can use a small table, with its extremely fast lookup, to find associated information. For example, you might have a state table. The states, themselves, do not allow for easy table access. You can't subscript a table using a state abbreviation. Instead, you can search the table for the particular value required. Listing 12.2 is one example of a state search against a state table.

LISTING 12.2 STATE NAME LOOKUP

```
000001 @OPTIONS MAIN,TEST
000002 Identification Division.
000003 Program-Id.   Chapt12b.
000004 Environment Division.
000005 Configuration Section.
000006 Source-Computer.   IBM-PC.
000007 Object-Computer.   IBM-PC.
000008 Data Division.
000009 Working-Storage Section.
000010 01  State-Table-Area.
000011     03  State-Table-Data.
```

continues

LISTING 12.2   CONTINUED

```
000012          05  Filler Pic X(22) Value "ALAlabama".
000013          05  Filler Pic X(22) Value "AKAlaska".
000014          05  Filler Pic X(22) Value "AZArizona".
000015          05  Filler Pic X(22) Value "ARArkansas".
000016          05  Filler Pic X(22) Value "CACalifornia".
000017          05  Filler Pic X(22) Value "COColorado".
000018          05  Filler Pic X(22) Value "CTConnecticut".
000019          05  Filler Pic X(22) Value "DCDistrict of Columbia".
000020          05  Filler Pic X(22) Value "DEDelaware".
000021          05  Filler Pic X(22) Value "FLFlorida".
000022          05  Filler Pic X(22) Value "GAGeorgia".
000023          05  Filler Pic X(22) Value "HIHawaii".
000024          05  Filler Pic X(22) Value "IDIdaho".
000025          05  Filler Pic X(22) Value "ILIllinois".
000026          05  Filler Pic X(22) Value "INIndiana".
000027          05  Filler Pic X(22) Value "IAIowa".
000028          05  Filler Pic X(22) Value "KSKansas".
000029          05  Filler Pic X(22) Value "KYKentucky".
000030          05  Filler Pic X(22) Value "LALouisiana".
000031          05  Filler Pic X(22) Value "MEMaine".
000032          05  Filler Pic X(22) Value "MDMaryland".
000033          05  Filler Pic X(22) Value "MAMassachusetts".
000034          05  Filler Pic X(22) Value "MIMichigan".
000035          05  Filler Pic X(22) Value "MNMinnesota".
000036          05  Filler Pic X(22) Value "MSMississippi".
000037          05  Filler Pic X(22) Value "MOMissouri".
000038          05  Filler Pic X(22) Value "MTMontana".
000039          05  Filler Pic X(22) Value "NENebraska".
000040          05  Filler Pic X(22) Value "NVNevada".
000041          05  Filler Pic X(22) Value "NHNew Hampshire".
000042          05  Filler Pic X(22) Value "NJNew Jersey".
000043          05  Filler Pic X(22) Value "NMNew Mexico".
000044          05  Filler Pic X(22) Value "NYNew York".
000045          05  Filler Pic X(22) Value "NCNorth Carolina".
000046          05  Filler Pic X(22) Value "NDNorth Dakota".
000047          05  Filler Pic X(22) Value "OHOhio".
000048          05  Filler Pic X(22) Value "OKOklahoma".
000049          05  Filler Pic X(22) Value "OROregon".
000050          05  Filler Pic X(22) Value "PAPennsylvania".
000051          05  Filler Pic X(22) Value "RIRhode Island".
000052          05  Filler Pic X(22) Value "SCSouth Carolina".
000053          05  Filler Pic X(22) Value "SDSouth Dakota".
000054          05  Filler Pic X(22) Value "TNTennessee".
000055          05  Filler Pic X(22) Value "TXTexas".
000056          05  Filler Pic X(22) Value "UTUtah".
000057          05  Filler Pic X(22) Value "VTVermont".
000058          05  Filler Pic X(22) Value "VAVirginia".
000059          05  Filler Pic X(22) Value "WAWashington".
000060          05  Filler Pic X(22) Value "WVWest Virginia".
```

```
000061              05  Filler Pic X(22) Value "WIWisconsin".
000062              05  Filler Pic X(22) Value "WYWyoming".
000063          03  State-Table Redefines State-Table-Data.
000064              05  State-Table-Occurrences  Occurs 51 Times.
000065                  10  State-Abbrev       Pic XX.
000066                  10  State-Name         Pic X(20).
000067 01  State-Subscript              Pic 99 Value Zeros.
000068 Procedure Division.
000069 Chapt12b-Start.
000070* Search For Texas, By Abbreviation
000071      Perform Varying State-Subscript From 1 By 1 Until
000072          State-Subscript > 51 Or
000073          State-Abbrev (State-Subscript) = "TX"
000074          Continue
000075      End-Perform
000076      If State-Subscript > 51
000077          Display "State Not Found"
000078      Else
000079          Display "TX = "
000080                  State-Name (State-Subscript)
000081      End-If
000082      Stop Run
000083          .
```

The Redefines clause allows the table to be loaded in Working-Storage. The search is
an inline Perform that continues until it reaches the end of the table or until it gets a
match. Before displaying the state description found, the subscript field is checked to
ensure it is within the table boundary. If it is not, you know that the abbreviation was not
found in the table.

12

The Search Statement

NEW TERM   COBOL provides a quick way to Search a table for particular values. For you to
use this feature, the table must have an associated index. An *index* is a system-
assigned data field that references the different elements of a table—you do not define
this field in your program. Although an index behaves like a numeric data item, you cannot adjust it using mathematical statements as you would normal numeric data items. An
index is specified by using the Indexed By clause on the same line as the Occurs clause.
Specify a unique data name after the words Indexed By.

The compiler vendor determines the actual contents of an index. In most
cases, it is an absolute offset in characters to the particular item within the
table. However, you may not reference the item as a number, and the index

does not contain an element number, even though it may be tested in perform loops as if it does. The compiler handles the actual interpretation of
the value for you.

```
000058      03  Month-Table Redefines Month-Descriptions.
000059          05  Month-Name    Pic X(9) Occurs 12 Times Indexed by
000060              Table-Index.
```

To manipulate the value of an index, you must use the Set statement. You may Set an
index to a particular value or adjust its value up or down by specific amounts.

```
000061      Set Table-Index To 1
000062      Set Table-Index Up by 2
000063      Set Table-Index Down by 1
```

Using index values provides faster table access than using a regular numeric
data item or numeric literal. You must remember, however, that you cannot
change an index value using standard mathematical statements. If you need
to adjust an index, use the Set statement.

An indexed table may be searched using the COBOL verb Search, which has two
formats. The first format searches the table from the top to the bottom. In the Search
statement, you specify the condition that causes the Search to end. Optionally, you may
specify some statements to perform if the Search does not find any items in the table
that satisfy your test condition.

When coding the Search statement, the data item that is specified for the Search is the
one for which the Occurs clause has been coded. The conditions that end the Search are
coded using When, in a manner very similar to that used with the Evaluate statement.
The statements that are executed when the Search fails are coded after the clause At
End. The Search proceeds from the present value of the associated index. Consequently,
you must be careful to Set the value of the table's index to 1 before the Search begins.
Failing to do so causes the Search to begin at an entry in the table other than the first.

If the state table is defined with the index Table-Index, the following code will perform
the same test as the inline Perform from the earlier example. In fact, the following
Search statement can replace the entire Procedure Division from Listing 12.2.

```
000215      Search State-Table-Occurrences
000216          At End Display "State Not Found"
000217          When State-Abbrev (Table-Index) = "TX"
```

```
000218                  Display "TX = "
000219                      State-Name (Table-Index)
000220      End-Search
```

When coding the Search statement, the At End condition, if present, must occur before any When clauses. At End is optional. If not coded, nothing happens when the Search ends without meeting your conditions.

You may use multiple When clauses within the Search statement. If any one of them is true, the statements after the associated When are executed. As soon as a When condition is true, the searching stops.

The End-Search explicit scope terminator is valid with the Search statement. I strongly suggest that you use it with every Search statement to clearly separate the code after the When from the rest of your program.

Remember that the index of a table has a special internal representation. The only COBOL statements you can use to address this index are the Set, Search, and Perform with Varying statements. If you want to do something in your program based on the actual element number of the found item, COBOL provides a method to increment another data item during the Search. This method involves the Tally clause. The item being incremented can be the index for another table or a numeric variable.

The Varying clause specifies the other data item. You should remember that this item is being adjusted by the Search in addition to the index specified for the table, not instead of that index.

12

Because the data item is incremented separately and independently of the table's defined index, it is important to initialize that data item in addition to the table's index. For example, if the numeric data item started with a value of 10 and the table element that satisfied the search was element 5, the resulting value in the numeric data item is 15, not 5 like you might expect.

```
000221      Move Zeros to Numeric-Data-Item
000222      Set Table-Index to 1
000223      Search State-Table-Occurrences
000224          Varying Numeric-Data-Item
```

```
000225                  At End Display "State Not Found"
000226                  When State-Abbrev (Table-Index) = "TX"
000227                      Display "TX = "
000228                              State-Name (Table-Index)
000229        End-Search
```

The Search statement, which starts at the front of the table and searches to the end, is
not very efficient on large tables. COBOL provides another format of the Search statement that allows much faster searching. This format is Search All. For a program to use
Search All, the table must be indexed and keyed. The elements of the table must be in
ascending or descending key sequence as specified in the field's definition. The key
fields are defined in the Data Division, on the same line as the Occurs clause. The previous example, using the state table, was sorted in ascending state-name sequence.
Therefore, Search All can be used against the state name. However, Search All cannot
be used on the state abbreviations because they are not in sequence. The definition of the
state table keyed on state name follows.

```
000199     03  State-Table Redefines State-Table-Data.
000200         05  State-Table-Occurrences  Occurs 51 Times
000201                                         Indexed By Table-Index
000202                                         Ascending Key State-Name.
000203             10  State-Abbrev       Pic XX.
000204             10  State-Name         Pic X(20).
```

Here's how the Search All statement is coded to find the abbreviation of a state name
such as Texas:

```
000230     Search All State-Table-Occurrences
000231          At End Display "State Not Found"
000232          When State-Name (Table-Index) = "Texas"
000233              Display "Texas = "
000234                      State-Abbrev (Table-Index)
000235        End-Search
```

The rules governing Search and Search All are not exactly the same. With Search All,
there may be only one When clause. The When clause must reference one of the key fields.
However, the When may be coded with one or more And statements. The And statements
allow you to test for multiple conditions and must also reference one of the key fields in
the table. The key field must immediately follow the word When.

The Search All performs a binary search. A binary search starts around the middle of
the table and determines whether the value is greater or less than the key being searched.
If the value is greater, the search looks in the higher half of the table. The program continues to split the table into smaller and smaller search areas until the Search is satisfied
or until no more items are in the table. Because of the binary search, the setting of the
table index to 1 before the Search is unnecessary. The initial value of the index is
ignored.

Listing 12.3 shows an example of Search All with When and And clauses. The table being searched contains multiple city and state entries allowing the program to find the state that corresponds with the city.

LISTING 12.3 SEARCH ALL EXAMPLE

```
000001 @OPTIONS MAIN,TEST
000002 Identification Division.
000003 Program-Id.  Chapt12e.
000004 Environment Division.
000005 Configuration Section.
000006 Source-Computer.  IBM-PC.
000007 Object-Computer.  IBM-PC.
000008 Data Division.
000009 Working-Storage Section.
000010 01  State-Table-Area.
000011     03  State-Table-Data.
000012         05  Filler Pic X(37) Value "ALBirmingham    Alabama".
000013         05  Filler Pic X(37) Value "ALMontgomery    Alabama".
000014         05  Filler Pic X(37) Value "AZPhoenix       Arizona".
000015         05  Filler Pic X(37) Value "AZTucson        Arizona".
000016     03  State-Table Redefines State-Table-Data.
000017         05  State-Table-Occurrences  Occurs 4 Times
000018             Indexed By Table-Index
000019             Ascending Key State-Abbrev City-Name.
000020             10  State-Abbrev      Pic XX.
000021             10  City-Name         Pic X(15).
000022             10  State-Name        Pic X(20).
000023 Procedure Division.
000024 Chapt12e-Start.
000025     Search All State-Table-Occurrences
000026         At End Display "State Not Found"
000027         When State-Abbrev (Table-Index) = "AZ"
000028         And  City-Name (Table-Index) = "Phoenix"
000029             Display "State = "
000030                     State-Name (Table-Index)
000031     End-Search
000032     Stop Run
000033       .
```

First, notice that the table is keyed by two key fields. This technique can be useful in case two states have cities with the same name. The key sequence, as defined, is city within state abbreviation. Second, notice the When and the And clauses in the Search All statement. Each clause refers to a key as defined on the Occurs line. This syntax is required for the Search All statement. Finally, realize that the Search does not stop until both conditions, the When and the And, are satisfied.

12

Multidimensional Tables

NEW TERM   Thus far, the tables discussed here have been one-dimensional. However, in COBOL tables can have up to seven dimensions. A *two-dimensional table* is a table within a table. You can visualize a two-dimensional table as a file within a drawer in a file cabinet. The file cabinet is the table. The first dimension is the drawer number, and the second is the file within the drawer. The table might be described in your data division as follows:

```
000040 01  File-Cabinet.
000041     03   Drawer-Number Occurs 3 Times Indexed By Drawer-Index.
000042         05  File-Number Pic 9(3) Occurs 10 Times Indexed By
000043                                  File-Index.
```

To reference a particular file number, a two-dimensional table reference is coded. This is accomplished by coding both index values within the parenthetical reference to the data item. For example, the following code references the fifth file in the third drawer:

```
000100     Display File-Number (3,5)
```

The comma is optional but helps to make the table reference more readable. The highest level index is specified first. Another example might make this syntax clearer.

```
000101     Set Drawer-Index To 3
000102     Set File-Index To 5
000103     Display File-Number (Drawer-Index, File-Index)
```

You may Search a multidimensional table using the Search verb. The higher-level index values must be Set before the basic, or lowest-level index can be searched. When you specify the table level to be searched in the Search statement, you do not need to provide the full reference. However, any When statements must specify the full qualification of the table entry.

```
000104     Set Drawer-Index To 2
000105     Search File-Number
000106         At End Display "File Not Found"
000107         When File-Number (Drawer-Index, File-Index) = 123
000108             Display "File Found"
000109     End-Search
```

In this example, File-Number is being searched. It is a table that exists as the second dimension of the larger table, Drawer-Number. Note that in the Search line the element of Drawer-Number is not specified. The Search statement uses the current index value associated with the Drawer-Number for its search. Also note that the When statement specifies the full table reference for the purposes of the test condition.

Now examine a more complex example of multidimensional tables. Consider this classic logic puzzle: "As I was going to St. Ives, I met a man with seven wives. Every wife had seven sacks, every sack had seven cats, and every cat had seven kits. Kits, cats, sacks and wives, how many were going to St. Ives?"

Ignore the basic question being asked by the puzzle. To describe this condition in a table, you might code:

```
000040 01  The-Man-On-The-Road.
000041     03  Wife              Occurs 7 Times Indexed By Wife-Index.
000042         05  Wife-Name               Pic X(20).
000043         05  Sack          Occurs 7 Times Indexed By Sack-Index.
000044             10  Sack-Color          Pic X(10).
000045             10  Cat       Occurs 7 Times Indexed By Cat-Index.
000046                 15  Cat-Name        Pic X(20).
000047                 15  Kitten Occurs 7 Times Indexed By Kitten-Index.
000048                     20  Kitten-Name Pic X(20).
```

Notice that the tables are not just tables within tables. The Wife-Name has the same level number as the Sack table, which allows the tracking of each wife and her associated sacks. Each Sack-Color has the same level number as the Cat table beneath it, which allows each sack color to be tracked.

How might you code a COBOL program to find which wife is carrying a kitten named "Hershey"? You need to search through each and every cat, in every sack, carried by every wife, until you either find a match or don't find the kitten in any sack. Listing 12.4 is one way to code the Search.

LISTING 12.4 SEARCH A MULTIDIMENSIONAL TABLE

```
000001 @OPTIONS MAIN,TEST
000002 Identification Division.
000003 Program-Id.  Chapt12g.
000004 Environment Division.
000005 Configuration Section.
000006 Source-Computer.  IBM-PC.
000007 Object-Computer.  IBM-PC.
000008 Data Division.
000009 Working-Storage Section.
000010 01  The-Man-On-The-Road.
000011     03  Wife              Occurs 7 Times
000012         Indexed By Wife-Index.
000013         05  Wife-Name               Pic X(20).
000014         05  Sack          Occurs 7 Times
000015         Indexed By Sack-Index.
000016             10  Sack-Color          Pic X(10).
000017             10  Cat       Occurs 7 Times
000018                 Indexed By Cat-Index.
000019                 15  Cat-Name        Pic X(20).
```

continues

12

LISTING 12.4   CONTINUED

```
000020                    15  Kitten Occurs 7 Times
000021                        Indexed By Kitten-Index.
000022                    20  Kitten-Name      Pic X(20).
000023 01  Found-Flag  Pic X Value Spaces.
000024     88  Kitten-Found Value "Y".
000025 Procedure Division.
000026 Chapt12g-Start.
000027     Move "Hershey" To Kitten-Name (1, 3, 2, 6)
000028     Move "Darlene" To Wife-Name (1)
000029     Move "Yellow"  To Sack-Color (1, 3)
000030     Perform With Test After
000031                 Varying Wife-Index From 1 By 1 Until
000032                 Wife-Index = 7 Or
000033                 Kitten-Found
000034       Perform With Test After
000035                   Varying Sack-Index From 1 By 1 Until
000036                   Sack-Index = 7 Or
000037                   Kitten-Found
000038         Perform With Test After
000039                     Varying Cat-Index From 1 By 1 Until
000040                     Cat-Index = 7 Or
000041                     Kitten-Found
000042           Set Kitten-Index To 1
000043           Search Kitten
000044             When
000045               Kitten-Name (Wife-Index, Sack-Index,
000046                       Cat-Index, Kitten-Index) =
000047               "Hershey" Set Kitten-Found To True
000048             End-Search
000049           End-Perform
000050         End-Perform
000051     End-Perform
000052     If Kitten-Found
000053       Display "Hershey found in the "
000054               Sack-Color (Wife-Index, Sack-Index)
000055               " Sack, Being carried by "
000056               Wife-Name (Wife-Index)
000057     Else
000058       Display "Hershey Escaped"
000059     End-If
000060     Stop Run
000061     .
```

Examine this program line by line. The entry to be searched for is first loaded into the table. In actuality, the full table would be loaded. The specific entry is loaded only as an example.

Next, note the use of the inline `Perform` statements, which allow nested `Perform` statements to search each dimension of the table. Remember that when using `Varying` with a `Perform`, the data item being varied is incremented before each loop through the `Perform`. Therefore, the behavior of the `Perform` has been changed to `Test After`. This change allows the different indices to remain set to the values they are on when the `Search` completes successfully. Notice also that no `At End` clause is coded in the `Search` statement. The clause is not necessary. Compile and run the program. Experiment with setting different locations for `"Hershey"`. Run the program in the debugger and watch what is happening. Remember to link the program with the debug option enabled.

Variable-Length Tables

Tables do not have to be of fixed length. You can define a table that contains from one to any number of entries. You might want to have a variable-length table for several reasons. For example, you might choose a variable-length table to shorten the response time on a `Search` or `Search All` statement.

You might have a table in which you don't know the maximum number of entries. It might be loaded from user input or from a data file. It might even be created during the course of a program's execution. If you always allow for the table's maximum size, you will be wasting time during the `Search` operations. Additionally, it will be virtually impossible to provide a sorted table for `Search All`. If your table has 1,000 entries, but you load it with only 100, the other 900 entries in the table must be in ascending sequence. One solution is to load the remaining entries with `High-Values`, but that approach wastes time. Instead, you should use a variable-length table.

You create a variable-length table by specifying `Depending On` in the `Occurs` clause on the item definition. You must have a data item defined that will contain the number of items in the table. This item is the one that the number of occurrences in the table depends on and can change during the course of the program. In addition to specifying the `Depending On` clause, you must specify the minimum and maximum number of occurrences in the table.

The following table contains dealer numbers and names from your antique store. You can have any number of dealers, but the number may fluctuate. You might need a table to find the dealer name with the associated dealer number.

```
000040 01  Dealer-Table.
000041     03  Dealers Occurs 1 To 1000 Times Depending On
000042                              Number-Of-Dealers
000043              Indexed By Dealer-Index
000044              Ascending Key Dealer-Number.
000045        05  Dealer-Number   Pic 9(4).
```

12

```
000046           05  Dealer-Name       Pic X(20).
000047 01 Number-Of-Dealers     Pic 9(4) Value 1.
```

A variable-length table must have at least one occurrence. The memory required to contain the maximum size the table may obtain is usually reserved by the compiler (some COBOL vendors dynamically allocate the storage space). You should be aware that some compilers limit the maximum size of a table. You should refer to your compiler documentation to find out what limit, if any, is specified for your compiler.

Variable-length tables may be specified only for the highest level of a table. If your table is multidimensional, the tables that make up the dimensions under the main table may not be variable length.

When this table is loaded, the Number-Of-Dealers has to be incremented in the program. You should not reference an element of the table that is higher in number than the Depending On data item. Doing so will cause a table-boundary violation.

Summary

In this hour, you learned the following:

- Tables are groups of like items arranged in such a way that individual elements of the group can be referenced.
- Table elements can be initialized to specific values in Working-Storage by setting up a data area with the various values and using the Redefines clause.
- Tables elements can be referenced by numeric literals, numeric data items, or index values.
- Index items may be specified by using Indexed By on the same line as the Occurs clause.
- Index items are not like normal numeric data items. You must use the Set statement to set or change the values of index items.
- Tables may be searched using the Search verb.
- For Search All, the items in the table must be in key sequence.
- Tables may be created with multiple dimensions. COBOL supports up to seven dimensions in a table.

• Tables do not have to contain a fixed number of elements. They can contain a variable number of elements. Variable-length tables are defined by specifying the `Depending On` clause in the table's definition.

Q&A

Q When I want to `Search` a table, how can I remember which part of the table to code after the `Search` statement?

A Look for the `Occurs` clause. All of your `Search` statements `Search` the named data items on the same line as the `Occurs` clause.

Q I tried to use `Search All`, but I can't seem to get it right. Can you give me some pointers?

A Some common mistakes are not specifying the key fields on the table. Other problems come from the data in the table not being in this key sequence. The key values can be either ascending or descending. When your table is created and data is loaded into it, if you are going to use `Search All`, you must ensure that the data in the table is in the proper sequence. Nothing in the COBOL language informs you that your table is out of sequence.

Q When I run my program, I get some strange results. I think I have a boundary violation, but the program is not reporting it. How do I get it to?

A With the Fujitsu Compiler you need to add the compiler option `CHECK(1)` to the top of the program. This option displays an error message the first time a boundary violation occurs and terminates the program. (See Program Chapt12z.Cob on the CD-ROM.)

Q What is a boundary violation?

A A boundary violation occurs when you try to access a table element that is out of the range of the table. If your table has 50 occurrences and you attempt to access an element with a subscript of 51, you will get a boundary violation. Some compilers report this error by default, and some do not. On those that do not, or where you have disabled boundary or index/subscript range checking, unpredictable results may occur.

Q My table searches using the `Search` verb are taking a long time. What can I do to speed them up?

A You can try to limit the search time by using `Search All` if it is feasible. If not, try limiting the table size to the actual number of items you have in the table by making the table variable length. You do this by using the `Depending On` clause with the `Occurs` clause.

12

Workshop

To help reinforce your understanding of the material presented in this hour, refer to the section "Quiz and Exercise Questions and Answers" that can be found on the CD. This section contains quiz questions and exercises for you to complete, as well as the corresponding answers.

PART II
File Handling

Hour

13   Sequential Files

14   Indexed Files

15   Reading Indexed File Records

16   Updating Indexed File Records

17   Sorting

Hour 13

Sequential Files

One of the many things that makes COBOL such a rich and powerful language is its ability to clearly, accurately, and quickly handle data files. Business deals with data files constantly. In this hour, you learn about one type of commonly used file: the sequential file. You learn

- How to define a sequential file in a COBOL program
- How to Open and Close the file
- How to create records in the file
- How to read records from a sequential file
- How to update existing records in a sequential file

In addition, COBOL uses some terms that you need to understand in order to discuss data file access.

NEW TERM   First, a *file* is made up of individual records. A *record* is a collection of individual fields or data items. The format or formats of the records in the file are defined in your COBOL program. A record is a Group Level item, made up of elementary data items or groups of elementary data items. The definition for a record is called a record layout, or record description. The layouts of the records used by the various files in your COBOL program are specified in the Data Division.

A file is simply a group of records. A *sequential file* is one that is accessed sequentially; that is, the records are retrieved from the file in order, from the first record in the file to the last. Records cannot be retrieved out of order. You may not jump ahead in the file, nor may you go backward.

When creating, or writing, a sequential file, you must write the records in order. The physical order of the records in the file is the order in which they were written.

Most PC-based compilers differentiate between two types of sequential files. The first is the default type, Record Sequential, and the other is Line Sequential. Line Sequential files are regular text files, created by Notepad or some other text editor. Your CONFIG.SYS and AUTOEXEC.BAT files are examples of Line Sequential files.

NEW TERM Line Sequential files contain records of varying length. Trailing space data in the record is not written (that is, it is truncated), thus saving space. Records are terminated with a platform-dependent delimiter. Under most PC-based operating systems, this delimiter is a Carriage Return and Line Feed, in ACSII a X"0D0A".

> On UNIX systems, Line Sequential files are terminated with a Line Feed only; in ASCII, a X"0A".

The hexadecimal, or internal representation, of these characters is X"0D", X"0A". Only textual data may be written to these files. Many implementations ignore characters less than spaces when they are written to these files. For example, Low-Values do not appear in your Line Sequential data file if you attempt to use them in the record.

Line Sequential files are good for reading or writing data that the user may edit with a standard text editor. If your files are for use only by your COBOL program and are not to be shared with other systems or if your files contain packed data such as usage COMP or COMP-3 data items, you should not use Line Sequential files.

NEW TERM The other type of file is a Record Sequential file, normally referred to simply as a Sequential file. The records in a Record Sequential file are not delimited. Each record in the file is adjacent to its immediate neighbors. Table 13.1 illustrates the difference between Line Sequential and Record Sequential files.

TABLE 13.1 LINE SEQUENTIAL VERSUS RECORD SEQUENTIAL ORGANIZATION

Line Sequential	Record Sequential
Line 1*CRLF*	Line 1********************
Record 1*CRLF*	Record 1******************
This is a Sequential record*CRLF*	This is a Sequential record

The *CRLF* under the `Line Sequential` column demonstrates the delimiters in each record of a `Line Sequential` file. The delimiter immediately follows the last character in the record that is greater than a space. Under the `Record Sequential` column, imagine that the * characters are actually spaces. With a `Record Sequential` file, the trailing spaces are written to the file, and there is no delimiter. The next record in the file starts immediately after the current record.

`Sequential` files have many uses. For example, they can hold the data necessary to load a table for use in the COBOL program. Such files often hold transactional data to be used in an update of a master file. You can also use `Sequential` files to exchange data between systems and computers. Printers are written to as if they were `Sequential` files.

A `Sequential` file might be a disk file or a tape file. It could even be a paper tape or punch card file. Any device that can be attached to the computer and read from or written to in a sequential fashion can contain a `Sequential` file. On the PC, most `Sequential` files are located on disk.

Connecting Your Program to a File

To access a `Sequential` file, you must establish a connection between the file and your program. This process requires two steps. The first establishes the hardware, file type, organization, and filename of the file you are accessing. The second defines the layout of the records in the file.

13

The `Select` Statement

The `Select` statement connects your program to a file. Several clauses can be coded with the `Select` statement. This section considers only the clauses that relate to `Sequential` files.

The `Select` statement is coded in the `Environment Division`, under the `Input-Output Section`, in a paragraph titled `File-Control`.

An internal filename is specified in the Select statement. This name is the name by which you refer to the file in your COBOL program. The filename may be up to 30 characters long.

The Assign clause associates the file with a named file on your system. The Assign clause can refer to a symbolic name or, in some cases, as on the PC, an actual physical filename. The symbolic name can later be associated with a specific file, using runtime options. In the case of IBM mainframes, these files are associated using Job Control Language (JCL). In this book, the actual physical filenames to be used are defined. The Organization clause specifies the type of file you are working with. For Sequential files, the type can be Sequential or Line Sequential.

The File Status clause associates the system returned File Status with a field in the Data Division. This field is two characters long and contains a status value that can be tested after every operation against the file.

The following example is the Select statement for a file called Name-File in your COBOL program. The organization is Line Sequential. The actual filename on the PC is NAME.TXT. The File Status is stored in a field named Name-File-Status. The Select clause starts in Area B (column 12).

```
000010 @OPTIONS MAIN,TEST
000020 Identification Division.
000030 Program-Id.  Chapt13a.
000031* File Creation Example
000043 Environment Division.
000050 Configuration Section.
000051 Source-Computer.  IBM-PC.
000055 Object-Computer.  IBM-PC.
000056 Input-Output Section.
000059 File-Control.
000060     Select Name-File Assign To "NAME.TXT"
000061         Organization Is Line Sequential
000062         File Status  Is Name-File-Status.
```

This program contains several new elements. Notice the new Section: Input-Output. It contains the paragraphs pertaining to external file I-O. The File-Control Paragraph is the heading under which your Select statements are coded.

I-O is shorthand for "Input-Output." *Input* is information that comes into your program. It might be user input, such as the data that is entered into a data entry program, or it might be a data file. *Output* is any information that your program produces. It can take many forms. Output might be data displayed on the screen or a data file, among other things.

The File Description

The File Description (FD) describes the attributes of the file and its associated data record or records.

With modern COBOL, the only relevant line is the actual FD line. The FD is coded in the Data Division of the File Section. The Record Description, or descriptions, immediately follow the FD. The FD contains the same filename as specified in the Select statement. Every file specified with a Select statement requires a File Description entry.

The record description must start with an 01 Group Level item. A file may have more than one record description, and each must follow the associated FD. Your file has only one field: Full-Name. The FD is coded as follows:

```
000065 Data Division.
000066 File Section.
000067 FD   Name-File.
000068 01   Name-Record.
000069      03  Full-Name   Pic X(30).
```

> The 01 level for this record can also be coded as 01 Name-Record Pic X(30) or as 01 Full-Name Pic X(30). However, as you will see when you start using this FD, this method is unclear in the program. A better approach is to name your record descriptions "record" and to name the individual fields that make up the record with names that are appropriate for their contents.

The rules for coding data items in the Record Description are nearly identical to those for dealing with Working-Storage. The data records can contain 88 level items and Redefines clauses. However, a few restrictions do apply. Any Value clauses specified are considered comments and do not set actual values within the fields. In addition, 77 level items may not be used in a Record Description. Occurs clauses may be used, even those that describe variable-length tables. However, the result is a variable-length record, and certain special rules must be followed. These records are discussed later in the hour.

13

> You should be aware that if you specify more than one Record Description for a file, these Record Descriptions are implicit Redefines. You can think of them as overlapping each other. Therefore, if you move data into a field in one Record Description, that data shows in all Record Descriptions for the file.

Opening the File

Now that the file is defined to the COBOL program, you may use it. The first step is to Open the file. Sequential files may be opened in four different modes.

Opening the file for Input allows you to read data from the file. If you open the file for Output, you can write data to the file. Opening the file I-O allows you to update records in the file, and opening the file Extend allows you to add records to the end of the file.

To open a file for Input, code as follows:

```
000090     Open Input Name-File
```

The Open will be successful if the file exists. The status value of a successful open is 00. This value is stored in the data item assigned by the File Status clause on the Select statement. If no File Status is defined, the program may end abnormally, with an error reported by the runtime system.

Standard File Status values contain two characters. The status returned under "normal" circumstances begins with a zero. If your file does not exist and you Open it Input, the File Status returned is 35.

If you don't want your program to report a serious file error when the file does not exist, you can code the Optional clause on the Select statement. When Optional is coded, the File Status reported for the Open of a file that does not exist is 05 and the Open is successful. The first Read of the file, however, reports that end of file has been reached. The Optional clause is coded in the Select statement as follows:

```
000058 Input-Output  Section.
000059 File-Control.
000060     Select Optional Name-File Assign To "NAME.TXT"
000061            Organization Is Line Sequential
000062            File Status  Is Name-File-Status.
```

File Status values are discussed as you learn the different file operations. For a complete list of File Status values that can be returned with the Fujitsu compiler, please see the *Cobol 85 User's Guide,* which is included with the Fujitsu compiler on the CD. If you prefer to use the Adobe Acrobat reader for viewing this document, the PDF format file is in the \SOFTCOPY\PDF directory of the CD.

Closing the File

When you are finished processing a file, you should release that file to the operating system so that other programs can use it. The Close statement syntax closely follows the Open statement. The filename being closed, as stated in the Select statement and FD, must be specified.

```
000100     Close Name-File
```

Most programmers do not check the File Status after the Close statement. However, the File Status values shown in Table 13.2.can be returned from the Close of a Sequential file.

TABLE 13.2 SEQUENTIAL FILE STATUS VALUES AFTER A CLOSE STATEMENT

Status	Meaning
00	Successful completion
30	Physical error, no other information available
42	Close issued for an unopened file
9x	Compiler-vendor defined

The last status, 9x, actually contains a 9 in the first position and a vendor-defined value in the second position. This value can be just about anything that the compiler vendor desires.

Writing to the File

Before you can accomplish anything meaningful with a Sequential file, you need to create it. To create the file, it is opened for Output. When a file that does not exist is opened for Output, it is created. If it does exist, it is replaced by an empty file. This concept is very important. When you Open a file for Output, you should intend to create a new file. The statement required to Open the name file for Output is

```
000091     Open Output Name-File
```

After the Open, the File Status is checked to confirm the Open. Any status other than 00 indicates an error with the Open.

13

TABLE 13.3 SEQUENTIAL FILE STATUS VALUES FOR OPEN IN OUTPUT MODE

Status	Meaning
00	Successful completion
30	Physical error, no other information available
9x	Compiler-vendor defined

The only error you are likely to encounter when opening a Sequential file for Output relates to the name chosen for your file or the media on which you are trying to create the file. For example, if you have a read-only CD in your CD-ROM drive and you attempt to Open a file Output on that drive, the File Status returned with the Fujitsu compiler is 90.

Data records are created in the file by using the Write statement. The only required operand with the Write statement is a *record identifier*. The record identifier is one of the 01 Group Level items coded under the FD.

> Remember, when writing to a file, never specify the filename, but rather the record identifier. The reason is that multiple record descriptions may exist for a particular file. Specifying the record description causes the program to Write the record in the format desired.

Several File Status values can be returned after a Write statement, as shown in Table 13.4.

TABLE 13.4 FILE STATUS VALUES FROM THE WRITE STATEMENT

Status	Meaning
00	Successful completion
30	Error, no other information available
34	Boundary error
48	Attempted to write to a file that is either not open or is not open in an appropriate mode for write
9x	Compiler-vendor defined

File Status 30 is a kind of catchall. Errors that may occur during the Write that are not captured any other way may report a File Status 30. Status 34 is reported if you exceed the maximum allowable size for the file on your platform or if the media you are writing to fills up. Status 48 is typically encountered when you have failed to Open the file or when you have opened it Input and are attempting to Write to the file.

The short program in Listing 13.1 demonstrates how to Open a file for Output, Accept names, and Write them to the file until F1 is pressed, and then Close the file and exit.

LISTING 13.1 FILE CREATION EXAMPLE

```
000001 @OPTIONS MAIN,TEST
000002 Identification Division.
000003 Program-Id.  Chapt13a.
000004* File Creation Example
000005 Environment Division.
000006 Configuration Section.
000007 Special-Names.
000008       Crt Status Is Keyboard-Status.
000009 Source-Computer.  IBM-PC.
000010 Object-Computer.  IBM-PC.
000011 Input-Output  Section.
000012 File-Control.
000013     Select Name-File Assign To "NAME.TXT"
000014         Organization Is Line Sequential
000015         File Status  Is Name-File-Status.
000016 Data Division.
000017 File Section.
000018 FD  Name-File.
000019 01  Name-Record.
000020     03  Full-Name   Pic X(30).
000021 Working-Storage Section.
000022 01  Keyboard-Status.
000023     03  Accept-Status   Pic 9.
000024     03  Function-key    Pic X.
000025         88 F1-Pressed   Value X"01".
000026     03  System-Use      Pic X.
000027 01  File-Error-Flag     Pic X Value Space.
000028     88  File-Error      Value "Y".
000029 01  Name-File-Status    Pic XX Value Spaces.
000030     88  Name-File-Success Value "00".
000031 01  Error-Message       Pic X(50) Value Spaces.
000032 Screen Section.
000033 01  Name-Entry Blank Screen.
000034     03  Line 01 Column 01 Value " Enter Name: ".
000035     03  Line 01 Column 14 Pic X(30) Using Full-Name.
000036     03  Line 05 Column 01 Pic X(50) From Error-Message.
000037     03  Line 20 Column 01 Value "Press F1 to Exit".
000038 Procedure Division.
000039 Chapt13a-Start.
000040     Perform Open-File
```

13

continues

LISTING 13.1   CONTINUED

```
000041     If Not File-Error
000042        Perform Process-Input Until F1-Pressed Or
000043                                    File-Error
000044        Perform Close-File
000045     End-If
000046     Stop Run
000047     .
000048 Open-File.
000049     Open Output Name-File
000050     If Not Name-File-Success
000051        Move Spaces To Error-Message
000052        String "Open Error " Name-File-Status
000053             Delimited By Size
000054             Into Error-Message
000055        Perform Display-And-Accept-Error
000056     End-if
000057     .
000058 Process-Input.
000059     Move Spaces To Full-Name
000060     Display Name-Entry
000061     Accept Name-Entry
000062     Move Spaces To Error-Message
000063     If Not F1-Pressed
000064        Perform Write-Record
000065     End-If
000066     .
000067 Write-Record.
000068     Write Name-Record
000069     If Name-File-Success
000070        Move "Record Written" To Error-Message
000071     Else
000072        String "Write Error " Name-File-Status
000073             Delimited By Size
000074             Into Error-Message
000075        Perform Display-And-Accept-Error
000076     End-if
000077     .
000078 Display-And-Accept-Error.
000079     Set File-Error To True
000080     Display Name-Entry
000081     Accept Name-Entry
000082     .
000083 Close-File.
000084     Close Name-File
000085     .
```

As you read through this program, notice the File Status checks after the Open and the Write. If an error of any kind occurs, the error flag is set and the status and type of error are displayed. Records are written to the file until someone presses the F1 key or a file error occurs.

After a Write, the contents of the file buffer cannot be counted on. The file buffer is the area described by the record description under the FD. Therefore, if you need to reference the contents of the data record after a Write, you need to store the record in Working-Storage. Simply create a Record Description that is a single elementary item, long enough to hold the data record. Then manipulate and use the record as defined in Working-Storage. When you Write the record, you can do one of two things. You can either move the Working-Storage version of the record to the record description and then issue the Write, or you can use the Write statement with the From clause. Using From causes the program to do an implied move. The data in Working-Storage is moved to the file buffer as the Write is processed.

Instead of the FD coded previously, you may use the following:

```
000018 FD   Name-File.
000019 01   Name-Record     Pic X(30).
```

Add the following line to Working-Storage.

```
000021 Working-Storage Section.
000022 01   Full-Name   Pic X(30) Value Spaces.
```

The only other change necessary is to the Write statement:

```
000068    Write Name-Record From Full-Name
```

Now you can reference Full-Name with the Display statement, after the Write is complete, without worrying about the integrity of the data in the file buffer.

Enter, compile, link, and run this program. After entering several names and exiting the program, use Notepad or some other text editor to open and examine Name.Txt in the \TYCOBOL folder. You can see that each record appears on a separate line.

What happens if you want to add data to the end of the file? Every time you run the program and the file is opened for Output, the previous data is lost. You can change the Open statement to Open the file Extend, instead of Output. When the file is opened Extend, new data records written to the file are added at the end of the file, after the existing records.

```
000049    Open Extend Name-File
```

When opening a file Extend, two new File Status values come into play. If the file does not exist, a File Status value of 35 is returned, which tells you that the file does

13

not exist. If you want to always add to the end of a file, this condition makes it difficult. When running the program, you may not know whether the file exists or not! Changing the `Select` clause to include `Optional` cures this problem. If you `Open` an `Optional` file `Extend` and the file does not exist, the file is created and a `File Status` value of `05` is returned.

Change the filename that `Name-File` is assigned to in the sample program to `"NAMES.TXT"`. Change the `Open` statement from `Output` to `Extend`. Then compile, link, and run the program. Notice the `File Status` of `35` that is returned when the program runs.

> If you run the program with the Fujitsu compiler, a `Non File` message appears before the program actually seems to run. These Fujitsu messages are nice for diagnosing problems but should be turned off when your program is fully debugged. To turn off this feature, you need to change a runtime option. When you run the program and the runtime options window appears, in the `Environment Variables Information` field type in `@NoMessage=YES`. Click Set and then click Save. Follow the prompts. Then click OK to run the program. The error message window is now disabled.

Add the word `Optional` to the `Select` statement:

```
000013    Select Optional Name-File Assign To "NAME.TXT"
```

Now compile and run the program. An `05` error is still reported. You need to change the `88` level conditional item for success to consider `00` and `05` as successful return codes.

```
000029 01  Name-File-Status      Pic XX Value Spaces.
000030     88  Name-File-Success Value "00" "05".
```

When you run the revised program, new records are added to the end of Names.Txt. Try exiting and running the program multiple times, examining the file created. (You can use Notepad or another text editor.) Note that new records are added to the end of the file.

Reading from the File

You may retrieve data from a sequential data file. Reading from a sequential data file requires that you `Open` the file for `Input`, or for `I-O`. Opening the file `I-O` is covered in following section, "Updating the File." The statement required to `Open` the file for `Input` is

```
000110    Open Input Name-File
```

When a file is Open for Input, you may only retrieve, or Read, data from the file. You may not update or write data to the file. A few new File Status values are reported when a file is opened for Input.

TABLE 13.5 SEQUENTIAL FILE STATUS VALUES FOR OPEN IN INPUT MODE

Status	Meaning
00	Successful completion.
05	Successful Open of an optional file that does not exist.
30	Physical error, no other information available.
35	Open failed on a non optional file. The file does not exist.
39	The file being opened is defined differently than the definition specified in this program.
41	The file being opened is already open.
9x	Compiler-vendor defined.

One of the new File Status values is 05. If a file with Optional coded on the Select statement is opened for Input and that file does not exist, the Open is successful and a return code of 05 is returned. The file is not created. This feature is useful when you have a program that expects input data, but where you may not always have any input data to provide. By making the file Optional, the Open never fails, and the file is not created when it is opened. Additionally, you do not have to create an empty file to satisfy the program's need for a file.

File Status 35 means that the file is not defined as Optional and does not exist.

File Status 39 means that the definition of the file being opened differs from that in the program. This condition usually does not affect Sequential files, but is possible.

File Status 41 means that you are attempting to Open a file that is already open.

You may retrieve data from an open file with the Read statement. Sequential files are read from the first record to the last. You may not skip forward in the file. Every record is read in order. Each Read returns the next record in the file.

When you code the Read statement, the filename is specified. You do not read using a record description. The simplest form of the Read statement is

```
000111     Read Name-File
```

This Read statement returns the next record in the file and places the contents in the record description defined for the file under the FD. Several File Status values can be returned from a Read statement with a Sequential file (see Table 13.6).

13

TABLE 13.6 SEQUENTIAL FILE STATUS VALUES FOR READ

Status	Meaning
00	Successful completion.
04	Successful; however, the record read is not the same length as the record defined in the FD.
10	The end of the file has been reached.
30	Physical error, no other information available.
46	The Read failed because the previous Read failed.
47	A Read was attempted on a file that is not Open for Input or I-O.
9x	Compiler-vendor defined.

File Status 04 is considered a successful Read. However, the record read has a different size than your program's definition.

File Status 10 means that you have reached the end of your input file and no record is returned. The previously read record was the last one in the file.

File Status 46 occurs when you attempt to Read a record and the previous Read has failed. This condition can occur if you happen to have reached end of file and then attempt to Read another record.

File Status 47 means that you have attempted to Read from a file that is either not Open or is Open Output or Extend, instead of Input or I-O.

The end-of-file condition can be detected in two ways. One method is to check the File Status after the Read. If it is 10, then you have reached the end of the file. Another way is to code the At End clause on the Read statement.

When At End is coded, the statements after the clause are executed when an end-of-file condition is detected. When using At End, I suggest you use the End-Read explicit terminator. In addition to coding At End, you may also code Not At End. This clause allows you to perform different statements depending on the status of end of file. If you are at the end of the file, you may want to do some special processing.

```
000120     Read Name-File
000121         At End Set All-Done To True
000122         Not At End Perform Process-Data
000123     End-read
```

You may also store the results of a Read statement in a data item in Working-Storage. This is similar to the Write statement with From where the record is written from another data item. For the Read statement, you specify Into and the name of the data item in which you wish to store the record read.

```
000124      Read Name-File Into Full-Name
```

Revise the program that wrote the Names.Txt file (see Listing 13.2). It should now Read
a new record every time the user presses Enter and quit when the end of file is reached or
the user presses F1.

LISTING 13.2   READ EXAMPLE

```
000001 @OPTIONS MAIN,TEST
000002 Identification Division.
000003 Program-Id.  Chapt13d.
000004* Read Example
000005 Environment Division.
000006 Configuration Section.
000007 Special-Names.
000008       Crt Status Is Keyboard-Status.
000009 Source-Computer.  IBM-PC.
000010 Object-Computer.  IBM-PC.
000011 Input-Output  Section.
000012 File-Control.
000013     Select Optional Name-File Assign To "NAMES.TXT"
000014          Organization Is Line Sequential
000015          File Status  Is Name-File-Status.
000016 Data Division.
000017 File Section.
000018 FD  Name-File.
000019 01  Name-Record         Pic X(30).
000020 Working-Storage Section.
000021 01  Full-Name           Pic X(30) Value Spaces.
000022 01  Keyboard-Status.
000023      03  Accept-Status   Pic 9.
000024      03  Function-key    Pic X.
000025          88 F1-Pressed   Value X"01".
000026      03  System-Use      Pic X.
000027 01  File-Error-Flag     Pic X Value Space.
000028      88  File-Error      Value "Y".
000029 01  Name-File-Status    Pic XX Value Spaces.
000030      88  Name-File-Success Value "00" "05".
000031      88  End-of-File     Value "10".
000032 01  Error-Message       Pic X(50) Value Spaces.
000033 Screen Section.
000034 01  Name-Entry Blank Screen.
000035      03  Line 01 Column 01 Value "       Name: ".
000036      03  Line 01 Column 14 Pic X(30) Using Full-Name.
000037      03  Line 05 Column 01 Pic X(50) From Error-Message.
000038      03  Line 20 Column 01 Value "Press F1 to Exit".
000039 Procedure Division.
000040 Chapt13d-Start.
```

continues

LISTING 13.2 CONTINUED

```
000041      Perform Open-File
000042      If Not File-Error
000043          Perform Process-File Until F1-Pressed Or
000044                                      File-Error Or
000045                                      End-Of-File
000046          Perform Close-File
000047      End-If
000048      Stop Run
000049      .
000050 Open-File.
000051      Open Input Name-File
000052      If Not Name-File-Success
000053          Move Spaces To Error-Message
000054          String "Open Error " Name-File-Status
000055                  Delimited By Size
000056                  Into Error-Message
000057          Perform Display-And-Accept-Error
000058      End-If
000059      .
000060 Process-File.
000061      Move Spaces To Full-Name
000062      Perform Read-File
000063      If Not File-Error
000064          Display Name-Entry
000065          Accept Name-Entry
000066      End-If
000067      Move Spaces To Error-Message
000068      .
000069 Read-File.
000070      Read Name-File Into Full-Name
000071          At End Move "End Of File" To Error-Message
000072      End-Read
000073      If Name-File-Success Or End-Of-File
000074          Continue
000075      Else
000076          Move Spaces To Error-Message
000077          String "Read Error " Name-File-Status
000078              Delimited by Size Into Error-Message
000079          End-String
000080          Perform Display-And-Accept-Error
000081      End-If
000082      .
000083 Display-And-Accept-Error.
000084      Set File-Error To True
000085      Display Name-Entry
000086      Accept Name-Entry
000087      .
000088 Close-File.
000089      Close Name-File
000090      .
```

Make note of the use of the File Status; also note the At End condition test on the Read statement. The Read Into is the Full-Name field, which is used by the Screen Section.

> When you run the program, you will note that the Full-Name field is cleared when the At End condition is encountered. This condition may or may not occur with other compilers. Some compilers leave the value of the last successfully read record in the input buffer, or record description. Most will not.

Updating the File

NEW TERM In addition to reading and writing, you may also update the file. Some very special restrictions apply to updating a Sequential file. Because Line Sequential File records can be of differing lengths and updated records are written to the original physical location, you may not update a Line Sequential file. Take a moment now to change the program that writes the file (Chapt13a.Cob, Listing.13.1) Change the filename from Names.Txt to Names.Seq. Change the Select statement from Line Sequential to Sequential. Create some records with this program so that you can update them with the next example (Listing 13.3).

To update the file, you must Open it for I-O. The File Status values returned by the Open are the same as those reported for opening the file for Input.

```
000125       Open I-O Name-File
```

After the file is Open, it is processed by Read statements as if it were Open for Input. However, you may now update a record by coding the Rewrite statement. Rewrite replaces the last record read with the new data that you have placed in the record description. Rewrite also supports the use of From to update the record from a data item in Working-Storage. The File Status values returned from a Rewrite on a Sequential file are the same as those that are returned as the result of a Write. The Rewrite statement also requires the record description and not the filename—exactly the same as the Write statement.

```
000125       Rewrite Name-Record From Full-Name
```

13

> You may not issue a Write statement against a Sequential file that is opened I-O. If you need to Write more records to a Sequential file, you must open it Extend.

The program in Listing 13.3 updates a Sequential file. If the user presses Enter, the program reads the next record. Pressing F1 ends the program; pressing F2 updates the last record with the name entered by the user. Enter, compile, link, and run this program. Experiment with its operation to see how the Rewrite statement updates records.

LISTING 13.3   UPDATE EXAMPLE

```
000001 @OPTIONS MAIN,TEST
000002 Identification Division.
000003 Program-Id.  Chapt13f.
000004* Update Example
000005 Environment Division.
000006 Configuration Section.
000007 Special-Names.
000008       Crt Status Is Keyboard-Status.
000009 Source-Computer.  IBM-PC.
000010 Object-Computer.  IBM-PC.
000011 Input-Output  Section.
000012 File-Control.
000013     Select Optional Name-File Assign To "NAMES.SEQ"
000014          Organization Is Sequential
000015          File Status  Is Name-File-Status.
000016 Data Division.
000017 File Section.
000018 Fd  Name-File.
000019 01  Name-Record        Pic X(30).
000020 Working-Storage Section.
000021 01  Full-Name          Pic X(30) Value Spaces.
000022 01  Keyboard-Status.
000023     03  Accept-Status   Pic 9.
000024     03  Function-Key    Pic X.
000025         88 F1-Pressed    Value X"01".
000026         88 F2-Pressed    Value X"02".
000027     03  System-Use      Pic X.
000028 01  File-Error-Flag     Pic X Value Space.
000029     88  File-Error      Value "Y".
000030 01  Name-File-Status    Pic XX Value Spaces.
000031     88  Name-File-Success Value "00" "05".
000032     88  End-Of-File      Value "10".
000033 01  Error-Message       Pic X(50) Value Spaces.
000034 Screen Section.
000035 01  Name-Entry Blank Screen.
000036     03  Line 01 Column 01 Value " Enter Name: ".
000037     03  Line 01 Column 14 Pic X(30) Using Full-Name.
000038     03  Line 05 Column 01 Pic X(50) From Error-Message.
000039     03  Line 20 Column 01
000040         Value "Press F1 to Exit    Press F2 to Update".
000041 Procedure Division.
000042 Chapt13f-Start.
```

```
000043     Perform Open-File
000044     If Not File-Error
000045         Perform Process-File Until F1-Pressed Or
000046                                   File-Error Or
000047                                   End-Of-File
000048         Perform Close-File
000049     End-If
000050     Stop Run
000051     .
000052 Open-File.
000053     Open I-O Name-File
000054     If Not Name-File-Success
000055         Move Spaces To Error-Message
000056         String "Open Error " Name-File-Status
000057             Delimited By Size
000058             Into Error-Message
000059         Perform Display-And-Accept-Error
000060     End-If
000061     .
000062 Process-File.
000063     Move Spaces To Full-Name
000064     Perform Read-File
000065     If Not File-Error
000066         Display Name-Entry
000067         Accept Name-Entry
000068         Move Spaces To Error-Message
000069         If F2-Pressed And Not End-Of-File
000070             Perform Rewrite-Record
000071         End-If
000072     End-If
000073     .
000074 Read-File.
000075     Read Name-File Into Full-Name
000076         At End Move "End Of File" To Error-Message
000077     End-Read
000078     If Name-File-Success Or End-Of-File
000079         Continue
000080     Else
000081         Move Spaces To Error-Message
000082         String "Read Error " Name-File-Status
000083             Delimited By Size Into Error-Message
000084         End-String
000085         Perform Display-And-Accept-Error
000086     End-If
000087     .
000088 Rewrite-Record.
000089     Rewrite Name-Record From Full-Name
000090     If Name-File-Success
000091         Move "Prior Record Updated" To Error-Message
```

continues

LISTING 13.3   CONTINUED

```
000092       Else
000093          Move Spaces To Error-Message
000094          String "Rewrite Error " Name-File-Status
000095             Delimited By Size Into Error-Message
000096          End-String
000097       End-If
000098       .
000099 Display-And-Accept-Error.
000100       Set File-Error To True
000101       Display Name-Entry
000102       Accept Name-Entry
000103       .
000104 Close-File.
000105       Close Name-File
000106       .
```

Take special note of the check for end of file before the attempt at Rewrite. This test prevents you from trying to Rewrite a record after the end of file has been reached. Read carefully through the program. If something is not clear, enter, compile, and run the program in Debug mode and watch what is happening.

Variable-Length Records

Sequential data files can contain variable-length records. These data records contain a table that is defined with an Occurs and Depending On. The numeric field that determines the number of occurrences may or may not appear in the data record. If it does appear in the record, it must appear before the table that it helps to define. If it does not, then the Read of the record will not be successful. If the field that determines the number of occurrences is not part of the data record, it must be initialized to the proper number of occurrences before the Read statement is executed. The following example shows a variable-length record, using a table with Occurs and Depending On. You may be limited in the absolute size of a data record. If your maximum number of occurrences exceeds the maximum record size for your system, even if your Depending On number creates a table that keeps your record under the maximum allowable size, your program will not compile.

```
000020 FD  Name-File.
000021 01  Name-Record.
000022     03  Name-Ctr      Pic 9(2).
000023     03  Name-Table Occurs 1 to 20 Times Depending On Name-Ctr.
000024         05  Name-Item Pic X(20).
```

Summary

In this hour, you learned the following:

- COBOL has very powerful and simple methods of handling Sequential file Input and Output.
- Files are identified to the COBOL program by using the Select statement and a file description entry, called an FD.
- Before files can be accessed, they must be opened with the Open statement.
- A special field can be defined to capture the status code of any file operation. This field is called the File Status field.
- Records can be created in a file with the use of the Write statement. The file must be opened Output or Extend to use Write.
- When writing to a file, the record description entry is specified, not the filename.
- You can add records to the end of a Sequential file by opening the file Extend and using the Write statement.
- To retrieve data written to a Sequential file, you must Open the file either Input or I-O, and use the Read statement.
- To update records in a Sequential file, Open the file for I-O and use the Rewrite statement. You cannot update records in a Line Sequential file, because the records are variable length.

Q&A

Q What is the difference between a Line Sequential file and a Sequential file?

A A Line Sequential file is one kind of Sequential file and is similar to a regular text file. Each record in a Line Sequential file is a line in a file and is delimited by a carriage return and line feed (or just a line feed in the UNIX world). The lines may be of various lengths. Each Read against a Line Sequential file returns a single line as a record. With a regular Sequential file, otherwise known as a Record Sequential file, records are read based on their length. If your records are 80 characters long, every Read returns exactly 80 characters. There are no "lines" and no delimiters separating the records.

Q When I use Optional in my Select statement and I Open the file Input, is it automatically created?

A No. To the program, it looks as if the file is there, but it contains no records. The first Read issued against the file results in an end-of-file condition. The file is not created.

13

Q If I want to always add records to the end of a file, can I `Open Extend` even if the file does not exist?

A Yes, but you must specify that the file is `Optional` on the `Select` statement. This syntax causes any missing file to be created.

Q I tried to create a `Line Sequential` file and then open it `I-O`. The compiler tells me that I can't do that with a `Line Sequential` file. Why not?

A The records in a `Line Sequential` file can be virtually any length. Updating records may involve shortening or lengthening them, which would mean shifting the entire remainder of the file forward and backward to adjust for the size difference. Imagine the overhead and time it would take to accomplish that on large files.

Workshop

To help reinforce your understanding of the material presented in this hour, refer to the section "Quiz and Exercise Questions and Answers" that can be found on the CD. This section contains quiz questions and exercises for you to complete, as well as the corresponding answers.

Hour 14

Indexed Files

An `Indexed` file is a file that allows access to data records by way of a `Key` field. The file is said to be "Indexed" by this `Key`. `Indexed` files are sometimes referred to as *keyed files*. In this hour, you learn the basics of `Indexed` file handling, such as

- Defining an `Indexed` file
- Handling `Primary` and `Alternate` `Keys`
- `Writing` records with an `Indexed` file
- Using `File` `Status` values
- Using `Declaratives`

A record in an `Indexed` file contains at least one `Key` field. This field is the index to the file. There must be at least one `Key` field that contains a value that is unique. This `Key` field is the `Primary` `Key`. Each record in the file is uniquely identified by this `Key`, which functions like a serial number. With this `Key` you can find and access the remainder of the record. The `Key` field may be anything from a name to a part number.

An Indexed file is similar to the index of a book. You can go to the index of the book, find a subject, and then go directly to the page on which that subject is discussed. An Indexed file allows you to go directly to a record based upon its Key.

COBOL is one of the few programming languages that incorporates Indexed file methods. Indexed files are very useful. Accessing Indexed files in COBOL is extremely simple and straightforward.

Different COBOL compilers provide different physical Indexed file structures, with varying efficiency. However, the definition and statements used to access an Indexed file are always the same.

Indexed files have many uses. You can use an Indexed file to validate user input. For example, you might store the account numbers of the different dealers in your store in an Indexed file. When an item is sold, you can ask the user for a dealer number. If the number is not in the file, you can issue an error message. This approach is much better than coding each dealer number in the program, where it has to be changed every time you gain or lose a dealer. Validating against a Sequential file is inefficient. With a Sequential dealer file, you might have to Read all the records in the file to validate the dealer number. With an Indexed file, you can determine whether the record is in the file with a single Read.

In addition to keeping the dealer number in the file, you can keep all of the information associated with a dealer in the data record. Doing so allows you to store only the dealer number in the sale transaction data and does not require you to enter or store all the dealer information in each sale record.

Indexed files are ideal for storing any information that you can identify by some Key field. The example in Hour 12 used a table of states. Using a table for this information is very efficient. However, if the number of states or their names chaage frequently, an Indexed file is a better idea. Always analyze your needs to determine which method gives the best performance and is easiest to maintain.

Indexed files need not be limited to a single Key field. For example, you might not know a dealer's number. If you want to find the dealer number in the file, you might have to Read the entire file, looking for that dealer's name. Indexed files may have Alternate Key fields. Unlike the Primary Key field, Alternate Key fields may or may not be unique. When you define the Key structure of the file in your COBOL program, you must specify whether any Alternate Key fields may contain duplicates.

Defining the Indexed File

Care should be taken in how you design your Indexed file and its Key structure. Changing the Key structure of an established Indexed file can be quite an undertaking. Your main (Primary) Key field must be unique. You should choose something that you know is not likely to change frequently and that identifies the data record. The Key field is either a single elementary item in your record description or a single group field. Most programmers put this Key field at the front of the file, which can facilitate debugging. In addition, some earlier compilers required this placement in support of the computer's native Indexed file structure. As an example, in this hour you create a dealer master file. The Key is the dealer number, and an Alternate Key is the dealer name. Both Keys are unique. Therefore, you can't have two dealers with the same name, nor can two dealers share the same dealer number.

You need to decide which information to track for each dealer. The fields used in the example in Hour 4, "Basic User Interface," are good items to track. These are

- Dealer number
- Name: last, first, and middle
- Address lines 1 and 2
- City, state, and postal code
- Home telephone
- Work telephone
- Other phone
- Start date (when someone became a dealer in your store)
- Last rent paid date
- Next rent due date
- Rent amount
- Consignment percent

The Select Statement for Indexed Files

The Select statement is where you define the Key data for the Indexed file. Several items coded on the Select relate to Indexed files.

- Organization Indexed—Specifies that this file is an Indexed file.
- Access Dynamic, Random, or Sequential—Specifies how the records in the file are to be retrieved and/or updated.
- Record Key—Specifies the field that is to be the Primary Key for the file. Only one Primary Key is allowed.

14

- Alternate Record Key—Specifies a field that is to act as an Alternate Key field for the file. A single file may have multiple Alternate Key statements.
- With Duplicates—If coded, the associated Alternate Record Key may contain duplicates; it does not have to uniquely identify the record as does the Primary Key field.

For an Indexed file, Organization Indexed must be included in the Select statement. One of the three access methods must be chosen. Sequential access causes the Indexed file to behave as a Sequential file. However, instead of reading records in their physical sequence in the file, they are returned in Primary Key sequence. Random access means that every record is retrieved by specifying a Key field. The records may be retrieved in any order. Dynamic access allows you to have the best of both Sequential and Random access. Data records may be accessed randomly via a Key, or you may position the data file at a particular record and then access the file sequentially. You may choose a starting position based on the Primary Key or Alternate Record Key, depending on which you have specified when positioning the file.

In this example, the dealer Indexed file uses Sequential access. The Select statement is coded as follows:

```
000058     Select Dealer-File Assign to "Dealer.Dat"
000059            Organization Indexed
000060            Access Sequential
000061            Record Key Dealer-Number of Dealer-Record
000062            Alternate Record Key Dealer-Name of Dealer-Record
000063            File Status Dealer-Status.
```

Be careful assigning the physical filename for the file. Some compilers store Indexed files in two components. The index portion might be stored separately from the data portion of the file. Compilers that use this method use a special file extension for the index portion of the file, for example .IDX. Therefore, you should be careful to check your documentation so that you do not assign a name with this extension to your file. The Fujitsu compiler stores the index and data in a single file.

Take note of the qualification of the Key fields. This example uses an Input file that has the same field names, making this qualification necessary.

The FD for your file follows.

```
000066 File Section.
000067 FD   Dealer-File.
000068 01   Dealer-Record.
000069      03   Dealer-Number        Pic X(8).
000070      03   Dealer-Name.
000071           05   Last-Name        Pic X(25).
000072           05   First-Name       Pic X(15).
000073           05   Middle-Name      Pic X(10).
000074      03   Address-Line-1       Pic X(50).
000075      03   Address-Line-2       Pic X(50).
000076      03   City                 Pic X(40).
000077      03   State-or-Country     Pic X(20).
000078      03   Postal-Code          Pic X(15).
000079      03   Home-Phone           Pic X(20).
000080      03   Work-Phone           Pic X(20).
000081      03   Other-Phone          Pic X(20).
000082      03   Start-Date           Pic 9(8).
000083      03   Last-Rent-Paid-Date  Pic 9(8).
000084      03   Next-Rent-Due-Date   Pic 9(8).
000085      03   Rent-Amount          Pic 9(4)V99.
000086      03   Consignment-Percent  Pic 9(3).
000087      03   Filler               Pic X(50).
```

Notice that the last item in the record description is a 50-character Filler area. This area
is provided for future growth in the file. Some time in the future, you might need to add
or expand other fields in the file. Leaving a Filler area for expansion makes it easier to
modify the layout of the file.

Creating an Indexed File from a Sequential File

To explore the different methods for working with Indexed files, you need to create one.
The CD-ROM contains a data file named DEALER.TXT. It is located in the \Datafile
directory. This file has several records that you can use to create a dealer file.

Listing 14.1 has two files assigned: the Input text file and the Output Indexed file. The
start of the program, Select, and FD statements are coded as follows:

LISTING 14.1   DEALER FILE CREATION

```
000001 @OPTIONS MAIN,TEST
000002 Identification Division.
000003 Program-Id.   Chapt14a.
000004* Dealer File Creation
```

14

continues

LISTING **14.1**   CONTINUED

```
000005 Environment Division.
000006 Configuration Section.
000007 Source-Computer.  IBM-PC.
000008 Object-Computer.  IBM-PC.
000009 Input-Output Section.
000010 File-Control.
000011     Select Dealer-File Assign To "Dealer.Dat"
000012             Organization Indexed
000013             Access Sequential
000014             Record Key Dealer-Number Of Dealer-Record
000015             Alternate Record Key Dealer-Name Of Dealer-Record
000016             File Status Dealer-Status.
000017     Select Dealer-Text Assign To "Dealer.TXT"
000018             Organization Is Line Sequential
000019             File Status Dealer-Text-Status.
000020
000021 Data Division.
000022 File Section.
000023 Fd   Dealer-File.
000024 01   Dealer-Record.
000025      03  Dealer-Number      Pic X(8).
000026      03  Dealer-Name.
000027          05  Last-Name      Pic X(25).
000028          05  First-Name     Pic X(15).
000029          05  Middle-Name    Pic X(10).
000030      03  Address-Line-1     Pic X(50).
000031      03  Address-Line-2     Pic X(50).
000032      03  City               Pic X(40).
000033      03  State-Or-Country   Pic X(20).
000034      03  Postal-Code        Pic X(15).
000035      03  Home-Phone         Pic X(20).
000036      03  Work-Phone         Pic X(20).
000037      03  Other-Phone        Pic X(20).
000038      03  Start-Date         Pic 9(8).
000039      03  Last-Rent-Paid-Date Pic 9(8).
000040      03  Next-Rent-Due-Date Pic 9(8).
000041      03  Rent-Amount        Pic 9(4)v99.
000042      03  Consignment-Percent Pic 9(3).
000043      03  Filler             Pic X(50).
000044 Fd   Dealer-Text.
000045 01   Text-Record.
000046      03  Dealer-Number      Pic X(8).
000047      03  Dealer-Name.
000048          05  Last-Name      Pic X(25).
000049          05  First-Name     Pic X(15).
000050          05  Middle-Name    Pic X(10).
000051      03  Address-Line-1     Pic X(50).
000052      03  Address-Line-2     Pic X(50).
000053      03  City               Pic X(40).
000054      03  State-Or-Country   Pic X(20).
000055      03  Postal-Code        Pic X(15).
```

```
000056          03  Home-Phone          Pic X(20).
000057          03  Work-Phone          Pic X(20).
000058          03  Other-Phone         Pic X(20).
000059          03  Start-Date          Pic 9(8).
000060          03  Last-Rent-Paid-Date Pic 9(8).
000061          03  Next-Rent-Due-Date  Pic 9(8).
000062          03  Rent-Amount         Pic 9(4)v99.
000063          03  Consignment-Percent Pic 9(3).
000064          03  Filler              Pic X(50).
000065
000066 Working-Storage Section.
000067 01  Dealer-Status       Pic XX Value Spaces.
000068 01  Dealer-Text-Status Pic XX Value Spaces.
000069 01  Record-Counter      Pic 9(5) Value Zeros.
```

To create the file you need to Open the Indexed file, you Open it Output for creation.

> Creating an Indexed file by opening it output and accessing it sequentially is
> normally the most efficient file creation method. In this case, the records
> being added must already be in Primary Key sequence. Doing so reduces
> the computer's overhead as it creates the index entries for the file. You have
> to remember, however, that the data records for the file must be written in
> Primary Key sequence. If a record is written out of sequence, an error 21 is
> reported. The sample data file provided contains records that are in Primary
> Key sequence.

```
000070 Procedure Division.
000071 Chapt14a-Start.
000072     Open Input Dealer-Text
000073     Open Output Dealer-File
```

The next step is to Read the Sequential file, creating Indexed file records as you go.

```
000074     Perform Until Dealer-Status Not = "00" Or
000075                  Dealer-Text-Status Not = "00"
000076        Read Dealer-Text
000077        If Dealer-Text-Status = "00"
000078           Write Dealer-Record From Text-Record
000079           If Dealer-Status Not = "00"
000080              Display
000081              "Write Error Dealer-Record " Dealer-Status
000082           Else
000083              Add 1 To Record-Counter
000084           End-If
000085        End-If
000086     End-Perform
```

14

```
000087      Close Dealer-Text Dealer-File
000088      Display
000089      "File Processed with " Record-Counter " Records Written"
000090      Stop Run
000091      .
```

Note the check of the File Status on the Write. Table 14.1 describes the File Status values that might be returned from a Write to an Indexed file opened for Output in Sequential access mode.

In addition to the File Status check, the code adds 1 to the record counter for every successful Write. At the end of the program, this value is displayed.

> It is always a good idea, especially when there is no special user interaction, to show the user that the program completed successfully. It is also useful to provide some accounting information such as the number of records processed. If a problem develops, a low or high record count could help diagnose the situation.

TABLE 14.1 Indexed File Status VALUES FOR Writes ON Open FOR Output WITH Sequential ACCESS

Status	Meaning
00	Successful completion.
30	Physical error, no other information available.
21	Primary Record Key value not in ascending Key sequence. This condition can occur when a duplicate record is encountered, or when the Primary Key is out of order.
34	Fatal error caused by the inability of the program to Write the record. Usually occurs because of an inaccurate Key field. Can also be caused by a hardware problem, such as running out of disk space, or secondary file allocations of space on some systems.
48	Attempt to Write to a file that is not opened for Output, Extend, or I-O.
9x	Compiler-vendor defined.

Running this program creates an Indexed file from the Sequential Input file. Notice the Perform loop and how the program terminates when there are no more Input records (as indicated by a non-zero status value on the Input text file) or an error occurs writing to the Output file. Any errors writing to the Output file are reported.

When the program is complete, the output should look like that shown in Figure 14.1.

FIGURE **14.1**

Results of running Chapt14a.

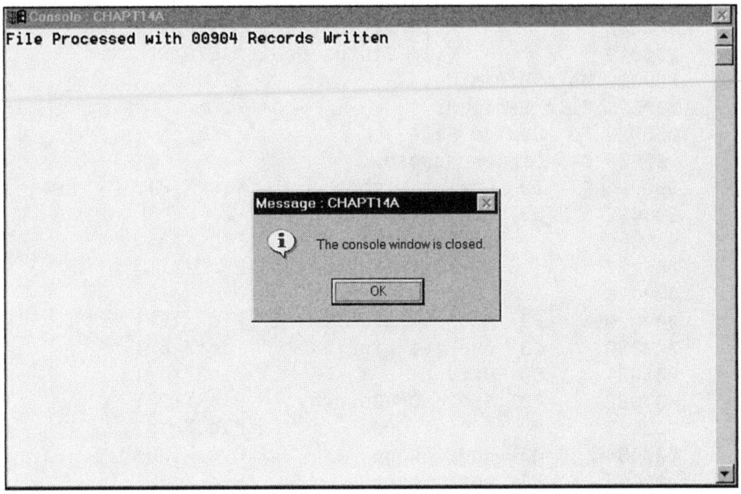

Creating Indexed File Records from User Input

Another common way to create an Indexed file is to have the user key the information for the data records into a program. Again, you want to create a new file, so you must Open the file Output. The program to accept user input and to Write to the Indexed file from that input might be coded as shown in Listing 14.2.

LISTING **14.2**   DEALER DATA ENTRY

```
000001 @OPTIONS MAIN,TEST
000002 Identification Division.
000003 Program-Id.  Chapt14b.
000004* Dealer Data Entry
000005 Environment Division.
000006 Configuration Section.
000007 Special-Names.
000008      Crt Status Is Keyboard-Status
000009      Cursor Is Cursor-Position.
000010 Source-Computer.  IBM-PC.
000011 Object-Computer.  IBM-PC.
000012 Input-Output Section.
000013 File-Control.
000014     Select Dealer-File Assign To "Dealer.Dat"
000015            Organization Indexed
000016            Access Sequential
```

14

continues

LISTING **14.2**   CONTINUED

```
000017              Record Key Dealer-Number Of Dealer-Record
000018              Alternate Record Key Dealer-Name Of Dealer-Record
000019              File Status Dealer-Status.
000020 Data Division.
000021 File Section.
000022 Fd  Dealer-File.
000023 01  Dealer-Record.
000024      03  Dealer-Number       Pic X(8).
000025      03  Dealer-Name.
000026          05  Last-Name       Pic X(25).
000027          05  First-Name      Pic X(15).
000028          05  Middle-Name     Pic X(10).
000029      03  Address-Line-1      Pic X(50).
000030      03  Address-Line-2      Pic X(50).
000031      03  City                Pic X(40).
000032      03  State-Or-Country    Pic X(20).
000033      03  Postal-Code         Pic X(15).
000034      03  Home-Phone          Pic X(20).
000035      03  Work-Phone          Pic X(20).
000036      03  Other-Phone         Pic X(20).
000037      03  Start-Date          Pic 9(8).
000038      03  Last-Rent-Paid-Date Pic 9(8).
000039      03  Next-Rent-Due-Date  Pic 9(8).
000040      03  Rent-Amount         Pic 9(4)v99.
000041      03  Consignment-Percent Pic 9(3).
000042      03  Filler              Pic X(50).
000043 Working-Storage Section.
000044 01  Keyboard-Status.
000045      03  Accept-Status Pic 9.
000046      03  Function-Key  Pic X.
000047          88  F1-Pressed Value X"01".
000048          88  F2-Pressed Value X"02".
000049      03  System-Use    Pic X.
000050 01  Cursor-Position.
000051      03  Cursor-Row    Pic 9(2) Value 1.
000052      03  Cursor-Column Pic 9(2) Value 1.
000053 01  Dealer-Status     Pic X(2) Value Spaces.
000054      88  Dealer-Success Value "00".
000055 01  Error-Message     Pic X(60) Value Spaces.
000056 01  Open-Error.
000057      03  Filler        Pic X(26)
000058          Value "Error Opening Dealer File ".
000059      03  Open-Error-Status  Pic X(2).
000060 01  Write-Error.
000061      03  Filler        Pic X(26)
000062          Value "Error Writing Dealer File ".
000063      03  Write-Error-Status Pic X(2).
000064 01  Work-Record.
```

```
000065      03   Dealer-Number          Pic X(8).
000066      03   Dealer-Name.
000067           05   Last-Name    Pic X(25).
000068           05   First-Name   Pic X(15).
000069           05   Middle-Name  Pic X(10).
000070      03   Address-Line-1         Pic X(50).
000071      03   Address-Line-2         Pic X(50).
000072      03   City                   Pic X(40).
000073      03   State-Or-Country       Pic X(20).
000074      03   Postal-Code            Pic X(15).
000075      03   Home-Phone             Pic X(20).
000076      03   Work-Phone             Pic X(20).
000077      03   Other-Phone            Pic X(20).
000078      03   Start-Date             Pic 9(8).
000079      03   Last-Rent-Paid-Date Pic 9(8).
000080      03   Next-Rent-Due-Date  Pic 9(8).
000081      03   Rent-Amount            Pic 9(4)v99.
000082      03   Consignment-Percent Pic 9(3).
000083
000084 Screen Section.
000085 01   Data-Entry-Screen
000086      Blank Screen, Auto
000087      Foreground-Color Is 7,
000088      Background-Color Is 1.
000089*
000090      03   Screen-Literal-Group.
000091           05   Line 01 Column 30 Value "Darlene's Treasures"
000092                Highlight Foreground-Color 4 Background-Color 1.
000093           05   Line 03 Column 30 Value "Tenant Entry Program"
000094                Highlight.
000095           05   Line 4  Column 01   Value "Number: ".
000096           05   Line 5  Column 01   Value "Name, Last: ".
000097           05   Line 5  Column 39   Value "First: ".
000098           05   Line 5  Column 62   Value "Middle: ".
000099           05   Line 6  Column 01   Value "Address 1: ".
000100           05   Line 7  Column 01   Value "Address 2: ".
000101           05   Line 8  Column 01   Value "City: ".
000102           05   Line 9  Column 01   Value "Country/State: ".
000103           05   Line 9  Column 36   Value "Postal Code: ".
000104           05   Line 11 Column 01   Value "Phone/Home: ".
000105           05   Line 11 Column 34   Value "Work: ".
000106           05   Line 12 Column 06   Value "Other: ".
000107           05   Line 14 Column 01   Value "Start Date: ".
000108           05   Line 14 Column 24   Value "Last Paid Date: ".
000109           05   Line 14 Column 51   Value "Next Rent Due on: ".
000110           05   Line 15 Column 01   Value "Rent Amount: ".
000111           05   Line 16 Column 01   Value "Consignment Percent: ".
000112           05   Line 22 Column 01   Value "F1-Exit    F2-Save".
000113*
```

14

continues

LISTING 14.2 CONTINUED

```
000114    03  Required-Reverse-Group Reverse-Video Required.
000115        05  Line 4 Column 13  Pic X(8)  Using Dealer-Number
000116            Of Work-Record.
000117        05  Line 5 Column 13  Pic X(25) Using Last-Name
000118            Of Work-Record.
000119        05  Line 5 Column 46  Pic X(15) Using First-Name
000120            Of Work-Record.
000121*
000122    03  Reverse-Video-Group Reverse-Video.
000123        05  Line 5  Column 70 Pic X(10) Using Middle-Name
000124            Of Work-Record.
000125        05  Line 6  Column 15 Pic X(50) Using Address-Line-1
000126            Of Work-Record.
000127        05  Line 7  Column 15 Pic X(50) Using Address-Line-2
000128            Of Work-Record.
000129        05  Line 8  Column 15 Pic X(40) Using City
000130            Of Work-Record.
000131        05  Line 9  Column 15 Pic X(20) Using State-Or-Country
000132            Of Work-Record.
000133        05  Line 9  Column 50 Pic X(15) Using Postal-Code
000134            Of Work-Record.
000135        05  Line 11 Column 13 Pic X(20) Using Home-Phone
000136            Of Work-Record.
000137        05  Line 11 Column 41 Pic X(20) Using Work-Phone
000138            Of Work-Record.
000139        05  Line 12 Column 13 Pic X(20) Using Other-Phone
000140            Of Work-Record.
000141        05  Line 14 Column 13 Pic 99/99/9999 Using Start-Date
000142            Of Work-Record.
000143        05  Line 14 Column 40 Pic 99/99/9999
000144            Using Last-Rent-Paid-Date Of Work-Record.
000145        05  Line 14 Column 69 Pic 99/99/9999
000146            Using Next-Rent-Due-Date Of Work-Record.
000147        05  Line 15 Column 14 Pic Z,ZZZ.99 Using Rent-Amount
000148            Of Work-Record.
000149        05  Line 16 Column 22 Pic ZZ9 Using Consignment-Percent
000150            Of Work-Record.
000151    03  Blink-Group Highlight Blink.
000152        05  Line 20 Column 01 Pic X(60) From Error-Message.
000153*
000154
000155 Procedure Division.
000156 Chapt14b-Start.
000157     Perform Open-File
000158     If Dealer-Success
000159         Initialize Work-Record
000160         Perform Process-Screen Until F1-Pressed Or
000161                                 Not Dealer-Success
000162         Perform Close-File
```

```
000163      End-If
000164      Stop Run
000165         .
000166  Process-Screen.
000167      Display Data-Entry-Screen
000168      Accept Data-Entry-Screen
000169      If F2-Pressed
000170          Perform Save-Record
000171      End-If
000172         .
000173  Save-Record.
000174      Move Corresponding Work-Record To Dealer-Record
000175      Write Dealer-Record
000176      If Not Dealer-Success
000177          Move Dealer-Status To Write-Error-Status
000178          Move Write-Error To Error-Message
000179          Perform Display-And-Accept-Error
000180      Else
000181          Initialize Work-Record
000182          Move 1 To Cursor-Row
000183                     Cursor-Column
000184      End-If
000185         .
000186  Open-File.
000187      Open Output Dealer-File
000188      If Not Dealer-Success
000189          Move Dealer-Status To Open-Error-Status
000190          Move Open-Error To Error-Message
000191          Perform Display-And-Accept-Error
000192      End-If
000193         .
000194  Close-File.
000195      Close Dealer-File
000196         .
000197  Display-And-Accept-Error.
000198      Display Data-Entry-Screen
000199      Accept Data-Entry-Screen
000200         .
```

When you examine this program, notice that it uses the same data names in the record in Working-Storage and in the data record. Using the same data names allows you to use Move Corresponding later in the program to fill in the record's data fields from the screen input. Because the same data names were used, they must be qualified in the Using clause by specifying the group of which the data item is a member.

In the program, the data file is Open Output, effectively creating a new file every time the program runs. Sequential access was chosen for performance reasons. However, try running the program and note what happens when you enter a record out of sequence. If you do, a File Status value of 21 is returned. The record was not written in proper Key sequence.

14

Indexed files may be opened Extend instead of Output and still use Sequential access. If this option is coded, records added to the file must still be in Primary Key sequence, and their Primary Key values must be greater than the last record in the file.

One way to avoid this problem is to Open the file with Random access instead of Sequential access. When Random access is used, records are added based on their Key value. They do not have to be added in sequence. COBOL and the Indexed file system work together to ensure that the records are properly added to the file. File Status 21 errors should no longer occur.

A new File Status value—22—is possible when an Indexed file is Open for Output with Random access. This File Status is returned when a record with a duplicate Key is added to the file. The Key causing the error can be either the Primary Key or the Alternate Key. This error is caused by duplicate Alternate Key values only when duplicates are not allowed on Alternate Keys. If duplicates are allowed on Alternate Keys and a duplicate record is written, the returned File Status is 02. When you code your programs, you need to allow for this status as a valid and successful status.

Change the program to use Random access, instead of Sequential, and recompile the program. The only thing you need to change is the Select statement.

```
000014      Select Dealer-File Assign to "Dealer.Dat"
000015          Organization Indexed
000016          Access Random
000017          Record Key Dealer-Number Of Dealer-Record
000018          Alternate Record Key Dealer-Name of Dealer-Record
000019          File Status Dealer-Status.
```

Now when you run the program, the order in which the records are added does not matter. Random access allows you to Write records in any position in the file.

Other Methods of Handling File Errors

Thus far, you have relied on the File Status values to indicate the success or failure of the Indexed file operations. In addition, two other methods for capturing error conditions are available when using Indexed files.

On the Write statement, you may code an Invalid Key clause. Any statements coded after this clause are executed when an Invalid Key condition occurs. These File Status values begin with a 2. When an Invalid Key condition is encountered, the associated operation is not successful. In this example, you can replace the code in lines 175 through 184 of Listing 14.2 with the following:

```
000175        Write Dealer-Record
000176          Invalid Key
000177            Move Dealer-Status To Write-Error-Status
000178            Move Write-Error To Error-Message
000179            Perform Display-And-Accept-Error
000180          Not Invalid Key
000181            Initialize Work-Record
000182            Move 1 To Cursor-Row
000183                      Cursor-Column
000184        End-Write
```

Notice the use of Invalid Key and Not Invalid Key. When you use Invalid Key, I suggest that you code the End-Write explicit scope terminator. You should remember that the Invalid Key condition is triggered only when a File Status value begins with a 2. I still suggest full and complete File Status value checking as the best way to capture all possible errors, including those for which the File Status value does not begin with a 2.

New Term   Another way to handle file errors is to use Declaratives. The use of Declaratives is specified in your program immediately after the Procedure Division by coding the word Declaratives. After the word Declaratives, a Section is coded for each file that is to have declarative logic executed when an error condition occurs. These must be Sections, not Paragraphs. Immediately after the Section header is a Use statement. It tells the program to execute the Declaratives in this section when a file error is detected for the specified file. A file error is defined as any returned File Status value in which the first character is not a zero.

You may separate the Sections within the Declaratives into Paragraphs. You need to remember a few simple rules. You may not Perform any code outside the Declaratives and End-Declaratives labels. However, you may Perform code from different Sections within the Declaratives. For example, you might have a common error-display paragraph that is coded in the Declaratives Section for one file and then performed in the Declaratives Sections for the other files. The Declaratives are not executed for Invalid Key conditions (that is, File Status values starting with 2) if the Invalid Key clause is coded for the file operation. Additionally, File Status 10 (end of file) does not trigger the Declaratives if the At End clause is coded on the Read statement.

The following code shows the Procedure Division from the previous example coded to use Declaratives.

```
000155 Procedure Division.
000156 Declaratives.
000157 Input-File-Error Section.
000158     Use After Standard Error Procedure On Dealer-File.
000159 Dealer-File-Error.
```

14

```
000160      String "Error On Dealer-File " Dealer-Status
000161        Delimited By Size Into Error-Message
000162      End-String
000163      Display Data-Entry-Screen
000164      Accept Data-Entry-Screen
000165        .
000166 End Declaratives.
000167 Chapt14d-Start Section.
000168      Perform Open-File
000169      If Dealer-Success
000170        Initialize Work-Record
000171        Perform Process-Screen Until F1-Pressed Or
000172                                Not Dealer-Success
000173        Perform Close-File
000174      End-If
000175      Stop Run
000176        .
000177  Process-Screen.
000178      Perform Display-And-Accept
000179      If F2-Pressed
000180        Perform Save-Record
000181      End-if
000182        .
000183 Save-Record.
000184      Move Corresponding Work-Record to Dealer-Record
000185      Write Dealer-Record
000186       Invalid Key
000187        Move Dealer-Status to Write-Error-Status
000188        Move Write-Error to Error-Message
000189        Perform Display-And-Accept
000190       Not Invalid Key
000191        Initialize Work-Record
000192        Move 1 to Cursor-Row
000193                 Cursor-Column
000194      End-Write
000195        .
000196 Display-And-Accept.
000197      Display Data-Entry-Screen
000198      Accept Data-Entry-Screen
000199        .
000200 Open-File.
000201      Open Output Dealer-File
000202        .
000203 Close-File.
000204      Close Dealer-File
000205        .
```

In the program, the screen Accept and Display were changed to use a common routine:
Display-And-Accept. However, it is not Performed from the Declaratives Section of
the program. You cannot Perform anything outside the Declaratives from within the
Declaratives.

Notice the use of the `Invalid Key` clause with the `Write` statement. Because `Invalid Key` is coded the `Declaratives` will be executed on any file error encountered other than an `Invalid Key` condition. Coding for the `Invalid Key` in addition to using `Declaratives` allows you to capture any and all file errors that might occur.

Summary

In this hour, you learned the following:

- `Indexed` files are those files whose records are keyed by specified `Key` fields.

- The `Primary Key` field of an `Indexed` file must be unique.

- One or more `Alternate Key` fields may be specified. They are not required. When specified, they may be defined as allowing duplicate records.

- When an `Indexed` file is opened for `Output` and the access mode specified is `Sequential`, any records written to the file must be written in `Primary key` sequence order.

- When an `Indexed` file is opened for `Output` and the access mode specified is `Random`, the records may be written in any order.

- `File Status` values may be checked to determine the result of `Indexed` file operations, such as `Open`, `Close`, and `Write`.

- In addition to `File Status` values, the `Invalid Key` clause can be coded to test for the `Invalid Key` condition.

- `Declaratives` allow you to code a common error-handling routine for any invalid `File Status` values returned for operations against the specified files.

Q&A

Q When using an `Indexed` file opened for `Output` with `Sequential` access, if I have to be so careful about adding records in the proper sequence, why would I ever want to use `Sequential` access?

A When processing large amounts of data, you will find that adding records in random order is much slower than adding them in `Sequential` order. For each `Add` in random order, the program must check whether the record already exists, add the record in the proper portion of the data file, and then adjust the index records accordingly. With `Sequential` access, the program need only verify that the `Key` value currently being written is greater than the last `Key` value written. All the records are in sequence and can be added efficiently. `Key` maintenance is simplified for the program as well.

14

Q **When I run the example program, I get a `File Status 22`. What does that mean?**

A Either the `Primary Key` value of the record you are adding is duplicated, or the `Alternate Key` is not specified to allow duplicates, and you have duplicated that `Key` value.

Q **I understand the various `File Status` values, but what does `Invalid Key` mean?**

A The `Invalid Key` clause is an easy way to catch a range of errors in `Indexed` file operations. These errors relate to problems associated with the `Key` values. `File Status` values that are associated with the `Invalid Key` condition begin with a `2`.

Q **I can see some good uses for `Declaratives`. But if they are a catch-all, how can I tell exactly what was happening when the error occurred?**

A You are right. Using `Declaratives` can save a lot of coding. However, because they will be executed for any error not explicitly coded for with an `At End` or `Invalid Key` clause, they are not very specific. You can compensate by setting up a common area where you store information like the filename and the type of operation being attempted, for example, `Open`, `Write`, `Close`. You can use this area to be specific when reporting errors that occur.

Workshop

To help reinforce your understanding of the material presented in this hour, refer to the section "Quiz and Exercise Questions and Answers" that can be found on the CD. This section contains quiz questions and exercises for you to complete, as well as the corresponding answers.

HOUR 15

Reading Indexed File Records

In the previous hour, you learned how to create an Indexed file. In this hour, you learn different ways to Read the records in the file. You will learn about

- The different access methods for Indexed files, such as Sequential, Random, and Dynamic.
- How to position the file using the Start statement.
- How to Read records randomly.
- How to Read records sequentially from an Indexed file.

Indexed files can provide superior performance and response time in your programs. Imagine how long the user would have to wait to recall the information for a dealer, when the dealer number is entered, if the program had to Read through all the records in a large file. Indexed files provide virtually instant access to the information if the Key field is known. Even if one of the Key fields in not known, Indexed files can still narrow the search and speed the location of the information.

Various Access Methods

As mentioned briefly in Hour 14, "Indexed Files," COBOL offers several ways to access an Indexed file, depending on the situation. Although these methods have much in common, to a large extent, the efficiency of Indexed file access varies with each COBOL compiler and the environment upon which it runs. In addition, these different access methods have specific performance advantages and disadvantages.

Sequential access, for example, allows the file to be processed from front to back, from lowest Primary Key to highest, using the same programming statements as a normal Sequential file. Sequential access can be put to good use when the entire file is to be processed. On the other hand, Random access provides instant access to a specific record and can be a very fast way to retrieve information from an Indexed file. Dynamic access allows both Sequential and Random access. Dynamic access offers the best of both worlds but has the disadvantage of being slightly more cumbersome than either Random or Sequential access.

Sequential Access

NEW TERM Think of an Indexed file as a book. Each record in the file is a page in the book. The Key for the records is the page number. Sequential access allows you to Read through the book, starting at the first page and ending after the last. You cannot jump ahead in the book. You cannot jump backward in the book. You can only go forward, page by page. You must Read every page, and you cannot skip any pages. If you close the book and Open it again, you must start over from the front of the book.

Sequential access of an Indexed file works exactly as described in this book analogy. Sequential access is specified in the Select statement for the file:

```
000058      Select Dealer-File Assign To "Dealer.Dat"
000059          Organization Indexed
000060          Access Sequential
000061          Record Key Dealer-Number Of Dealer-Record
000062          Alternate Record Key Dealer-Name Of Dealer-Record
000063          File Status Dealer-Status.
```

In order to Read data from an Indexed file, it must be opened for Input. The Open statement is very simple:

```
000101      Open Input Dealer-File
```

When applied against an Indexed file, with Access Sequential, this Open statement allows you to Read data records from the Indexed file. The Read statement operates exactly the same way with an Indexed file Open with Sequential access as it does with a regular Sequential file. Each subsequent Read statement returns the next record in the

15

file, in Primary Key sequence. The At End condition is true if a Read is attempted after the last record of a file is read. The File Status returned is 10 if the end of file is reached.

The program in Listing 15.1 returns a record in the file every time the user presses Enter until the answer to the question Read another record? is N or the end of file is reached.

> Before running this program, you might want to re-run the program in Listing 14.1 to create the file from the provided DEALER.TXT file.

LISTING 15.1   SEQUENTIALLY READ AN INDEXED FILE

```
000001 @OPTIONS MAIN,TEST
000002 Identification Division.
000003 Program-Id.  Chapt15a.
000004* Sequentially Read An Indexed File
000005 Environment Division.
000006 Configuration Section.
000007 Source-Computer.  IBM-PC.
000008 Object-Computer.  IBM-PC.
000009 Input-Output Section.
000010 File-Control.
000011     Select Dealer-File Assign To "Dealer.Dat"
000012             Organization Indexed
000013             Access Sequential
000014             Record Key Dealer-Number
000015             Alternate Record Key Dealer-Name
000016             File Status Dealer-Status.
000017 Data Division.
000018 File Section.
000019 Fd   Dealer-File.
000020 01   Dealer-Record.
000021      03  Dealer-Number         Pic X(8).
000022      03  Dealer-Name.
000023          05  Last-Name    Pic X(25).
000024          05  First-Name   Pic X(15).
000025          05  Middle-Name  Pic X(10).
000026      03  Address-Line-1        Pic X(50).
000027      03  Address-Line-2        Pic X(50).
000028      03  City                  Pic X(40).
000029      03  State-Or-Country      Pic X(20).
000030      03  Postal-Code           Pic X(15).
000031      03  Home-Phone            Pic X(20).
000032      03  Work-Phone            Pic X(20).
000033      03  Other-Phone           Pic X(20).
```

continues

LISTING 15.1   CONTINUED

```
000034     03   Start-Date          Pic 9(8).
000035     03   Last-Rent-Paid-Date Pic 9(8).
000036     03   Next-Rent-Due-Date  Pic 9(8).
000037     03   Rent-Amount         Pic 9(4)v99.
000038     03   Consignment-Percent Pic 9(3).
000039     03   Filler              Pic X(50).
000040 Working-Storage Section.
000041 01  Dealer-Status    Pic X(2) Value Spaces.
000042     88  Dealer-Success Value "00".
000043 01  Show-Next-Record  Pic X Value "Y".
000044 01  Process-Flag      Pic X Value Spaces.
000045     88  End-Process     Value "Y".
000046 Screen Section.
000047 01  Data-Entry-Screen
000048     Blank Screen, Auto
000049     Foreground-Color Is 7,
000050     Background-Color Is 1.
000051*
000052     03   Screen-Literal-Group.
000053          05   Line 01 Column 30 Value "Darlene's Treasures"
000054               Highlight Foreground-Color 4 Background-Color 1.
000055          05   Line 03 Column 30 Value "Tenant Display Program"
000056               Highlight.
000057          05   Line 4  Column 01   Value "Number: ".
000058          05   Line 5  Column 01   Value "Name, Last: ".
000059          05   Line 5  Column 39   Value "First: ".
000060          05   Line 5  Column 62   Value "Middle: ".
000061          05   Line 6  Column 01   Value "Address 1: ".
000062          05   Line 7  Column 01   Value "Address 2: ".
000063          05   Line 8  Column 01   Value "City: ".
000064          05   Line 9  Column 01   Value "Country/State: ".
000065          05   Line 9  Column 36   Value "Postal Code: ".
000066          05   Line 11 Column 01   Value "Phone/Home: ".
000067          05   Line 11 Column 34   Value "Work: ".
000068          05   Line 12 Column 06   Value "Other: ".
000069          05   Line 14 Column 01   Value "Start Date: ".
000070          05   Line 14 Column 24   Value "Last Paid Date: ".
000071          05   Line 14 Column 51   Value "Next Rent Due on: ".
000072          05   Line 15 Column 01   Value "Rent Amount: ".
000073          05   Line 16 Column 01   Value "Consignment Percent: ".
000074          05   Line 22 Column 01
000075               Value "Display next Record? (Y/N):".
000076*
000077     03   Required-Reverse-Group Reverse-Video.
000078          05   Line 4 Column 13  Pic X(8)  From Dealer-Number.
000079          05   Line 5 Column 13  Pic X(25) From Last-Name.
000080          05   Line 5 Column 46  Pic X(15) From First-Name.
000081          05   Line 5  Column 70 Pic X(10) From Middle-Name.
000082          05   Line 6  Column 15 Pic X(50) From Address-Line-1.
```

15

```
000083          05  Line 7  Column 15 Pic X(50) From Address-Line-2.
000084          05  Line 8  Column 15 Pic X(40) From City.
000085          05  Line 9  Column 15 Pic X(20) From State-Or-Country.
000086          05  Line 9  Column 50 Pic X(15) From Postal-Code.
000087          05  Line 11 Column 13 Pic X(20) From Home-Phone.
000088          05  Line 11 Column 41 Pic X(20) From Work-Phone.
000089          05  Line 12 Column 13 Pic X(20) From Other-Phone.
000090          05  Line 14 Column 13 Pic 99/99/9999 From Start-Date.
000091          05  Line 14 Column 40 Pic 99/99/9999
000092              From Last-Rent-Paid-Date.
000093          05  Line 14 Column 69 Pic 99/99/9999
000094              From Next-Rent-Due-Date.
000095          05  Line 15 Column 14 Pic Z,ZZZ.99 From Rent-Amount.
000096          05  Line 16 Column 22 Pic ZZ9 From Consignment-Percent.
000097          05  Line 22 Column 29 Pic X Using Show-Next-Record.
000098*
000099
000100 Procedure Division.
000101 Chapt15a-Start.
000102      Perform Open-File
000103      If Dealer-Success
000104          Perform Process-Screen Until Show-Next-Record = "N" Or
000105                                        Show-Next-Record = "n" Or
000106                                        End-Process
000107          Perform Close-File
000108      End-If
000109      Stop Run
000110          .
000111  Process-Screen.
000112      Read Dealer-File
000113       At End Set End-Process To True
000114       Not At End
000115           Perform Display-And-Accept
000116      End-Read
000117          .
000118 Display-And-Accept.
000119      Display Data-Entry-Screen
000120      Accept Data-Entry-Screen
000121          .
000122 Open-File.
000123      Open Input Dealer-File
000124          .
000125 Close-File.
000126      Close Dealer-File
000127          .
```

When you run this program, notice that the records are read in Primary Key sequence. The names do not appear in alphabetical order; instead you see the lowest account number and progress to the higher ones.

The Start Statement

With a book, you can open to any page and begin reading. The same is true of an Indexed file accessed in Sequential mode. You can Start at any position within the file and then Read records. You cannot go backward, and if you Close the file, you have to Start over. But you can begin reading anywhere in the file by using the Start statement.

The Start statement allows you to specify the position in the file where the next Read will occur. With the Start statement, you specify the file you want to position—and the location—in reference to the Key field. Before issuing the Start, you place a value in the Key field to control the positioning. You can Start the file on a record equal to the Key field, greater than the Key field, greater than or equal to the Key field, or not less than the Key field. You may not specify less than in the Start statement. For example, if you want to begin processing on the account numbers beginning with the letter C, you can code the following statements after the Open and before any Read statements:

```
000412          Move "C" to Dealer-Number
000413          Start Dealer-File Key Not < Dealer-Number
```

> Most compilers allow you to code the Start statement without using the Invalid Key clause and without having Declaratives associated with the file. The COBOL standard requires the presence of either Declaratives or an Invalid Key clause. To ensure that your program can compile on standard COBOL compilers, you should either use Declaratives or specify the Invalid Key clause.

One new File Status value (status 23) can be returned when you use the Start statement to position an Indexed file for a Sequential Read. Status 23 means record not found. This status is returned after a Start statement if a record cannot be found that matches the requested position in the file. This File Status is returned if there are no greater keys in the file or the specific Key was not found when Start with Key = is used.

To Start processing the file with account numbers that begin with C, you can use the following code in the Procedure Division:

```
000098 Chapt15b-Start.
000099      Perform Open-File
000100      If Dealer-Success
000101        Move "C" To Dealer-Number
000102        Start Dealer-File Key Not < Dealer-Number
000103            Invalid Key Set End-Process To True
000104        End-Start
000105        Perform Process-Screen Until Show-Next-Record = "N" Or
```

```
000106                                  Show-Next-Record = "n" Or
000107                                  End-Process
000108          Perform Close-File
000109      End-If
000110      Stop Run
000111      .
```

15

An interesting aspect of the Start statement is that it allows you to begin sequentially reading the Indexed file based on the Alternate Key field. This approach is like creating a new page-numbering scheme for your book and then rearranging the pages in the book in the new sequence. COBOL allows you to perform the same task using Indexed files and the Start statement. Instead of specifying the Primary Key on the Start statement, you may specify an Alternate Key field. The following example shows the Procedure Division code necessary to Start reading the file on the Alternate Key, beginning with last names that begin with H.

```
000098 Chapt15c-Start.
000099      Perform Open-File
000100      If Dealer-Success
000101          Move "H" To Dealer-Name
000102          Start Dealer-File Key Not < Dealer-Name
000103              Invalid Key Set End-Process To True
000104          End-Start
000105          Perform Process-Screen Until Show-Next-Record = "N" Or
000106                                  Show-Next-Record = "n" Or
000107                                  End-Process
000108          Perform Close-File
000109      End-If
000110      Stop Run
000111      .
```

When you run the program with this code inserted, the first name that is displayed begins with an H. Each subsequent Read returns the records in name sequence, not in account number sequence as you saw before. The Start statement specifies where to Start in the file and in which Key sequence to Read the file.

What if you want to Start at the beginning of the file, using the Alternate Key? You don't know what the lowest Key value in the file is, and you want to code a Start statement that ensures access to every record in the file. In this case, use the Start statement but place Low-Values in the Key field. When starting, use the not < phrase, not the > phrase. Using not < ensures that the next record read is the one with Low-Values or something greater in it.

The Start statement might be coded as follows:

```
000099      Move Low-Values To Dealer-Name
000100      Start Dealer-File Key Not < Dealer-Name
000101          Invalid Key Set End-Process To true
```

If you know the specific record Key you want to Start on, you may use Start with Key = the Key field after it has been filled with the appropriate starting Key, for example:

```
000099        Move "Jennings" To Last-Name
000100        Move "Shelly" To First-Name
000101        Move "Martin" To Middle-Name
000102        Start Dealer-File Key = Dealer-Name
000103            Invalid Key Set End-Process To True
```

If the name does not exist, you get a File Status 23 and the Invalid Key condition is true. If the name does exist, the very next Read contains the record with this Key value.

> The Start statement does not return the record; it only positions the file for the next Read. A Read statement must be executed to retrieve a data record, even after a successful Start.

Random Access

NEW TERM You have learned how to access records sequentially from an Indexed file. Another method that can be used to Read records from the file is Random access. Random access is similar to deciding which page of a book to open to, opening exactly on that page, reading it, and then closing the book. You may not read the next page or the preceding page without first closing and reopening the book, but only the page you specified.

The Select statement necessary for Random access is

```
000058        Select Dealer-File Assign To "Dealer.Dat"
000059            Organization Indexed
000060            Access Random
000061            Record Key Dealer-Number Of Dealer-Record
000062            Alternate Record Key Dealer-Name Of Dealer-Record
000063            File Status Dealer-Status.
```

When reading from the file using Random access, you must place a value in the Key field of the file being read. A simple Move statement is all you need.

```
000101        Move "L3460" To Dealer-Number
```

The next Read statement for the file returns the record identified by dealer number L3460.

```
000102        Read Dealer-File
```

If the file contains no record matching the Key specified, a File Status of 23 is returned, which is an Invalid Key condition. You may code the Invalid Key clause after the Read to handle these conditions if you desire.

15

```
000102      Read Dealer-File
000103        Invalid Key Display "No Dealer Record Found"
000104        Not Invalid Key Perform Process-Record
000105      End-Read
```

> If a Read is not successful, the content of your data record area is not protected. If data was in the area from a previous Read or a value was in the Key field, it may not be there after an unsuccessful Read attempt.

I suggest the use of the End-Read explicit scope terminator whenever you use the Invalid Key clause.

Unless otherwise specified, the Read statement assumes that you are reading via the Primary Key field. It is entirely permissible to Read records from an Indexed file opened in Random mode by the Alternate Key field. When you Read via the Alternate Key, the specific Key field desired must be coded in the Read statement. You must remember to Move the data value required to identify the desired record into the Alternate Key field before the Read.

```
000100      Move "Alan"    To First-Name
000101      Move "Aaron"   To Middle-Name
000102      Move "Holmes" To Last-Name
000103      Read Dealer-File Key Dealer-Name
000104          Invalid Key Display "Record Not Found"
000105          Not Invalid Key Perform Process-Record
000106      End-Read
```

If a matching record is not found, a File Status of 23 is returned in the File Status field if one is defined. Declaratives may be specified for the file and will be executed in case of a Read that is not successful. The Key clause specifies the Key field to be used for the Random Read.

Some files may be defined with an Alternate Key that allows duplicates. If a Random Read is attempted against such a Key and a record is identified that has an identical Alternate Key to another record in the file, a File Status of 02 is returned. The record returned is the oldest in the file, the first record added with this Alternate Key value.

> The At End clause is not valid for use on a Read statement when the file is Open for Random access. You will never reach the end of the file, the record being read will exist, or it will not.

Random reads are useful when you know the Key information of the record you are trying to retrieve. Random reads are an extremely fast way to retrieve the data record and can be handy in programs that are used to retrieve information about a specific item or individual.

Dynamic Access

NEW TERM   Dynamic access is the slowest and most versatile of the access methods used to retrieve records from an Indexed file. This type of access is the slowest because of the overhead required for the program to keep track of its position in the file. Dynamic access allows you to retrieve records both randomly and sequentially.

The Select statement used to specify Dynamic access is coded as follows:

```
000058      Select Dealer-File Assign to "Dealer.Dat"
000059             Organization Indexed
000060             Access Dynamic
000061             Record Key Dealer-Number of Dealer-Record
000062             Alternate Record Key Dealer-Name of Dealer-Record
000063             File Status Dealer-Status.
```

When Dynamic access is specified, you can perform Random reads using exactly the same method as if the file were Open with Random access.

To Read records from the file sequentially from an Indexed file Open with Dynamic access, you must first position the file at a valid record. Correct positioning can be accomplished in three ways.

One method is to issue a Random Read using the desired Key field. If the Read is successful, then you may continue to Read subsequent records from the file sequentially in the order of the Key that was used for the Random Read. Obviously, you need some way to differentiate between a Random Read and a Sequential Read designed to retrieve the next record in the file.

To indicate that the next record in sequence should be returned, you issue a Read statement with the Next clause.

```
000101      Read Dealer-File Next Record
```

> The word *record* is optional and is specified only to make the code more readable.

The At End clause may be coded to detect the end of file. The Invalid Key clause is not valid on a Read statement with the Next clause. Some additional File Status values may be returned after a Read Next statement is executed. In addition to the File Status values returned as a result of a Read statement, Table 15.1 explains two new File Status values that may be returned after the Read Next statement.

TABLE 15.1 ADDITIONAL FILE STATUS VALUES RETURNED FROM A READ WITH NEXT

Status	Meaning
46	The prior Read or Start statement was unsuccessful, and the next record cannot be determined.
47	The file is not Open for Input.

The second method that can be used to position the file for a Sequential Read is to issue a Start statement. The Start statement works as previously discussed and sets the position in the file for the next Read Next statement.

> Use caution when reading randomly from an Indexed file that is Open with Dynamic access. Any previous Start statements do not retain the associated Key or file positioning. Any subsequent Read Next statements may not return the record you expect in the Key sequence you expect. A successful Read repositions the file and possibly changes the Key by which the file is being read.

The third method to position the file at a valid record is simply to Open the file. When you Open an Indexed file with Dynamic access, the next record pointer is set to the beginning of the file. Subsequent Read statements with the Next clause return records in Primary Key sequence.

The program in Listing 15.2 uses both Sequential and Random access. This program allows the user to input the information for the Key fields and then choose how to retrieve the record by using the function keys. The program uses the Start statement to determine which Key to use for reading sequentially. A function key is provided to clear the screen input.

This first part of the program identifies it and specifies the Special Names necessary to capture and set the cursor position and to capture the various function keys you want to detect.

LISTING 15.2 DYNAMIC ACCESS EXAMPLE

```
000001 @OPTIONS MAIN,TEST
000002 Identification Division.
000003 Program-Id.  Chapt15d.
000004* Dynamic Access Example
000005 Environment Division.
000006 Configuration Section.
000007 Special-Names.
000008       Crt Status Is Keyboard-Status
000009       Cursor Is Cursor-Position.
000010 Source-Computer.  IBM-PC.
000011 Object-Computer.  IBM-PC.
```

The file is described here. Notice the access mode is Dynamic. This mode allows you to retrieve records either sequentially or randomly from the file.

```
000012 Input-Output Section.
000013 File-Control.
000014     Select Dealer-File Assign To "Dealer.Dat"
000015            Organization Indexed
000016            Access Dynamic
000017            Record Key Dealer-Number
000018            Alternate Record Key Dealer-Name
000019            File Status Dealer-Status.
000020 Data Division.
000021 File Section.
000022 Fd   Dealer-File.
000023 01   Dealer-Record.
000024      03  Dealer-Number       Pic X(8).
000025      03  Dealer-Name.
000026          05  Last-Name    Pic X(25).
000027          05  First-Name   Pic X(15).
000028          05  Middle-Name  Pic X(10).
000029      03  Address-Line-1      Pic X(50).
000030      03  Address-Line-2      Pic X(50).
000031      03  City                Pic X(40).
000032      03  State-Or-Country    Pic X(20).
000033      03  Postal-Code         Pic X(15).
000034      03  Home-Phone          Pic X(20).
000035      03  Work-Phone          Pic X(20).
000036      03  Other-Phone         Pic X(20).
000037      03  Start-Date          Pic 9(8).
000038      03  Last-Rent-Paid-Date Pic 9(8).
000039      03  Next-Rent-Due-Date  Pic 9(8).
000040      03  Rent-Amount         Pic 9(4)v99.
000041      03  Consignment-Percent Pic 9(3).
000042      03  Filler              Pic X(50).
```

The various working fields are described here in Working-Storage. Notice the File Status value clause is coded with an 88 level condition. The condition specified for Dealer-Success to be true is the range of File Status values from 00 through 09. Any File Status value that begins with 0 indicates a successful operation.

```
000043 Working-Storage Section.
000044 01  Dealer-Status     Pic X(2) Value Spaces.
000045      88  Dealer-Success Value "00" Thru "09".
```

The Keyboard-Status and Cursor-Position fields allow you to capture the key that was pressed and to position the cursor on the first field when the screen is cleared.

```
000046 01  Keyboard-Status.
000047      03  Accept-Status Pic 9.
000048      03  Function-Key  Pic X.
000049          88  F1-Pressed Value X"01".
000050          88  F2-Pressed Value X"02".
000051          88  F3-Pressed Value X"03".
000052          88  F4-Pressed Value X"04".
000053          88  F5-Pressed Value X"05".
000054          88  F6-Pressed Value X"06".
000055      03  System-Use    Pic X.
000056 01  Cursor-Position.
000057      03  Cursor-Row    Pic 9(2) Value 1.
000058      03  Cursor-Column Pic 9(2) Value 1.
```

The screen description uses the Error-Message to hold any error messages you might need to issue.

```
000059 01  Error-Message Pic X(50) Value Spaces.
```

The Screen Section describes the input screen. Notice that the only fields that can be used as input are the Number and Name fields. Text has been added to describe the functions of the various keys that are captured.

```
000060 Screen Section.
000061 01  Data-Entry-Screen
000062      Blank Screen, Auto
000063      Foreground-Color is 7,
000064      Background-Color is 1.
000065      03  Screen-Literal-Group.
000066          05  Line 01 Column 30 Value "Darlene's Treasures"
000067              Highlight Foreground-Color 4 Background-Color 1.
000068          05  Line 03 Column 30 Value "Tenant Entry Program"
000069              Highlight.
000070          05  Line 4  Column 01  Value "Number: ".
000071          05  Line 5  Column 01  Value "Name, Last: ".
000072          05  Line 5  Column 39  Value "First: ".
000073          05  Line 5  Column 62  Value "Middle: ".
000074          05  Line 6  Column 01  Value "Address 1: ".
000075          05  Line 7  Column 01  Value "Address 2: ".
```

```
000076        05  Line 8  Column 01  Value "City: ".
000077        05  Line 9  Column 01  Value "Country/State: ".
000078        05  Line 9  Column 36  Value "Postal Code: ".
000079        05  Line 11 Column 01  Value "Phone/Home: ".
000080        05  Line 11 Column 34  Value "Work: ".
000081        05  Line 12 Column 06  Value "Other: ".
000082        05  Line 14 Column 01  Value "Start Date: ".
000083        05  Line 14 Column 24  Value "Last Paid Date: ".
000084        05  Line 14 Column 51  Value "Next Rent Due on: ".
000085        05  Line 15 Column 01  Value "Rent Amount: ".
000086        05  Line 16 Column 01  Value "Consignment Percent: ".
000087        05  Line 22 Column 01  Value "F1-Read Random Number".
000088        05  Line 22 Column 23  Value "F2-Read Random Name".
000089        05  Line 22 Column 56  Value "F3-Read Next Number".
000090        05  Line 23 Column 01  Value "F4-Read Next Name".
000091        05  Line 23 Column 23  Value "F5-Clear".
000092        05  Line 23 Column 56  Value "F6-Exit".
000093  03  Required-Reverse-Group Reverse-Video.
000094        05  Line 4 Column 13  Pic X(8)  Using Dealer-Number.
000095        05  Line 5 Column 13  Pic X(25) Using Last-Name.
000096        05  Line 5 Column 46  Pic X(15) Using First-Name.
000097        05  Line 5  Column 70 Pic X(10) Using Middle-Name.
000098        05  Line 6  Column 15 Pic X(50) From Address-Line-1.
000099        05  Line 7  Column 15 Pic X(50) From Address-Line-2.
000100        05  Line 8  Column 15 Pic X(40) From City.
000101        05  Line 9  Column 15 Pic X(20) From State-Or-Country.
000102        05  Line 9  Column 50 Pic X(15) From Postal-Code.
000103        05  Line 11 Column 13 Pic X(20) From Home-Phone.
000104        05  Line 11 Column 41 Pic X(20) From Work-Phone.
000105        05  Line 12 Column 13 Pic X(20) From Other-Phone.
000106        05  Line 14 Column 13 Pic 99/99/9999 From Start-Date.
000107        05  Line 14 Column 40 Pic 99/99/9999 From Last-Rent-Paid-Date.
000108        05  Line 14 Column 69 Pic 99/99/9999 From Next-Rent-Due-Date.
000109        05  Line 15 Column 14 Pic Z,ZZZ.99 From Rent-Amount.
000110        05  Line 16 Column 22 Pic ZZ9 From Consignment-Percent.
000111        05  Line 20 Column 01 Pic X(50) Using Error-Message.
```

The first portion of the actual program opens the dealer file. If the Open fails, an error message is displayed and processing stops. If the Open is successful, then the file is processed until the user presses the F6 key to exit.

```
000112 Procedure Division.
000113 Chapt15d-Start.
000114     Perform Open-File
000115     If Not Dealer-Success
000116         String "Error Opening Dealer File "
000117               Dealer-Status
000118               Delimited By Size
000119               Into Error-Message
000120         End-String
000121     Perform Display-And-Accept
```

```
000122      Else
000123          Initialize Dealer-Record
000124          Perform Process-File Until F6-Pressed
000125          Perform Close-File
000126      End-If
000127      Stop Run
000128      .
```

The Process-File Paragraph displays the screen and accepts the user input. The
Paragraph tests, via an Evaluate statement, for the different keystrokes that can be
pressed and performs the appropriate function.

```
000129 Process-File.
000130      Perform Display-And-Accept
000131      Evaluate True
000132        When F1-Pressed
000133            Perform Read-Random-Number
000134        When F2-Pressed
000135            Perform Read-Random-Name
000136        When F3-Pressed
000137            Perform Read-Next-Number
000138        When F4-Pressed
000139            Perform Read-Next-Name
000140        When F5-Pressed
000141            Perform Clear-Screen
000142        When F6-Pressed
000143            Continue
000144        When Other
000145            Continue
000146      End-Evaluate
000147      .
```

The Read-Random-Number Paragraph reads the dealer file randomly via the Primary
Key of the file. Notice that no specific Key is specified. If none is specified, then the
Primary Key is used. If an error occurs, the exact error is reported to the user via the
error message. The only error that you should see reported, baring hardware problems, is
23 for record not found. There is no Move of data to the Key field because this step is
automatically handled by the Screen Section.

```
000148 Read-Random-Number.
000149      Read Dealer-File
000150        Invalid Key
000151            String "Error on Random Read Number "
000152                  Dealer-Status
000153                  Delimited By Size
000154                  Into Error-Message
000155      End-Read
000156      .
```

The `Read-Random-Name` `Paragraph` is nearly identical to the `Read-Random-Number` `Paragraph`. The only real difference is that the `Alternate` `Key` field is specified, so the `Read` is attempted using that `Key`.

```
000157 Read-Random-Name.
000158      Read Dealer-File Key Dealer-Name
000159        Invalid Key
000160          String "Error on Random Read Name "
000161                Dealer-Status
000162                Delimited By Size
000163                Into Error-Message
000164      End-Read
000165        .
```

The `Read-Next-Number` `Paragraph` does two things. First is does a `Start` on the file to position it on the next dealer number. The `Key` specified is the dealer number. If the `Start` fails, the reason for the failure is reported to the user in the error message.

If the `Start` statement is successful, a `Read` with the next clause is attempted. If the end of the file is reached, it is reported to the user.

```
000166 Read-Next-Number.
000167      Start Dealer-File Key > Dealer-Number
000168        Invalid Key
000169          String "Start Error Number "
000170                Dealer-Status
000171                Delimited By Size
000172                Into Error-Message
000173      End-Start
000174      If Dealer-Success
000175        Read Dealer-File Next
000176          At End
000177            Move "End of File, Read by Number" To Error-Message
000178        End-Read
000179      End-If
000180        .
```

The `Read-Next-Name` `Paragraph` performs a similar `Start` and `Read`. The `Start` statement uses the `Dealer-Name` field instead of the `Dealer-Number`. The only difference in the `Read` with `Next` statements in the two paragraphs is the text of the error reported. The `Read` with `Next` need not specify the `Key` being used; it is assumed from the last successful `Read` or `Start` operation.

```
000181 Read-Next-Name.
000182      Start Dealer-File Key > Dealer-Name
000183        Invalid Key
000184          String "Start Error Name "
000185                Dealer-Status
000186                Delimited By Size
000187                Into Error-Message
```

```
000188        End-Start
000189        If Dealer-Success
000190           Read Dealer-File Next
000191              At End
000192                 Move "End of File, Read by Name" To Error-Message
000193           End-Read
000194        End-If
000195        .
```

The Clear-Screen Paragraph clears the dealer record that is used by the screen description and sets the cursor positioning so that the cursor appears in the first field on the screen.

```
000196 Clear-Screen.
000197        Initialize Dealer-Record
000198        Move 01 To Cursor-Row Cursor-Column
000199        .
```

The Display-And-Accept Paragraph displays the screen and accepts the user input. This Paragraph also clears any remaining error messages after accepting the user input.

```
000200 Display-And-Accept.
000201        Display Data-Entry-Screen
000202        Accept Data-Entry-Screen
000203        Move Spaces To Error-Message
000204        .
```

The Open and Close statements grant Input access to the file and release the file to the operating system when the program is finished with the file.

```
000205 Open-File.
000206        Open Input Dealer-File
000207        .
000208 Close-File.
000209        Close Dealer-File
000210        .
```

There are some more advanced ways to use the Start statement. For example, imagine that you are scrolling through the file by name. However, you want to jump to the next record with a last name that begins with the next letter in the alphabet. The Start statement offers a simple way to accomplish that task.

As you know, with Start you must specify the Key field you want to Start on. You may, however, use just a portion of that field and not specify the entire field. For example, change the Record Description of the Dealer-Record to look like this:

```
000022 FD  Dealer-File.
000023 01  Dealer-Record.
000024     03  Dealer-Number        Pic X(8).
000025     03  Dealer-Name.
```

```
000026                05  Last-Name.
000027                    10  Last-Name-First-Letter    Pic X.
000028                    10  Last-Name-Remainder       Pic X(24).
000029                05  First-Name   Pic X(15).
000030                05  Middle-Name  Pic X(10).
000031           03  Address-Line-1         Pic X(50).
000032           03  Address-Line-2         Pic X(50).
000033           03  City                   Pic X(40).
000034           03  State-or-Country       Pic X(20).
000035           03  Postal-Code            Pic X(15).
000036           03  Home-Phone             Pic X(20).
000037           03  Work-Phone             Pic X(20).
000038           03  Other-Phone            Pic X(20).
000039           03  Start-Date             Pic 9(8).
000040           03  Last-Rent-Paid-Date    Pic 9(8).
000041           03  Next-Rent-Due-Date     Pic 9(8).
000042           03  Rent-Amount            Pic 9(4)V99.
000043           03  Consignment-Percent    Pic 9(3).
000044           03  Filler                 Pic X(50).
```

Now, when you want to position the file for reading the next record that has a last name that begins with the next letter of the alphabet, you can issue the following Start statement:

```
000101     Start Dealer-File Key > Last-Name-First-Letter
```

If the current last name is "Berg", the next record returned after a Read with Next will have a last name of "Colvin".

The only rule you need to remember is that the field you use must Start is in the same position in the record as the actual Key field.

Summary

In this hour, you learned the following:

- Indexed files can be read randomly or sequentially. Random reads are made directly with a known Key, and Sequential reads are made serially, one after the other, based on the Key sequence of the file.
- You can specify the starting position for Sequential reads by using the Start statement.
- The Start statement is valid for both Sequential access and Dynamic access.
- When a Random Read is issued and a matching record is not found, a File Status 23 is returned. Another way to detect this condition is to use the Invalid Key clause of the Read statement because any File Status that begins with 2 indicates an Invalid Key condition.

- Dynamic access allows you to access an Indexed file randomly or sequentially. The statement to Read a record sequentially is the Read statement with the Next clause.

- A Start statement does not return the data record contents; it only positions the file for the next Read.

15

Q&A

Q **If I am reading an Indexed file with Access Sequential, how do I ensure that I am reading from the beginning of the file?**

A Simply opening the file positions you at the front of the file. If you want to be certain, you can Move Low-Values to the Key field and issue a Start statement with Key Not < Your-Key. The very next Read Starts at the front of the file.

Q **I understand that Sequential access allows me to Read the records in an Indexed file sequentially. Because Dynamic access is slower, why would I ever need to use Dynamic access?**

A Although both Dynamic access and Sequential access allow you to Read sequentially through an Indexed file, in some cases you may need to execute a Random Read against the same file that you are reading sequentially. Dynamic access allows you to do both. I suggest that you evaluate the requirements of your program carefully and choose the most appropriate access method.

Q **How can I ensure that Read with Next reads the file in Key sequence by the Alternate Key field?**

A Issue a Start statement that uses the Alternate Key or do a Random Read using the Alternate Key.

Q **If both Start and a Random Read position the file so that a Read with Next performs Sequential reads, why do I need to use Start?**

A The Read statement with the Next clause can work only if the file is positioned on a record. This condition happens in one of three ways: opening the file, a successful Random Read, or a successful Start. If you do not know the Key value of a record that exists in the file, you cannot perform a successful Random Read. If your Read or Start fails, the Read statement with the Next clause that follows will also fail.

Workshop

To help reinforce your understanding of the material presented in this hour, refer to the section "Quiz and Exercise Questions and Answers" that can be found on the CD. This section contains quiz questions and exercises for you to complete, as well as the corresponding answers.

Hour 16

Updating Indexed File Records

A large part of business programming involves updating records in data files. Information is constantly changing, and the files containing this information require frequent updates. In the examples using the dealer file, you are keeping up with information such as address and telephone number that could change. To keep these files current, records have to be updated. Updating an Indexed file record is fairly simple. In this hour, you learn about updating Indexed files and also about working with Relative files. The following topics are covered:

- Opening a file for I-O (simultaneous Input and Output)
- Writing records
- Rewriting records
- Deleting records
- Working with Relative files; similarities and differences with Indexed files

Opening for I-0

You know that when you Open a file Output, you are creating a new file. The only records it contains are those written after the Open statement. Any records that may have been in the file are lost. If you want to add records to a file, you know that you can Open the file Extend. To retrieve records from a file, you Open it Input. Updating records in an Indexed file requires that you be able to Read a record so that you can present its contents to the user for modification. You also need to be able to Write the new record, or update the existing record if a change has been made. Opening for Output or Extend won't accomplish either of these goals.

COBOL provides an Open mode that allows you to Read records from an Indexed file, Write new records, and update existing records. This Open mode is I-0, meaning Input-Output. The File Status values returned when opening a file I-0 are the same as those returned when opening the file for Input.

All the statements used when reading from an Indexed file that is Open Input apply when the file is Open I-0. You may specify Sequential, Random, or Dynamic access. You may Read records from the file as if it were Open Input. You may Write new records to the file using Write as if the file were Open Output. (There are some special considerations for writing to an Indexed file Open I-0 when the Organization is Sequential—these are discussed shortly.) Finally, you may update existing records.

Writing Records

One way to update an Indexed file is to add new records to the file with the Write statement. The way the Write statement works depends on the access method used and Open mode of the file. Remember that access can be Sequential, Random, or Dynamic.

You may not Open the file I-0 with Sequential access mode and Write records. If you attempt to do so, a File Status of 48 is returned. This status is returned because you cannot Write to an Indexed file with Sequential access that is opened for I-0. If you need to add a record to an Indexed file with Sequential access, you should Open the file for Extend instead of I-0. When writing to the file, you must ensure that the primary Key of the record being written is greater than the last record in the file. If not, you receive a File Status 21, record out of sequence, error. The primary Key controls the sequence of records for Sequential Write operations. Keep in mind that although Sequential access is pretty fast and has its place, you probably don't want to try to add records to an Indexed file Open in Sequential mode.

When you use Random access and have the file Open I-0, you may Write new records to the file. The order of the writes does not matter. If a duplicate primary Key is encountered, a File Status of 22 is returned. Your new record does not replace the existing record. If you have Alternate Record Keys and duplicates are not allowed—but one is encountered during the Write—a File Status 22 is also returned. In this case, it is not possible to determine which Key is being duplicated by the Write: the primary or one of the Alternate Key fields. If duplicates are allowed on the Alternate Key and one is encountered as the result of a Write statement, a File Status of 02 is returned.

Another potential File Status value that can be returned from this type of operation is a 24. This value means that you have attempted to Write outside the externally defined boundary of the file. Focus on the term *externally defined*. Some systems define Indexed files outside the program. The files must be defined to the operating system, and specific size limitations may apply. In this case, if the maximum size of the file is exceeded, a File Status 24 is returned.

16

Remember that any File Status that begins with 2, such as 22, is also an Invalid Key condition and that you may code the Invalid Key clause with the Write. The COBOL standard requires that you either code the Invalid Key clause or have Declaratives defined for the file when performing a Write against an Indexed file.

For the Write statement, Dynamic and Random access work the same way. Writes to an Indexed file that is Open I-O with Dynamic access are identical to writes to a file that is Open with Random access. You may not Open an Indexed file with Dynamic access for Extend.

The Write statement is coded the same as with Sequential files. You specify the record description to be written, not the file name. The only additional check that may be coded with Indexed files is the Invalid Key clause.

```
000101     Write Dealer-Record From Dealer-Work
000102            Invalid Key Perform Invalid-Dealer-Write
000103     End-Write
```

Remember that the From, when used with Write, moves the contents of Dealer-Work into the record area defined by Dealer-Record.

Rewriting Records

One very useful feature of Indexed files and COBOL is the capability to update an existing data file record. The Rewrite statement replaces an existing record with a new record. This statement is especially useful for updating information that is likely to change or changes frequently. When an address changes for one of your dealers, you update the dealer file by rewriting that dealer's record. The behavior of the Rewrite statement depends on the type of access you have selected for the file. The Rewrite statement is available only when the file is Open I-O.

When the file is defined with `Sequential` access, the `Rewrite` statement overlays the last record read with the new data record. You should be aware of some issues.

First, a `Rewrite` can be performed only if the last statement executed against the file was a `Read` statement, and the `Read` was successful. If you attempt to `Rewrite` a record when access is `Sequential`, without first reading a record, the `Rewrite` fails. The `File Status` reported for this failure is `43`, which simply means that the last statement executed for the file was not a successful `Read`. This failure occurs even after a successful `Rewrite` statement if you attempt to execute another `Rewrite` without first performing a `Read`.

Second, when rewriting a record you may not change the primary `Key`. For this example, that means you cannot `Read` the dealer file, change the dealer's number, and then `Rewrite` the record. Any attempt to do so results in a `File Status 21` for record out of sequence.

When using `Indexed` files, regardless of the access mode specified, you cannot change the primary `Key`. Think about the implications for your programs if this practice were allowed. You might have a purchase file that matches merchandise to dealers. In this file, rather than keeping all of the information relating to the dealer, you just keep the dealer number (for file maintenance). If a dealer's address changes, all you have to do is change the dealer file. Because the purchase file refers only to the dealer number, nothing needs to change in it. Now imagine what would happen if you were allowed to change the dealer number in the dealer master file. Your number in the purchase file would not be changed! This condition would break the link between the dealer file and the purchase file. You might use that dealer number again, and then the purchase file would point to the wrong dealer! Any time you feel you must change the primary `Key` of an `Indexed` file, you need to consider all the places in your system that might use the `Key`. You may then add the record with your new primary `Key` and `Delete` the one with the old primary `Key`. (Deleting records is discussed in the "Deleting Records" section in this hour.)

When `Random` or `Dynamic` access is selected for the `Indexed` file, the `Rewrite` statement becomes less restrictive. The `Rewrite` does not have to be preceded by a successful `Read` statement. The primary `Key` determines the placement of the record in the file. When you execute the `Rewrite` statement, if the primary `Key` does not exist for the record you are rewriting, then the `File Status` is set to `23`—record not found—and an `Invalid Key` condition occurs. If you `Rewrite` a record and cause a duplicate `Alternate Key` condition, a `File Status` of `22` is returned and an `Invalid Key` condition occurs.

I suggest that you always Read the record that you are going to Rewrite. Because the Rewrite statement allows you to replace a record without regard to its contents, erasing information in your data record with a Rewrite is relatively easy. Imagine that you want to change a dealer's phone number. If you fill in a record with dealer number and phone number and then Rewrite the record, all of the other information in the record is lost. It is replaced by the values that you may have had initialized or have left over from a previous, but unrelated, Read statement. The best practice is to Read the record, move in the fields being updated, and then Rewrite the record.

The act of rewriting a record does not change the current record positioning in the file. Therefore, you can change the contents of a record, even changing the Alternate Key value by which you are reading. The next record you Read is then based on what that Key used to be and not the new value. For example, if you are reading the dealer file by Alternate Key value and you change a last name from "Smith" to "Jones", your next Read returns the record after "Smith", not the record after "Jones".

16

The following snippet of code reads a record, moves in replacement values, and then rewrites that record. The Invalid Key clause on the Rewrite statement is coded to either catch records that do not exist and disallowed duplicate Alternate Key values.

```
000201     Move "A1366" To Dealer-Number Of Dealer-Record
000202     Read Dealer-File
000203         Invalid Key Move "Dealer Not Found" To Error-Message
000204         Set File-Error To True
000205     End-Read
000206     If Not File-Error
000207        Move "(909) 555-1212" To Home-Phone Of Dealer-Record
000208        Rewrite Dealer-Record
000209           Invalid Key Move Spaces To Error-Message
000210           String "Error Rewriting Dealer File " Dealer-Status
000211                             Delimited By Size Into Error-Message
000212                   Set File-Error To True
000213        End-Rewrite
000214     End-If
```

It should be obvious that you would never code a telephone number update with a literal in a program, as was done in the preceding example. The example is for illustration only. In reality, this telephone number would come from user input or a transaction record. Coding items such as this, using a literal, is known as *hard coding*. This term describes something that is coded in the program to always occur. Imagine the frustration of trying to

debug the preceding situation if you left this code in a program that actually accepted and updated telephone numbers. No matter what the user
entered, dealer number A1366 would always have the same telephone number!

Deleting Records

On occasion you may wish to remove, or delete, records from your Indexed files. Like
the Rewrite statement, the Delete statement is valid only when the file is Open I-O. The
Delete statement removes the records from the file. The primary Key of the file is the
determining factor in deleting a record. Unlike the Write and Rewrite statements, when
a Delete statement is coded, the filename is specified, for example:

```
000215      Delete Dealer-File
```

When Organization is Sequential, the record deleted is the last record read. The
Delete statement is valid only when the last operation against the file is a successful
Read statement. If not, the Delete returns a File Status value of 43. Because a Delete
cannot return File Status values beginning with a 2 when the file is Open with
Sequential access, coding Invalid Key on such a Delete is not allowed.

When Dynamic or Random access is selected for the file, the Delete statement, like the
Rewrite, becomes a little less restrictive. The record being deleted need not have been
previously read. Simply fill in the primary Key information in the record description for
the file and issue the Delete statement. If the record does not exist, a File Status of 23
is returned and an Invalid Key condition exists. You may code the Invalid Key clause
on a Delete statement if the access mode of the file against which the Delete is being
processed is Random or Dynamic.

Some programmers fall into the trap of thinking that they can Delete
records via the Alternate Key. They fill in the Alternate Key information
and then issue the Delete statement. This technique does not work. The
Delete statement applies only to the record identified by the primary Key of
the data file from which it is to be deleted.

Issuing a Delete statement does not disturb the file positioning if you are reading
sequentially through an Indexed file. The next Read follows the previously issued Read
statement.

Relative Files

Relative files are cousins to Indexed files. Relative files behave like Indexed files except the Primary Key for the file is not part of the data record and there are no Alternate keys. Relative files are keyed by a Relative record number. The first record in a Relative file is record 1. A Relative file is like a giant array against which you may perform Indexed file-type operations. The Select statement for the Relative file defines its Organization and tells the program the name of the data field in Working-Storage that contains the record number that is the Key for the file.

```
Select Rel-File Assign To "Relative.Dat"
               Organization Relative
               Access Dynamic
               Relative Key Is Rel-Work-Num
               File Status Rel-Status.
```

The field that defines the Key is specified with the Relative Key clause, not the Record Key clause as was the case for an Indexed file. The Relative Key can be any unsigned integer data item.

When using Sequential access for a Relative file and writing records, the Key of the record just written is stored in the field identified in the Select statement as the Relative Key. You must take care to make your Relative Key field large enough to handle the greatest number of records you expect to have in the file. If the field is too small and you attempt to Write a record whose Key value exceeds the maximum for the file, an Invalid Key condition occurs and the File Status is set to 24.

When reading a Relative file with Sequential access, the Relative Key of the record just read is stored in the Relative Key field. If the Key for the last record read exceeds the maximum value that your field can hold, an At End condition occurs and the File Status value is set to 14.

The short program in Listing 16.1 illustrates Relative files and their use.

LISTING 16.1 RELATIVE FILE ACCESS EXAMPLE

```
000001 @OPTIONS MAIN,TEST
000002 Identification Division.
000003 Program-Id.  Chapt16a.
000004* Relative File Access Example
000005 Environment Division.
000006 Configuration Section.
000007 Special-Names.
000008      Crt Status Is Keyboard-Status
```

continues

LISTING 16.1 CONTINUED

```
000009        Cursor Is Cursor-Position.
000010 Source-Computer.  IBM-PC.
000011 Object-Computer.  IBM-PC.
000012 Input-Output Section.
```

Because the file is assigned using Optional, it will be created if it does not exist. Notice the use of Organization Relative and the Relative Key clause. Note also that Relative-Key is not a field in the data record. There is nothing special about the name Relative-Key. It was chosen because the name describes the field's purpose. You could easily name the field, Record-Number, Relative-Record-Number, or Field-A.

```
000014        Select Optional Relative-File Assign To "Relative.Dat"
000015            Organization Relative
000016            Access Dynamic
000017            Relative Key Relative-Key
000018            File Status Relative-Status.
000019 Data Division.
000020 File Section.
000021 Fd  Relative-File.
000022 01  Relative-Record.
000023      03  Relative-Data Pic X(20).
```

Relative-Key is defined in Working-Storage as a two-character unsigned numeric field. Because the size is limited to two digits, the maximum Relative Key the file can have is 99.

```
000024 Working-Storage Section.
000025 01  Relative-Key   Pic 99 Value Zeros.
000026 01  Relative-Status    Pic X(2) Value Spaces.
000027      88  Relative-Success Value "00" Thru "09".
000028 01  Keyboard-Status.
000029      03  Accept-Status Pic 9.
000030      03  Function-Key  Pic X.
000031          88  F1-Pressed Value X"01".
000032          88  F2-Pressed Value X"02".
000033          88  F3-Pressed Value X"03".
000034          88  F4-Pressed Value X"04".
000035          88  F5-Pressed Value X"05".
000036          88  F6-Pressed Value X"06".
000037          88  F7-Pressed Value X"07".
000038          88  F8-Pressed Value X"08".
000039      03  System-Use    Pic X.
000040 01  Cursor-Position.
000041      03  Cursor-Row    Pic 9(2) Value 1.
000042      03  Cursor-Column Pic 9(2) Value 1.
000043 01  Error-Message Pic X(50) Value Spaces.
```

The following table creates the initial Relative file if the program detects that no such
file exists.

```
000044 01  Table-Area.
000045     03  Table-Values.
000046         05  Filler Pic X(20) Value "Entry 1".
000047         05  Filler Pic X(20) Value "Entry 2".
000048         05  Filler Pic X(20) Value "Entry 3".
000049         05  Filler Pic X(20) Value "Entry 4".
000050         05  Filler Pic X(20) Value "Entry 5".
000051         05  Filler Pic X(20) Value "Entry 6".
000052         05  Filler Pic X(20) Value "Entry 7".
000053         05  Filler Pic X(20) Value "Entry 8".
000054         05  Filler Pic X(20) Value "Entry 9".
000055         05  Filler Pic X(20) Value "Entry 10".
000056     03  Load-Table Redefines Table-Values.
000057         05  Basic-Table Pic X(20) Occurs 10 Times.
000058 Screen Section.
000059 01  Data-Entry-Screen
000060     Blank Screen, Auto
000061     Foreground-Color Is 7,
000062     Background-Color Is 1.
000063*
000064     03  Screen-Literal-Group.
000065         05  Line 01 Column 25 Value "Relative File Example"
000066             Highlight Foreground-Color 4 Background-Color 1.
000067         05  Line 4  Column 01  Value "Current Relative Key: ".
000068         05  Line 5  Column 01  Value "Relative Data: ".
000069         05  Line 22 Column 01  Value "F1-Read Random Number".
000070         05  Line 22 Column 23  Value "F2-Start Number".
000071         05  Line 22 Column 56  Value "F3-Read Next Number".
000072         05  Line 23 Column 01  Value "F4-Delete Record".
000073         05  Line 23 Column 23  Value "F5-Write Record".
000074         05  Line 23 Column 56  Value "F6-Rewrite Record".
000075         05  Line 24 Column 01  Value "F7-Clear".
000076         05  Line 24 Column 23  Value "F8-Exit".
000077     03  Required-Reverse-Group Reverse-Video.
000078         05  Line 4 Column 23  Pic 9(2)  Using Relative-Key.
000079         05  Line 5 Column 16  Pic X(25) Using Relative-Data.
000080         05  Line 20 Column 01 Pic X(50) From  Error-Message.
000081*
000082 Procedure Division.
```

The Invalid Key clause captures errors whose status value begins with a 2.
Declaratives are coded to capture any other errors that might occur, such as attempting
a sequential Read after the end of file is reached.

```
000083 Declaratives.
000084 Relative-File-Error Section.
000085     Use After Standard Error Procedure On Relative-File
000086        .
```

```
000087 Relative-Error.
000088     String "Error on Relative.Dat "
000089           Relative-Status
000090           Delimited By Size
000091           Into Error-Message
000092     End-String
000093     .
000094 End Declaratives.
```

This next segment of code performs the Open of the file and, if it is successful, continues to the processing loop, where the user interacts with the program.

```
000095 Chapt16a-Start.
000096     Perform Open-File
000097     If Not Relative-Success
000098         String "Error Opening Relative File "
000099               Relative-Status
000100               Delimited By Size
000101               Into Error-Message
000102         End-String
000103         Move Spaces To Relative-Data
000104         Perform Display-And-Accept
000105     Else
000106         Move Spaces To Relative-Data
000107         Perform Process-File Until F8-Pressed
000108         Perform Close-File
000109     End-If
000110     Stop Run
000111     .
```

The processing loop continues to execute until the user presses the F8 key. Each time through the loop, the key pressed is tested and the appropriate action is performed.

```
000112 Process-File.
000113     Perform Display-And-Accept
000114     Evaluate True
000115       When F1-Pressed
000116           Perform Read-Random-Number
000117       When F2-Pressed
000118           Perform Start-Number
000119       When F3-Pressed
000120           Perform Read-Next-Number
000121       When F4-Pressed
000122           Perform Delete-Number
000123       When F5-Pressed
000124           Perform Write-Record
000125       When F6-Pressed
000126           Perform Rewrite-Record
000127       When F7-Pressed
000128           Perform Clear-Screen
000129       When F8-Pressed
```

```
000130              Continue
000131       When Other
000132              Continue
000133       End-Evaluate
000134       .
```

The `Read-Random-Number` paragraph performs a random `Read` against the `Relative` file.
You can tell that this is a random `Read` and not a sequential `Read` because there is no
`Next`. The record whose `Relative` record number matches that of the `Relative-Key` field
is returned.

```
000135 Read-Random-Number.
000136       Read Relative-File
000137         Invalid Key
000138           String "Error on Random Read Number "
000139                   Relative-Status
000140                   Delimited By Size
000141                   Into Error-Message
000142       End-Read
000143       .
```

As with an `Indexed` file, the `Start` statement positions the file for the next `Read`. `Start`,
`Read`, `Write`, `Rewrite`, and `Delete` can be used in this program because `Dynamic` access
was specified on the `Select` statement. What do you think would happen if you tried to
`Start` the file with this `Start` statement and a `Relative Key` value of zeros? That `Key`
value can't exist in a `Relative` data file. The program will try to position the file on this
`Key` value but it will fail. An `Invalid Key` condition will exist with a `File Status` value
of 23.

```
000144 Start-Number.
000145       Start Relative-File Key = Relative-Key
000146         Invalid Key
000147           String "Start Error Number "
000148                   Relative-Status
000149                   Delimited By Size
000150                   Into Error-Message
000151         Not Invalid Key
000152           String "Start Successful "
000153                   Relative-Status
000154                   Delimited By Size
000155                   Into Error-Message
000156       End-Start
000157       .
```

The `Read` statement with `Next` returns the next record in the file. If you just did the `Start` as
coded in this program, the record specified by that `Start` is returned, not the one after it as
you might expect. Remember that `Start` only positions the file and does not return a record.

```
000158 Read-Next-Number.
000159     Read Relative-File Next
000160         At End
000161             Move "End of File " To Error-Message
000162     End-Read
000163         .
```

Delete removes the Relative record whose Relative record number is set in the Relative-Key field. Be aware that if the fifth record of the file is deleted in this method, the sixth record does *not* become the fifth, and so on. The result is a *missing* record in the Relative file. If you try to do a random Read, Delete, or Rewrite on this record now, you receive a File Status 23. If you Write the record again, it is created in its previous physical location in the file.

```
000164 Delete-Number.
000165     Delete Relative-File
000166     Invalid Key
000167         String "Delete Error "
000168                Relative-Status
000169                Delimited By Size
000170                Into Error-Message
000171     Not Invalid Key
000172         Move "Record Deleted" To Error-Message
000173         Perform Clear-Screen
000174     End-Delete
000175         .
```

The Write statement adds a record to the Relative file whose Relative record number is that of the Relative-Key field. Some performance issues are related to the use of Relative files. For example, if your Relative file contained records where the highest Relative record number was 50 and you wrote a record with Relative record number 1,000,050, the system would have to reserve the space for one million records between Relative record 50 and Relative record 1,000,050. This can take quite a long time.

If the record you are writing already exists, a File Status of 22 is returned and an Invalid Key condition exists.

```
000176 Write-Record.
000177     Write Relative-Record
000178     Invalid Key
000179         String "Write Error "
000180                Relative-Status
000181                Delimited By Size
000182                Into Error-Message
000183     Not Invalid Key
000184         Move "Write Successful"
000185                To Error-Message
000186     End-Write
000187         .
```

The Rewrite statement replaces the record whose Relative record number is the number in Relative-Key. If you attempt to Rewrite a Relative record number that does not exist, a File Status 23 is returned.

```
000188 Rewrite-Record.
000189     Rewrite Relative-Record
000190         Invalid Key
000191           String "Rewrite Error "
000192                  Relative-Status
000193                  Delimited By Size
000194                  Into Error-Message
000195         Not Invalid Key
000196           Move "Rewrite Successful"
000197              To Error-Message
000198     End-Rewrite
000199     .
```

The Clear-Screen and Display-And-Accept paragraphs help with the interface to the user. Clear-Screen is executed in two places: after the F7 key is pressed and during the process of creating the file so that the last Record Key is not left on the display.

```
000200 Clear-Screen.
000201     Initialize Relative-Record
000202     Move Zeros To Relative-Key
000203     Move 01 To Cursor-Row Cursor-Column
000204     .
000205 Display-And-Accept.
000206     Display Data-Entry-Screen
000207     Accept Data-Entry-Screen
000208     Move Spaces To Error-Message
000209     .
```

The Open statement opens the file for Input and Output. Because the file was made Optional, it is created the first time it is opened if it does not already exist. A File Status of 05 is returned, which tells the program to create some base records so that you don't have to. In this case, the program creates 10 records, using a table defined in Working-Storage.

```
000210 Open-File.
000211     Open I-O Relative-File
000212     If Relative-Status = "05"
000213        Perform Create-Base-File Varying Relative-Key
000214                            From 1 By 1
000215                            Until Relative-Key  > 10  Or
000216                            Not Relative-Success
000217        Perform Clear-Screen
000218     End-If
000219     .
```

The Create-Base-File paragraph creates 10 records in the Relative file. This step gives you a simple file to work with when you run the program.

```
000220 Create-Base-File.
000221     Write Relative-Record From Basic-Table (Relative-Key)
000222        Invalid Key
000223          String "Creation Write Error "
000224                 Relative-Status
000225                 Delimited By Size
000226                 Into Error-Message
000227          Perform Display-And-Accept
000228     End-Write
000229        .
```

The Close is coded to release the file to the operating system.

```
000230 Close-File.
000231     Close Relative-File
000232        .
```

Enter, compile, link, and try running this program. As you run the program, scroll forward through the file until you reach the end. Then press the F3 key again to Read another record. Notice that File Status 46 is returned. This status value means that a sequential Read was attempted, but no next record is established—the end of the file has been reached! If Declaratives are not coded to capture this error, you might not know about it.

Experiment with deleting different Relative record numbers and adding new ones. Try deleting a record and then writing a new record to the same Relative Key. Try starting on a Relative record number that you have deleted. Experiment with the different things you can do and observe the results. Do things happen the way you expect? If not, why not? If necessary, follow the program with the debugger and observe what is happening inside the program.

Summary

In this hour, you learned the following:

- You may update an Indexed file by opening the file I-O or Extend. Opening Extend limits you to adding new records. To update existing records, you must Open the file I-O.

- When using Sequential access, you can Rewrite or Delete a record only when the last operation for the file is a successful Read statement.

- When using Dynamic or Random access, you can Delete or Rewrite a record without first reading it. You must use caution when performing a Rewrite in this manner so as not to erase information in the record that you want to keep.

- `Write` statements return a `File Status 22` if a record already exists in the file with the same primary `Key` or `Alternate Key` that does not allow duplicates.
- If a `Rewrite` or `Delete` is executed for a record that does not exist, a `File Status` of `23` is returned.
- Unlike `Write` and `Rewrite`, the `Delete` statement is coded with the filename, not the record description name, as the identifier for the operation.
- `Relative` files are similar to `Indexed` files. The difference is that the `Key` is always a `Relative` record number, and the field that contains this number is not a part of the data record. The `Key` field is identified in the `Select` statement as a `Relative Key` instead of a `Record Key`.
- Deleting `Relative` records does not cause the remaining records to be renumbered. Instead, the location where that record was located is cleared, and another record with the same `Relative` record number may be written in that place.
- `Declaratives` can be useful for capturing file errors that are missed by the coding of the `Invalid Key` or `At End` condition.

Q&A

Q When I want to update an `Indexed` file, can I `Open` it with `Sequential` access, or must I `Open` it with `Random` or `Dynamic`?

A You may `Open` the file with `Sequential` access. Depending on the updates being applied, `Sequential` may be the most efficient access method. You have to remember that you cannot perform random reads when the file is `Open` with `Sequential` access. Records may be rewritten only after a successful `Read`.

Q I understand `Relative` files, but I can't think of a good use for them. Can you give me some examples?

A You can use a `Relative` file as an alternative to a table when you don't know the number of records that will be in the table. This use is not always very efficient as far as access time goes, but is a viable solution. Obviously, you will have to code your own `Search` of the file, as you cannot use the `Search` verb against a `Relative` file. I have also used `Relative` files for storing `Key` values when paging through an `Indexed` file. This method allows me to display a page of data, saving the `Key` field for the first item on the screen in a `Relative` file. Then if the user wants to page backward or return to a specific page, I use the page number as the `Relative Key` to read the `Relative` file and find the `Indexed` file `Record Key` that last started that page.

Q Can I `Open` a regular `Record Sequential` file and address it as if it were a `Relative` file?

A You must be very careful because only a few compiler vendors allow this technique. Usually, some compiler-dependent internal record identifier is associated with a `Relative` file, and becomes part of the record. Opening a `Record Sequential` file as a `Relative` file can cause problems and will most likely result in a `File Status 39`.

Q When writing to a `Relative` file `Open` with `Sequential` access, I get a `File Status 24`. What does that mean?

A It means that your `Relative Record Key` field is too small. If it is defined as `Pic 9(2)` and you attempt to write the 100th record, you receive a `File Status 24`.

Q I know that my `Relative` file has more than 1,000 records, but I can only `Read` the first 999. Then I get an `At End` condition. How can this be?

A You must be accessing the file with `Sequential` access. Your `Relative Record Key` field is too small. When the maximum value it can hold is reached when reading a file, a status `14` is returned, which is a valid `At End` condition. Increase the size of your `Relative Record Key` field.

Workshop

To help reinforce your understanding of the material presented in this hour, refer to the section "Quiz and Exercise Questions and Answers" that can be found on the CD. This section contains quiz questions and exercises for you to complete, as well as the corresponding answers.

Hour 17

Sorting

One of the tasks frequently required in business is data file sorting. Reports are created from data files in different sequences, allowing business professionals to analyze information and make sound business decisions. Sorting data frequently occurs within the normal business process. In this hour, various aspects of sorting are covered, including topics such as

- The Sort Work File
- The Sort Key
- The Using and Giving clauses
- Preprocessing Input, using the Input Procedure
- Post-Sort processing, using the Output Procedure

Sometimes data is sorted prior to being loaded to an Indexed file. As you found out in Hour 14, "Indexed Files," you cannot Write records to an Indexed file Open for Output with Sequential access unless the data is in primary Key sequence. Sorting the data file can help in the quick creation of the Indexed file.

Data might also be sorted for update purposes. When updating a master file, you might collect transactional data from many sources. This data is then sorted in the same sequence as the master file that the data is updating. This process creates an orderly and fast update sequence. Within the transactions, you might want certain transactions to be applied before others. For example, you might want all ordering transactions for an item to be processed before any sales transactions. Sorting can ensure that the input data is in the proper sequence.

Sorting a File

COBOL provides very easy and efficient sorting methods. You need not write your own program to sort the data in the desired sequence. With a simple statement, COBOL allows you to sort a data file. You may even sort the data file in place. That is, you can take a file, sort it, and not create a separate output file.

Each sort in your program uses a Sort Work File, which contains the records as they are sorted by the system. You must declare these files in your program with a Select statement, like any other file. File organization and access modes are not specified for the file. However, you must select a unique filename.

In Fujitsu COBOL, Sort Work Files are not assigned to a physical file. The physical filename in the Sort Work File Assign statement is for internal purposes only. When the actual Sort Work File is created, Fujitsu creates it in the directory defined by your TEMP= environment variable. Other COBOL compilers may require you to specify a physical filename for the Sort Work File.

Your Sort Work File Select might look something like this:

```
000010      Select Sort-Work Assign to Symbolic-Sort-Name.
```

Symbolic-Sort-Name is not defined in your program. Fujitsu uses it to keep track of the file internally, but assigns its own temporary Sort Work File with a system-determined unique name.

In addition to the Select statement, a special File Section entry is required under the Data Division. This entry is the Sort Description, or SD. The SD is coded in exactly the same manner as an FD, but identifies the file as a Sort Work File to the system. A typical SD is coded as follows:

```
000020 SD  Sort-Work.
000021 01  Sort-Record.
000022     03  Sort-Field-1          Pic X(20).
```

```
000023      03  Sort-Field-2           Pic X(20).
000024      03  Filler                 Pic X(20).
```

As you can see, there is no special difference between an SD and an FD. The SD simply refers to the Sort Work File.

The Using and Giving Clauses

The simplest sort reads an input file, sorts the records, and creates an output file. The records in the three files have the same record layout. The following program sorts the Dealer.TXT file that you have used in previous examples. This Line Sequential file is now in dealer-number sequence, but the sort puts it in last name, first name, and middle name sequence. This sort sorts in place, meaning that it does not create a new file from Dealer.TXT, but rather replaces Dealer.TXT with a version of itself, sorted in a different sequence.

This work is accomplished by the Sort statement, with a Using and Giving clause. The Sort statement specifies the name of the Sort Work File, which is the file that is actually being sorted, and the data fields that are to be used as the Key fields for sorting. When sorting, any number of fields may be specified as Key fields—the fields that are used to control the Sort sequence. The order of the Sort is also specified. The Sort may be in Ascending or Descending sequence on the various Key data fields involved.

Using specifies the data file to be used as input into the Sort. Giving specifies the data file that is to be the output of the Sort. When utilizing the Sort statement, the input and output files cannot be Open by the program. The Sort will take care of all I-O against these files, including the Open, Close, Read, Write, and Close statements. Listing 17.1 is a simple program to sort the Dealer.TXT file in the manner described.

The first part of the program is the normal housekeeping and the Select for the input file for the sort.

LISTING 17.1 SIMPLE SORT EXAMPLE

```
000001 @OPTIONS MAIN,TEST
000002 Identification Division.
000003 Program-Id.   Chapt17a.
000004* Simple Sort Example
000005 Environment Division.
000006 Configuration Section.
000007 Source-Computer.   IBM-PC.
000008 Object-Computer.   IBM-PC.
000009 Input-Output Section.
```

continues

LISTING 17.1   CONTINUED

```
000010 File-Control.
000011     Select Dealer-Text Assign To "Dealer.TXT"
000012           Organization Line Sequential
000013           Access Sequential.
```

The next Select is for the Sort Work File. The name chosen, Sort-Work, is not significant. Any valid filename will work as well. Sort-Work is descriptive, and it is a good
programming practice to name your files as descriptively as possible. Note that the physical filename that the Sort Work File is assigned to is not enclosed in quotation marks.
It is not a physical name, but rather is a symbolic name used internally by the compiler.

```
000014     Select Sort-Work Assign To Dealer-Sort-Work.
```

The FD for the input file is the regular, normal FD.

```
000015 Data Division.
000016 File Section.
000017 Fd  Dealer-Text.
000018 01  Dealer-Record.
000019     03  Dealer-Number        Pic X(8).
000020     03  Dealer-Name.
000021         05  Last-Name   Pic X(25).
000022         05  First-Name  Pic X(15).
000023         05  Middle-Name Pic X(10).
000024     03  Address-Line-1       Pic X(50).
000025     03  Address-Line-2       Pic X(50).
000026     03  City                 Pic X(40).
000027     03  State-Or-Country     Pic X(20).
000028     03  Postal-Code          Pic X(15).
000029     03  Home-Phone           Pic X(20).
000030     03  Work-Phone           Pic X(20).
000031     03  Other-Phone          Pic X(20).
000032     03  Start-Date           Pic 9(8).
000033     03  Last-Rent-Paid-Date  Pic 9(8).
000034     03  Next-Rent-Due-Date   Pic 9(8).
000035     03  Rent-Amount          Pic 9(4)v99.
000036     03  Consignment-Percent  Pic 9(3).
000037     03  Last-Sold-Amount     Pic S9(7)v99.
000038     03  Last-Sold-Date       Pic 9(8).
000039     03  Sold-To-Date         Pic S9(7)v99.
000040     03  Commission-To-Date   Pic S9(7)v99.
000041     03  Filler               Pic X(15).
```

The SD describes the Sort Work File record. For convenience, the same record layout as
the input file has been used.

```
000042 Sd  Sort-Work.
000043 01  Sort-Record.
```

```
000044        03   Dealer-Number          Pic X(8).
000045        03   Dealer-Name.
000046             05   Last-Name    Pic X(25).
000047             05   First-Name   Pic X(15).
000048             05   Middle-Name  Pic X(10).
000049        03   Address-Line-1        Pic X(50).
000050        03   Address-Line-2        Pic X(50).
000051        03   City                  Pic X(40).
000052        03   State-Or-Country      Pic X(20).
000053        03   Postal-Code           Pic X(15).
000054        03   Home-Phone            Pic X(20).
000055        03   Work-Phone            Pic X(20).
000056        03   Other-Phone           Pic X(20).
000057        03   Start-Date            Pic 9(8).
000058        03   Last-Rent-Paid-Date Pic 9(8).
000059        03   Next-Rent-Due-Date  Pic 9(8).
000060        03   Rent-Amount           Pic 9(4)v99.
000061        03   Consignment-Percent Pic 9(3).
000062        03   Last-Sold-Amount    Pic S9(7)v99.
000063        03   Last-Sold-Date        Pic 9(8).
000064        03   Sold-To-Date          Pic S9(7)v99.
000065        03   Commission-To-Date  Pic S9(7)v99.
000066        03   Filler                Pic X(15).
000067 Working-Storage Section.
000068 Procedure Division.
000069 Chapt17a-Start.
```

The Sort statement is very simply stated. The filename specified after Sort is always the Sort Work File and must be described with an SD entry in the File Section. The fields you wish to sort on are specified after either Ascending or Descending Key, depending on whether you want to have the fields sorted from lowest value to highest or from highest to lowest.

The Using clause specifies the input file to be used by the Sort. Giving specifies the file that is to be created by the Sort. The files specified with Using and Giving can be the same.

```
000070        Sort Sort-Work Ascending Key Last-Name Of Sort-Record
000071                                      First-Name Of Sort-Record
000072                                      Middle-Name Of Sort-Record
000073             Using Dealer-Text
000074             Giving Dealer-Text
000075        Display "Sort Complete"
000076        Stop Run
000077             .
```

Notice that the program had no Open, Close, Read or Write statements. The Sort performs all of these operations automatically. Sorting files in COBOL is extremely simple!

Enter, compile, and run this program. Use a text editor, such as Notepad or WordPad to edit the Dealer.TXT file after running the program. Notice the sort sequence of the data file.

Change the program to sort the file in Descending Key sequence instead of Ascending Key sequence. The Sort statement is the only one that needs to change:

```
000070     Sort Sort-Work Descending Key Last-Name Of Sort-Record
000071                                    First-Name Of Sort-Record
000072                                    Middle-Name Of Sort-Record
```

Compile the program with the changes and run it again. Edit the output with WordPad again and notice how the sort sequence changes.

The Sort statement can sort using complex combinations of Ascending and Descending Key fields. For example, you can sort the dealer file Descending by state and the names Ascending under state.

```
000070     Sort Sort-Work Descending Key State-Or-Country Of Sort-Record
000071                     Ascending  Key Last-Name Of Sort-Record
000072                                    First-Name Of Sort-Record
000073                                    Middle-Name Of Sort-Record
```

The input and output files from a sort need not be the same file type. In Hour 14, an Indexed file was created from the Line Sequential file Dealers.TXT. You used a regular COBOL program to handle the Open, Read, Write, and Close statements. This same task can be accomplished with a Sort. You simply need to specify the Indexed file as the output in the Giving clause of the Sort statement.

> When an Indexed file is specified in the Giving clause of a Sort statement, the Sort Key must be the same as the Primary Key of the Indexed file. In addition, the SD must match the FD for record size and the location and length of the Primary Key field.

Listing 17.2 creates the Indexed Dealer.Dat file from the Line Sequential Dealer.TXT file, using a Sort.

LISTING 17.2 CREATE AN INDEXED FILE FROM A SEQUENTIAL FILE USING SORT

```
000001 @OPTIONS MAIN,TEST
000002 Identification Division.
000003 Program-Id.  Chapt17d.
000004* Create An Indexed File From A Sequential File Using Sort
000005 Environment Division.
```

```
000006 Configuration Section.
000007 Source-Computer.   IBM-PC.
000008 Object-Computer.   IBM-PC.
000009 Input-Output Section.
000010 File-Control.
```

The Select statements are provided for all three files: the Line Sequential input file, the Indexed output file, and the Sort Work File.

```
000011      Select Dealer-Text Assign To "Dealer.TXT"
000012             Organization Line Sequential
000013             Access Sequential.
000014      Select Dealer-File Assign To "Dealer.Dat"
000015             Organization Is Indexed
000016             Record Key Dealer-Number Of Dealer-Record
000017             Alternate Key Dealer-Name Of Dealer-Record
000018             Access Is Sequential.
000019      Select Sort-Work Assign To Dealer-Sort-Work.
```

The File Section of the Data Division contains the FD and SD, File and Sort Definitions. Notice that the record layouts have been simplified to contain only the essential data to complete the desired Sort operation.

```
000020 Data Division.
000020 Data Division.
000021 File Section.
000022 Fd  Dealer-File.
000023 01  Dealer-Record.
000024      03  Dealer-Number       Pic X(8).
000025      03  Dealer-Name.
000026          05  Last-Name   Pic X(25).
000027          05  First-Name  Pic X(15).
000028          05  Middle-Name Pic X(10).
000029      03  Filler          Pic X(318).
000030 Fd  Dealer-Text.
000031 01  Text-Record         Pic X(376).
000032 Sd  Sort-Work.
000033 01  Sort-Record.
000034      03  Dealer-Number       Pic X(8).
000035      03  Dealer-Name.
000036          05  Last-Name   Pic X(25).
000037          05  First-Name  Pic X(15).
000038          05  Middle-Name Pic X(10).
000039      03  Filler          Pic X(318).
000040 Working-Storage Section.
000041 Procedure Division.
000042 Chapt17d-Start.
```

The Sort statement is coded so that the Sort Key fields and sequence match the Sort Key of the output file. If they do not, the compiler issues a warning and the program does not compile.

```
000043        Sort Sort-Work Ascending Key Dealer-Number Of Sort-Record
000044            Using Dealer-Text
000045            Giving Dealer-File
000046        Display "Sort Complete"
000047        Stop Run
000048            .
```

If you compile and run this program, it creates a new Dealer.Dat file from the `Line Sequential` file Dealer.TXT. This method of creating the `Indexed` file, unlike the version from Hour 14, is not sensitive to the order of the data in the input file. The `Sort` statement takes care of that problem and creates the `Indexed` file in the proper sequence.

Manipulating Data During the `Sort`

In addition to the simple sorts discussed in the previous section, COBOL allows you to manipulate the data going into and coming out of the `Sort`. This feature allows a single program to read a data file, manipulate the data to a great degree, sort it, and produce output based on this data.

This diversity is handled by coding `Input` and `Output` procedures on the `Sort`. These procedures permit you to create a `Sort` file from various input sources—not just from a single input file. When utilizing the `Input` and `Output` procedure, the `Sort` file does not need to have the same record layout as the input file. The output file does not need to have the same layout as the `Sort` file. In fact, in some cases the output file is not created at all!

The `Input` `Procedure`

The `Input Procedure` allows you to restrict the records that are used in the `Sort`. When an `Input Procedure` is specified, you are responsible for the file handling necessary to build the `Sort` records. However, you do not code any `Open`, `Close`, or `Write` statements for the `Sort Work File`.

The `Input Procedure` specified is performed to create the `Sort` records, which are released to the `Sort`. The `Input Procedure` is performed only once for each `Sort` statement coded. You must handle the necessary processing loop. When the `Input Procedure` is complete, the `Sort Work File` is sorted in the sequence specified.

The statement that writes records to the `Sort Work File` is the `Release` statement, and its coding is similar to the `Write` statement. You may `Release` a `Sort` record by using the `From` clause to build the `Sort` record in `Working-Storage` if desired. As with the `Write` statement, the data in the record description area of the `Sort` record cannot be relied on after a `Release` statement is executed.

By using the Input Procedure, you can create a Sort Work File and output file such that the record layouts differ, unlike Using and Giving in which the record layouts had to be the same.

Listing 17.3 illustrates the use of an Input Procedure to select dealer records with a state of "CA" from the file. Only the name and address information is selected for the Sort Work File and output file.

LISTING 17.3 SORT EXAMPLE WITH AN INPUT PROCEDURE

```
000001 @OPTIONS MAIN,TEST
000002 Identification Division.
000003 Program-Id.  Chapt17e.
000004* Sort Example With An Input Procedure.
000005 Environment Division.
000006 Configuration Section.
000007 Source-Computer.  IBM-PC.
000008 Object-Computer.  IBM-PC.
000009 Input-Output Section.
```

Select statements are coded for all three files: the Indexed input file, Dealer.Dat; the output Line Sequential file, Address.TXT; and the Sort Work File.

```
000010 File-Control.
000011     Select Dealer-File Assign To "Dealer.Dat"
000012            Organization Indexed
000013            Record Key Dealer-Number Of Dealer-Record
000014            Alternate Record Key Dealer-Name Of Dealer-Record
000015            Access Sequential
000016            File Status Dealer-Status.
000017     Select Address-File Assign To "Address.Txt"
000018            Organization Line Sequential
000019            Access Sequential.
000020     Select Sort-Work Assign To Dealer-Sort-Work.
000021 Data Division.
000022 File Section.
```

Notice that the FD for the dealer file does not match the SD for the Sort Work File. The FD for the output file simply has the same number of characters reserved in the record as the Sort Work File. Because the Giving clause is being used to create the file, the individual fields that make up the record need not be defined.

```
000023 Fd  Dealer-File.
000024 01  Dealer-Record.
000025     03  Dealer-Number        Pic X(8).
000026     03  Dealer-Name.
000027         05  Last-Name    Pic X(25).
000028         05  First-Name   Pic X(15).
```

```
000029           05  Middle-Name Pic X(10).
000030      03  Address-Line-1      Pic X(50).
000031      03  Address-Line-2      Pic X(50).
000032      03  City                Pic X(40).
000033      03  State-Or-Country    Pic X(20).
000034      03  Postal-Code         Pic X(15).
000035      03  Home-Phone          Pic X(20).
000036      03  Work-Phone          Pic X(20).
000037      03  Other-Phone         Pic X(20).
000038      03  Start-Date          Pic 9(8).
000039      03  Last-Rent-Paid-Date Pic 9(8).
000040      03  Next-Rent-Due-Date  Pic 9(8).
000041      03  Rent-Amount         Pic 9(4)v99.
000042      03  Consignment-Percent Pic 9(3).
000043      03  Last-Sold-Amount    Pic S9(7)v99.
000044      03  Last-Sold-Date      Pic 9(8).
000045      03  Sold-To-Date        Pic S9(7)v99.
000046      03  Commission-To-Date  Pic S9(7)v99.
000047      03  Filler              Pic X(15).
000048 Sd  Sort-Work.
000049 01  Sort-Record.
000050      03  Dealer-Name.
000051           05  Last-Name   Pic X(25).
000052           05  First-Name  Pic X(15).
000053           05  Middle-Name Pic X(10).
000054      03  Address-Line-1      Pic X(50).
000055      03  Address-Line-2      Pic X(50).
000056      03  City                Pic X(40).
000057      03  State-Or-Country    Pic X(20).
000058      03  Postal-Code         Pic X(15).
000059 Fd  Address-File.
000060 01  Address-Record          Pic X(225).
```

The File Status field and other necessary fields are coded in Working-Storage.

```
000061 Working-Storage Section.
000062 01  Done-Flag   Pic X Value Spaces.
000063      88  All-Done      Value "Y".
000064 01  Dealer-Status Pic XX Value "00".
000065 Procedure Division.
```

Declaratives capture any unexpected file errors on the input file. Although none are expected, it is a good practice to code for them. The All-Done flag is Set to true if any errors are encountered. This flag status terminates the Input Procedure loop coded later in the program.

```
000066 Declaratives.
000067 Dealer-File-Error Section.
000068     Use After Standard Error Procedure On Dealer-File.
000069 Dealer-Error.
000070     Display "Unhandled error on Dealer File " Dealer-Status
```

```
000071      Set All-Done To True
000072         .
000073 End Declaratives.
000074 Chapt17e-Start.
```

The Sort statement sorts the Sort Work File based on the last, first, and middle names.
Because the file was organized to appear in this sequence with a Group Level item, you
could change the Sort Key to Dealer-Name Of Sort-Record and achieve the same
result. The statement as coded is a little more explicit, however.

The Input Procedure name is not significant. You may call it anything that you desire.
One common mistake is to assume that the Input Procedure will be executed repeatedly until the input file has been read. In fact, the Input Procedure is performed only
once.

```
000075      Sort Sort-Work Ascending  Key Last-Name Of Sort-Record
000076                                     First-Name Of Sort-Record
000077                                     Middle-Name Of Sort-Record
000078          Input Procedure Sort-In
000079          Giving Address-File
000080      Display "Sort Complete"
000081      Stop Run
000082         .
```

The Input Procedure, Sort-In, handles the Open, Read, and Close statements of the
input file. Notice that if the state is not "CA", the Sort record is not released, which limits the Sort to records where the state is "CA". Using an Input Procedure to select the
desired records can speed processing of large volumes of data.

By using the same field names in the Dealer-Record and Sort-Record, you are able to
utilize Move with Corresponding. Notice that more fields are defined in the Dealer-
Record than in Sort-Record, yet Move with Corresponding correctly moves only those
fields where the field names match.

Note the Close of the input file after processing is complete. No Open or Close statements are coded for the Sort Work File. The only operation relating to the Sort Work
File releases the record to the Sort.

```
000083 Sort-In.
000084      Open Input Dealer-File
000085      Perform Until All-Done
000086          Read Dealer-File
000087              At End Set All-Done To True
000088              Not At End
000089              If State-Or-Country Of Dealer-Record = "CA"
000090                  Move Corresponding Dealer-Record To Sort-Record
000091                  Release Sort-Record
000092              End-If
```

```
000093          End-Read
000094          End-Perform
000095          Close Dealer-File
000096             .
```

The Output Procedure

The Input Procedure processed data before the Sort. If you want to process data after
the Sort, you may code an Output Procedure with your Sort statement. The Output
Procedure is responsible for all necessary file access. The Output Procedure is frequently used to create a printed report after input data is sorted. The Output Procedure
does not necessarily have to create a sorted output file.

Like the Input Procedure, the Output Procedure is performed only once. It is executed
immediately after the Sort Work File is sorted into the desired sequence. You are
responsible for coding the processing loop necessary for the Output Procedure to work
properly.

In the Output Procedure, you may Read records from the Sort Work File. You do not
code normal Open, Read, or Close statements. The Sort positions the file properly and
handles any necessary internal Open and Close operations. The Return statement
retrieves records from the sorted Sort Work File. Return behaves the same as a
Sequential Read. You must code an At End clause to detect the end of file. You may
Return the record into another data area, just as you can with Read, by using Return
with an Into clause.

In Hour 16, "Updating Indexed File Records," the exercise was to modify the record
layout of the dealer file to add four fields: Last-Sold-Amount, Last-Sold-Date,
Sold-To-Date and Commission-To-Date. These fields were to be initialized to zeros.
Running the program in Listing 17.2 (Chap17d) that creates the Indexed Dealer.Dat file
erases that file and eliminates the work you did zeroing those fields. This happens
because the input text file does not include the new fields. You may run the program you
created again to fix the problem, or you may modify the Sort program to include an
Output Procedure that initializes these fields as they are written. The program in Listing
17.4 does just that, and counts the records returned from the Sort. This count is displayed after the Output Procedure is executed.

The program has all of the normal Select and File Section entries.

LISTING 17.4 SORT EXAMPLE WITH AN OUTPUT PROCEDURE

```
000001 @OPTIONS MAIN,TEST
000002 Identification Division.
000003 Program-Id.  Chapt17f.
000004* Sort Example With Output Procedure
000005 Environment Division.
000006 Configuration Section.
000007 Source-Computer.  IBM-PC.
000008 Object-Computer.  IBM-PC.
000009 Input-Output Section.
000010 File-Control.
000011     Select Dealer-Text Assign To "Dealer.TXT"
000012             Organization Line Sequential
000013             Access Sequential.
000014     Select Dealer-File Assign To "Dealer.Dat"
000015             Organization Is Indexed
000016             Record Key Dealer-Number Of Dealer-Record
000017             Alternate Key Dealer-Name Of Dealer-Record
000018             Access Is Sequential
000019             File Status Is Dealer-Status.
000020     Select Sort-Work Assign To Dealer-Sort-Work.
000021 Data Division.
000022 File Section.
000023 Fd  Dealer-File.
000024 01  Dealer-Record.
000025     03  Dealer-Number       Pic X(8).
000026     03  Dealer-Name.
000027         05  Last-Name   Pic X(25).
000028         05  First-Name  Pic X(15).
000029         05  Middle-Name Pic X(10).
000030     03  Address-Line-1      Pic X(50).
000031     03  Address-Line-2      Pic X(50).
000032     03  City                Pic X(40).
000033     03  State-Or-Country    Pic X(20).
000034     03  Postal-Code         Pic X(15).
000035     03  Home-Phone          Pic X(20).
000036     03  Work-Phone          Pic X(20).
000037     03  Other-Phone         Pic X(20).
000038     03  Start-Date          Pic 9(8).
000039     03  Last-Rent-Paid-Date Pic 9(8).
000040     03  Next-Rent-Due-Date  Pic 9(8).
000041     03  Rent-Amount         Pic 9(4)v99.
000042     03  Consignment-Percent Pic 9(3).
000043     03  Last-Sold-Amount    Pic S9(7)v99.
000044     03  Last-Sold-Date      Pic 9(8).
000045     03  Sold-To-Date        Pic S9(7)v99.
000046     03  Commission-To-Date  Pic S9(7)v99.
000047     03  Filler              Pic X(15).
```

17

continues

LISTING **17.4**   CONTINUED

```
000048 Fd  Dealer-Text.
000049 01  Text-Record          Pic X(376).
000050 Sd  Sort-Work.
000051 01  Sort-Record.
000052     03  Dealer-Number        Pic X(8).
000053     03  Dealer-Name.
000054         05  Last-Name   Pic X(25).
000055         05  First-Name  Pic X(15).
000056         05  Middle-Name Pic X(10).
000057     03  Filler          Pic X(318).
```

Working-Storage contains the flag used to control the processing loop of the Output
Procedure and a field for the record count from the Sort.

```
000058 Working-Storage Section.
000059 01  Record-Count     Pic 9(5) Value Zeros.
000060 01  Dealer-Status    Pic XX   Value "00".
000061 01  Done-Flag        Pic X    Value Spaces.
000062     88  All-Done               Value "Y".
```

Declaratives are coded to handle any errors that might occur when creating the
Indexed file. None are likely to occur; however, coding the Declaratives will make you
aware of any error conditions that occur.

```
000063 Procedure Division.
000064 Declaratives.
000065 Dealer-File-Error Section.
000066     Use After Standard Error Procedure On Dealer-File.
000067 Dealer-Error.
000068     Display "Unhandled error on Dealer File " Dealer-Status
000069     Set All-Done To True
000070     .
000071 End Declaratives.
```

This particular Sort does not require an Input Procedure. However, in COBOL you
may use an Input Procedure and an Output Procedure in the same Sort statement.

```
000072 Chapt17f-Start.
000073     Sort Sort-Work Ascending Key Dealer-Number Of Sort-Record
000074         Using Dealer-Text
000075         Output Procedure Sort-Out
000076     Display "Sort Complete with " Record-Count " Records."
000077     Stop Run
000078     .
```

The Output Procedure controls the creation of the Indexed Dealer-File. You are
responsible for coding all necessary Open, Write, and Close statements. The Return
statement, like Read, uses the name defined in the FD, not the record description, to

describe the data being returned. The At End clause handles the end-of-file processing. Regular record processing occurs after the Not At End clause. Notice the use of the End-Return explicit scope terminator.

```
000079 Sort-Out.
000080    Open Output Dealer-File
000081    Perform Until All-Done
000082       Return Sort-Work Into Dealer-Record
000083          At End Set All-Done To True
000084          Not At End
000085             Add 1 To Record-Count
000086             Move Zeros To Last-Sold-Amount
000087                            Last-Sold-Date
000088                            Sold-To-Date
000089                            Commission-To-Date
000090          Write Dealer-Record
000091       End-Return
000092    End-Perform
000093    Close Dealer-File
000094       .
```

In these Sort examples, the various record sizes and layouts of the input file, output file, and Sort Work File have been the same. However, when using Sort, you may use records of varying sizes. The only restriction is that no input record may be longer than the Sort work record, and if variable-length records are used, none may be shorter than the shortest allowed record in the Sort Work File. If you wanted to sort the dealer file into a text file and shorten the output record to not include some of the extra information at the end of the file, you could modify the FD on the output file to terminate after the last desired field.

When sorting a file, you may encounter duplicate Sort Keys. Duplicates are allowed and will cause no problems. The order of the records with the duplicate Key fields in the Sort file is undetermined. You can control the order, forcing the duplicates to appear in the same order as the input file, by adding the word Duplicates, which is short for Duplicates In Order, to the Sort statement.

```
000073    Sort Sort-Work Ascending Key Dealer-Number Of Sort-Record
000074          With Duplicates
000075          Using Dealer-Text
000076          Output Procedure Sort-Out
```

Summary

In this hour, you learned the following:

- Files can be sorted quickly and easily by using the Sort statement.
- The input file can be simply specified with a Using clause, and the output file with a Giving clause. No Open, Read, Write, or Close statements need to be coded for a simple sort that utilizes Using and Giving.
- Sort Work Files must have Select statements under File-Control and entries under the File Section. The entry under the File Section, however, is not the normal FD, but instead is an SD.
- You can use an Input Procedure to manipulate and select records for the Sort.
- When using an Input Procedure, you must handle the Open, Read, and Close statements associated with the input file or files.
- Records are written to the Sort Work File in the Input Procedure by coding the Release statement.
- Records can be returned directly from the Sort Work File by using an Output Procedure.
- The Output Procedure does not necessarily have to create a sorted output file. Any logic you desire may be executed in the Output Procedure.
- The Return statement can read sorted records from the Sort Work File.
- You can use any combination of Using, Giving, Input Procedure, and Output Procedure with a Sort statement.

Q&A

Q What happens to the Sort Work File when the Sort is finished?

A On most systems, the Sort Work File is automatically deleted after the processing associated with the Sort statement is complete.

Q I need to manipulate some fields for the Sort. Should I modify them in the Input Procedure or in the Output Procedure?

A If any of the fields you are modifying are used as Sort Keys, you should modify them in the Input Procedure. Remember that records are not sorted as they go into the Input Procedure, so modifying the Sort Key will not adversely affect the Sort.

Q **I noticed that in the examples, there were no performs outside of the Input and Output Procedures. Am I restricted in what may be performed?**

A Only slightly. You may not execute another Sort statement within an Input or Output Procedure. Also you may not execute a Return within an Input Procedure, and you may not execute a Release in an Output Procedure. Otherwise, you are free to code any kind of statements or logic you desire. Just remember that the Input and Output Procedures are performed only once per sort.

Q **I'm still a little unclear. Which file is actually sorted? Is it the input file?**

A No, it's not the input file. The Sort Work File is the one that is sorted, which explains why you can manipulate data before the sort, using an Input Procedure. Using a Sort Work File also ensures that records returned from the Sort in the Output Procedure are in sorted sequence.

17

Workshop

To help reinforce your understanding of the material presented in this hour, refer to the section "Quiz and Exercise Questions and Answers" that can be found on the CD. This section contains quiz questions and exercises for you to complete, as well as the corresponding answers.

PART III
Business Processing

Hour

18 Master File Updating

19 Reporting

20 Advanced Reporting

HOUR 18

Master File Updating

Much of business processing is centered on updating a central repository of information. Transactions that are captured from a variety of locations are accumulated and applied to a master file. A typical transaction in your little shop might be a sale transaction. You need to update the dealer master file with this sale to capture the commission that you are to collect for handling the sale. In this hour, you learn the basics of transaction entry and master file update. The following topics are covered:

- Collecting transactional data
- Data validation
- `Sequential` file updating
- `Indexed` file updating

Updating a master file requires you to collect transactional data that is as accurate as possible. There is an old saying in the computer industry: GIGO—Garbage In, Garbage Out. The programmer's job is to ensure that the transactional data is as accurate as it can be. Having accurate data can aid in making processing efficient and accurate.

```
000072                 Using Transaction-Date.
000073          05  Line 5 Column 16  Pic X(4)
000074                 Using Transaction-Type.
000075          05  Line 6 Column 16  Pic X(8)
000076                 Using Transaction-Dealer.
000077          05  Line 7 Column 16  Pic ZZ,ZZZ.99-
000078                 Using Transaction-Price
000079                 Blank When Zero.
000080          05  Line 8 Column 16  Pic ZZ9
000081                 Using Transaction-Qty
000082                 Blank When Zero.
000083       03  Highlight-Display Highlight.
000084          05  Line 20 Column 01 Pic X(50) From Error-Message
000085                 Foreground-Color 5 Background-Color 1.
```

After opening the transaction file, the processing loop is performed until the user exits by pressing F3 or a serious file error occurs.

```
000086 Procedure Division.
000087 Chapt18a-Start.
000088     Perform Open-File
000089     If Not File-Error
000090         Initialize Trans-Record
000091         Perform Process-Input Until F3-Pressed Or
000092                                     File-Error
000093         Perform Close-File
000094     End-If
000095     Stop Run
000096     .
```

The Open with Extend allows the user to enter some data and then exit the program. When the user returns to the data entry task, the new transactions will be added to the end of the file. By opening the file Extend instead of Output, you prevent the previously entered transactions from being lost.

```
000097 Open-File.
000098     Open Extend Trans-File
000099     If Not Trans-File-Success
000100         Move Trans-File-Status To Open-Status
000101         Move Open-Error-Message To Error-Message
000102         Perform Display-And-Accept-Error
000103     End-If
000104     .
```

The Process-Input Paragraph displays the screen and accepts the user input. It then determines the appropriate action based on the key that is pressed. The Continue statement after the F3 lets the program fall through the end of the Evaluate and thus the Paragraph. Because the Perform of this Paragraph is testing for F3, you do not need to Perform any action when F3 is pressed. You may omit checking for the F3 key, and the program will still function, as it will fall into the Other condition. However, accounting for all valid function keys is a good practice. This approach makes it much easier if you later need to add another function key. By accounting for each function key in the Evaluate, you can decide which one is still available for use.

```
000105 Process-Input.
000106     Display Data-Entry-Screen
000107     Accept Data-Entry-Screen
000108     Move Spaces To Error-Message
000109     Evaluate True
000110        When F1-Pressed
000111            Perform Write-Record
000112        When F4-Pressed
000113            Initialize Trans-Record
000114        When F3-Pressed
000115            Continue
000116        When Other
000117            Continue
000118     End-Evaluate
000119     .
```

After a successful Write, the record is cleared so that no leftover data remains on the screen. The error message on the screen is updated to indicate a successful record Write, and the cursor is positioned for the next record entry.

```
000120 Write-Record.
000121     Write Trans-Record
000122     If Trans-File-Success
000123         Initialize Trans-Record
000124         Move "Record Written" To Error-Message
000125         Move "0101" To Cursor-Position
000126     Else
000127         Move Trans-File-Status To Write-Status
000128         Move Write-Error-Message To Error-Message
000129         Perform Display-And-Accept-Error
000130     End-If
000131     .
```

The Display-And-Accept-Error Paragraph is used whenever a serious error should terminate processing. What the user keys to terminate the Accept does not matter, as the program will end shortly after executing this paragraph. The File-Error condition is checked in determining when the processing loop should end.

```
000132 Display-And-Accept-Error.
000133     Set File-Error To True
000134     Display Data-Entry-Screen
000135     Accept Data-Entry-Screen
000136     .
000137 Close-File.
000138     Close Trans-File
000139     .
```

18

Data Validation

This program, as written, has some problems. Although it allows the user to enter the required data to create a transaction file that can be used for update, there is a lot of room for input error.

The program will Accept dates that may or may not be dates. The user may key any number he or she desires into the date field. The dealer number is not converted to upper-case, although the dealer numbers are all in uppercase letters with numbers. The user may enter any dealer number he or she can imagine, and there is no assurance that the dealer being entered is in the dealer file.

The category is not checked for validity, nor is it converted to uppercase. All of these fields are in need of some type of data validation.

Data validation is what the programmer, and thus the program, does to ensure that the data being entered is as valid and accurate as possible. You can do several things to this program to ensure that the user enters accurate data.

Although the date entered should be checked for validity, you are not checking it in this program. Date validation will be covered in Hour 21, "Date Manipulation."

I suggest that you code a data validation paragraph after the Accept and before the Write. You should not Write the data record unless it passes all data validations.

Add the following flag field to Working-Storage:

```
000040 01  Validate-Flag          Pic X Value Spaces.
000041     88  Validation-Passed  Value "Y".
```

Then change the Evaluate statement where the save record key is detected to Perform a data validation paragraph and check the status of that validation before carrying out the record Write.

```
000104     Evaluate True
000105         When F1-Pressed
000106             Perform Validate-Data
000107             If Validation-Passed
000108                 Perform Write-Record
000109             End-If
000110         When F4-Pressed
000111             Initialize Trans-Record
000112         When F3-Pressed
000113             Continue
```

```
000114          When Other
000115             Continue
000116       End-Evaluate
```

The first thing you can do to help ensure accurate information is to convert the `Pic X`
fields to uppercase with an `Inspect` statement. However, the entire transaction record
does not need to be converted. Inspecting two fields means executing the `Inspect` twice,
which is wasteful. Instead, change the record description of the transaction file as follows. This code does not change the position or length of any data in the record. It does,
however, group the fields so that a single `Inspect` can convert them both to uppercase.

```
000020 01  Trans-Record.
000021     03  Transaction-Date   Pic  9(8).
000022     03  Transaction-Text.
000023         05  Transaction-Type   Pic  X(4).
000024         05  Transaction-Dealer Pic  X(8).
000025     03  Transaction-Price  Pic S9(7)V99.
000026     03  Transaction-Qty    Pic  9(3).
000027     03  Filler             Pic  X(40).
```

Now you may use the `Inspect` instruction on the field `Transaction-Text` and convert
both fields to uppercase.

```
000119 Validate-Data.
000120     Inspect Transaction-Text Converting
000121            "abcdefghijklmnopqrstuvwxyz" To
000122            "ABCDEFGHIJKLMNOPQRSTUVWXYZ"
```

Now that the fields are uppercase, you can validate the category against a list of valid
categories. If the category entered is not on the list, you can issue a warning message to
the user and position the cursor on the field in error.

The starting assumption is that the data is valid. A flag is set if any invalid data is
encountered.

```
000124     Move "Y" to Validate-Flag
000125     If Not (Transaction-Type = "ANTI" Or "CRAF" Or "HOLI"Oor "JEWL"
000126            Or "MISC" Or "XMAS")
000127       Set Validation-Error To True
000128       Move "0516" to Cursor-Position
000129       Move
000130       "Invalid Category Must be ANTI CRAF HOLI JEWL MISC or XMAS"
000131       To Error-Message
000132     End-If
```

This simple validation prevents the user from accidentally entering garbage into the
transaction file.

18

Another field that can be validated is the dealer number. If a copy of the dealer master file exists on the computer where the data entry is being performed, you can check the dealer number against the dealer file by doing a Random Read on the dealer file.

First, add the Select and FD for the dealer file. Random access is used because you will be making a single keyed Read against the file for every dealer number entered.

```
000017      Select Dealer-File Assign to "Dealer.Dat"
000018             Organization Indexed
000019             Access Random
000020             Record Key Dealer-Number
000021             Alternate Record Key Dealer-Name
000022             File Status Dealer-Status.
```

For brevity, in this example the normal COBOL verbiage has been removed and only the relevant portions of the code are presented.

```
000034 FD  Dealer-File.
000035 01  Dealer-Record.
000036     03  Dealer-Number          Pic X(8).
000037     03  Dealer-Name.
000038         05  Last-Name    Pic X(25).
000039         05  First-Name   Pic X(15).
000040         05  Middle-Name  Pic X(10).
000041     03  Address-Line-1     Pic X(50).
000042     03  Address-Line-2     Pic X(50).
000043     03  City               Pic X(40).
000044     03  State-or-Country   Pic X(20).
000045     03  Postal-Code        Pic X(15).
000046     03  Home-Phone         Pic X(20).
000047     03  Work-Phone         Pic X(20).
000048     03  Other-Phone        Pic X(20).
000049     03  Start-Date         Pic 9(8).
000050     03  Last-Rent-Paid-Date Pic 9(8).
000051     03  Next-Rent-Due-Date  Pic 9(8).
000052     03  Rent-Amount        Pic 9(4)V99.
000053     03  Consignment-Percent Pic 9(3).
000054     03  Last-Sold-Amount   Pic S9(7)V99.
000055     03  Last-Sold-Date     Pic 9(8).
000056     03  Sold-to-Date       Pic S9(7)V99.
000057     03  Commission-to-Date Pic S9(7)V99.
000058     03  Filler             Pic X(15).
```

Several fields must be added to Working-Storage to handle the file.

```
000077 01  Dealer-Status     Pic X(2) Value Spaces.
000078     88  Dealer-Success Value "00" Thru "09".
```

```
000083 01  Dealer-Open-Error-Message.
000084     03  Filler          Pic X(31) Value "Error Opening Dealer File ".
000085     03  Open-Dealer-Status   Pic XX     Value Spaces.
```

Add the statements necessary to handle opening the file at the beginning of the program and closing the file at the end. There is no need to Open the file if the transaction file Open fails.

```
000121     Perform Open-File
000122     If Not File-Error
000123         Perform Open-Dealer-File
000124     End-If
```

The paragraph that opens the dealer file is coded as follows:

```
000142 Open-Dealer-File.
000143     Open Input Dealer-File
000144     If Not Dealer-Success
000145         Move Dealer-Status To Open-Dealer-Status
000146         Move Dealer-Open-Error-Message To Error-Message
000147         Perform Display-And-Accept-Error
000148     End-if
000149     .
```

Don't forget to close the file at the end of the program.

```
000129     Perform Close-File
000130     Perform Close-Dealer-File
```

Now that you have access to the file, you need to code the logic necessary in the validation paragraph.

```
000181     Move Transaction-Dealer To Dealer-Number
000182     Read Dealer-File
000183         Invalid Key
000184             Set Validation-Error To True
000185             Move "0616" to Cursor-Position
000186             Move "Invalid Dealer Number Entered" To Error-Message
000187     End-Read
```

These validations greatly reduce the chance of erroneous data entering the system. Data validations such as these are very common in business systems.

Updating a Master File

The two common methods used to update master files with transaction data are Sequential update and Random update. Each style has advantages and disadvantages. The Sequential update is easy to recover from if an error occurs during the update process. The Random update can apply transactions in any order. These update styles are discussed in detail in the following two sections.

18

Every file update should include some type of control statistics, which you can use to find and correct any problems that occur with the update. In the following examples, the dealer master is updated with sales transactions. To save you time, a sample transaction file has been prepared for each update. The total number of transactions, the number of rejected transactions, and the commission amount are reported.

Updating a Sequential Master File

Updating a Sequential file involves several elements. The main advantage of such an update is that transactions are processed against a Sequential Input file, creating a new master file as Output. If something happens in the update process, the original Input master file is untouched. Sequential updates require every master file record to be read and then written to an Output master file. If you are dealing with many transactions, this approach makes sense. However, if only a single transaction exists, the entire Input master file must still be read and written. Additionally, in a multiuser or network environment, where multiple users might need access to the master file simultaneously, you must prohibit this access until the update process is complete.

When updating a Sequential file, master and transaction files must be in the same order. The files must be sorted by the field that identifies the master record to the transaction record. There might be multiple transactions for a single master record. The programmer must ensure that all transactions for a master record have been applied before the Output master file record is written and the next master file Input record is read.

The Sequential update proceeds as follows: A record is read from the transaction file and the master file. One of three things can be true. If the transaction key matches the master file key, then an update needs to be applied. If the transaction file key is less than the master file key, then no matching master file record exists and the transaction is rejected. If the transaction key is greater than the master file key, then no further transactions, if any, occur for that master record. It should be written to the Output master, and the next master record Read.

As records are read and processed, one of two things can happen. Either the end of the master file is reached before the end of the transaction file, or the end of the transaction file is reached before the end of the master file. When the end of the transaction file is reached, any remaining master file records can be written directly to the new master file. If the end of the master file is reached first, then any transactions remaining are rejected, as no more master file records are available for updating.

In this update, rejected transactions are saved to a file. When the problem with the transactions is corrected, then they can be applied in a later update. As a good programmer, you should never terminate an update process just because you don't know what to do.

Nothing short of a hardware failure should terminate your update. Writing the rejects to another file isolates the invalid transactions so that the problem can be researched and repaired. For these examples, the only error that rejects a transaction is when no matching master file record exists.

Walking through a Sequential update program is the best way to understand the process, as shown in Listing 18.2. The program starts as would any other COBOL program.

LISTING 18.2 SEQUENTIAL FILE UPDATE

```
000001 @OPTIONS MAIN,TEST
000002 Identification Division.
000003 Program-Id.  Chapt18c.
000004* Sequential File Update
000005 Environment Division.
000006 Configuration Section.
000007 Source-Computer.  IBM-PC.
000008 Object-Computer.  IBM-PC.
000009 Input-Output  Section.
```

The files used by the program are all Line Sequential files. By making the files Optional, you need not worry about any Open failures. If a file does not exist, it is created. The files Trans.Seq and Dealer.Seq are provided on the CD-ROM, and after you install the CD-ROM, they will exist in the \DATAFILE directory of your hard drive as well. Copy these files into the \TYCOBOL folder. These files are properly formatted and sorted in dealer number sequence. The transaction file contains numerous records, some duplicate dealer numbers, and some contain invalid data. The Dealer.Out file is the new master file, and Reject.Txt contains any rejected transactions.

```
000010 File-Control.
000011     Select Optional Trans-File Assign To "Trans.Seq"
000012         Organization Is Line Sequential.
000013     Select Optional Dealer-File Assign To "Dealer.Seq"
000014         Organization Is Line Sequential.
000015     Select Optional Dealer-Out Assign To "Dealer.Out"
000016         Organization Is Line Sequential.
000017     Select Optional Reject-File Assign To "Reject.Txt"
000018         Organization Is Line Sequential.
```

The record layouts for the Output master and the reject file do not need to be coded. When the records are written, they will be written from the master and transaction Input file record areas.

```
000019 Data Division.
000020 File Section.
```

18

```
000021 Fd  Trans-File.
000022 01  Trans-Record.
000023     03  Transaction-Date    Pic  9(8).
000024     03  Transaction-Text.
000025         05  Transaction-Type   Pic   X(4).
000026         05  Transaction-Dealer Pic   X(8).
000027     03  Transaction-Price  Pic S9(7)v99.
000028     03  Transaction-Qty    Pic  9(3).
000029     03  Filler             Pic  X(40).
000030 Fd  Reject-File.
000031 01  Reject-Record             Pic X(72).
000032 Fd  Dealer-File.
000033 01  Dealer-Record.
000034     03  Dealer-Number           Pic X(8).
000035     03  Dealer-Name.
000036         05  Last-Name    Pic X(25).
000037         05  First-Name   Pic X(15).
000038         05  Middle-Name  Pic X(10).
000039     03  Address-Line-1       Pic X(50).
000040     03  Address-Line-2       Pic X(50).
000041     03  City                 Pic X(40).
000042     03  State-Or-Country     Pic X(20).
000043     03  Postal-Code          Pic X(15).
000044     03  Home-Phone           Pic X(20).
000045     03  Work-Phone           Pic X(20).
000046     03  Other-Phone          Pic X(20).
000047     03  Start-Date           Pic 9(8).
000048     03  Last-Rent-Paid-Date  Pic 9(8).
000049     03  Next-Rent-Due-Date   Pic 9(8).
000050     03  Rent-Amount          Pic 9(4)v99.
000051     03  Consignment-Percent  Pic 9(3).
000052     03  Last-Sold-Amount     Pic S9(7)v99.
000053     03  Last-Sold-Date       Pic 9(8).
000054     03  Sold-To-Date         Pic S9(7)v99.
000055     03  Commission-To-Date   Pic S9(7)v99.
000056     03  Filler               Pic X(15).
000057 Fd  Dealer-Out.
000058 01  Dealer-Out-Record         Pic X(376).
```

Working-Storage contains the fields necessary to process the records and to collect the statistics.

```
000059 Working-Storage Section.
000060 01  Current-Commission     Pic S9(7)v99 Value Zeros.
000061 01  Total-Commission       Pic S9(7)v99 Value Zeros.
000062 01  Transactions-Read      Pic 9(5) Value Zeros.
000063 01  Transactions-Rejected  Pic 9(5) Value Zeros.
```

Hour 21 is devoted to the intricacies of date processing. However, for this program the most recent transaction date is being stored in the master record. Because the dates are stored in month, day, year format, it is impossible to compare them directly to determine which date is the most recent. The value "01042000:" evaluates to less than "08111999", when in actuality the former is a later date. Work-Date and Reverse-Date in lines 64 through 71 are provided to allow the formatting of the dates in year, month, day format for comparison.

```
000064 01  Work-Date.
000065     03  Work-MM          Pic 9(2).
000066     03  Work-DD          Pic 9(2).
000067     03  Work-YYYY        Pic 9(4).
000068 01  Reverse-Date.
000069     03  Work-YYYY        Pic 9(4).
000070     03  Work-MM          Pic 9(2).
000071     03  Work-DD          Pic 9(2).
000072 01  Compare-Date-1       Pic 9(8).
000073 01  Compare-Date-2       Pic 9(8).
```

These edit fields are used for formatting the audit counts that are displayed at the end of the program.

```
000074 01  Edit-Count           Pic ZZ,ZZ9.
000075 01  Edit-Amt             Pic Z,ZZZ,ZZZ.99-.
```

The program starts by reading a single record from each file. The Read may result in an At End condition if the files don't exist. This condition does not terminate the update process or cause any problems. The absence of transactions becomes apparent when the counts are displayed at the end of the process. The Read Paragraphs move High-Values into the data records when the end of file is reached. This value serves a dual purpose. First, it is the indicator that is used to terminate the update process. When both files have been completely read, then both data records are High-Values. Second, if one file reaches the end first, any comparisons with the remaining file's data result in the remaining data values being less. This status ensures that no attempt is made to read past the end of the master file or transaction file.

```
000076 Procedure Division.
000077 Chapt18c-Start.
000078     Display "Begin Process Chapt18c"
000079     Open Output Reject-File
000080             Dealer-Out
000081       Input  Trans-File
000082             Dealer-File
000083     Perform Read-Dealer
000084     Perform Read-Trans
```

The process is performed until both records contain High-Values; that is, each reaches the end of the file. When both files have been completely read, the update process is complete. The files may then be closed and the processing statistics displayed.

```
000085     Perform Process-Files Until
000086         Trans-Record = High-Values And
000087         Dealer-Record = High-Values
```

```
000088        Close Reject-File
000089              Dealer-Out
000090              Trans-File
000091              Dealer-File
000092        Move Transactions-Read To Edit-Count
000093        Display "Processing Complete"
000094        Display "Transactions Read " Edit-Count
000095        Move Transactions-Rejected To Edit-Count
000096        Display "Transactions Rejected " Edit-Count
000097        Move Total-Commission To Edit-Amt
000098        Display "Total Commission  " Edit-Amt
000099        Stop Run
000100        .
000101
```

The Process-Files Paragraph is where the actual update process occurs. The current transaction record is compared to the master record. Based on the results of the compare, one of three things can happen. If the current dealer number is less than that of the transaction file, then the process is finished with the present master record and it can be written to the Output file.

```
000102 Process-Files.
000103     Evaluate True
000104        When Dealer-Number < Transaction-Dealer
000105           Perform Write-Dealer-Out
000106           Perform Read-Dealer
```

If the dealer number in the master file is greater than the current transaction, then this transaction cannot be applied to a dealer record and is rejected. After each valid transaction is applied, a new one is read. If a dealer number in the master file is greater than the dealer number in the transaction file, there was no matching dealer number for the transaction.

```
000107        When Dealer-Number > Transaction-Dealer
000108           Perform Write-Reject
000109           Perform Read-Trans
```

If the dealer number in the master file matches the dealer number in the transaction file, then the dealer record can be updated. After this transaction is used to update the master file record, a new transaction is read. Notice that no new master file record is read because multiple transactions might apply for each master file record. Transactions must be read and applied until no more match. When a transaction is read that has a higher dealer number, then the existing master file record can be written to the Output file. It does not matter in the least if the record has been modified or not. All master records must be written to the new Output file.

```
000110        When Dealer-Number = Transaction-Dealer
000111           Perform Apply-Transaction
```

```
000112          Perform Read-Trans
000113     End-Evaluate
000114     .
```

This `Paragraph` is where the master file fields are updated with the appropriate fields from the transaction record. First the `Sold-To-Date` is incremented by the proper amount. The `Compute` statement takes care of multiplying the unit price by the quantity and adding the result to the master field. The second `Compute` figures the commission on this item based on the consignment percentage that is stored in the dealer file. The percentage is divided by `100` because it was stored as a whole number. After the consignment amount is computed, it is added to the master file record and to the audit totals.

```
000115 Apply-Transaction.
000116     Compute Sold-To-Date = Sold-To-Date +
000117          (Transaction-Qty * Transaction-Price)
000118     Compute Current-Commission Rounded =
000119          (Transaction-Qty * Transaction-Price) *
000120          (Consignment-Percent / 100)
000121     Add Current-Commission To Commission-To-Date
000122                         Total-Commission
```

The last sale date from the master file is reversed so that it can be properly compared. This step is done simply, and the result is stored in a temporary field that is used in the comparison. The transaction date is similarly reversed. Then the two dates are compared, and if the transaction date is after the last sold date in the master file, the transaction date is moved to the master record. It is very important to remember that the nonreversed date is moved to the record. This step ensures that all the dates are in the same format.

```
000123     Move Last-Sold-Date To Work-Date
000124     Move Corresponding Work-Date To Reverse-Date
000125     Move Reverse-Date To Compare-Date-1
000126     Move Transaction-Date To Work-Date
000127     Move Corresponding Work-Date To Reverse-Date
000128     Move Reverse-Date To Compare-Date-2
000129     If Compare-Date-2 > Compare-Date-1
000130        Move Transaction-Date To
000131             Last-Sold-Date
000132     End-If
000133     .
```

The following `Paragraphs` are performed from elsewhere in the program. Notice that when a reject record is written, the count of rejected records is incremented. Note also that as each file is read, if the end of file is reached, `High-Values` is moved into the record area. This step is the key to controlling the process. By having `High-Values` in the record, no compare can be greater than that of the value in the data record, and no further data records will be read. As each transaction record is read, the count of transactions is incremented. It is important to realize that this counter is incremented only when the

18

Read is successful, not At End of file. A frequent error when accumulating these types of counts is to increment the counter for the Read that resulted in an end of file condition.

```
000134 Write-Dealer-Out.
000135     Write Dealer-Out-Record From Dealer-Record
000136        .
000137 Write-Reject.
000138     Add 1 To Transactions-Rejected
000139     Write Reject-Record From Trans-Record
000140        .
000141 Read-Dealer.
000142     Read Dealer-File
000143         At End
000144             Move High-Values To Dealer-Record
000145     End-Read
000146        .
000147 Read-Trans.
000148     Read Trans-File
000149         At End
000150             Move High-Values To Trans-Record
000151         Not At End
000152             Add 1 To Transactions-Read
000153     End-Read
000154        .
```

As you can see, the Sequential update is straightforward and can be written in relatively few lines of code. After the Sequential update is complete, the original master file must be replaced with the new Output file. This step can occur after the counts are validated and the user is satisfied with the results. If the update process is interrupted for any reason, you can restart the Sequential update from the beginning with no ill effects.

Enter, compile, and run the sample program in Listing 18.2. The Output screen from this program, if it is properly coded, is shown in Figure 18.1.

Updating an Indexed Master File

Random updates are applied against Indexed master files. The update is called Random because the transactions do not need to be in any particular order. Each transaction is matched and applied against a master file record. This type of update is much easier to program than a Sequential file update.

Although a Sequential file update may seem less efficient, as it has to Read and Write every master file record, in many cases the Indexed file update is less efficient. Because the transaction records are not in any particular sequence, after each update is applied, the master file record must be rewritten. If many transaction records exist for a particular master file record, this process can be very inefficient.

FIGURE 18.1

Results of running the program in Listing 18.2.

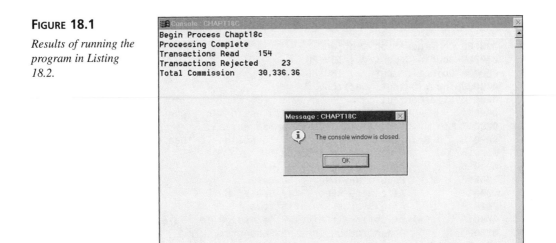

```
Console : CHAPT18C
Begin Process Chapt18c
Processing Complete
Transactions Read     154
Transactions Rejected    23
Total Commission     30,336.36
```

Message : CHAPT18C

The console window is closed.

OK

The advantages to this type of update relate to the relative ease of programming such an update. The process is simple and easy to follow. The transaction file is processed from beginning to end. As each transaction record is read, the related master file record is read. If the master file record is not found, then the transaction is rejected and the program moves on to the next transaction. If the master file does exist, the transaction is applied and the master file record is rewritten. When all transactions have been processed, the update is complete.

One disadvantage occurs when a problem develops during the update. It is virtually impossible to back out the transactions that have been applied. You must either determine the last successful transaction or restore a backup copy of the master file and reapply the update.

Review the following program that updates the Indexed file Dealer.Dat from Trans.Txt. These files are included on the CD-ROM in the \DATAFILE directory.

The example in Listing 18.3 uses one less file than the Sequential update did. There is no Output master file. The Indexed dealer file is accessed in Random mode.

LISTING 18.3 INDEXED FILE UPDATE

```
000001 @OPTIONS MAIN,TEST
000002 Identification Division.
000003 Program-Id.  Chapt18d.
000004* Indexed File Update
000005 Environment Division.
```

continues

LISTING 18.3 CONTINUED

```
000006 Configuration Section.
000007 Source-Computer.  IBM-PC.
000008 Object-Computer.  IBM-PC.
000009 Input-Output  Section.
000010 File-Control.
000011     Select Optional Trans-File Assign To "Trans.Txt"
000012         Organization Is Line Sequential.
000013     Select Optional Dealer-File Assign To "Dealer.Dat"
000014         Organization Indexed
000015         Access Random
000016         Record Key Dealer-Number
000017         Alternate Record Key Dealer-Name
000018         File Status Dealer-Status.
000019     Select Optional Reject-File Assign To "Reject.Txt"
000020         Organization Is Line Sequential.
000021 Data Division.
000022 File Section.
000023 Fd  Trans-File.
000024 01  Trans-Record.
000025     03  Transaction-Date   Pic  9(8).
000026     03  Transaction-Text.
000027         05  Transaction-Type   Pic  X(4).
000028         05  Transaction-Dealer Pic  X(8).
000029     03  Transaction-Price  Pic S9(7)v99.
000030     03  Transaction-Qty    Pic  9(3).
000031     03  Filler             Pic  X(40).
000032 Fd  Reject-File.
000033 01  Reject-Record          Pic X(72).
000034 Fd  Dealer-File.
000035 01  Dealer-Record.
000036     03  Dealer-Number          Pic X(8).
000037     03  Dealer-Name.
000038         05  Last-Name   Pic X(25).
000039         05  First-Name  Pic X(15).
000040         05  Middle-Name Pic X(10).
000041     03  Address-Line-1     Pic X(50).
000042     03  Address-Line-2     Pic X(50).
000043     03  City               Pic X(40).
000044     03  State-Or-Country   Pic X(20).
000045     03  Postal-Code        Pic X(15).
000046     03  Home-Phone         Pic X(20).
000047     03  Work-Phone         Pic X(20).
000048     03  Other-Phone        Pic X(20).
000049     03  Start-Date         Pic 9(8).
000050     03  Last-Rent-Paid-Date Pic 9(8).
000051     03  Next-Rent-Due-Date Pic 9(8).
000052     03  Rent-Amount        Pic 9(4)v99.
000053     03  Consignment-Percent Pic 9(3).
000054     03  Last-Sold-Amount   Pic S9(7)v99.
```

```
000055       03  Last-Sold-Date        Pic 9(8).
000056       03  Sold-To-Date          Pic S9(7)v99.
000057       03  Commission-To-Date    Pic S9(7)v99.
000058       03  Filler                Pic X(15).
000059 Working-Storage Section.
000060 01  Current-Commission          Pic S9(7)v99 Value Zeros.
000061 01  Total-Commission            Pic S9(7)v99 Value Zeros.
000062 01  Transactions-Read           Pic 9(5) Value Zeros.
000063 01  Transactions-Rejected       Pic 9(5) Value Zeros.
000064 01  Work-Date.
000065       03  Work-MM               Pic 9(2).
000066       03  Work-DD               Pic 9(2).
000067       03  Work-YYYY             Pic 9(4).
000068 01  Reverse-Date.
000069       03  Work-YYYY             Pic 9(4).
000070       03  Work-MM               Pic 9(2).
000071       03  Work-DD               Pic 9(2).
000072 01  Compare-Date-1              Pic 9(8).
000073 01  Compare-Date-2              Pic 9(8).
000074 01  Used-Transaction-Flag       Pic X Value Spaces.
000075       88  Used-This-Tran        Value "Y".
000076 01  Edit-Count                  Pic ZZ,ZZ9.
000077 01  Edit-Amt                    Pic Z,ZZZ,ZZZ.99-.
```

Three new fields are necessary in Working-Storage: one to note when the transaction file has reached end of file, another to return the File Status value of operations against the dealer Indexed file, and a flag that is set in case an error occurs on the Indexed file that is captured by the Declaratives. If such an error exists, processing the update should terminate. The only error that can occur here is a critical error caused by a serious problem with the Indexed file, such as a hardware failure.

```
000078 01  Dealer-Status           Pic XX Value Zeros.
000079       88  Dealer-Success    Value "00" Thru "09".
000080 01  Trans-Flag              Pic X Value Spaces.
000081       88  End-Of-Trans      Value "Y".
000082 01  Dealer-Flag             Pic X Value Spaces.
000083       88  Dealer-Error      Value "Y".
000084 Procedure Division.
000085 Declaratives.
000086 Dealer-File-Error Section.
000087     Use After Standard Error Procedure On Dealer-File
000088         .
000089 Dealer-Error-Paragraph.
000090     Display "Error on Dealer File " Dealer-Status
000091     Set Dealer-Error To True
000092         .
```

18

The processing loop is simple. The files are opened, and then the transaction file is read and processed until the end of file is reached or an error occurs in the Indexed dealer file.

```
000093 End Declaratives.
000094 Chapt18d-Start.
000095     Display "Begin Process Chapt18d"
000096     Open Output Reject-File
000097          Input   Trans-File
000098          I-O     Dealer-File
000099     Perform Process-Files Until End-Of-Trans Or Dealer-Error
000100     Close Reject-File
000101          Trans-File
000102          Dealer-File
000103     Move Transactions-Read To Edit-Count
000104     Display "Processing Complete"
000105     Display "Transactions Read " Edit-Count
000106     Move Transactions-Rejected To Edit-Count
000107     Display "Transactions Rejected " Edit-Count
000108     Move Total-Commission To Edit-Amt
000109     Display "Total Commission   " Edit-Amt
000110     Stop Run
000111          .
000112
000113 Process-Files.
000114     Read Trans-File
000115          At End Set End-Of-Trans To True
000116          Not At End
000117               Add 1 To Transactions-Read
000118               Perform Attempt-Transaction
000119     End-Read
000120          .
```

Before a master file record can be updated, the program must use a Read statement to determine whether the corresponding record exists in the master file. If the Read fails because of an invalid key, then the record is written to the reject file. If the Read is successful, the master file is updated, using the same logic as in the Sequential update, and then rewritten.

```
000121 Attempt-Transaction.
000122     Move Transaction-Dealer To Dealer-Number
000123     Read Dealer-File
000124          Invalid Key
000125               Perform Write-Reject
000126          Not Invalid Key
000127               Perform Apply-Transaction
000128     End-Read
000129          .
000130 Apply-Transaction.
000131     Compute Sold-To-Date = Sold-To-Date +
```

```
000132               (Transaction-Qty * Transaction-Price)
000133      Compute Current-Commission Rounded =
000134               (Transaction-Qty * Transaction-Price) *
000135               (Consignment-Percent / 100)
000136      Add Current-Commission To Commission-To-Date
000137                              Total-Commission
000138      Move Last-Sold-Date To Work-Date
000139      Move Corresponding Work-Date To Reverse-Date
000140      Move Reverse-Date To Compare-Date-1
000141      Move Transaction-Date To Work-Date
000142      Move Corresponding Work-Date To Reverse-Date
000143      Move Reverse-Date To Compare-Date-2
000144      If Compare-Date-2 > Compare-Date-1
000145         Move Transaction-Date To
000146             Last-Sold-Date
000147      End-If
000148      Rewrite Dealer-Record
000149      .
000150 Write-Reject.
000151      Add 1 To Transactions-Rejected
000152      Write Reject-Record From Trans-Record
000153      .
```

As you can see, the Indexed file update is very easy to follow and can be efficient. However, if the potential exists for many transaction records to be applied against a single master file record, this approach can be less efficient than a simple Sequential update.

Summary

In this hour, you learned the following:

- How data validation can eliminate problems that might occur later during an update process.

- Several methods for validating user entered data. These include checking the entry against an internal table and validating against an Indexed file.

- Two common file update procedures, Sequential and Random, and the advantages and disadvantages of each.

- How each of these updates is coded and data is processed.

- The importance of reporting errors, continuing processing when possible, and accumulating audit totals.

- Why the most efficient update method depends on the types and numbers of transactions being applied.

18

Q&A

Q When updating a `Sequential` file, what do I need to watch for?

A Common mistakes include not processing the remaining records in the file that does not reach end of file first and writing the new master record before all transactions are applied.

Q Can I apply the techniques for master file updating to other updates?

A Yes. The `Random` update, in particular, is very similar to the updates that occur in interactive programs in which users are entering data and updating a master file record with each entry.

Q Can't I just ignore data validation for user input and then take care of the validation in the update program?

A Sure, but it's not a good idea. Many systems, people, and procedures can come between you and the input of the transactional data. Tracing problems to their source can be very difficult, so you are better off having as much up-front data validation as possible. However, if you do encounter an error caused by invalid data in a transaction record, don't abort the update process. Store the invalid data for later problem diagnosis.

Q I really think the `Sequential` update is confusing. Can I use a `Random` update all the time instead?

A Maybe and maybe not. Your master file may not be an `Indexed` file. Additionally, you may find that a `Sequential` update is many times more efficient than a `Random` update, depending on the transactions you are processing.

Workshop

To help reinforce your understanding of the material presented in this hour, refer to the section "Quiz and Exercise Questions and Answers" that can be found on the CD. This section contains quiz questions and exercises for you to complete, as well as the corresponding answers.

Hour 19

Reporting

Business today relies on computers. More specifically, business today relies on the reports generated by computers. Computers are fantastic for gathering, storing, sorting, analyzing, and generally processing information. Ultimately the results of this activity must be made available to the end user. This hour covers the basics of creating a report, including topics such as

- The importance of reports
- Report layout design
- Defining report records in `Working-Storage`
- Writing `Before` and `After Advancing`
- Page breaks

Historically, programs presented output to the user in the form of printed reports. Even today, the printed report is the primary means of data presentation in business. Nevertheless, reports are not always printed on paper. They can be saved to files, sent via email, faxed, or displayed on the screen via a Web browser. Today users receive reports via a nearly infinite variety of methods.

Reports range from large inventory listings that show each and every item to month-end and year-end summary reports that give a snapshot of a company's financial status. When you go shopping and the computer prints your receipts, you are receiving a report. When you open your bank statement, you are looking at a computer-generated report. Reporting is extremely fundamental to the business process.

Regardless of the delivery method, the basics of reporting have remained the same. The result of the data processing must be delivered to the user in a clear, concise, and easy-to-understand format.

Creating Reports

An important part of any business-programming task is creating reports. COBOL has some simple features built into the language to aid in report creation. You are already aware of the different data-editing capabilities of the language. These play a big part in the reporting process. To make reports readable and easy to understand, the various data fields are edited. Instead of representing 12 dollars and 99 cents as 00001299, a good report will show $12.99. Dates should be displayed in the format that users expect. In the United States, this format is MM/DD/YYYY or MM/DD/YY. Showing a report-creation date of 990317 is cryptic and hard to understand; 03/17/99 more readily identifies the information as a date to the user. Try to keep your reporting as plain, simple, and clear as possible.

Designing Your Report Layout

The most important step in developing a useful report is planning. Before you can write a program that creates a report, you must decide how the final report should look. This planning tool is called the report layout. The report layout can be anything from a loose sketch on a piece of paper to a tightly controlled formalized report description. Reports are frequently designed on report layout forms. A report layout form is simply a paper form with horizontal and vertical lines, corresponding to lines and columns on the page. A typical page printed on a modern laser printer is 80 columns wide and 60 lines long. The examples in this book adhere to the 80-by-60 standard. Reports usually have heading lines that describe the contents of the report and give information about its creation. Page numbers are usually included. It is a good idea to include information such as the name of the program that created the report with the date and time the report was produced.

The first reporting example creates a report from the dealer file. This report shows the dealer name, last rent paid date, next rent due date, and rent amount. One line is printed per entry. The report has a title, page number, and headings. The layout is as follows:

```
Created by: CHAPT19A       Dealer File Rent Report        Page XXXX
Created on: MM/DD/YY
At:         HH:MM:SS


                                 Last Rent  Next Rent       Rent
Name                                  Paid        Due     Amount


XXXXXXXXXXXXXXXXXXXXXXXXXXXXXXXXXXXXXXXXX MM/DD/YYYY MM/DD/YYYY $$$,$$$.99
```

When creating a report, each horizontal print line is represented by a print record. The records are created in `Working-Storage`. A typical report has one or more heading lines followed by detail lines. The detail line contains the report details, hence the name. The following `Working-Storage` entries describe the report lines used for this first report.

```
000050 01  Heading-Line-1.
000051     03  Filler      Pic X(12) Value "Created by:".
000052     03  Filler      Pic X(8)  Value "CHAPT19A".
000053     03  Filler      Pic X(11) Value Spaces.
000054     03  Filler      Pic X(23) Value "Dealer File Rent Report".
000055     03  Filler      Pic X(10) Value Spaces.
000056     03  Filler      Pic X(5)  Value "Page".
000057     03  Page-No     Pic Z(4)9 Value Zeros.
000058 01  Heading-Line-2.
000059     03  Filler      Pic X(12) Value "Created on:".
000060     03  Date-MM     Pic 99.
000061     03  Filler      Pic X     Value "/".
000062     03  Date-DD     Pic 99.
000063     03  Filler      Pic X     Value "/".
000064     03  Date-YY     Pic 99.
000065 01  Heading-Line-3.
000066     03  Filler      Pic X(12) Value "At:".
000067     03  Time-HH     Pic 99.
000068     03  Filler      Pic X     Value ":".
000069     03  Time-MM     Pic 99.
000070     03  Filler      Pic X     Value ":".
000071     03  Time-SS     Pic 99.
000072 01  Heading-Line-4.
000073     03  Filler      Pic X(41) Value Spaces.
000074     03  Filler      Pic X(27) Value "Last Rent  Next Rent".
000075     03  Filler      Pic X(4)  Value "Rent".
000076 01  Heading-Line-5.
000077     03  Filler  Pic X(44) Value "Name".
000078     03  Filler  Pic X(29) Value "Paid        Due        Amount".
000079 01  Detail-Line.
000080     03  Detail-Name        Pic X(40)      Value Spaces.
000081     03  Filler             Pic X          Value Spaces.
000082     03  Last-Rent-Paid-Date Pic 99/99/9999.
000083     03  Filler             Pic X          Value Spaces.
000084     03  Next-Rent-Due-Date  Pic 99/99/9999.
000085     03  Filler             Pic X          Value Spaces.
000086     03  Rent-Amount        Pic $$$,$$$.99.
```

19

Notice the use of literals and `Filler` areas in the different print line descriptions. You can see the print lines as they are described in `Working-Storage` and how they relate to the visual representation of the report layout. Edit patterns are used for many of the fields.

Creating a report is accomplished by writing the different heading and detail lines to the printer. The printer is merely another `Sequential` file as far as the COBOL program is concerned. Many compilers use a special name to `Assign` in the `Select` statement when defining a printer to the program. This name is `Printer`. The `Select` statement for Chapt19a follows.

```
000011    Select Report-File Assign To Printer.
```

The newly defined `Report-File` must have a corresponding `FD` in the program.

```
000020 FD  Report-File.
000021 01  Report-Record Pic X(80).
```

Notice that the report record does not have a special record layout. All records are written to the `Report-File` using `Write` with `From`.

When creating a report, the file assigned to the `Printer` is opened for `Output` in the program.

The `Write` Statement and Reports

The COBOL `Write` statement has several options that make creating printed reports easy. These clauses—`Before` and `After`—position the print on the page.

The `Before` and `After` clauses allow you to `Write` print records `Before` and `After` `Advancing` the specified number of print lines. In addition, these clauses allow you to `Write` your print records `Before` or `After` a `Page` break.

For example, the normal print logic is to print a line `After Advancing` a single line. This clause causes the printer to scroll down a single line and then print the print line. The corresponding code follows.

```
000138    Write Report-Record from Detail-Line After Advancing 1
```

The word `Advancing` is optional and may be omitted. When it is time to print the next print line, the process is repeated. If you want a double-spaced report, you can `Write` all of your print lines `After Advancing` 2. If you want to `Write` a print line exactly where the printer is positioned, without skipping down a line, you can either `Write After Advancing 0`, or `Write Before Advancing 1`.

Creating a report requires you to control the line spacing of the printer. It's not the same as choosing single or double spacing. The programmer is required to control every action that the printer takes when printing a report. When you `Write` to the `Printer`, you send the print line that you want to have printed, along with the action you want the printer to take in reference to that line. If you send every line to the `Printer` with `After Advancing 0`, then all the print lines print on top of one another because the printer does not advance the paper.

`After Advancing` causes the printer to advance to the next print line before writing the record. After the record is written, the printer remains positioned on that same print line. This clause allows you to print over that line again. You may intend to do so, or it may happen to you by accident! If you print a line `After Advancing 1` and then print another line `After Advancing 0`, the second line prints over the first.

`Before Advancing` does just the opposite. When `Before` is used, the print line is written to the `Printer`, and then the specified printer control is performed. When `Before Advancing` is used, unless a value of zero is specified, the printer is always positioned on a blank line.

The number of lines to advance does not need to be a numeric literal. You can also use a numeric data item. The value must not be a negative number.

```
000101     Write Report-Record After Advancing Lines-To-Feed
```

In addition to `Advancing` a number of lines, you can execute a `Write` and cause the printer to advance to a new `Page`. This type of `Write` is frequently performed when writing a heading line.

```
000147     Write Report-Record From Heading-Line-1 After Page
```

This statement causes the printer to advance to a new `Page` and then print your heading line.

`Before Advancing` works exactly as you would expect. It first prints the line and then advances the specified number of lines or `Page`. As you can see, you would not want to use `Before Advancing` when printing a heading line. Consider the following instruction:

```
000147     Write Report-Record From Heading-Line-1 Before Page
```

If you execute line 147, the printer prints your heading line and then advances to a new `Page`! This result is not exactly what you had in mind.

If the `Before` or `After` is omitted when writing to a `Printer`, the compiler assumes `After 1`.

Programming for Page Breaks

One of the issues that you face when creating reports is the proper printing of the heading and detail lines. Ideally, the headings should be at the top of each page, with a page number, followed by the detail. When the page is full, you should advance to a new

19

Page, printing a set of headings and then more detail, until the report is complete. Starting a new page is called a page break.

To control this process, you have to count lines and pages. You need to know how many lines can be printed on a page. As print lines are written to the Printer, the counter is incremented. When the maximum number of lines that can be on a page is reached, a new page with headings is printed. One method programmers use is to Write the first heading lines when the Printer is opened. I dislike this approach, as it causes a report to be printed when, in fact, there may be no data to print. Instead, I like the alternative approach.

The second approach involves an initial value in the line counter that is higher than the maximum number of lines on the page. This method allows the normal program logic to examine the line counter before printing the detail line and to print a new page and heading lines before printing the report detail if the maximum line count has been exceeded. The advantage to this approach is that no heading lines will be printed unless there is a detail record to be printed under them. The page counter starts at zero and is incremented before each set of report headings is printed.

The following program fulfills the reporting requirements described earlier in the hour. Notice that the Report-File is assigned to the reserved name Printer. Printer is not a data item declared anywhere in your program. See Listing 19.1.

LISTING 19.1 A SIMPLE REPORT

```
000001 @OPTIONS MAIN,TEST
000002 Identification Division.
000003 Program-Id.  Chapt19a.
000004* Simple Report
000005 Environment Division.
000006 Configuration Section.
000007 Source-Computer.  IBM-PC.
000008 Object-Computer.  IBM-PC.
000009 Input-Output  Section.
000010 File-Control.
000011     Select Report-File Assign To Printer.
000012     Select Dealer-File Assign To "Dealer.Dat"
000013        Organization Indexed
000014        Access Sequential
000015        Record Key Dealer-Number
000016        Alternate Record Key Dealer-Name
000017        File Status Dealer-Status.
000018 Data Division.
000019 File Section.
000020 Fd  Report-File.
000021 01  Report-Record Pic X(80).
000022 Fd  Dealer-File.
000023 01  Dealer-Record.
000024     03  Dealer-Number       Pic X(8).
000025     03  Dealer-Name.
```

```
000026              05  Last-Name    Pic X(25).
000027              05  First-Name   Pic X(15).
000028              05  Middle-Name Pic X(10).
000029         03  Address-Line-1       Pic X(50).
000030         03  Address-Line-2       Pic X(50).
000031         03  City                 Pic X(40).
000032         03  State-Or-Country     Pic X(20).
000033         03  Postal-Code          Pic X(15).
000034         03  Home-Phone           Pic X(20).
000035         03  Work-Phone           Pic X(20).
000036         03  Other-Phone          Pic X(20).
000037         03  Start-Date           Pic 9(8).
000038         03  Last-Rent-Paid-Date Pic 9(8).
000039         03  Next-Rent-Due-Date   Pic 9(8).
000040         03  Rent-Amount          Pic 9(4)v99.
000041         03  Consignment-Percent Pic 9(3).
000042         03  Last-Sold-Amount     Pic S9(7)v99.
000043         03  Last-Sold-Date       Pic 9(8).
000044         03  Sold-To-Date         Pic S9(7)v99.
000045         03  Commission-To-Date   Pic S9(7)v99.
000046         03  Filler               Pic X(15).
000047 Working-Storage Section.
000048 01  Dealer-Status             Pic XX Value Zeros.
000049      88  Dealer-Success  Value "00" Thru "09".
```

The heading and detail lines are described here in Working-Storage.

```
000050 01  Heading-Line-1.
000051      03  Filler     Pic X(12) Value "Created by:".
000052      03  Filler     Pic X(8)  Value "CHAPT19A".
000053      03  Filler     Pic X(11) Value Spaces.
000054      03  Filler     Pic X(23) Value "Dealer File Rent Report".
000055      03  Filler     Pic X(10) Value Spaces.
000056      03  Filler     Pic X(5)  Value "Page".
000057      03  Page-No    Pic Z(4)9 Value Zeros.
000058 01  Heading-Line-2.
000059      03  Filler     Pic X(12) Value "Created on:".
000060      03  Date-MM    Pic 99.
000061      03  Filler     Pic X     Value "/".
000062      03  Date-DD    Pic 99.
000063      03  Filler     Pic X     Value "/".
000064      03  Date-YY    Pic 99.
000065 01  Heading-Line-3.
000066      03  Filler     Pic X(12) Value "At:".
000067      03  Time-HH    Pic 99.
000068      03  Filler     Pic X     Value ":".
000069      03  Time-MM    Pic 99.
000070      03  Filler     Pic X     Value ":".
000071      03  Time-SS    Pic 99.
000072 01  Heading-Line-4.
000073      03  Filler     Pic X(41) Value Spaces.
```

19

```
000074      03  Filler      Pic X(27) Value "Last Rent  Next Rent".
000075      03  Filler      Pic X(4)  Value "Rent".
000076 01  Heading-Line-5.
000077      03  Filler   Pic X(44) Value "Name".
000078      03  Filler   Pic X(29) Value "Paid       Due         Amount".
000079 01  Detail-Line.
000080      03  Detail-Name      Pic X(40)        Value Spaces.
000081      03  Filler           Pic X            Value Spaces.
000082      03  Last-Rent-Paid-Date Pic 99/99/9999.
000083      03  Filler           Pic X            Value Spaces.
000084      03  Next-Rent-Due-Date Pic 99/99/9999.
000085      03  Filler           Pic X            Value Spaces.
000086      03  Rent-Amount      Pic $$$,$$$.99.
```

The necessary counters for tracking the number of lines printed and the page number are coded next. Notice that the initial value of Line-Count is 99. The Max-Lines data item contains the maximum number of lines that is desired per page. Because 99 is greater than this value, a page break is triggered for the first detail record encountered.

```
000087 01  Line-Count          Pic 99          Value 99.
000088 01  Page-Count          Pic 9(4)        Value Zeros.
000089 01  Max-Lines           Pic 99          Value 60.
```

Some working fields are set up here to handle date and time formatting for the report headings.

```
000090 01  Date-And-Time-Area.
000091      03  Work-Date          Pic 9(6).
000092      03  Work-Date-X        Redefines Work-Date.
000093          05  Date-YY        Pic 99.
000094          05  Date-MM        Pic 99.
000095          05  Date-DD        Pic 99.
000096      03  Work-Time          Pic 9(8).
000097      03  Work-Time-X        Redefines Work-Time.
000098          05  Time-HH        Pic 99.
000099          05  Time-MM        Pic 99.
000100          05  Time-SS        Pic 99.
000101          05  Filler         Pic XX.
000102
000103 Procedure Division.
000104 Declaratives.
000105 Dealer-File-Error Section.
000106     Use After Standard Error Procedure On Dealer-File
000107         .
000108 Dealer-Error-Paragraph.
000109     Display "Error on Dealer File " Dealer-Status
000110         .
000111 End Declaratives.
```

The program first opens the files, including the Printer file. If the input file Open is successful, the program retrieves the date and time and places these in the heading lines. No report records are written yet. The Start statement allows the printing of the report in name sequence. The file is then processed one record at a time until there is no longer a successful return code on the dealer file.

```
000112 Chapt19a-Start.
000113     Display "Begin Process Chapt19a"
000114     Perform Open-Files
000115      If Dealer-Success
000116        Perform Fill-Initial-Headings
000117        Perform Start-Alternate-Key
000118        Perform Process-File Until Not Dealer-Success
000119        Perform Close-Files
000120     End-If
000121     Stop Run.
000122 Start-Alternate-Key.
000123     Move Low-Values To Dealer-Name
000124     Start Dealer-File Key Not < Dealer-Name
000125     .
```

The Process-File paragraph merely reads the input data file. If it is not the end of file, data from the record that was just read is printed. If it is the end of file, nothing happens in this Paragraph, but because the dealer File Status is set to 10 for end of file, the processing loop terminates.

```
000126 Process-File.
000127     Read Dealer-File
000128         At End Continue
000129         Not At End
000130             Perform Print-This-Record
000131     End-Read
000132     .
```

The first thing that happens before the detail record can be printed is the formatting of the name. In the dealer file, the name is split into its three parts—first, last, and middle. The report requires them to be in a single field. After that, the fields in the dealer record that are also in the detail line are moved with a simple Move with Corresponding. The only fields moved from the dealer file are Last-Rent-Paid-Date, Next-Rent-Due-Date and Rent-Amount. These three fields are the only fields that the two records have in common.

```
000133 Print-This-Record.
000134     Perform Format-Name
000135     Move Corresponding Dealer-Record To Detail-Line
```

After the detail record is constructed, the line counter is checked to see whether a new page with a set of headings is necessary. If the line count is reached, or exceeded, the heading line is printed.

```
000136     If Line-Count >= Max-Lines
000137         Perform Heading-Routine
000138     End-If
```

19

Why not just check for = when comparing the line count? The reason is that not all reporting tasks print a single print line per detail record. In some cases, multiple print lines are created for a single input record. The user does not want the detail for a single item to span multiple pages, so the line counter is checked only before the first detail Write for a particular input record. The number of actual print lines may exceed the maximum the next time it is checked, and the equal condition may never occur, causing the program to print multiple pages of report without the appropriate page breaks.

After checking for a new page, and printing the heading lines if necessary, the detail line may be printed. Notice that the detail line is printed After Advancing a single line. The report is single-spaced. Always add the proper number of lines to the line counter after printing the detail lines.

```
000139     Write Report-Record From Detail-Line After 1
000140     Add 1 To Line-Count
000141       .
```

The heading routine is interesting. The first thing that happens is that the page counter is incremented and moved to the appropriate field in the heading record for printing. Remember that the initial value specified in Working-Storage was zero. Notice the check for page 1. It is executed because the printer is positioned at a new page when the report starts printing. Sending a page break to the printer on the first page is a waste of paper, and annoys most users. This check allows the first line to either print after a page break, if this is not the first page, or on the first line of the current page if it is. After Zero causes the printer to print only the current line and not change the paper position.

```
000142 Heading-Routine.
000143     Add 1 To Page-Count
000144     Move Page-Count To Page-No
000145     If Page-Count = 1
000146         Write Report-Record From Heading-Line-1 After Zero
000147     Else
000148         Write Report-Record From Heading-Line-1 After Page
000149     End-If
```

The second and third heading lines print After 1 line and follow the first one. However, an extra space is desired before the fourth heading line. Therefore, it is printed using After 2. This clause causes the printer to skip two lines and then print the detail line.

```
000150     Write Report-Record From Heading-Line-2 After 1
000151     Write Report-Record From Heading-Line-3 After 1
000152     Write Report-Record From Heading-Line-4 After 2
```

Notice the apparently strange printing of heading line 5 (see lines 153 and 154). First, it is printed `After 1` and then again `Before 2`. What does this coding accomplish? On older impact printers, before the day of lasers, this common technique was used to over-strike a print line and make the printing appear **bold**. With Windows-based printing, the line is physically printed only once. Printing `Before 2` inserts a blank line between the last heading line and the first detail line on the page the second time the line is printed. An alternative to this approach is to `Move` spaces to the print record and then print `After 1` again.

```
000153      Write Report-Record From Heading-Line-5 After 1
000154      Write Report-Record From Heading-Line-5 Before 2
```

When printing your heading lines, you do not have to count lines after every print. Simply move the total number of lines advanced to the line counter to reset the count.

```
000155      Move 7 To Line-Count
000156      .
```

The name formatting that occurs here simply strings the three names into one. It is not as good a routine as it might be. If embedded spaces occur in any of the names, this method does not properly assemble the full name. A technique for properly handling this type of situation is discussed in Hour 22, "Other Intrinsic Functions."

```
000157 Format-Name.
000158      Move Spaces To Detail-Name
000159      String First-Name   Delimited By Space
000160             " "          Delimited By Size
000161             Middle-Name  Delimited By Space
000162             " "          Delimited By Size
000163             Last-Name    Delimited By Space
000164             Into Detail-Name
000165      End-String
000166      .
```

This next paragraph is the one that accepts the system date and time and formats them for the report. Because the formats of the fields are in the reverse order of what people are used to looking at, the `Move Corresponding` handles moving the appropriate fields to the heading record, where they are formatted in a more normal order. Remember that the date returned has only the last two digits of the year and should not be used in any calculations. However, using the two-digit date for cosmetic purposes on a report is acceptable.

```
000167 Fill-Initial-Headings.
000168      Accept Work-Date From Date
000169      Accept Work-Time From Time
000170      Move Corresponding Work-Date-X To
000171                          Heading-Line-2
```

19

```
000172        Move Corresponding Work-Time-X To
000173                         Heading-Line-3
000174      .
000175 Open-Files.
000176      Open Output Report-File
000177           Input Dealer-File
000178      .
000179 Close-Files.
000180      Close Report-File
000181           Dealer-File
000182      .
```

Compile, link, and run the program. If you allow the report to finish printing, it will be nearly 100 pages, so cancel it if you don't want the whole document to print. As you run the program, you need to adjust the printer font, which defaults to a small seven dots per inch. Fujitsu provides a runtime option that you can change to adjust the print size to a more standard size for the PC. (This option is not available if you installed the 16-bit version of the compiler.) Selecting the TYPE-PC font results in larger, monospaced print.

- Select the program from WINEXEC. The runtime environment setup window appears.
- Choose the Environment Setup menu option.
- Select the Keyword menu item.
- Click @CBR_PrinterANK_Size.
- Click the Selection button.
- Click in the field to the left of the Set button and position the cursor after the = sign.
- Enter **TYPE-PC** after the =. The entire line should now say @CBR_PrinterANK_Size=TYPE-PC.
- Click the Set button.
- Click the Save button.
- Select OK when asked whether you want to add the entry to the INI file. This setting is in effect only for the execution of this particular program name.

When you next run the program, it will print with a more reasonable font size.

Printing reports usually does not involve this simple one-data-record, one-print-record approach. Sometimes multiple data records are read from various files to construct a single print line. At other times, reporting programs limit the data records that are being reported by allowing the user to specify certain selection criteria.

What if you want the program to print only those dealers with numbers that begin with the letter C? When you design and code your programs, remember to keep them clear and easy to follow. Don't use strange, inappropriate data names. Try to keep things self-explanatory. If your program is properly written, using a structured approach, future modification will be a minor task. What change is necessary to ensure that the program selects only dealer records with numbers that start with the letter C? Because of the structured approach used, the change is very simple:

```
000285     Read Dealer-File
000286          At End Continue
000287          Not At End
000288              If Dealer-Number (1:1) = "C"
000289                  Perform Print-This-Record
000290              End-If
000291     End-read
```

For this single selection, the If statement around the Perform will suffice. If you have more complex selection logic, you can Perform a Paragraph that sets a switch you can check to see whether this particular record was selected.

```
000285     Read Dealer-File
000286          At End Continue
000287          Not At End
000288                  Perform Check-Record
000289              If Use-Record
000290                  Perform Print-This-Record
000291              End-If
000292     End-Read
```

Occasionally, you might want to underline a line on a report. To do so, define a new line in Working-Storage.

```
000020 01 Underline-Line     Pic X(80) Value all "_".
```

Then, when printing the line you wish to underline, make sure not to advance a line afterward. For example, use After Advancing 0. The printer remains at the beginning of the last print line printed. Then print the Underline-Line with the normal After Advancing clause.

```
000040     Write Report-Record From Underline-Line After Advancing 1
```

Reports are frequently written as the Output Procedure from a Sort. In this situation, instead of a record Read, you are executing a Return on the Sort record. Functionally, nothing is really different from coding a program for a report. All the report-printing logic is contained within the Output Procedure. The exercise at the end of this hour requires you to write a report in the Output Procedure of a program that uses Sort.

During the development process of a system, you might want to look at a report without

19

actually printing it. Because a report file assigned and written to `Printer` is just another `Sequential` file as far as the compiler is concerned, you can change the `Select` statement and create a file instead. Instead of assigning the `Report-File` to `Printer`, change the `Assign` to something similar to `"PRINT.IMG"`. The report is written to the file, instead of the printer. You can view the file in your favorite text editor, make necessary adjustments, and then run the program again.

Summary

In this hour, you learned the following:

- Reporting is an important programming function.
- Reports consist of heading lines and detail lines.
- A report is simply another `Sequential` file as far as the compiler is concerned.
- Reports can be written to the `Printer` or to another `Sequential` file.
- When printing a report, the programmer is responsible for controlling the printer. This task is accomplished using `Write`, with the `Before` and `After` clauses.
- When creating reports, the programmer must keep track of the number of lines on a page and the number printed to control the occurrence of page breaks.
- Reporting makes extensive use of the data-editing features of COBOL to produce clear, easy-to-understand documents.

Q&A

Q If a report file is just a `Sequential` file, why can't I just `Write Line Sequential` records to the `Printer`?

A You can. However, you lose the advantage of being able to simply single, double, and triple space. You can't cause a page break, and you can't do things like overprinting and underlining. The printer control features of COBOL provide this flexibility.

Q When I execute a `Write Print-Record After 1` and then follow it up with a `Write Print-Record Before 1`, what happens?

A The first `Write` advances the printer to the next line and then prints the record. The next `Write` prints on top of the last print line and then advances to the next blank line.

Q **Can I make the printer advance backward?**

A No. All Advancing is in a forward direction. But you can control whether the printer Advancing occurs Before or After your print line is written.

Q **When I print to a file and I try to underline something, I still get two records in the file. Why?**

A In actuality you really have two records. By controlling the Advancing when you Write to a Printer, the result just looks like one line because the printer does not move after printing the first line.

Workshop

To help reinforce your understanding of the material presented in this hour, refer to the section "Quiz and Exercise Questions and Answers" that can be found on the CD. This section contains quiz questions and exercises for you to complete, as well as the corresponding answers.

19

HOUR 20

Advanced Reporting

To make good use of the data collected on a daily basis, the data must be analyzed and reported. Quick reactions to trends and activity can lead to greater profits or prevent disaster. However, simple reports showing detailed activity do not always help businesses react. Consequently, you frequently need to produce more than a report of detailed data items.

This hour covers concepts relating to advanced reporting, including topics such as

- The definition of control breaks
- Determining the proper hierarchy of control breaks
- Subtotaling
- Walking through a program with control breaks

Advanced reports often contain summary information that is gathered from individual transactions. This summary reporting can yield a tremendous amount of information in a short, concise format, usually in the form of totals and subtotals. A single report might contain several levels of information. For example, the transactions that are applied to the dealer file might be analyzed before the update is applied, thus accomplishing several tasks.

The business owner can see the impact of the transactions before they are applied. Any invalid data is exposed, and the problem can be corrected before the actual update is applied. The totals from the report can be compared with the totals produced by the update process as an audit to ensure that both processes are operating properly.

The example for this hour reports totals for quantity, amount, and commission for each transaction type, within each date, for each dealer. It also reports a grand total. There may be multiple transactions for a particular transaction type for a specific day, and because this report is a summary report, the individual record detail is not printed. This type of reporting involves control breaks.

NEW TERM   A *control break* is what happens in a program that produces the types of totals just described. The program branches out and performs the special subtotal processing when a change or break occurs in the sequence of data items being tested. This break in sequence causes the control break.

Reporting with Control Breaks

Control breaks are directly related to the sequence that is desired for the report. Examine the report layout designed for the current example.

```
Created by: CHAPT20A        Transaction Summary by Dealer      Page  ZZZ9
Created on: MM/DD/YY
At:         HH:MM:SS


                                            Qty      Amount   Commission

*    Total  XXXXXXXXXXX Tran Type XXX…XXX ZZZZ9 $$$,$$$.99- $$$,$$$.99-
**   Total  XXXXXXXXXXX Tran Date XXX…XXX ZZZZ9 $$$,$$$.99- $$$,$$$.99-

***Total   XXXXXXXXXXX Dealer Name XXX…XXX ZZZZ9 $$$,$$$.99- $$$,$$$.99-

****Grand Totals                          ZZZZ9 $$$,$$$.99- $$$,$$$.99-
```

Determining the Number and Hierarchy of Control Breaks

The subtotal levels determine the number and hierarchy of control breaks. This sequence is one of the most fundamental to the process. In this hour's example, the levels are grand totals, dealer totals, transaction date totals, and transaction type totals. They are listed from highest level to smallest level to help explain what is happening in the program.

The grand total is the only total not dependent on the contents of the data. It is generated after all of the data is processed. However, this condition counts as the highest level control break. The next level is the dealer level. Anytime a new dealer is encountered in the data, this break is triggered. The third break is the transaction date break. If a new transaction date is encountered, then this control break is activated. The final level is the transaction type level. This break occurs whenever a new transaction type is encountered in the data. To summarize, the program has four control-break levels. The highest level is the grand total level. The next level is the dealer level. The level that occurs under the dealer level is the date level, and the level under that is the type level.

This hierarchy might appear to be reversed. Because transaction type appears on the report first, you might think that transaction type is the first level. This is a common conceptual error. As you examine the logic in the example program, it will become apparent why you must think of these levels as proceeding from the highest level to the lowest and not the lowest to the highest.

One important issue relating to control breaks is the Sort sequence. The data must be sorted in sequence of the control-break hierarchy. The Sort sequence for the example is dealer name, transaction date, and then transaction type. As you can see, the control-break levels required for the report determine this sequence. If you attempt to create control-break levels that differ from the Sort sequence of the Input data, your report program will not function properly. The data will be out of order, or items that should be grouped together will instead appear multiple times.

Subtotaling

When control breaks are used, subtotals are usually associated with each level of control break. Programmers use several methods to accumulate these subtotals. Some programmers, after retrieving a record, Add the item to every subtotal field defined for the program. This process can be very inefficient. A better approach is to Add the subtotals to the next highest level of subtotal when the control break for that level is processed.

In the current example, when a type break occurs, the accumulated subtotals for type are added to the date subtotal field. When a date break occurs, the date field subtotals are added to the dealer subtotals. When a dealer break occurs, then the dealer subtotals are added to the grand totals. Each level feeds the preceding level, which makes for very efficient processing.

20

One common mistake relating to subtotals involves the failure of the programmer to reset the value after using the subtotal. After the subtotal is
added to the next highest level, the subtotal field should be cleared—reset
to zero. Another mistake is not initializing the subtotal fields to zero in
Working-Storage to begin with. The best and most efficient method for initializing these values at the start of the program is to use the Value clause
when the item is defined.

The order of operations should be as follows: Write the subtotal record to the report, Add
the subtotal to the next highest level, and then zero the subtotal field that was just
processed. If this process occurs for every control break, the totals are always correct.

Walking Through a Program with Control Breaks

NEW TERM   On several occasions in the previous hours, segments of a program were inter-
mixed with the text. Most modern programming uses this procedure, called a
program *walk through*, as a way to explain what a program is doing and why. The walk
through is often used as a peer review of a programmer's work. Sometimes the walk
through finds programming inefficiencies that can be corrected; other times the activity
uncovers serious programming flaws. Walk-through participants often discover interesting tips and techniques that they can use in other programs.

In this walk through of a program with multiple levels of control breaks, the reasons
behind the code are explained in detail. In addition, tips and cautions that you can use in
your future control break programming are presented.

Start the walk through by examining the initial program setup and the data files used by
the program. As usual with a report program, you have an Input data file and an assign-
ment to the printer file. This program also has a reference to the Indexed file Dealer.Dat
and a Sort Work file. The Dealer.Dat file is required to retrieve the dealer name from the
dealer file. The transaction data, on which the report is based, does not contain the dealer
name. The Sort Work file is used by the Sort. The transaction data cannot possibly be in
the correct sequence for the report, because it does not contain the dealer name. The
Sort is used to prepare the Input file and get it in the same sequence as the control
break hierarchy previously decided on.

```
000001 @OPTIONS MAIN,TEST
000002 Identification Division.
000003 Program-Id.  Chapt20a.
000004* Control Breaks
000005 Environment Division.
000006 Configuration Section.
```

```
000007 Source-Computer.   IBM-PC.
000008 Object-Computer.   IBM-PC.
000009 Input-Output  Section.
000010 File-Control.
```

Access to the dealer file is Random. Because the Input data records are out of order, you need to Read a dealer record for each Input data record to fill in the corresponding dealer name.

```
000011      Select Dealer-File Assign To "Dealer.Dat"
000012          Organization Indexed
000013          Access Random
000014          Record Key Dealer-Number
000015          Alternate Record Key Dealer-Name Of Dealer-Record
000016          File Status Dealer-Status.
000017      Select Report-File Assign To Printer.
```

The Input data file for this program is Trans1.Txt. This data file is provided on the CD-ROM in the \DATAFILE folder.

The file was carefully constructed and contains data for several dealers who are in the dealer master file. There are multiple dates, but not enough to make the report extremely large. One dealer in the transaction file does not correspond to an existing dealer in the dealer master file. The format of the transaction file is the same as that used in previous hours.

```
000018      Select Optional Trans-File Assign To "Trans1.TXT"
000019          Organization Is Line Sequential.
000020      Select Sort-File Assign To Sort-Work.
000021 Data Division.
000022 File Section.
000023 Fd  Dealer-File.
000024 01  Dealer-Record.
000025      03  Dealer-Number         Pic X(8).
000026      03  Dealer-Name.
000027          05  Last-Name   Pic X(25).
000028          05  First-Name  Pic X(15).
000029          05  Middle-Name Pic X(10).
000030      03  Address-Line-1        Pic X(50).
000031      03  Address-Line-2        Pic X(50).
000032      03  City                  Pic X(40).
000033      03  State-Or-Country      Pic X(20).
000034      03  Postal-Code           Pic X(15).
000035      03  Home-Phone            Pic X(20).
000036      03  Work-Phone            Pic X(20).
000037      03  Other-Phone           Pic X(20).
000038      03  Start-Date            Pic 9(8).
000039      03  Last-Rent-Paid-Date Pic 9(8).
000040      03  Next-Rent-Due-Date    Pic 9(8).
000041      03  Rent-Amount           Pic 9(4)v99.
```

20

```
000042      03  Consignment-Percent Pic 9(3).
000043      03  Last-Sold-Amount    Pic S9(7)v99.
000044      03  Last-Sold-Date      Pic 9(8).
000045      03  Sold-To-Date        Pic S9(7)v99.
000046      03  Commission-To-Date  Pic S9(7)v99.
000047      03  Filler              Pic X(15).
000048 Fd  Report-File.
000049 01  Report-Record Pic X(80).
000050 Fd  Trans-File.
000051 01  Trans-Record.
000052      03  Transaction-Date    Pic  9(8).
000053      03  Transaction-Date-X Redefines Transaction-Date.
000054          05  Trans-Month     Pic 99.
000055          05  Trans-Day       Pic 99.
000056          05  Trans-Year      Pic 9(4).
000057      03  Transaction-Type    Pic  X(4).
000058      03  Transaction-Dealer Pic  X(8).
000059      03  Transaction-Price   Pic S9(7)v99.
000060      03  Transaction-Qty     Pic  9(3).
000061      03  Filler              Pic  X(40).
```

The Sort file is one of the most important areas of the program. It contains a single record for every record in the transaction file. Several fields in the record do not exist in the Input file. The record layout of the Sort file is not a copy of the Input file record. The Sort Key is also very important. Notice that the organization of the Sort Key matches the hierarchy that was previously discussed for the report.

The names chosen for the elementary items under the date field are significant. They match the names of the fields in the transaction record; however, they are in a different order. To Sort by date and to arrange the oldest date first in the file and the newest date last, you must use the date format as defined in the Sort record. You must use Year, Month, and then Day to force the Sort into the proper sequence.

Commission is also stored in this field, although that item is not included in the Input data record. The Commission field is computed during the Input Procedure of the Sort. Because the dealer record contains the consignment percentage that is used for computing this field and is read to retrieve the dealer name, calculating the commission at this point makes sense. You could also perform the calculation in the Output Procedure; however, that would mean an additional special Read of the dealer file, which is inefficient. Because you are already going to Sort on dealer name, the Read must be issued for the dealer file in the Input Procedure. While the dealer file record is available, the fields used by the program for calculating the commission are utilized.

```
000062 Sd  Sort-File.
000063 01  Sort-Record.
000064      03  Sort-Key.
000065          05  Dealer-Name.
```

```
000066                    10   Last-Name              Pic X(25).
000067                    10   First-Name             Pic X(15).
000068                    10   Middle-Name            Pic X(10).
000069               05   Sort-Trans-Date.
000070                    10   Trans-Year             Pic 9(4).
000071                    10   Trans-Month            Pic 9(2).
000072                    10   Trans-Day              Pic 9(2).
000073               05   Sort-Trans-Type             Pic X(4).
000074          03   Sort-Trans-Price            Pic S9(6)v99.
000075          03   Sort-Trans-Qty              Pic 9(3).
000076          03   Sort-Commission             Pic S9(6)v99.
```

The various heading lines are coded next.

```
000077 Working-Storage Section.
000078 01   Heading-Line-1.
000079       03   Filler      Pic X(12) Value "Created by:".
000080       03   Filler      Pic X(8)  Value "CHAPT20A".
000081       03   Filler      Pic X(8) Value Spaces.
000082       03   Filler      Pic X(29)
000083            Value "Transaction Summary by Dealer".
000084       03   Filler      Pic X(7) Value Spaces.
000085       03   Filler      Pic X(5)  Value "Page".
000086       03   Page-No     Pic Z(4)9 Value Zeros.
000087 01   Heading-Line-2.
000088       03   Filler      Pic X(12) Value "Created on:".
000089       03   Date-MM     Pic 99.
000090       03   Filler      Pic X     Value "/".
000091       03   Date-DD     Pic 99.
000092       03   Filler      Pic X     Value "/".
000093       03   Date-YY     Pic 99.
000094 01   Heading-Line-3.
000095       03   Filler      Pic X(12) Value "At:".
000096       03   Time-HH     Pic 99.
000097       03   Filler      Pic X     Value ":".
000098       03   Time-MM     Pic 99.
000099       03   Filler      Pic X     Value ":".
000100       03   Time-SS     Pic 99.
000101 01   Heading-Line-4.
000102       03   Filler      Pic X(51) Value Spaces.
000103       03   Filler      Pic X(6)  Value "   Qty".
000104       03   Filler      Pic X(12) Value "     Amount".
000105       03   Filler      Pic X(10) Value "Commission".
```

The Blank-Line data item is coded so that you can place blank lines after certain heading lines and not have to worry about the complexities introduced when Before Advancing is used with After Advancing on the Write statement.

```
000106 01   Blank-Line       Pic X(80) Value Spaces.
```

20

Some programmers use a separate total line description for every total line. This approach makes sense when the layout of the different columns of data is different. For example, one technique that makes reports more readable is to offset the totals by one or more positions from the column of detail data. This simple report does not require an offset, so a single total line is used.

> The total here uses numeric edited data items with the $ symbol, which displays the field on the report with a leading dollar sign. This edit pattern produces at least one dollar sign on the report and thereby limits the size of your data field to one position less that the total number of $ defined. For example, the dollar amounts in these examples can contain a maximum value of 99,999.99, which is one significant position smaller than the 999,999.99 you might expect when you examine the numeric edited data item Picture clause.

```
000107 01  Total-Line.
000108     03  Total-Description  Pic X(51)          Value Spaces.
000109     03  Total-Qty          Pic Z(4)9.
000110     03  Filler             Pic X             Value Spaces.
000111     03  Total-Amt          Pic $$$,$$$.99-.
000112     03  Filler             Pic X             Value Spaces.
000113     03  Total-Commission   Pic $$$,$$$.99-.
```

Because only a single total line is used, you must have different data items in which to build the different total descriptions. An alternative to this method is to String the various total descriptions together when required. As much as possible you should avoid this type of coding. The String statement requires much more computing overhead than the simple Move required to construct these descriptions.

```
000114 01  Desc-Type.
000115     03  Filler             Pic X(11) Value "*   Total".
000116     03  Desc-Type-Type     Pic X(4).
```

Notice the use of Trans-Month, Trans-Day, and Trans-Year in the Desc-Date Group Level item. These field names are the same as those in the transaction record, the Sort record, and the save data areas that are defined shortly. This feature allows you to use Move with Corresponding to reverse the saved date so that it is presented to the users in a more familiar manner. End users feel more comfortable with reports that present data as they are used to seeing it; for example, MM/DD/YYYY instead of YYYY/MM/DD.

```
000117 01  Desc-Date.
000118     03  Filler             Pic X(11) Value "**  Total".
000119     03  Trans-Month        Pic 99.
000120     03  Filler             Pic X Value "/".
```

```
000121      03  Trans-Day            Pic 99.
000122      03  Filler               Pic X Value "/".
000123      03  Trans-Year           Pic 9(4).
000124 01  Desc-Dealer.
000125      03  Filler               Pic X(11) Value "*** Total".
000126      03  Desc-Dealer-Name     Pic X(30).
```

The save fields help detect the different control breaks. The High-Values assigned as values to the alphabetic data items ensure that the first record read causes a control break. When compared against these fields, the data record will be different. The program uses High-Values to detect the fact that this record is the first record read and that the save fields are to be initialized with the fields from this data record.

Some programmers handle this condition differently. They code a special Read for the first data record and initialize the control break save fields. This method requires two Read or Sort return statements for a file, instead of a single statement. Although this approach is conceptually correct, I have found that the single Read leads to programs that are clearer and easier to maintain. A common mistake that programmers make when using a special "seed" Read, as it is called, is the failure to process the first record in the file and Add its data values to the required subtotal. Failure to process the first and last records in a file are common mistakes programmers make when handling control breaks.

Notice that the save fields are defined in exactly the same order as the Sort Key in the Sort record. This feature permits an easier Move when initializing the fields the first time. The entire contents of the Sort Key can be moved instead of individually moving fields.

```
000127 01  Save-Fields.
000128      03  Save-Dealer-Name                 Value High-Values.
000129           05  Last-Name      Pic X(25).
000130           05  First-Name     Pic X(15).
000131           05  Middle-Name    Pic X(10).
000132      03  Save-Date-X.
000133           05  Trans-Year     Pic 9(4).
000134           05  Trans-Month    Pic 9(2).
000135           05  Trans-Day      Pic 9(2).
000136      03  Save-Type          Pic X(4)     Value High-Values.
```

20

The Accumulators group contains the various fields that are used in the different levels of subtotal. Notice the use of the same name for every total field used. This feature allows an Add with Corresponding to accumulate the various subtotals. You will have a group of subtotals for every level of control break identified for the report.

```
000137 01  Accumulators.
000138      03  Grand-Totals.
000139           05  Total-Qty         Pic 9(5)      Value Zeros.
000140           05  Total-Amt         Pic S9(6)v99  Value Zeros.
000141           05  Total-Commission  Pic S9(5)v99  Value Zeros.
```

```
000142      03   Dealer-Totals.
000143           05   Total-Qty        Pic 9(5)          Value Zeros.
000144           05   Total-Amt        Pic S9(6)v99      Value Zeros.
000145           05   Total-Commission Pic S9(5)v99      Value Zeros.
000146      03   Date-Totals.
000147           05   Total-Qty        Pic 9(5)          Value Zeros.
000148           05   Total-Amt        Pic S9(6)v99      Value Zeros.
000149           05   Total-Commission Pic S9(5)v99      Value Zeros.
000150      03   Type-Totals.
000151           05   Total-Qty        Pic 9(5)          Value Zeros.
000152           05   Total-Amt        Pic S9(6)v99      Value Zeros.
000153           05   Total-Commission Pic S9(5)v99      Value Zeros.
```

As it did in Hour 19, "Reporting," the line count starts at 99, thus causing a page break and the printing of headings when the first line of print is produced. The different date and time fields print, in the heading, the date and time the report is produced.

```
000154 01   Line-Count            Pic 99           Value 99.
000155 01   Page-Count            Pic 9(4)         Value Zeros.
000156 01   Max-Lines             Pic 99           Value 60.
000157 01   Date-And-Time-Area.
000158      03   Work-Date             Pic 9(6).
000159      03   Work-Date-X           Redefines Work-Date.
000160           05   Date-YY          Pic 99.
000161           05   Date-MM          Pic 99.
000162           05   Date-DD          Pic 99.
000163      03   Work-Time             Pic 9(8).
000164      03   Work-Time-X           Redefines Work-Time.
000165           05   Time-HH          Pic 99.
000166           05   Time-MM          Pic 99.
000167           05   Time-SS          Pic 99.
000168           05   Filler           Pic XX.
```

The String-Pointer field and the String statements assemble a single name from the three parts of the name that are stored in the Sort record. The name is assembled in the Output Procedure so that it can remain in Last, First, Middle name order during the Sort.

Two separate portions of the program use the Done-Flag field. The first controls the Input Procedure for the Sort, and the second controls the processing in the Output Procedure.

```
000169 01   String-Pointer        Pic 99 Value Zeros.
000170 01   Done-Flag             Pic X Value Spaces.
000171      88   All-Done              Value "Y".
000172 01   Dealer-Status         Pic XX Value Zeros.
000173      88   Dealer-Success   Value "00" Thru "09".
000174 Procedure Division.
```

`Declaratives` catch any unexpected problems that might occur in the `Indexed` dealer file.

```
000175 Declaratives.
000176 Dealer-File-Error Section.
000177     Use After Standard Error Procedure On Dealer-File
000178        .
000179 Dealer-Error-Paragraph.
000180     Display "Error on Dealer File " Dealer-Status
000181        .
000182 End Declaratives.
000183 Chapt20a-Start.
000184     Display "Begin Process Chapt20A"
```

The `Sort` statement ensures that the `Input` data is in the same order as the hierarchy of the control breaks. The `Sort-Key` Group Level item of `Sort-Record` defines this hierarchy. The `Sort` can be coded specifying the individual fields used in the `Sort`, but the method shown is slightly more efficient. The `Sort` needs to handle only the single field and does not need to compare multiple fields.

```
000185     Sort Sort-File Ascending Key Sort-Key
000186         Input Procedure Sort-In
000187         Output Procedure Print-Report
000188     Stop Run
000189        .
```

The `Input Procedure`, `Sort-In`, handles the `Input` operations related to the file being sorted and constructs the `Sort-Record` that is to be sorted. The `Process-Input-Records` `Paragraph` is performed repeatedly until the `All-Done` condition is `Set` to true. This flag indicates that all records in the `Input` file have been processed and released to the `Sort`. After the `Input Procedure` is complete, the `Input` files are closed.

```
000190 Sort-In.
000191     Open Input Trans-File
000192                 Dealer-File
000193     Perform Process-Input-Records Until All-Done
000194     Close Trans-File
000195           Dealer-File
000196        .
```

This `Paragraph` performs the actual `Read` of the `Input` file and, if a record is retrieved, performs the `Paragraph` that processes the data and releases it to the `Sort`. If the end of file is reached, all records have been processed and the `All-Done` flag is set so that the `Input Procedure` will end.

```
000197 Process-Input-Records.
000198     Read Trans-File
000199         At End Set All-Done To True
000200         Not At End
```

20

```
000201                   Perform Move-And-Release-Input
000202          End-Read
000203              .
```

The Move-And-Release-Input Paragraph builds the individual Sort record from the available Input data. It reads the dealer file to retrieve the name and consignment percentage. The actual consignment amount for this transaction is then computed and moved to the appropriate Sort record field. This computation is done here instead of in the Output Procedure so that there can be a single Read of the dealer file for each record. Because the Sort requires the dealer name, it is read in the Input Procedure. If the commission were not computed here, another Read of the dealer master would be required in the Output Procedure to retrieve the consignment percentage.

Recall that the date format of the transaction date in the Sort record is the "reverse" of that in the Input record. The Sort record format is YYYYMMDD, and the Input record is MMDDYYYY.

After the necessary fields are moved, the record is released to the Sort.

```
000204 Move-And-Release-Input.
000205* Reverse The Date
000206          Move Corresponding Transaction-Date-X To
000207                                  Sort-Trans-Date
000208* Move The Data
000209          Move Transaction-Price  To Sort-Trans-Price
000210          Move Transaction-Qty    To Sort-Trans-Qty
000211          Move Transaction-Type   To Sort-Trans-Type
000212* Read Dealer File To Retrieve Name And Consignment Percent
000213          Perform Retrieve-Dealer-Record
000214* Move The Name And Compute Consignment
000215          Move Dealer-Name Of Dealer-Record To
000216               Dealer-Name Of Sort-Record
000217          Compute Sort-Commission Rounded =
000218                  (Transaction-Qty * Transaction-Price) *
000219                  (Consignment-Percent / 100)
000220* Release The Record
000221          Release Sort-Record
000222              .
```

The Retrieve-Dealer-Record Paragraph fills in the required information for the Sort. If the dealer record is not found, the word **UNKNOWN** is moved into the field, and a default consignment percentage of 10 is applied.

```
000223 Retrieve-Dealer-Record.
000224          Move Transaction-Dealer To Dealer-Number Of Dealer-Record
000225          Read Dealer-File
000226              Invalid Key
000227                  Move "**UNKNOWN**" To
000228                       Dealer-Name Of Dealer-Record
```

```
000229               Move 10 To Consignment-Percent
000230       End-Read
000231         .
```

Print-Report is the Output Procedure from the Sort. It contains the meat of the control break program. After some initial housekeeping of opening the report file and filling in the date and time for the headings, each record from the sorted file is returned and processed until all records have been processed.

```
000232 Print-Report.
000233       Open Output Report-File
000234       Move Space To Done-Flag
000235       Perform Fill-Initial-Headings
000236       Perform Return-Process-Records Until All-Done
000237       Close Report-File
000238         .
```

The Return-Process-Records Paragraph handles the actual returning of the Sort records and the decisions made based on the values of the various data fields in the Input records.

> Always include the final processing described here after the At End condition is encountered on your Input file. Programmers frequently fail to process the final required control breaks and instead terminate the program when this end-of-file condition occurs. Note the order of the break processing at the end of file. The lowest-level break is processed first, then the next highest, and so on. This sequence is required so that every subtotal on the report is properly printed and processed into the next level's subtotal fields.

If the end of file is not reached, the program checks for a change in one of the fields that defines the control breaks.

```
000239 Return-Process-Records.
000240       Return Sort-File
000241           At End
000242               Perform Type-Break
000243               Perform Date-Break
000244               Perform Dealer-Break
000245               Perform Print-Grand-Totals
000246               Set All-Done To True
000247           Not At End
000248               Perform Check-For-Break
000249       End-Return
000250         .
```

20

The Check-For-Break paragraph examines the values of the various data fields, comparing them against the save fields. If a control break occurs, the appropriate break is processed. The order of the checks is significant. The first check compares the save field value against High-Values. If it is High-Values, then this data record is the first record into the Output Procedure. The Key fields from this data record are moved to the save fields.

Next the different levels that were defined for this report are checked. The levels are checked in a particular order. The highest level item is checked first.

> The order of control break checks really is important. Many programmers check the lowest level of break first. This is a common mistake. In this example, the lowest level of break is the item type. If a new record is read with a different date but the same item type, a problem could occur if the breaks are checked from the lowest level. There would be no break at the item type level, and the program would continue as if there were no control break, producing erroneous results.

Notice that if a break is detected at a high level, the lower level breaks are performed. They are performed from lowest level to highest level. This sequence allows the individual lines that make up the report for the data records prior to the current record to be printed. Each subtotal is executed and accumulated into the next higher level. Performing each subtotal under the break, in order from lowest to highest, accounts for all accumulated records.

```
000251 Check-For-Break.
000252     Evaluate True
000253        When  Save-Dealer-Name = High-Values
000254              Move Sort-Key To Save-Fields
000255        When  Dealer-Name Of Sort-Record Not = Save-Dealer-Name
000256              Perform Type-Break
000257              Perform Date-Break
000258              Perform Dealer-Break
000259        When  Sort-Trans-Date Not = Save-Date-X
000260              Perform Type-Break
000261              Perform Date-Break
000262        When  Sort-Trans-Type Not = Save-Type
000263              Perform Type-Break
000264        When  Other
000265              Continue
000266     End-Evaluate
```

After any required control break processing, the data for the lowest level is accumulated. This accumulation occurs any time a valid Input record is returned. The only special computation at the detail level in this example is that of expanding the total amount based on the quantity and the individual price.

```
000267      Perform Accumulate-Details
000268         .
000269 Accumulate-Details.
000270      Add Sort-Trans-Qty To Total-Qty Of Type-Totals
000271      Add Sort-Commission To Total-Commission Of Type-Totals
000272      Compute Total-Amt Of Type-Totals =
000273             Total-Amt Of Type-Totals +
000274             (Sort-Trans-Qty * Sort-Trans-Price)
000275         .
```

When a break occurs, the prior subtotals are printed first. The subtotals from the previous records are then added to the next higher level.

Using Add with Corresponding on the various subtotals helps to eliminate coding errors. Programmers have a good habit of copying programming statements from other areas of code. This coding shortcut can, however, lead to errors. Imagine that instead of using Add with Corresponding, the individual subtotals were added. Then the programmer copied this code for the logic for the next control break but failed to change one of the data names in the Add statements. The program would compile and run because all the data names are properly declared, but the results would be wrong. Using Add with Corresponding also eliminates the possibility of forgetting to add one of the many subtotals. It also makes future maintenance of the program easier. Suppose the report is modified to add another subtotal. All the programmer has to do is add the field to the four different Group Level subtotal items in Working-Storage. The control break logic need not change. Writing programs for future maintainability is the goal of any good programmer.

After the next level of subtotal is added, the Initialize verb resets the current level of subtotal fields to zero. The sequence of events works because the last data record returned has not yet had its values added to any subtotals. That step occurs after any control break processing.

20

The final step of any control break logic is to set the value of the save field, which is used in comparisons to check for control breaks, to the value of the newly returned record.

All control breaks perform along the same lines. They print their appropriate data lines, increment the next higher subtotal, initialize their own subtotals, and move the data value that defines the break into the save area.

```
000276 Type-Break.
000277     Perform Print-Type-Total
000278     Add Corresponding Type-Totals To Date-Totals
000279     Initialize Type-Totals
000280     Move Sort-Trans-Type To Save-Type
000281         .
000282 Date-Break.
000283     Perform Print-Date-Total
000284     Add Corresponding Date-Totals To Dealer-Totals
000285     Initialize Date-Totals
000286     Move Sort-Trans-Date To Save-Date-X
000287         .
000288 Dealer-Break.
000289     Perform Print-Dealer-Total
000290     Add Corresponding Dealer-Totals To Grand-Totals
000291     Initialize Dealer-Totals
000292     Move Dealer-Name Of Sort-Record To Save-Dealer-Name
000293         .
```

In Print-Type-Total, the subtotal line is created and written to the printer. The line count is checked and the heading lines are printed if necessary. Notice the use of Move with Corresponding. This statement ensures that all subtotal fields are moved to the subtotal line.

```
000294 Print-Type-Total.
000295     Move Corresponding Type-Totals To Total-Line
000296     Move Save-Type To Desc-Type-Type
000297     Move Desc-Type To Total-Description
000298     If Line-Count > Max-Lines
000299         Perform Heading-Routine
000300     End-If
000301     Write Report-Record From Total-Line After 1
000302     Add 1 To Line-Count
000303         .
```

The Print-Date-Total Paragraph works like the Print-Type-Total Paragraph with the exception of the extra print line printed before and after the total. The line count is checked against two less than the maximum number of lines to allow for the extra lines and to ensure that no page contains more than 60 lines—the value defined as the maximum number of print lines. The Blank-Line is used to print a blank line after the total line. This blank line is required because the very next print line could be one of the single-spaced type subtotals, and you do not want that line to appear without spacing immediately after the date subtotal.

```
000304 Print-Date-Total.
000305     Move Corresponding Date-Totals To Total-Line
000306     Move Corresponding Save-Date-X To Desc-Date
000307     Move Desc-Date To Total-Description
000308     If Line-Count > Max-Lines - 2
```

```
000309          Perform Heading-Routine
000310       End-If
000311       Write Report-Record From Total-Line After 2
000312       Write Report-Record From Blank-Line After 1
000313       Add 3 To Line-Count
000314          .
```

The Print-Dealer-Total Paragraph must perform the additional task of formatting the name field for printing. The multiple String statements allow for a normalized name even in the absence of a middle name in the data record. If the middle name is missing and a single String statement constructs the name, two spaces—the space that follows the first name and the one that should follow the middle name—separate the first and last names. By checking the value of the middle name before issuing the String verb, you can avoid this problem. String-Pointer controls and contains the position used in the next String statement.

```
000315 Print-Dealer-Total.
000316       Move Corresponding Dealer-Totals To Total-Line
000317       Move Spaces To Desc-Dealer-Name
000318       Move 1 To String-Pointer
000319       String First-Name Of Save-Dealer-Name
000320                          Delimited By Space
000321          Into Desc-Dealer-Name
000322          With Pointer String-Pointer
000323       End-String
000324       If Middle-Name Of Save-Dealer-Name
000325          > Spaces
000326          String " " Delimited By Size
000327               Middle-Name Of Save-Dealer-Name
000328                 Delimited By Spaces
000329             Into Desc-Dealer-Name
000330             With Pointer String-Pointer
000331          End-String
000332       End-If
000333       String " " Delimited By Size
000334            Last-Name Of Save-Dealer-Name
000335              Delimited By Spaces
000336          Into Desc-Dealer-Name
000337          With Pointer String-Pointer
000338       End-String
000339       Move Desc-Dealer To Total-Description
000340       If Line-Count > Max-Lines - 1
000341          Perform Heading-Routine
000342       End-If
000343       Write Report-Record From Total-Line After 1
000344       Write Report-Record From Blank-Line After 1
000345       Add 2 To Line-Count
000346          .
```

20

The `Print-Grand-Totals` Paragraph simply moves and prints the grand totals for the report.

```
000347 Print-Grand-Totals.
000348     Move Corresponding Grand-Totals To Total-Line
000349     Move "****Grand Totals" To Total-Description
000350     If Line-Count > Max-Lines - 1
000351         Perform Heading-Routine
000352     End-If
000353     Write Report-Record From Total-Line After 2
000354     .
```

The `Heading-Routine` Paragraph is performed when the maximum line count is exceeded. The page counter is incremented. If this page is the first page of the report, a page eject is not coded. For all subsequent pages in the report, a new page is started for each heading.

The `Fill-Initial-Headings` Paragraph is performed at the beginning of the `Output Procedure` to fill in the date and time that the report is created.

```
000355 Heading-Routine.
000356     Add 1 To Page-Count
000357     Move Page-Count To Page-No
000358     If Page-Count = 1
000359         Write Report-Record From Heading-Line-1 After Zero
000360     Else
000361         Write Report-Record From Heading-Line-1 After Page
000362     End-If
000363     Write Report-Record From Heading-Line-2 After 1
000364     Write Report-Record From Heading-Line-3 After 1
000365     Write Report-Record From Heading-Line-4 After 2
000366     Write Report-Record From Blank-Line     After 1
000367     Move 6 To Line-Count
000368     .
000369 Fill-Initial-Headings.
000370     Accept Work-Date From Date
000371     Accept Work-Time From Time
000372     Move Corresponding Work-Date-X To
000373                         Heading-Line-2
000374     Move Corresponding Work-Time-X To
000375                         Heading-Line-3
000376     .
```

The first page of the printed output follows.

```
Created by: CHAPT20A        Transaction Summary by Dealer        Page    1
Created on: 08/23/98
At:         21:38:43
```

			Qty	Amount	Commission
*	Total	CRAF	8	$558.88	$55.89
**	Total	01/02/1999	8	$558.88	$55.89
*	Total	ANTI	3	555.11	$55.51
*	Total	CRAF	2	$195.40	$19.54
*	Total	MISC	1	$96.25	$9.63
**	Total	04/30/1999	16	$846.76	$84.68
*	Total	ANTI	16	$1,542.11	$154.21
*	Total	CRAF	6	$587.43	$58.74
*	Total	JEWL	9	$1,652.13	$165.21
*	Total	MISC	7	$711.34	$71.13
**	Total	10/12/1999	38	$4,493.01	$449.29
*	Total	HOLI	6	$244.08	$24.41
*	Total	JEWL	1	$89.93	$8.99
**	Total	01/03/2000	7	$334.01	$33.40
***Total		**UNKNOWN**	69	$6,232.66	$623.26
*	Total	ANTI	12	$1,320.72	$858.46
*	Total	HOLI	1	$131.19	$85.27
*	Total	MISC	5	$383.50	$249.28
*	Total	XMAS	3	$145.71	$94.71
**	Total	01/02/1999	21	$1,981.12	$1,287.72

20

*	Total	ANTI	9	$577.17	$375.16
*	Total	CRAF	2	$85.94	$55.86
*	Total	JEWL	3	$464.37	$301.84
*	Total	XMAS	9	$751.31	$488.35
**	Total	04/30/1999	23	$1,878.79	$1,221.21
*	Total	ANTI	6	$727.74	$473.03
*	Total	CRAF	5	$999.20	$649.48
*	Total	JEWL	1	$97.48	$63.36
**	Total	10/12/1999	12	$1,824.42	$1,185.87
*	Total	CRAF	8	$1,291.36	$839.38
*	Total	XMAS	1	$33.37	$21.69
**	Total	01/03/2000	9	$1,324.73	$861.07
*	Total	MISC	13	$1,387.05	$901.58
**	Total	02/07/2000	13	$1,387.05	$901.58
***Total		Doug Mitchell Berg	78	$8,396.11	$5,457.45

The final report produced by the program has multiple dealers per page. If your business keeps a separate file for each dealer, you must start a new page for each new dealer. The simple solution might seem to be to perform the heading routine after a dealer break. This solution is not a good one, though, because the dealer being processed might be the last dealer in the file and you will produce a report where the last page contains headings only. Instead, after the dealer break, Move 99 to the line count field to cause a page break when the next line is printed. The result is a clean, clear report.

Control breaks can be a confusing subject for programmers. If the reporting requirements are not properly analyzed before the program is written, or if the programmer has a poor understanding of control breaks, these programs can become convoluted and difficult to debug and maintain.

A program based on properly analyzed reporting requirements, with clear, concise control break logic, produces reliable and accurate results and, compared to a report where the logic is based on an improper or incomplete analysis, is much easier to maintain.

Summary

In this hour, you learned the following:

- Control breaks occur when the criteria defining the subtotal structure of a report change.
- Control breaks are a normal part of everyday business reporting.
- Proper analysis of the reporting requirements is required up-front to create a reliable reporting program that uses control breaks.
- The Input data for a program that uses control breaks must be sorted in the same hierarchy as that of the control breaks. The Sort proceeds from the highest control break level to the lowest.
- One common mistake is the failure to properly process the first record in the Input file.
- Another common mistake is the failure to properly add the subtotal fields at each control break. Using Add with Corresponding can help to eliminate this problem.
- Occasionally, programmers fail to program for the required processing that must occur at the end of the Input file. When the end of the Input file is reached, every level of control break should be triggered. Each must be processed from lowest level to highest level.
- When a control break occurs at a particular level, all the breaks for the lower levels must be processed first. They must be processed from lowest level to highest.

20

Q&A

Q **What are some of the important things I need to remember when creating a control break program?**

A The data must be sorted in sequence of the hierarchy of your control breaks. A subtotal area must be defined for each level of control break. Save fields must be defined in order to check for a new control break. The subtotal fields must be reset each time they are printed.

Q How often are programs requiring control breaks used in the business world?

A Nearly every report used in business requires the use of some level of control break. Many of these reports contain only subtotal data. Some combine detail and subtotal data on the same report.

Q What are some common mistakes made when writing a program that uses control breaks?

A Failure to process the first and/or last data records are the most common errors. Failure to properly add and then initialize the subtotal fields are also common errors.

Workshop

To help reinforce your understanding of the material presented in this hour, refer to the section "Quiz and Exercise Questions and Answers" that can be found on the CD. This section contains quiz questions and exercises for you to complete, as well as the corresponding answers.

PART IV
Miscellaneous Functions

Hour

21   Date Manipulation

22   Other Intrinsic Functions

HOUR 21

Date Manipulation

An integral part to most business processes is date manipulation. Dates are important to business for a number of reasons. Virtually everything related to business is tied in some way to a date. From birth dates to expiration dates, dates affect business. Transaction dates track when transactions were created and applied. Payment due dates track when a payment is due or past due. Birth dates are used to determine age. Accounting systems use dates for reporting income and expense. In this hour, concepts relating to date manipulation are covered. The topics include

- Calendar history and the year 2000 problem
- Determining the current system date
- The Current-Date Intrinsic Function
- Finding the number of days between dates
- Determining the day of the week
- Date validation
- Converting to Greenwich mean time
- Calculating the date of Easter

Modern COBOL (since 1989) provides a wealth of Functions for working with and manipulating dates. Before 1989 the only way to determine the system date was to use the Accept verb with the From Date and Day clauses. This technique returned only a two-digit date. In 1989 the 1985 COBOL standard was revised to include a new set of features called Intrinsic Functions. Among these Functions were several relating to date manipulation. These provided several methods to help solve the problem related to dates and the year 2000.

The infamous year 2000 problem stems from the fact that most computer programs use only two digits to represent the year. With the year 2000, this two-digit year is 00. This representation causes problems when compared to previous years, for example 99. The logic of programs is affected because this comparison should show that 2000 is greater than 1999, but 00 compares to be less than 99. The program does not perform correctly in this case.

The 1989 extension to the COBOL standard provided a solution to the problem of retrieving the full 4-digit year from the system. Although every program must be checked and changed, the language provides the necessary tools to accomplish the task.

Determining the Current System Date

One function that many programs require is the capability to determine today's date. COBOL uses three different, but related, clauses with the Accept verb to obtain the date.

The first method returns the Gregorian date, which is the date as you are used to seeing it. Pope Gregory XIII instituted the Gregorian calendar in 1582, and it was slowly adopted by the entire world. This calendar is a modification of the Julian calendar that had become incorrect over time. The date correction involved with the change to the Gregorian calendar did not interrupt the weekly cycle of days, but did adjust the day of the month. The Julian calendar had been in use since 45 B.C. and used a standard year of 365 days with every fourth year being a leap year. Over the centuries, the extra days that were slowly added to the calendar caused a problem. When the Gregorian calendar was introduced, a 10-day adjustment was made to the calendar to account for the extra days that had been added to the calendar. Pope Gregory's decree stated that Thursday, October 4, 1582, should be followed by Friday October 15, 1582.

Because of the adjustment in the calendar, any weekday calculations on dates before 1582 must be adjusted, or considered inaccurate. It's not likely that you will need to calculate a date that far back for normal programming, but it does make for a good trivia question!

At this juncture, the current method of figuring leap years was introduced. Using the knowledge of the day, it was determined that every fourth year should be a leap year; however, to avoid the addition of extra days caused by the Julian calendar, every year that ended in a even century, such as 1800 and 1900, would not be a leap year. Except, that is, years divisible by 400. Thus the year 2000 is a leap year.

The three different standard Accept statements related to date processing are

```
000100      Accept The-Date From Date
000101      Accept The-Day  From Day
000102      Accept The-Weekday From Day-Of-Week
```

The first returns the date in a format known as Year-Month-Day. The field The-Date is defined as a six-digit numeric field. The first two numbers represent the last two digits of the current year. The next two represent the month, and the last two the day of the month. This format has been in use since the early days of COBOL. When adding the capability for COBOL to retrieve the current date with a four-digit year, the standards committee had the foresight not to change the behavior of these features. Doing so would have broken countless programs. Instead, the committee devised another, better way to handle the situation.

The second format returns the Julian date. The Julian date is a five-digit numeric field. It contains the two-digit year and a three-digit number corresponding to the day of the year. January 1 is day 1; December 31, in a non-leap year, is day 365. In years with a leap year, the last day is 366. Programmers frequently used this format because it took up little of the precious memory and disk storage that was available in early computing.

The third format returns the current day of the week. The value is a single-digit numeric field. For example, 1 is returned for Monday, 2 for Tuesday, and 3 for Wednesday. This format makes it easy to set up a table in working storage that can be referenced to display the name of the present weekday on your screens and on your reports.

The new method for retrieving the current system date and time uses a new feature called an Intrinsic Function. This hour covers only the date-related Functions. The remainder of these very powerful and useful Functions are covered in Hour 22, "Other Intrinsic Functions."

The Current-Date Intrinsic Function

Intrinsic Functions are used like literals. They are invoked by coding the word Function followed by the name of the Intrinsic Function to be used. The Function for returning the current system date and time is Current-Date. Function Current-Date is one of the few Intrinsic Functions that return an alphanumeric value. This Function returns a field that is 21 characters long. The first eight positions are the

21

current date in Year-Month-Day format, using four digits to represent the year. The next
eight positions represent the current system time in Hour-Minute-Second-Hundredths
format. The final five characters return the offset from Greenwich mean time (GMT) for
time-zone conversion. GMT is the accepted baseline for all time-zone calculations. In
computing environments where this value is not available, it is not returned. In a
Windows NT or Windows 95 environment, the Fujitsu compiler returns the offset from
GMT.

Run the small program in Listing 21.1 and examine the results.

LISTING 21.1   USING THE CURRENT-DATE INTRINSIC FUNCTION

```
000001 @OPTIONS MAIN,TEST
000002 Identification Division.
000003 Program-Id.  Chapt21a.
000004 Environment Division.
000005 Configuration Section.
000006 Source-Computer.   IBM-PC.
000007 Object-Computer.   IBM-PC.
000008 Data Division.
000009 Working-Storage Section.
000010 01  Current-Date-Group.
000011     03   Todays-Date.
000012          05   Today-YYYY        Pic 9(4).
000013          05   Today-MM          Pic 9(2).
000014          05   Today-DD          Pic 9(2).
000015     03   Time-Now.
000016          05   Time-Hour         Pic 99.
000017          05   Time-Minutes      Pic 99.
000018          05   Time-Seconds      Pic 99.
000019          05   Time-Hundredths   Pic 99.
000020     03   GMT-Offset.
000021          05   GMT-Direction     Pic X.
000022          05   GMT-Hours         Pic 99.
000023          05   GMT-Minutes       Pic 99.
000024 Procedure Division.
000025 Chapt21a.
000026     Move Function Current-Date To Current-Date-Group
000027     Display "Today = " Todays-Date
000028     Display "Time  = " Time-Now
000029     Display "GMT offset = " GMT-Offset
000030     Stop Run
000031     .
```

The field Current-Date-Group is further divided into the individual fields. Dividing the
group in this manner gives you access to each field individually. The GMT-Direction is
either a plus sign or a minus sign (+ or -), indicating the conversion that was applied to

GMT to achieve local time. Therefore, to convert back to GMT, you must adjust the time in the opposite direction. If the `GMT-Direction` field is - and the `GMT-Hours` field is 5, you must add 5 hours to the current time to arrive at GMT.

If you want to use the `Current-Date Intrinsic Function` but require only the date, not the time values, you can use reference modification. For example, you can code:

```
000101     Move Function Current-Date (1:8) to Date-Only
```

When using the current date for other than cosmetic reasons, it is best to use the `Current-Date Intrinsic Function`.

Days Between Dates

One task frequently required when working with dates is computing the number of days between dates. This value can be useful in a number of applications. For example, you might require a dealer to bring in new merchandise every 90 days. To derive the next date that a dealer needs to add merchandise, you can add 90 days to the last date the dealer did so. When working with a date in `Year-Month-Day` format, adding days can be a daunting task.

Adding 90 days might not seem to be a difficult calculation. Simply add 3 months, and that date should be close enough. But many applications require more precision. For instance, you might be writing a program for an ice cream factory. The ice cream might have a shelf life of 37 days. This number of days must be added to the date of manufacture to determine the expiration date.

Another task might be determining the age of an item. Given two dates in `Year-Month-Day` format, you might need to determine the age of the item.

COBOL provides some date-related `Intrinsic Functions` that make these types of computations easy to accomplish. These `Functions` are `Integer-Of-Date` and `Date-Of-Integer`. `Integer-Of-Date` accepts a single argument: the date in `Year-Month-Day` format, using a four-digit year. The `Function` returns the number of days since December 31, 1600. Day 1 is January 1, 1601. The standards committee chose this date because integer day 1, January 1, 1601, is a Monday. Monday is day 1 in the `Day-Of-Week` format of the `Accept` verb.

When arguments are specified with `Intrinsic Functions`, the argument follows the `Function` name and is enclosed in parentheses. The numeric-returning `Intrinsic Functions`, such as `Integer-Of-Date` and `Date-Of-Integer`, must be used in a mathematical statement—that is, within a mathematical expression such as `Compute`. Unlike the alphanumeric-returning `Current-Date Function`, you cannot use these `Functions` in a `Move` statement. Listing 21.2 shows the conversion of 12/31/1999 into an integer date.

21

LISTING 21.2 INTEGER-OF-DATE EXAMPLE

```
000001 @OPTIONS MAIN,TEST
000002 Identification Division.
000003 Program-Id.  Chapt21b.
000004 Environment Division.
000005 Configuration Section.
000006 Source-Computer.  IBM-PC.
000007 Object-Computer.  IBM-PC.
000008 Data Division.
000009 Working-Storage Section.
000010 01  Integer-Version-Of-Date   Pic 9(7) Value Zeros.
000011 01  Date-To-Convert           Pic 9(8) Value 19991231.
000012 Procedure Division.
000013 Chapt21b.
000014     Compute Integer-Version-Of-Date =
000015             Function Integer-Of-Date (Date-To-Convert)
000016     Display "Integer Date Version of " Date-To-Convert
000017             " is " Integer-Version-Of-Date
000018        .
```

You can use the opposite procedure to convert a date from an integer date to a regular Gregorian date in the format YYYYMMDD.

```
000019     Compute Date-To-Convert =
000020     Function Date-Of-Integer (Integer-Version-Of-Date)
```

Determining the days between particular dates becomes easy. Simply convert each date to an integer date and compute the difference. Likewise, if you want to compute a date that is a certain number of days in the future, convert the date to an integer, add the number of days, and reconvert the result to a date.

The program in Listing 21.3 will Accept two dates and reports the number of days between them. Try compiling it and determining how many days old you are!

LISTING 21.3 DAYS BETWEEN DATES

```
000001 @OPTIONS MAIN,TEST
000002 Identification Division.
000003 Program-Id.  Chapt21c.
000004* Days Between Dates
000005 Environment Division.
000006 Configuration Section.
000007 Source-Computer.  IBM-PC.
000008 Object-Computer.  IBM-PC.
000009 Data Division.
000010 Working-Storage Section.
000011 01  First-Date                Value Zeros.
```

```
000012        03   Date-MM              Pic 99.
000013        03   Date-DD              Pic 99.
000014        03   Date-YYYY            Pic 9(4).
000015 01  Second-Date                  Value Zeros.
000016        03   Date-MM              Pic 99.
000017        03   Date-DD              Pic 99.
000018        03   Date-YYYY            Pic 9(4).
000019 01  Days-Between                 Pic S9(12) Value Zeros.
000020 01  Integer-First-Date           Pic  9(12).
000021 01  Integer-Second-Date          Pic  9(12).
000022 01  Date-Formatting-Items.
000023        03   YYYYMMDD-Format-Date.
000024           05   Date-YYYY          Pic 9(4).
000025           05   Date-MM            Pic 99.
000026           05   Date-DD            Pic 99.
000027        03   YYYYMMDD-Format-Date-N Redefines
000028             YYYYMMDD-Format-Date  Pic 9(8).
000029        03   Format-Indicator-F    Pic X(8) Value "MMDDYYYY".
000030        03   Format-Indicator-S    Pic X(8) Value "MMDDYYYY".
000031 Screen Section.
000032 01  Date-Entry Blank Screen Auto.
000033        03   Line 01 Column 01 Value "Enter First Date: ".
000034        03   Line 01 Column 21 Pic X(8) From Format-Indicator-F
000035                                      To    First-Date.
000036        03   Line 03 Column 01 Value "Enter Second Date: ".
000037        03   Line 03 Column 21 Pic X(8) From Format-Indicator-S
000038                                      To    Second-Date.
000039        03   Line 05 Column 01 Value "Days between dates: ".
000040        03   Line 05 Column 21 Pic -Zzz,ZZ9 From Days-Between.
000041 Procedure Division.
000042 Chapt21c-Start.
000043        Display Date-Entry
000044        Accept Date-Entry
000045        Move Corresponding First-Date To YYYYMMDD-Format-Date
000046        Compute Integer-First-Date =
000047             Function Integer-Of-Date (YYYYMMDD-Format-Date-N)
000048        Move First-Date To Format-Indicator-F
000049        Move Corresponding Second-Date To YYYYMMDD-Format-Date
000050        Compute Integer-Second-Date =
000051             Function Integer-Of-Date (YYYYMMDD-Format-Date-N)
000052        Move Second-Date To Format-Indicator-S
000053        Compute Days-Between = Integer-Second-Date -
000054                               Integer-First-Date
000055        Display Date-Entry
000056        Stop Run
000057        .
```

21

When you run the program, notice the use of the separate From and To fields in the screen definition. This syntax allows you to prompt the user for the proper date format.

Determining the weekday of any given date is an easy operation in COBOL. An even easier method that uses another COBOL-provided `Intrinsic Function` is demonstrated later in this hour.

Validating Dates

In Hour 18, "Master File Updating," you wrote a transaction file data entry program. This program used transaction dates. No checks were performed on the dates that the user entered, and invalid data could enter the transaction file.

Whenever possible you should ensure that invalid data cannot enter the systems that you design and code. Correcting invalid data after it has been accepted can be a very time-consuming and complex task. Prevention is the order of the day.

Dates are a particularly sensitive area for business. Ensuring that the dates entered are valid is very important. Date validation is simple to accomplish.

When validating a date, you must first ensure that it has been entered in the proper format by checking the values in the individual fields that make up the date. First, check the month value to determine whether it is between 1 and 12. Any value outside that range is obviously invalid.

Then you must check the value of the day to determine whether it falls within the prescribed value for the particular month with which it is associated. Each month, with the exception of February, has a set number of days. A table of maximum day values is the simplest method of validating the day.

To properly validate days in February, you must determine whether the year being checked is a leap year. The rules for determining a leap year are simple. Any year evenly divisible by 4, except those years evenly divisible by 100 and not evenly divisible by 400, is a leap year. The year 2000 is a leap year because it is evenly divisible by 400. The year 1900, although evenly divisible by 4, was not a leap year because it was evenly divisible by 100 and not by 400.

After you determine that the month and day are valid, you can check the full date to determine whether it falls within your desired range. For example, you might want to `Accept` a date and then ensure that it falls within 30 days of the current date. Any date that falls outside that range is invalid.

After determining that the month and day are valid, you can convert the day to an integer and check it against the integer value of the current date.

One thing you should do before using the Intrinsic Function for converting the entered date to an integer is ensure that the year entered is 1601 or
greater. Any invalid value passed as an argument to the Intrinsic Function
Integer-Of-Date causes the Function to abnormally terminate your program.

The program in Listing 21.5 accepts a date in MM/DD/YYYY format and validates the date.
It then checks to ensure that the date is within 30 days of the current date. The validity
and range are reported on the screen before the program ends.

LISTING 21.5 DATE VALIDATION

```
000001 @OPTIONS MAIN,TEST
000002 Identification Division.
000003 Program-Id.  Chapt21e.
000004* Validate A Date
000005 Environment Division.
000006 Configuration Section.
000007 Source-Computer.  IBM-PC.
000008 Object-Computer.  IBM-PC.
000009 Data Division.
000010 Working-Storage Section.
000011 01  Date-Validation-Work-Fields.
000012     03  Date-To-Validate      Pic 9(8) Value Zeros.
000013     03  Date-To-Validate-X Redefines Date-To-Validate.
000014         05  Date-MM           Pic 99.
000015         05  Date-DD           Pic 99.
000016         05  Date-YYYY         Pic 9(4).
000017     03  YYYYMMDD-Format-Date  Pic 9(8) Value Zeros.
000018     03  YYYYMMDD-Format-Date-X Redefines YYYYMMDD-Format-Date.
000019         05  Date-YYYY         Pic 9(4).
000020         05  Date-MM           Pic 99.
000021         05  Date-DD           Pic 99.
```

The Day-Table has an entry containing the number of days in the corresponding month.
Only the second entry, February, requires modification if the year being tested is a leap
year.

```
000022     03  Day-Table-Values     Pic X(24) Value
000023         "312831303130313130313031".
000024     03  Day-Table Redefines Day-Table-Values.
000025         05  Days-In-Month     Pic 99   Occurs 12 Times.
```

21

The work fields below are used in the process of validating the dates. The remainder fields are used with division statements to determine whether the year in question is a leap year.

```
000026 01  Valid-Status          Pic X(40) Value Spaces.
000027 01  Work-Number           Pic 9(5) Value Zeros.
000028 01  Work-Remainder        Pic 9(5) Value Zeros.
000029 01  Work-Remainder-100    Pic 9(5) Value Zeros.
000030 01  Work-Remainder-400    Pic 9(5) Value Zeros.
000031 01  Today-Date            Pic 9(8) Value Zeros.
000032 01  Today-Integer         Pic 9(7) Value Zeros.
000033 01  Test-Integer          Pic 9(7) Value Zeros.
000034 01  Test-Range            Pic 9(7) Value Zeros.
000035 Screen Section.
000036 01  Date-Entry Blank Screen Auto.
000037     03  Line 01 Column 01 Value "Enter Date: ".
000038     03  Line 01 Column 13 Pic 99/99/9999 Using Date-To-Validate.
000039     03  Line 01 Column 24 Pic X(40) From Valid-Status.
000040 Procedure Division.
000041 Chapt21e-Start.
000042     Display Date-Entry
000043     Accept Date-Entry
```

The first part of the program determines whether the year entered is a leap year. The first step is to set up the three conditions that must be checked.

```
000044     Divide Date-YYYY Of Date-To-Validate-X By 4
000045         Giving Work-Number Remainder
000046             Work-Remainder
000047     Divide Date-YYYY Of Date-To-Validate-X By 100
000048         Giving Work-Number Remainder
000049             Work-Remainder-100
000050     Divide Date-YYYY Of Date-To-Validate-X By 400
000051         Giving Work-Number Remainder
000052             Work-Remainder-400
```

The conditions are then tested. If Work-Remainder is zeros, the date was divisible by 4, which it must be to be a leap year. Then if the date is not divisible by 100 or if the date is divisible by 400, it is a leap year. The appropriate number of days is moved to the table for February.

```
000053     If Work-Remainder = Zeros And
000054       (Work-Remainder-100 Not = Zeros Or
000055        Work-Remainder-400 = Zeros)
000056           Move 29 To Days-In-Month (2)
000057     Else
000058           Move 28 To Days-In-Month (2)
000059     End-If
```

The conditions that make the date an invalid date are checked. If any of these conditions is true, the date is invalid. To be valid, the month must be between 1 and 12. The year

must be greater than 1600 or else the Intrinsic Functions related to Integer-Of-Date
fails. The day must be at least 1 and not greater than the maximum number of days in the
month.

```
000060     If Date-MM Of Date-To-Validate-X  > 12 Or
000061         Date-MM Of Date-To-Validate-X  < 01 Or
000062         Date-YYYY Of Date-To-Validate-X < 1601 Or
000063         Date-DD Of Date-To-Validate-X Not > Zero Or
000064         Date-DD Of Date-To-Validate-X >
000065         Days-In-Month (Date-MM Of Date-To-Validate-X)
000066         Move "Invalid Date" To Valid-Status
000067     End-If
```

If the date was not marked invalid by a message in the Valid-Status field, then the
number of days between the dates can be checked.

When comparing the two dates, you will have no idea which is greater. When you do the
subtraction of the two integer dates, you could end up with either a positive or a negative
number. To make the comparison easy, the result of the subtraction is stored in an
unsigned field. This step causes the value to be stored without a sign and treated in comparisons as a positive number.

```
000068     If Valid-Status = Spaces
000069         Move Corresponding Date-To-Validate-X To
000070                           YYYYMMDD-Format-Date-X
000071         Move Function Current-Date (1:8) To Today-Date
000072         Compute Test-Range =
000073             Function Integer-Of-Date (YYYYMMDD-Format-Date) -
000074             Function Integer-Of-Date (Today-Date)
000075         If Test-Range > 30
000076            Move "Date Valid, but out of Range" To Valid-Status
000077         End-If
000078     End-If
```

If there were no errors, a message to that effect is displayed for the user.

```
000079     If Valid-Status = Spaces
000080        Move "Date Valid and Within Range" To Valid-Status
000081     End-If
000082     Display Date-Entry
000083     .
```

The previous examples use the remainder of a division to calculate the day of the week
and to determine whether a year is a leap year. In COBOL a simpler method can achieve
the same results. When you want to use a remainder only and are not concerned about
the whole result of the division, you can use the Intrinsic Function Rem. Rem returns
the remainder of the first argument divided by the second. When you are concerned only
with the remainder, using the Function Rem is more efficient than coding the necessary
Working-Storage and Divide statement.

21

`Function Rem` simplifies the day of the week calculation so that it consists of only the
following lines of code:

```
000065      Compute Remainder-Days =
000066               (Function Rem (Integer-First-Date 7) + 1)
000067      Move The-Day (Remainder-Days) To Weekday-First
```

Notice that the arguments for the `Function` are enclosed in parentheses after the
`Function` name.

> When multiple arguments are specified with an `Intrinsic Function`, they
> may be separated by a comma. This visual clue sometimes makes the argu-
> ments easier to pick out when examining source code. For example, the
> `Function Rem` noted above, can be coded as `Function Rem (Integer-First-`
> `Date, 7)`.

Another interesting calculation is the conversion from local time to GMT using the values returned from the `Current-Date Intrinsic Function`. The problem in this conversion comes from the fact that when you subtract or add the time differential, the date
may change. Doing math on time fields is tricky under normal circumstances. With the
added complexity of a possibly changing date, the task can seem rather challenging.
Times are tricky to work with because they are not normal base 10 numbers. When you
add to the minutes, anything over `59` requires the hour to be incremented by 1. If you are
subtracting and need to borrow from the hours, you must add `59` to the minutes, not `10`
as in more conventional math. Consequently, normal computational formulas won't solve
the problem.

One simple way to solve the problem is to convert the current time into seconds since
midnight `12/31/1600`. The solution is relatively easy if you use these equivalencies:
`86,400` seconds in a day; `3,600` seconds in an hour; and `60` seconds in a minute.
Multiply the date by `86,400`; the hour by `3,600`; and the minutes by `60`; then add the current time seconds to the result. The current time is now in seconds. Perform the same
type of math against the GMT offset, as reported by the `Current-Date Intrinsic`
`Function`, and either add or subtract the amount of seconds from the current date in seconds.

The only remaining difficulty is to return the resulting seconds to a conventional date and
time. Listing 21.6 shows the program required to perform the calculation. Find the number of the day by dividing the resulting seconds by `86,400` and save the remainder, as it
is the time. Convert this integer date to a Gregorian date. Divide the remaining seconds
by `3,600` to find the hour, again saving the remainder. Then divide the remainder of that

calculation by 60 to find the minutes. The remainder of this computation is the seconds!
Simple.

LISTING 21.6   CONVERT LOCAL TIME TO GMT

```
000001 @OPTIONS MAIN,TEST
000002 Identification Division.
000003 Program-Id.   Chapt21g.
000004* Convert Local Time To Gmt
000005 Environment Division.
000006 Configuration Section.
000007 Source-Computer.  IBM-PC.
000008 Object-Computer.  IBM-PC.
000009 Data Division.
000010 Working-Storage Section.
000011 01   Current-Date-Group.
000012      03   Todays-Date.
000013           05   Today-YYYY      Pic 9(4).
000014           05   Today-MM        Pic 9(2).
000015           05   Today-DD        Pic 9(2).
000016      03   Todays-Date-N Redefines Todays-Date Pic 9(8).
000017      03   Time-Now.
000018           05   Time-Hour       Pic 99.
000019           05   Time-Minutes    Pic 99.
000020           05   Time-Seconds    Pic 99.
000021           05   Time-Hundredths Pic 99.
000022      03   GMT-Offset.
000023           05   GMT-Direction   Pic X.
000024           05   GMT-Hours       Pic 99.
000025           05   GMT-Minutes     Pic 99.
000026 01   Display-Date.
000027      03   Today-MM             Pic 9(2).
000028      03   Filler               Pic X Value "/".
000029      03   Today-DD             Pic 9(2).
000030      03   Filler               Pic X Value "/".
000031      03   Today-YYYY           Pic 9(4).
000032 01   Display-Time.
000033      03   Time-Hour            Pic 99.
000034      03   Filler               Pic X Value ":".
000035      03   Time-Minutes         Pic 99.
000036      03   Filler               Pic X Value ":".
000037      03   Time-Seconds         Pic 99.
000038 01   Total-Seconds             Pic 9(15) Value Zeros.
000039 01   Work-Number               Pic 9(15) Value Zeros.
000040 01   Work-Remainder            Pic 9(15) Value Zeros.
000041 01   GMT-Offset                Pic 9(15) Value Zeros.
000042 Procedure Division.
000043 Chapt21g.
```

21

continues

LISTING 21.6   CONTINUED

```
000044      Move Function Current-Date To Current-Date-Group
000045* Convert Today To Seconds
000046      Compute Work-Number =
000047             Function Integer-Of-Date (Todays-Date-N)
000048      Compute Total-Seconds = (Work-Number * 86400) +
000049                           (Time-Hour Of Time-Now * 3600) +
000050                           (Time-Minutes Of Time-Now * 60) +
000051                           Time-Seconds Of Time-Now
000052      Compute Work-Number = (GMT-Hours * 3600) +
000053                           (GMT-Minutes * 60)
000054* We Need To Change By The Opposite Of The Direction From Gmt
000055      If GMT-Direction = "+"
000056         Subtract Work-Number From Total-Seconds
000057      Else
000058         Add Work-Number To Total-Seconds
000059      End-If
000060* Convert The Time In Seconds Back To A Date And Time
000061      Divide Total-Seconds By 86400 Giving Work-Number
000062                           Remainder Work-Remainder
000063      Compute Todays-Date-N =
000064             Function Date-Of-Integer (Work-Number)
```

This next computation uses the remainder from the last division and stores the new remainder in Work-Number, which is used in the next calculation. Although the names don't match their Function, this technique saves having to move the fields before the next calculation.

```
000065      Divide Work-Remainder By 3600 Giving Time-Hour Of Time-Now
000066                           Remainder Work-Number
000067      Divide Work-Number By 60 Giving Time-Minutes Of Time-Now
000068                           Remainder Time-Seconds Of Time-Now
000069      Move Corresponding Todays-Date To Display-Date
000070      Move Corresponding Time-Now To Display-Time
000071      Display "Current GMT " Display-Date " " Display-Time
000072      Stop Run
000073         .
```

Other Kinds of Dates

Occasionally, you may need to use the Julian date instead of the Gregorian date. The Intrinsic Functions provide an easy way to convert to and from the Julian date. These Functions are similar to the Date-Of-Integer and Integer-Of-Date Functions.

The `Functions` related to the Julian date are `Day-Of-Integer` and `Integer-Of-Day`. These `Functions` make conversion to and from the Gregorian date simple. If you want to convert from Gregorian date, use the `Function Integer-Of-Date` to find the integer date of the day in question. Then, using that integer, execute the `Function Day-Of-Integer`. The Julian date is returned in YYYYDDD format, where YYYY is the full four-digit year and DDD is the day of the year.

To convert from Julian date to Gregorian date, use the `Function Integer-Of-Day` to determine the integer date; then use the `Function Date-Of-Integer` to find the Gregorian date.

Fun with Dates

Now that you know how to do nearly everything there is to do with dates, you can have some fun. You can create your own calendar program. You can determine the holidays and print these on the calendar. Most holidays fall on specific days of the month or on the closest Monday to that day. The only really tricky holiday to figure is the date for Easter.

In 325 A.D., the Council of Nicaea determined that Easter should be celebrated on the first Sunday after the first full moon after the vernal equinox. If the full moon fell on a Sunday, causing it to coincide with the Passover, it would be celebrated the following Sunday.

Problems soon beset this method because of the difference between the solar year and the lunar year, known as the epact. Over time, the difference became increasingly pronounced. It was the problem of fixing the date of Easter that ultimately led to the calendar reform of 1582.

The method for calculating the date of Easter is fairly complex. However, because it has a series of steps that follow a specific set of rules, a program can be created that accurately calculates the date.

The algorithm chosen first appeared in volume 1 of *The Art of Computer Programming* by Donald Knuth. The steps are as follows:

- First, the current position in the metonic cycle is determined by the remainder of the full four-digit year divided by 19. Every 19 years, the phases of the moon repeat on the same calendar days of the year. This cycle is the metonic cycle, and the result of this computation is known as the "golden number."

- Next, the century number is determined by dividing the year by 100, disregarding the remainder, and adding 1.

21

- Next, the number of years that the leap year was dropped in the even centuries is determined. Remember that if the century is divisible by 100 and not by 400, the year, which is divisible by 4, is not a leap year. The number of years in which this condition occurs is determined by multiplying the century previously computed by 3, dividing the result by 4, and subtracting 12. The remainder portion of the division is discarded. After 1900 and until the year 2100, this number is 3—the number of even centuries without a leap year since calendar reform. (Recall that 1600 was a leap year, 1700 was not, 1800 was not, 1900 was not, and 2000 is.)

- A special correction is computed to synchronize Easter with the orbit of the moon. This value is 8 times the century, plus 5, divided by 25. The remainder is discarded, and 5 is subtracted from the result of the division.

- A factor is determined to adjust the date to the next Sunday. This factor is computed by multiplying the full four-digit year by 5 and dividing the result by 4. Again, the remainder is discarded. The number of skipped leap years plus 10 is then subtracted from the result.

- Next, the epact is computed. It is the remainder of 11 times the golden number, plus 20, plus the correction factor, minus the number of skipped leap years, all divided by 30. The epact is always a positive number. If you achieve a negative result, change the sign to positive. In the COBOL program, you can just compute the value into an unsigned field.

- If the epact is 24, or if the epact is 25 and the golden number is greater than 11, 1 is added to the epact.

- The day of the first full moon in March is then computed. This value is 44 minus the epact. If the result of this subtraction is less than 21, then 30 is added to it.

- This day is then advanced to the following Sunday by subtracting the remainder of the sum of this date and the correction factor divided by 7 from the day plus 7. That is, day plus 7 minus remainder, or ((Day + Correction) / 7).

- If this resulting day is greater than 31, then Easter falls in April instead of March and 31 is subtracted from the day.

Taking this type of algorithm and creating a program that performs the task is the COBOL programmer's job. Chapt21h.Cob, shown in Listing 21.7, computes the date of Easter for any given year.

LISTING 21.7   EASTER DATE CALCULATION

```
000001 @OPTIONS MAIN,TEST
000002 Identification Division.
000003 Program-Id.   Chapt21h.
```

```
000004* Compute The Date Of Easter For The Given Year
000005 Environment Division.
000006 Configuration Section.
000007 Source-Computer.  IBM-PC.
000008 Object-Computer.  IBM-PC.
000009 Data Division.
000010 Working-Storage Section.
000011 01  Easter-Work-Fields.
000012     03  The-Year          Pic 9(4) Value Zeros.
000013     03  Easter-Date       Pic 9(8) Value Zeros.
000014     03  Easter-Date-X Redefines Easter-Date.
000015         05  Easter-Month  Pic 99.
000016         05  Easter-Day    Pic 99.
000017         05  Easter-Year   Pic 9(4).
000018     03  Golden-Number     Pic 9(6).
000019     03  Century           Pic 9(3).
000020     03  Skipped-Leap-Year Pic 9(6).
000021     03  Correction        Pic 9(8).
000022     03  Factor            Pic 9(8).
000023     03  Epact             Pic 9(8).
000024 01  Temp-Work             Pic 9(8).
000025 01  Temp-Work-1           Pic 9(8).
000026 Screen Section.
000027 01  Date-Entry Blank Screen Auto.
000028     03  Line 01 Column 01 Value "Enter Year: ".
000029     03  Line 01 Column 14 Pic 9(4) Using The-Year.
000030     03  Line 03 Column 01 Value "Easter is: ".
000031     03  Line 03 Column 15 Pic 99/99/9999 From Easter-Date.
000032 Procedure Division.
000033 Chapt21h-Start.
000034     Display Date-Entry
000035     Accept Date-Entry
000036     Move The-Year To Easter-Year
000037*
000038     Compute Golden-Number = Function Rem (The-Year 19)
000039     Add 1 To Golden-Number
000040*
000041     Divide The-Year By 100 Giving Century
000042     Add 1 To Century
000043*
000044     Compute Temp-Work = 3 * Century
000045     Divide Temp-Work By 4 Giving Skipped-Leap-Year
000046     Subtract 12 From Skipped-Leap-Year
000047*
000048     Compute Temp-Work = (8 * Century) + 5
000049     Divide Temp-Work By 25 Giving Correction
000050     Subtract 5 From Correction
000051*
000052     Compute Temp-Work = 5 * The-Year
```

21

continues

LISTING 21.7   CONTINUED

```
000053      Divide Temp-Work By 4 Giving Factor
000054      Subtract Skipped-Leap-Year From Factor
000055      Subtract 10 From Factor
000056*
000057      Compute Temp-Work = (11 * Golden-Number) + 20
000058                      + Correction - Skipped-Leap-Year
000059      Compute Epact = Function Rem (Temp-Work 30)
000060*
000061      If Epact = 25 And Golden-Number > 11 Or
000062         Epact = 24
000063         Add 1 To Epact
000064      End-If
000065*
000066      Compute Temp-Work = 44 - Epact
000067      If Temp-Work < 21
000068         Add 30 To Temp-Work
000069      End-If
000070*
000071      Compute Temp-Work-1 = Factor + Temp-Work
000072      Compute Easter-Day =  Temp-Work + 7 -
000073             Function Rem (Temp-Work-1 7)
000074*
000075      If Easter-Day > 31
000076         Move 4 To Easter-Month
000077         Subtract 31 From Easter-Day
000078      Else
000079         Move 3 To Easter-Month
000080      End-If
000081      Move The-Year To Easter-Year
000082*
000083      Display Date-Entry
000084      Stop Run
000085      .
```

Summary

In this hour, you learned the following:

- COBOL provides several powerful Functions for date processing.

- Today's date, time, and offset from Greenwich mean time can be determined with the Intrinsic Function Current-Date.

- When using Intrinsic Functions, the argument or arguments are enclosed in parentheses after the name of the Function.

- The Function Integer-Of-Date returns a value that is the number of days since December 31, 1600, for the date used as the argument.

- When using the Intrinsic Functions for dates, the Gregorian date format is YYYYMMDD and the Julian date format is YYYYDDD.

- The current state of the calendar is directly related to the 1582 calendar reform that corrected the number of days in the year, by adjusting the years that have a leap year, in an effort to solidify and correct the calculation of Easter.

- You can use the Intrinsic Function Rem instead of the Divide statement to find the remainder of a division.

Q&A

Q Why did the standards committee choose January 1, 1601, as day 1 in the COBOL calendar?

A It was the closest year to calendar reform that began on a Monday. When accepting the current weekday from the system, 1 is the value returned for Monday.

Q When I want to figure out what the date is 90 days from now, what is the easiest method?

A Convert the date to an integer, using the Function Integer-Of-Date, and then add 90. Convert that number back to a date using the Function Date-Of-Integer.

Q What happens if I use an invalid date as an argument for one of the date Intrinsic Functions?

A The Function fails, and in most COBOL implementations your program ends abnormally.

Q My program won't compile when I try to code Move Function Integer-Of-Date (The-Date) to Integer-Date. Why not?

A Numeric Intrinsic Functions must be used in mathematical expressions.

Workshop

To help reinforce your understanding of the material presented in this hour, refer to the section "Quiz and Exercise Questions and Answers" that can be found on the CD. This section contains quiz questions and exercises for you to complete, as well as the corresponding answers.

21

Hour **22**

Other Intrinsic Functions

In Hour 21, "Date Manipulation," you learned about the Intrinsic Functions associated with date processing. In addition to these functions, COBOL comes equipped with a wealth of additional Intrinsic Functions that fill the need for a variety of items such as

- Mathematical and statistical Functions
- Financial application Functions
- String manipulation Functions
- Miscellaneous Functions such as random number generation

These functions bring features to COBOL that, prior to their introduction in 1989, had to be designed and coded by programmers, sometimes using complex algorithms. Many of these functions can help make programming much easier for the COBOL programmer.

Mathematical Functions

The first subset of Functions relates to trigonometric Functions. These Functions can be used for calculations normally reserved for scientific programming languages such as FORTRAN. Many governments and universities rely on COBOL as their main programming language. Having these Functions available from COBOL means that these institutions don't have to develop these processes in other programming languages.

> The trigonometric Functions and the square root Function are approximations. Different compilers can produce different results for these Functions.

> Explaining trigonometric Functions is beyond the scope of this book. However, this section does explain the values returned and the methods used to obtain those values.

Each trigonometric Function accepts a single argument, which is specified within parentheses following the Function name. These Functions are

- Cosine   Function Cos
- Sin   Function Sin
- Tangent   Function Tan
- Arcsin   Function Asin
- Arccosine   Function Acos
- Arctangent   Function Atan

The Cosine Function returns a numeric value in the range of plus or minus 1. As with all numeric Intrinsic Functions, the value is returned by using the Function in an arithmetic statement such as Compute. The argument used with the Cos Function must be numeric and is specified in radians. For example, to find the cosine of .785 radians, you code the following:

```
000100     Compute The-Cosine = Function Cos (.785)
```

The value returned is .707388269.

22

Because the argument is in radians, you might need to convert an angle to radians. You may approximate the radians with the following `Compute` statement (pi is approximated and is the value that is divided by 180):

```
000101     Compute Radians = Angle * (3.14159265358979324 / 180)
```

The `Sin Function` returns a numeric value in the range of plus or minus 1 that approximates the value of the `Sin` of the argument. As with Cosine, the argument value is specified in radians. To find the `Sin` of `.875` radians, code the following:

```
000102     Compute The-Sin = Function Sin (.875)
```

The `Tan Function` returns a numeric value that approximates the value of the Tangent of the argument. The argument value is specified in radians. To find the Tangent of `.785` radians, code the following:

```
000103     Compute The-Tangent = Function Tan (.785)
```

The `Asin` and `Acos Functions` return an approximation of the ArcSin and ArcCosine of the argument. The argument must fall within the range of plus or minus 1. The value returned is in radians. To figure the Acos of `.707388269`, code the following:

```
000104     Compute The-Arc-Cosine = Function Acos (.707388269)
```

The `Atan Function` returns an approximation of the ArcTangent of the specified argument. The value is returned in radians.

Two different logarithm `Functions` are provided. These numeric `Functions` accept a single numeric argument. The `Log Function` returns an approximation of the natural logarithm of the specified argument. The `Log10 Function` returns an approximation of logarithm to base 10 of the argument. The argument must be a positive number.

You can use the `Factorial Function` to find the factorial of an argument. The argument specified must be either zero or a positive integer. When the argument specified is zero, a value of 1 is returned from the `Function`; otherwise, the factorial is returned. Make sure that the numeric field you are computing the result into is large enough to contain the value. To compute the factorial of 7, code the following:

```
000105     Compute The-Factorial = Function Factorial (7)
```

The examples thus far have used numeric literals as the arguments for the `Functions`. You may also use any numeric data item defined in the `Data Division` of your COBOL program.

The Sqrt Function approximates the square root of the argument. For example, if you have a number stored in Numeric-Field and you want to determine its square root, you may code the following:

```
000106      Compute Square-Root = Function Sqrt (Numeric-Field)
```

COBOL has two Functions that can find the integer portion of a numeric field. The two Functions differ in how they handle negative numbers. The first Function, Integer-Part, returns the integer portion of the argument. For example:

```
000107      Compute The-Integer-Part = Function Integer-Part (-1.9)
```

returns negative 1 in The-Integer-Part. Any decimal positions are removed.

If the argument were 1.9, the value returned would be 1.

The sister Function, Integer, returns the greatest integer value that is less than or equal to the argument. With Integer, the example

```
000108      Compute The-Integer-Part = Function Integer (-1.9)
```

returns a value of negative 2. Negative 2 is the greatest integer value that is less than or equal to negative 1.9. For positive numbers, the two Functions, Integer-Part and Integer, return the same result.

In Hour 21, you learned about the Rem Function. This Function returns the remainder of the first argument divided by the second. You may be interested to know that the actual calculation performed to return this value is

```
000109      Compute Remainder = First-Argument -
000110      (Second-Argument *
000111      Function Integer-Part (First-Argument/Second-Argument))
```

A Function that is very similar to Rem, and often used erroneously instead, is Mod. Mod accepts two arguments, and returns an integer that is the value of the first argument using the second argument as the modulus. For positive numbers, the value returned is the same as that of Rem. However, when negative numbers are involved, the values returned by Mod and Rem differ because of the slight variation in the calculation used to arrive at the Mod result. The calculation for Mod uses Integer rather than Integer-Part.

```
000112      Compute Mod-Value = First-Argument -
000113            (Second-Argument *
000114             Function Integer (First-Argument/Second-Argument))
```

To find 14 modulus 7, the statement is coded as follows:

```
000115      Compute Mod-Value = Function Mod (14 7)
```

Statistical Functions

The COBOL Intrinsic Functions are rich in statistical analysis tools. There are Functions for Max, Min, Mean, Median, Midrange, Range, Sum, Variance, and Standard-Deviation. Two related Functions are Ord-Max and Ord-Min.

The Function Max returns the maximum value from a list of arguments. For example, if you have three numeric fields—Field-1, Field-2, and Field-3—you can determine the minimum value stored in the fields.

> For this section, only numeric values are discussed with the statistical Functions. Many of these Functions accept alphanumeric arguments. Alphanumeric argument values are covered in the upcoming "String Functions" section.

```
000116      Compute Max-Value = Function Max (Field-1 Field-2 Field-3)
```

Similarly, the Min Function returns the minimum value of the arguments specified for the Function.

Ord-Max and Ord-Min are related to Max and Min. Instead of returning the highest or lowest value, Ord-Max and Ord-Min return the relative position of the argument in the list that contains the highest or lowest value. Table 22.1 shows the various values returned from Max, Min, Ord-Max, and Ord-Min when Field-1 is 10, Field-2 is 30, and Field-3 is 15.

TABLE 22.1 VALUES RETURNED BY FUNCTIONS MAX, MIN, ORD-MAX, AND ORD-MIN

Function	Value Returned
Function Max (Field-1, Field-2, Field-3)	30
Function Min (Field-1, Field-2, Field-3)	10
Function Ord-Max (Field-1, Field-2, Field-3)	2
Function Ord-Min (Field-1, Field-2, Field-3)	1

The Functions Mean and Midrange are closely related. Both Functions return numeric values. The Mean Function returns the average value of all of the arguments specified for the Function. The Midrange Function returns the average value of the highest and lowest argument values. Arguments are specified just as for the Max Function.

The Median Function sorts the values of the arguments and returns the value of the argument that is in the middle of the sorted list. If Field-1 has a value of 3, Field-2 has a value of 300 and Field-3 has a value of 10, the following code returns a value of 10:

```
000117      Compute The-Median = Function Median (Field-1 Field-2 Field-3)
```

If the three fields are arranged in sorted order, the middle value is 10.

The Range Function returns the range of numbers involved in the argument list. The Function returns a number that is the difference between the highest and lowest value in the argument list. If you have arguments where the lowest value is 10 and the highest value is 20, the range is 10.

The Sum Function adds all the arguments specified together and reports that result. The following two lines of code produce identical results:

```
000118      Compute The-Result = Function Sum (Field-1 Field-2 Field-3)
000119      Add Field-1, Field-2, Field-3 Giving The-Result
```

The Standard-Deviation Function returns an approximation of the standard deviation of the arguments. If all the arguments have the same value, 0 is returned; otherwise, the algorithm is fairly involved. First, the mean of the arguments is calculated. Then the square of the difference between the mean and each argument is summed. This sum is divided by the number of arguments and the absolute value of the square root is the result.

The Variance Function returns a numeric value that approximates the variance between the list of arguments specified. It is simply the square of the standard deviation of the list of arguments.

These Functions can be very useful in statistical calculations. Prior to the introduction of these Functions, the COBOL programmer had to write the lines of code necessary to complete these often-complex calculations. If the number of arguments changed, the program required significant modification. These Intrinsic Functions make for much easier program maintenance.

In addition to accepting a list of data items, you might have a set of items that vary in number. Sometimes you might need to calculate the Min of three numbers and other times the Min of five numbers. Obviously, you don't want to have to code two different Functions for this purpose.

The statistical Functions, Max, Min, Ord-Max, Ord-Min, Mean, Median, Midrange, Standard-Deviation, Sum, and Variance, accept a table as the argument. The Elementary Level of the table must be specified. If the entire table is to be processed, the subscript specified is the word All. By using a variable-length table defined with the

Depending On clause, you can process a variable number of items with these Functions. For example, you might have the following table defined:

```
000011 01  Work-Table.
000012     03  Work-Entry Pic 9(3) Occurs 1 To 20 Times
000013         Depending On Num-Entries.
000014 01  Num-Entries    Pic 9(3) Value 3.
```

Assume that the first element of the table is equal to 5, the second is equal to 20, and the third 10. The following line finds the minimum value in the table:

```
Compute Result = Function Min (Work-Entry (All))
```

When a Function Ord-Min or Ord-Max is used with a table, the element that is the Min or the Max is returned. Function Ord-Min provides a simple method to find the element of the table that contains the lowest value.

Financial Functions

Financial institutions are heavy users of COBOL. Many different financial algorithms have been coded in COBOL over the years. Two of these are now available as Intrinsic Functions: Annuity and Present-Value.

The Annuity Function returns the approximate value of the ratio of an annuity paid at the end of each period for the number of periods specified to an initial investment of 1. The number of periods is specified in the second argument. The rate of interest is specified by the first argument, and is applied at the end of the period, before payment. The actual calculation is

When Argument-1 (interest rate) is 0, the value is 1/Argument-2.

When Argument-1 is not 0, the value is Argument-1/(1 - (1 + Argument-1) ** (-Argument-2)). (Remember that ** specifies an exponent).

You can use the Annuity Function to calculate a monthly payment on a loan, as shown in Listing 22.1.

LISTING 22.1   DEMONSTRATE THE ANNUITY FUNCTION

```
000001 @OPTIONS MAIN,TEST
000002 Identification Division.
000003 Program-Id.  Chapt22b.
000004* Annuity Example
000005 Environment Division.
000006 Configuration Section.
```

continues

LISTING 22.1 CONTINUED

```
000007 Source-Computer.  IBM-PC.
000008 Object-Computer.  IBM-PC.
000009 Data Division.
000010 Working-Storage Section.
000011 01  Loan-Amt         Pic 9(6)v99    Value Zeros.
000012 01  Interest-Rate    Pic 9(3)v99    Value Zeros.
000013 01  Loan-Years       Pic 9(3)       Value Zeros.
000014 01  Payment-Amt      Pic 9(6)v99    Value Zeros.
000015 01  Monthly-Interest Pic 9(3)v9(9)  Value Zeros.
000016 Screen Section.
000017 01  Data-Entry Blank Screen Auto.
000018     03  Line 01 Column 01 Value "Enter Principal: ".
000019     03  Line 01 Column 18 Pic Z(6).99 Using Loan-Amt.
000020     03  Line 03 Column 1  Value "Enter Interest Rate: ".
000021     03  Line 03 Column 22 Pic Z(2)9.99 Using Interest-Rate.
000022     03  Line 04 Column 1  Value "Number of Years of Loan: ".
000023     03  Line 04 Column 26 Pic ZZ9 Using Loan-Years.
000024     03  Line 06 Column 1  Value "Monthly Payment: ".
000025     03  Line 06 Column 18 Pic Z(3),Z(3).99 From Payment-Amt.
000026 Procedure Division.
000027 Chapt22b-Start.
000028     Display Data-Entry
000029     Accept Data-Entry
000030     Compute Monthly-Interest Rounded = (Interest-Rate / 12) / 100
000031     Compute Payment-Amt Rounded = Loan-Amt *
000032          Function Annuity (Monthly-Interest, Loan-Years * 12)
000033     Display Data-Entry
000034     Stop Run
000035     .
```

Before the calculation can occur, all the variables must have the same relationship. Since the monthly payment is to be determined, all items are changed into their monthly equivalents. In line 30, the interest rate is divided by 12 to give the monthly interest rate. It is again divided by 100 because the Annuity Function accepts the rate as a positive value and actual rate. When someone says the interest rate of 7.25, he or she means 7.25%, which is an actual rate of .0725. To keep data entry simple for the user, the rate is accepted at the percentage level and then changed to an actual rate.

In lines 31 and 32, where the Annuity Function is used, the number of years of the loan is multiplied by 12 to find the number of months of the loan. You do not have to calculate this value outside the Function. The value is determined as part of the Function calculation.

The other financial Function is Present-Value. Present-Value is the number that the principal must be to achieve a certain goal value at the end of the period for the specified interest rate. It is used frequently in bond calculation to determine the initial purchase price of a bond. Generally, bonds return a fixed specified rate of return monthly before paying back a specified principal. When deciding whether a bond is worthwhile, the buyer has to consider what kind of return he or she could make on the investment at a fixed interest rate. Consider the following example: If you give me a certain amount of money now, I will give you $1,000.00 at the end of the year. If you can earn 5% on your money right now, what is the present value of the $1,000.00 I will give you in the future?

The Function to compute this amount is

```
000100     Compute Result = Function Present-Value (.05 1000)
```

The value returned is $952.38. If I want you to give me any more than this amount, then the deal is not lucrative for you. You could make more money placing the money in a regular certificate of deposit.

Consider a more realistic investment situation. If you were to put $100 a year into an investment fund for 20 years at a rate of return of 4.5%, what is the present value of that money? In other words, what would you have to invest now as a single value to have the same amount of money at the end of 20 years? Considering the $100 every year for 20 years, you would put in a total of $2,000. How much would you have to put in today as a lump sum to achieve the same net value after 20 years?

One way to code the problem is

```
000017     Compute Result = Function Present-Value (.045,
000018             100, 100, 100, 100, 100
000019             100, 100, 100, 100, 100
000020             100, 100, 100, 100, 100
000021             100, 100, 100, 100, 100)
```

This methods appears cumbersome. The Present-Value Function accepts a table as an argument. Instead of coding the problem as shown, you can create a table and populate it with $100.00 in each element. The Function could then be simplified to

```
000022     Compute Result =
000023     Function Present-Value (.045, Value-Element (All))
```

Interestingly, rather than put away $100.00 a year for 20 years, you could start with $1,300.79 and reach the same net value at maturity.

String Functions

Several Intrinsic Functions can be used in string processing. Some of these Functions were described for numeric usage, but can also be used with alphanumeric arguments for string processing. The Functions related to working with strings are Length, Min, Max, Ord-Min, Ord-Max, Char, Ord, Upper-Case, Lower-Case, Reverse, Numval, and Numval-C.

The Length Function returns a numeric value that corresponds to the length of the argument. It may seem to have limited value, but actually the Function can be quite valuable. For instance, you might have a routine that centers a field. The method used might count backward from the end until a character greater than spaces is encountered. Then using that count, divide it in half and shift the field over to the right by that amount. Coding the program for a particular field is quite easy. But what if you want to reuse the code in another program with a different field length? You would have to change the routine for that field length. Instead, you could use the Length Function in the routine to determine the field length and never have to change the routine to use it in new programs.

Consider the program in Listing 22.2 for this purpose.

LISTING 22.2   CENTER A FIELD

```
000001 @OPTIONS MAIN,TEST
000002 Identification Division.
000003 Program-Id.  Chapt22d.
000004* Center A String
000005 Environment Division.
000006 Configuration Section.
000007 Source-Computer.  IBM-PC.
000008 Object-Computer.  IBM-PC.
000009 Data Division.
000010 Working-Storage Section.
000011 01  String-Length        Pic 9(6) Value Zeros.
000012 01  Counter              Pic 9(6) Value Zeros.
000013 01  String-To-Center     Pic X(60) Value
000014     "Teach Yourself COBOL in 24 Hours".
000015 01  Centered-String      Pic X(60) Value Spaces.
000016 Procedure Division.
000017 Chapt22d-Start.
000018     If String-To-Center > Spaces
000019         Compute String-Length =
000020                 Function Length (String-To-Center)
000021         Perform Varying Counter From
000022            String-Length By -1 Until
000023            String-To-Center (Counter:1) > Spaces
000024            Continue
000025         End-Perform
000026         Compute Counter Rounded = (String-Length - Counter) / 2
000027         Move String-To-Center To
000028                 Centered-String (Counter:)
000029     End-If
```

22

```
000030      Display "Centered-String=" Centered-String
000031      Stop Run.
000032        .
```

First, notice that the centering attempt is not made unless the field contains some data. Then the length of the field is calculated using the Length Function.

> Some people think the Length Function returns the number of characters in a field less the trailing blanks. This is not the case. Even if the field contains spaces, the Length Function returns the full field defined length.

If you need to change the size of the field to be centered, simply modify the two fields in Working-Storage, String-To-Center and Centered-String, to have a new length. Because you are using the Length Function to find this field length, nothing else in the program needs to change.

Another use for the Length Function is to return the actual length of a variable-length table. When you use the Function with a table, the actual used length is returned. For example, if your table is defined as

```
000011 01  Variable-Table.
000012      03  Table-Items Occurs 1 To 500 Times
000013                  Depending On Table-Occurrences.
000014          05  Table-Element   Pic 9(3).
000015 01  Table-Occurrences        Pic 9(3) Value 237.
```

You can determine the actual utilized length of the table using the Length Function as follows:

```
000019      Compute Item-Length = Function Length (Variable-Table)
```

The Min, Max, Ord-Min, and Ord-Max Functions work with alphanumeric data items in the same way that they work with numeric items. You can use the Min and Max Functions to find the minimum and maximum values in a series of strings stored in a table. Or you can use Ord-Max and Ord-Min to determine which elements of a table have the greatest and least value.

The Char Function accepts a numeric argument and returns the character that corresponds with that numeric value in the collating sequence in use by the program. For example, if the following statement is executed, the letter "X" is returned.

```
000016      Move Function Char (89) to Character-Returned
```

The converse Function is the Ord Function. When passed a character, the Ord Function returns the numeric position of the character in the computer's collating sequence. The following line of code returns the position in the collating sequence of the letter "Q".

```
000017     Compute Position-Returned = Function Ord ("Q")
```

> Obviously, these Functions do not have to be used with numeric and alphanumeric literals. You could use these Functions with data items as the arguments of the Functions—for example, Function Ord (Character-Item). However, with the Ord Function only a single character field is valid.

The Upper-Case Function converts an alphanumeric data item to uppercase. The argument can be any Elementary or Group Level alphanumeric data item. Each character within the field is converted to all capital letters.

```
000018     Move Function Upper-Case (Input-Field) To Output-Field
```

A related Function, Lower-Case, converts a data item to all lowercase characters.

```
000019     Move Function Lower-Case (Input-Field) To Output-Field
```

A very interesting and useful Function is the Reverse Function. The Reverse Function reverses the order of the characters in the argument. For example, your program might contain the following Working-Storage entries:

```
000010 01  Input-Field      Pic X(15) Value "COBOL".
000011 01  Output-Field     Pic X(15) Value Spaces.
```

If you code the following:

```
000025     Move Function Reverse (Input-Field) To Output-Field
```

Output-Field will contain "   LOBOC". You may be asking yourself how you can use this Function. In Hour 7, "Manipulating String Data," you used the String statement to construct a full name from a first, middle, and last name. A difficulty arose when the first name field had more than one name. Names such as Daisy Mae were not correctly used in the full name, as Delimited By Space was coded with the String statement. One way to correct this problem is to know the name within the name field. For example, the name field might be defined as Pic X(25), and "Daisy Mae" might be the value of the field. In this case, the field length is 25, but the name within the field is 9 characters long.

The Inspect statement enables you to easily determine the number of leading spaces, but determining the number of trailing spaces is not so easy. The Reverse Function allows you to reverse the order of the characters in Input-Field so that what were trailing spaces become leading spaces. You may then use the Inspect statement to count the spaces.

```
000025     Move Function Reverse (Input-Field) To Output-Field
000026     Inspect Output-Field Tallying
000027            Trailing-Spaces For Leading Spaces
```

The field, Trailing-Spaces, is initialized to Zero in Working-Storage.

You can use this technique, along with the Length Function, to properly assemble names regardless of the various field lengths as shown in Listing 22.3.

LISTING 22.3   ASSEMBLE FIRST AND LAST NAME INTO A FULL NAME

```
000001 @OPTIONS MAIN,TEST
000002 Identification Division.
000003 Program-Id.   Chapt22h.
000004*Assemble Full Name From First And Last
000005 Environment Division.
000006 Configuration Section.
000007 Source-Computer.   IBM-PC.
000008 Object-Computer.   IBM-PC.
000009 Data Division.
000010 Working-Storage Section.
000011 01   First-Name      Pic X(15)      Value Spaces.
000012 01   Last-Name       Pic X(25)      Value Spaces.
000013 01   Work-Field      Pic X(15)      Value Spaces.
000014 01   Full-Name       Pic X(51)      Value Spaces.
000015 01   Trailing-Spaces Pic 9(3)       Value Zeros.
000016 01   Field-Length    Pic 9(3)       Value Zeros.
000017 Screen Section.
000018 01   Data-Entry Blank Screen Auto.
000019      03  Line 01 Column 1  Value "First Name: ".
000020      03  Line 01 Column 13 Pic X(15) Using First-Name.
000021      03  Line 03 Column 1  Value "Last Name: ".
000022      03  Line 03 Column 13 Pic X(25) Using Last-Name.
000023      03  Line 06 Column 1  Value "Full Name: ".
000024      03  Line 06 Column 13 Pic X(51) From Full-Name.
000025 Procedure Division.
000026 Chapt22h-Start.
000027     Display Data-Entry
000028     Accept Data-Entry
000029     Move Function Reverse (First-Name) To Work-Field
000030     Inspect Work-Field Tallying Trailing-Spaces For
000031                     Leading Spaces
000032     Compute Field-Length = Function Length (First-Name)
000033     String First-Name (1:Field-Length - Trailing-Spaces)
000034            " "
000035            Last-Name
```

continues

LISTING 22.3 CONTINUED

```
000036           Delimited By Size, Into Full-Name
000037     Display Data-Entry
000038     Stop Run
000039       .
```

Lines 29 through 31 determine the number of trailing spaces. Line 32 determines the full length of the input field. The difference between these two fields is used with the String statement for assembling the name.

On occasion, you may need to read input data prepared by another system or programming language. As is often the case, the numeric fields passed to you by these systems are edited fields. That is, instead of numbers such as 0001000, the numbers are passed as 10.00 or " 10.00". You can spend quite some time creating a complex routine using String and Unstring statements, along with Inspect, to return this field to a proper numeric value. Fortunately, COBOL provides a much simpler method of converting these edited fields back into numbers.

Two related Functions handle this type of data conversion. These are Numval and Numval-C. When passed a valid edited numeric field, Numval returns a numeric value that is equal to the numeric value of the input field. Numval cannot handle input with currency symbols, commas, CR, or DB. Numval is simply coded as shown here:

```
000025     Compute Converted-Value = Function Numval (Field-To-Convert)
```

Numval-C accepts a second argument, which is the currency symbol to expect in the input field. If this argument is omitted, the currency symbol for the current character set is used. In addition to handling the currency, Numval-C handles embedded commas and the CR and DB characters that might appear at the end of a numeric edited field.

```
000026     Compute Converted-Value =
000027     Function Numval-C (Field-To-Convert "$")
```

If Numval-C is so much more capable than Numval, you may wonder why you would ever want to use Numval. Because Numval-C can handle many more types of input characters, it has to do more work and is therefore slower. Normally, you want the best performance possible from your programs. If the fields you are converting to numbers do not have commas or currency, you will see faster results by using Numval instead of Numval-C.

Miscellaneous Functions

22

The two remaining Intrinsic Functions are When-Compiled and Random. The When-Compiled Function returns the date and time the program was compiled. The format of the value returned is the same as that of the Current-Date Function. This Function can be useful on a multiuser or complex environment to make sure the version of the program being executed is the one you think it is. The following code displays the compilation date of a program:

```
000100      Display Function When-Compiled (1:8)
```

The Random Function returns a pseudo-random value that is less than one but greater than or equal to zero. The value is not truly random, but is a good approximation. The Function accepts a single integer argument that is the "seed" value for the random number Function. If you need to reproduce a series of random numbers, simply code the Random Function with the same starting seed value. After the initial execution of the Function, the argument should be omitted. Many programmers use the time as the initial seed value when a random number is desired.

To create a valid, random, whole number from the decimal value returned by the Random Function, you must multiply the value by your maximum value and then add 1. For example, to generate a random number, (Random-Number Pic 9(3)) between 1 and 500, you may code the following:

```
000100      Compute Random-Generate = Function Random (Seed-Number)
000101      Compute Random-Number = (Random-Generate * 500) + 1
```

> You might be tempted to code a one-step process for random number generation, such as Compute Random-Number = ((Function Random (Seed-Number) * 500) + 1. If you do, the highest random number generated is 451. The reason is that the compiler bases the precision of the random generation on the size of the data items used in the Compute statement. Because Random-Number and all of the other variables used are whole numbers with no decimal positions, the largest number returned from the Random Function is .9. Obviously, .9 times 500 is 450, and 450 plus the 1 yields 451. To avoid this problem, it is best to declare a separate data item with a high level of precision for the Random Function and then do the multiplication in a separate step.

The Random Function is frequently used to generate a data file of random selections from another file. Listing 22.4 uses the time as the seed value and generates a series of random numbers between 1 and 21.

LISTING 22.4   DEMONSTRATE RANDOM FUNCTION

```
000001 @OPTIONS MAIN,TEST
000002 Identification Division.
000003 Program-Id.   Chapt22j.
000004*Random Function
000005 Environment Division.
000006 Configuration Section.
000007 Source-Computer.  IBM-PC.
000008 Object-Computer.  IBM-PC.
000009 Data Division.
000010 Working-Storage Section.
000011 01  Random-Seed      Pic 9(8)      Value Zeros.
000012 01  Random-Number    Pic 99        Value Zeros.
000013 01  Random-Generate  Pic V9(18)    Value Zeros.
000014 Procedure Division.
000015 Chapt22j-Start.
000016     Move Function Current-Date (9:8) To Random-Seed
000017     Compute Random-Generate = Function Random (Random-Seed)
000018     Compute Random-Number = (Random-Generate * 21) + 1
000019     Display Random-Number
000020     Perform 19 Times
000021         Compute Random-Generate = Function Random
000022         Compute Random-Number = (Random-Generate * 21) + 1
000023         Display Random-Number
000024     End-Perform
000025     Stop Run
000026         .
```

Summary

In this hour, you learned the following:

- That numerous useful Intrinsic Functions are available to the COBOL programmer

- How to use advanced mathematical Functions such as Sin, Cos, Tan, Log, and Log10

- How to use the different statistical Intrinsic Functions such as Max, Min, Median, Range, Midrange, and Standard-Deviation

- The purpose and use of the financial Functions, Annuity and Present-Value

- How to handle string data with the following Functions: Length, Reverse, Upper-Case, and Lower-Case

- How to determine when your program was compiled with the When-Compiled Function

- How to generate pseudorandom numbers with the Random Function

Q&A

Q **How closely do the trigonometric Functions approximate their real values?**

A The answer depends on the compiler vendor. The approximations are very good, but may be different and accurate to different numbers of decimal positions with different compilers. You cannot count on identical answers from different compilers.

Q **I want to find the standard deviation between a list of values from a data file. I don't know how many different items there will be. How can I accomplish the task?**

A You can define a variable-length table with occurrences depending on a data value that you increment for each item loaded into the table. You need to know the maximum number of items you will be handling. After the table is loaded, you may use it with the subscript (All) as the argument for the Standard-Deviation Function.

Q **What can the Annuity Function help me compute?**

A One thing that you can compute with the Annuity Function is the monthly payment of a fixed-rate mortgage.

Q **Does the Length Function return the number of characters in a field or the field size?**

A The Length Function returns the size of the field passed as an argument to the Function. The contents of the field do not figure in the calculation.

Q **The Random Function returns an extremely small number. How do I use this number to calculate a larger random number?**

A You multiply the small number by the maximum number you want to generate and then add 1 to the result. If Zero is a valid value for your number, instead of adding 1 to the result, simply multiply by 1 more than the highest number you want to generate. Do not round the result.

Workshop

To help reinforce your understanding of the material presented in this hour, refer to the section "Quiz and Exercise Questions and Answers" that can be found on the CD. This section contains quiz questions and exercises for you to complete, as well as the corresponding answers.

PART V
Advanced Topics

Hour

23   The Call Interface

24   The Graphical User Interface

Hour **23**

The `Call` Interface

COBOL programs may execute other COBOL programs or even programs written in a different source language. The COBOL standard defines a simple method for accomplishing this task: the `Call` statement. In this hour, you learn how to write a program that calls another program and how to write the program that is called. You learn the information necessary to successfully interface and communicate between calling and called programs, such as

- How to `Call` another program
- Passing data to a called program from a calling program `By Reference` and `By Content`
- Coding the `Linkage Section` and the `Procedure Division` to allow a program to be called
- Static versus dynamic calls
- The importance of synchronizing the calling parameters and the `Linkage Section`, and how to use `Copybooks` to accomplish this task

Calling Other Programs

One important necessity of computer programming is the ability to reuse programming logic. If you have a really neat date-validation routine, you don't want to have to cut the paragraph out of one program and paste it into another. The data items used by the routine might have names that conflict with the data items in the new program. You have to remember to copy not only the routine but also the logic that performs it and the Working-Storage items used by the routine.

Instead of doing all of this work, COBOL allows you to Call other programs, passing and returning data values in the process. A Call is similar to a Perform. The called program is executed and then control returns to the calling program immediately after the Call statement.

The simplest form of calling a program involves the execution of another program without any program-to-program communication. An example of this approach is a menu program.

> **NEW TERM**   A *menu* is a screen or window that is displayed with a list of items from which the user may choose. A menu program typically performs little function and is used merely to allow the user to choose an option to be executed. Normally, making a menu choice causes the menu program to call a program that performs the associated function.

A menu program can be the control center for your application. A normal system is made up of related programs. A menu allows the user to choose the desired function from a list.

Simple Program Calling

The menu program being considered is the calling program. The *calling program* is simply the program that issues the Call statement, causing another program to be executed. No special setup is required for a calling program in general. With Fujitsu COBOL, the very first program that issues a Call must be compiled as a *Main* program, just as all the programs and examples have been so far.

The menu program in Listing 23.1 calls two of the examples from previous hours. The programs being called require a few simple changes, so they are given new names for this example. The first program being called is the telephone-number-formatting program from Hour 8, "Conditional Statements," Chapt08a, which appeared in Listing 8.1. It has been renamed Chapt23b. The second program being called is the days-between-dates program from Hour 21, "Date Manipulation," Chapt21c, which appeared in Listing 21.3. It has been renamed Chapt23c.

LISTING 23.1 MENU PROGRAM

```
000001 @OPTIONS MAIN,TEST
000002 Identification Division.
000003 Program-Id.  Chapt23a.
000004 Environment Division.
000005 Configuration Section.
000006 Source-Computer.  IBM-PC.
000007 Object-Computer.  IBM-PC.
000008 Special-Names.
000009     Crt Status Is Keyboard-Status.
000010 Data Division.
000011 Working-Storage Section.
000012 01  Dummy-Field        Pic X Value Spaces.
000013 01  Keyboard-Status.
000014     03  Accept-Status Pic 9.
000015     03  Function-Key  Pic X.
000016         88  F1-Pressed Value X"01".
000017         88  F2-Pressed Value X"02".
000018         88  F3-Pressed Value X"03".
000019     03  System-Use    Pic X.
000020 01  Done-Flag          Pic X Value Spaces.
000021     88  All-Done       Value "Y".
000022 Screen Section.
000023 01  Main-Screen
000024     Blank Screen, Auto, Required,
000025     Foreground-Color Is 7,
000026     Background-Color Is 1.
000027     03  Line 1 Column 29 Value "Program Selection Menu".
000028     03  Line 3 Column 1  Value "F1  Telephone Number Format".
000029     03  Line 5 Column 1  Value "F2  Days Between Dates".
000030     03  Line 7 Column 1  Value "F3  Exit".
000031     03  Line 9 Column 1  Pic X To Dummy-Field Secure.
000032 Procedure Division.
000033 Chapt023a-Start.
000034     Perform Until All-Done
000035       Display Main-Screen
000036       Accept Main-Screen
000037       Evaluate True
000038         When F1-Pressed
000039             Call "Chapt23b"
000040         When F2-Pressed
000041             Call "Chapt23c"
000042         When F3-Pressed
000043             Set All-Done To True
000044         When Other
000045             Continue
000046       End-Evaluate
000047     End-Perform
000048     Stop Run
000049     .
```

Notice the definition of Dummy-Field. The program must have some field to use in conjunction with the Accept statement. Dummy-Field is defined not to actually collect any user information, but simply as a field to Accept so the function key pressed may be captured.

The Call statements that cause the other programs to be executed are in lines 39 and 41. These called programs are often referred to as *subprograms* because they are called from a *Main* program.

The Call statement demonstrated here is the simplest form of the statement. It causes the subprogram specified to be executed. When the subprogram finishes its processing, control returns to the calling program at the statement immediately following the Call.

The subprograms require some special setup also. First, copy the original programs to the new program names. Then you need to make some minor modifications. Remove the @OPTIONS line at the top of the subprograms. You do not want the subprograms to be compiled as Main programs as the directive specifies. Omitting the MAIN causes the programs to be compiled as subprograms.

A new statement is required to return from the called program to the calling program. Replace the Stop Run in the programs with Exit Program. Exit Program causes control to return immediately to the calling program. Any files that are open in the subprogram are automatically closed as if a Close statement were executed. The only difference is that no Declaratives are processed, even if they are coded. Remember also, when changing the programs, to change the Program-Id to reflect the new names. After making the necessary changes, the two subprograms should appear as shown in Listings 23.2 and 23.3.

LISTING 23.2   CALLED PHONE NUMBER FORMAT PROGRAM

```
000001 Identification Division.
000002 Program-Id.   Chapt23b.
000003* Intelligent Telephone Number Format
000004 Environment Division.
000005 Configuration Section.
000006 Source-Computer.   IBM-PC.
000007 Object-Computer.   IBM-PC.
000008 Data Division.
000009 Working-Storage Section.
000010 01   Phone-Number        Pic 9(10) Value Zeros.
000011 01   Formatted-Number    Pic X(14) Value "(XXX) XXX-XXXX".
000012 01   Formatted-Alternate Pic X(8)  Value "XXX-XXXX".
000013 01   The-Edited-Number   Pic X(14) Value Spaces.
000014 Screen Section.
000015 01   Phone-Entry Blank Screen.
```

```
000016        03  Line 01 Column 01 Value " Enter Phone Number: ".
000017        03  Line 01 Column 22 Pic Z(10) Using Phone-Number.
000018        03  Line 03 Column 01 Value "Edited Phone Number: ".
000019        03  Line 03 Column 22 Pic X(14) From The-Edited-Number.
000020 Procedure Division.
000021 Chapt23b-Start.
000022     Display Phone-Entry
000023     Accept  Phone-Entry
000024     If Phone-Number > 9999999
000025* Number Large Enough To Contain Area Code
000026         Inspect Formatted-Number
000027           Replacing First "XXX"  By Phone-Number (1:3)
000028                    First "XXX"  By Phone-Number (4:3)
000029                    First "XXXX" By Phone-Number (7:4)
000030         Move Formatted-Number To The-Edited-Number
000031     Else
000032* Number Not Large Enough To Contain An Area Code
000033         Inspect Formatted-Alternate
000034           Replacing First "XXX"  By Phone-Number (4:3)
000035                    First "XXXX" By Phone-Number (7:4)
000036         Move Formatted-Alternate To The-Edited-Number
000037     End-If
000038     Display Phone-Entry
000039     Accept Phone-Entry
000040     Exit Program
000041     .
```

23

In addition to replacing Stop Run with Exit Program, an Accept is added in both programs before the Exit Program statement. If you fail to add this Accept, the program will run, but then return directly to the menu program without pausing to display its output.

LISTING 23.3 CALLED DAYS BETWEEN DATES PROGRAM

```
000001 Identification Division.
000002 Program-Id.   Chapt23c.
000003* Days Between Dates
000004 Environment Division.
000005 Configuration Section.
000006 Source-Computer.  IBM-PC.
000007 Object-Computer.  IBM-PC.
000008 Data Division.
000009 Working-Storage Section.
000010 01  First-Date           Value Zeros.
000011     03  Date-MM          Pic 99.
```

continues

LISTING 23.3   CONTINUED

```
000012        03   Date-DD               Pic 99.
000013        03   Date-YYYY             Pic 9(4).
000014 01   Second-Date                 Value Zeros.
000015        03   Date-MM               Pic 99.
000016        03   Date-DD               Pic 99.
000017        03   Date-YYYY             Pic 9(4).
000018 01   Days-Between                Pic S9(12) Value Zeros.
000019 01   Integer-First-Date          Pic  9(12).
000020 01   Integer-Second-Date         Pic  9(12).
000021 01   Date-Formatting-Items.
000022        03   YYYYMMDD-Format-Date.
000023           05   Date-YYYY          Pic 9(4).
000024           05   Date-MM            Pic 99.
000025           05   Date-DD            Pic 99.
000026        03   YYYYMMDD-Format-Date-N Redefines
000027           YYYYMMDD-Format-Date    Pic 9(8).
000028        03   Format-Indicator-F    Pic X(8) Value "MMDDYYYY".
000029        03   Format-Indicator-S    Pic X(8) Value "MMDDYYYY".
000030 Screen Section.
000031 01   Date-Entry Blank Screen Auto.
000032        03   Line 01 Column 01 Value "Enter First Date: ".
000033        03   Line 01 Column 21 Pic X(8) From Format-Indicator-F
000034                                         To    First-Date.
000035        03   Line 03 Column 01 Value "Enter Second Date: ".
000036        03   Line 03 Column 21 Pic X(8) From Format-Indicator-S
000037                                         To    Second-Date.
000038        03   Line 05 Column 01 Value "Days between dates: ".
000039        03   Line 05 Column 21 Pic -Zzz,ZZ9 From Days-Between.
000040 Procedure Division.
000041 Chapt23c-Start.
000042     Display Date-Entry
000043     Accept Date-Entry
000044     Move Corresponding First-Date To YYYYMMDD-Format-Date
000045     Compute Integer-First-Date =
000046            Function Integer-Of-Date (YYYYMMDD-Format-Date-N)
000047     Move First-Date To Format-Indicator-F
000048     Move Corresponding Second-Date To YYYYMMDD-Format-Date
000049     Compute Integer-Second-Date =
000050            Function Integer-Of-Date (YYYYMMDD-Format-Date-N)
000051     Move Second-Date To Format-Indicator-S
000052     Compute Days-Between = Integer-Second-Date -
000053                            Integer-First-Date
000054     Display Date-Entry
000055     Accept Date-Entry
000056     Exit Program
000057     .
```

After you alter the programs and have created Chapt23a.Cob (refer to Listing 23.1), you need to compile the programs. The process for compiling and linking a main program that calls subprograms can be complex. Fujitsu provides a simple method—called a *Project*—to accomplish the task. Follow these steps to create your Project file and compile the programs.

1. Start Programming Staff.

2. Choose the Project Menu option and then click Open.

3. Next to File Name, type **\Tycobol\Chapt23a.Prj**.

4. Click the Open button. (Under Windows 3.1, click OK.)

5. Click the Yes button when asked whether you want to create the file.

6. A Target Files dialog box is displayed. Click the Add button to add Chapt23a.Exe to the Project.

7. Click the OK button to accept the Project.

The next few steps select the source files that make up the project. These are the dependencies.

8. Under Dependent Files, type **\Tycobol\Chapt23a.Cob** and click the Add button.

9. The file is shown in the box under Dependent Files. Highlight the program by clicking on it. You need to specify that this file is the Main program. After selecting the program, click the Main Program button. The box to the left of the program name turns from white to red.

10. Change the filename in the Dependent Files field to **\Tycobol\Chapt23b.cob** and click the Add button.

11. Do the same for Chapt23c.

12. Click the OK button to accept the dependent files. A window appears onscreen with a title of Chapt23a.Prj, and several icons appear in the window. (See Figure 23.1.) Click the Build button to compile and link all the files in the project.

13. A message indicates that the Make has ended. Close that window. (Click OK under Windows 3.1.)

14. If your program has any compile errors, you must fix them and then click the Build button to compile and link the programs again. If the compile is clean, close the Edit window. (Under Windows 3.1, a clean compile does not show the Edit window.)

15. You are now ready to run the program. Click the Execute button to run the program. (Under Windows 3.1, the Execute button starts the debugger, so instead select the Utilities menu, choose Winexec, and type **Chapt23a.Exe**).

23

FIGURE 23.1

The Project window.

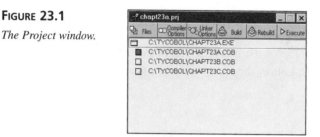

Run the program. Try the different menu options. Notice that if you select a program from the menu more than once, your last input is displayed and the program does not start in a fresh state. The telephone number reformat program does not function properly, because Working-Storage is left intact between calls of the subprograms. This condition can cause problems in many programs, especially if any Value clause items that you are counting on for proper program function are specified in Working-Storage.

A simple method to correct this problem is to code the clause Is Initial after the name of the program on the Program-Id line of the called program. Is Initial causes any Working-Storage items with a Value clause to be reinitialized to that value when the program is called. The utility provided by the ability to code Is Initial is one reason that you should always code a Value clause on Working-Storage items. Add the Is Initial clause after the name of the program on the Program-Id line of Chapt23b and Chapt23c.

```
000002 Program-Id.  Chapt23b Is Initial.
```

Then rebuild your project and try the programs again. Notice that they operate properly.

> To rebuild a project after you have closed the project, select the Project menu item from Programming Staff. Then choose Open and open the desired project. Then you can use the previously explained procedure to build and rebuild the open project. Rebuilding forces a recompile on all programs. Build recompiles only those programs that changed since the last build.

Passing Data Between Programs

In addition to simply calling a subprogram, you can pass data to and from the subprogram. A good example of this technique appears in the date-validation program coded in Hour 21. This program is an ideal candidate for a called subprogram. You can pass the date to be validated and a status flag that the called program can set to indicate the validity of the date.

When passing data to a subprogram, the Call statement is altered slightly with the addition of the Using clause. The various Call parameters are specified after the Using clause. COBOL passes the memory address of these data items to the subprogram, which then has access to those data items. The Call parameters may be any literals or data items. The program in Listing 23.4 accepts a date and then calls a date-validation program based on the validation program coded in Hour 21 to validate the date.

LISTING 23.4   DATE ENTRY, CALLING VALIDATION PROGRAM

```
000001 @OPTIONS MAIN,TEST
000002 Identification Division.
000003 Program-Id.  Chapt23d.
000004* Enter A Date For Validation
000005 Environment Division.
000006 Configuration Section.
000007 Source-Computer.  IBM-PC.
000008 Object-Computer.  IBM-PC.
000009 Data Division.
000010 Working-Storage Section.
000011 01   Passed-Date.
000012      03  Date-To-Validate      Pic 9(8).
000013      03  Date-To-Validate-X Redefines Date-To-Validate.
000014          05  Date-MM          Pic 99.
000015          05  Date-DD          Pic 99.
000016          05  Date-YYYY        Pic 9(4).
000017 01   Valid-Status        Pic X(40) Value Spaces.
000018 Screen Section.
000019 01   Date-Entry Blank Screen Auto.
000020      03  Line 01 Column 01 Value "Enter Date: ".
000021      03  Line 01 Column 13 Pic 99/99/9999 Using Date-To-Validate.
000022      03  Line 01 Column 24 Pic X(40) From Valid-Status.
000023 Procedure Division.
000024 Chapt23d-Start.
000025      Initialize Date-To-Validate
000026      Display Date-Entry
000027      Accept Date-Entry
000028      Call "Chapt23e" Using Passed-Date Valid-Status
000029      Display Date-Entry
000030      .
```

Notice the addition in line 28 of the Using clause with two Call parameters being passed to the called program, Chapt23e (see Listing 23.5). Nothing else is necessary for a calling program to pass data to a called program.

The Linkage Section

The called program must have some way to find the data being passed by the calling program. Remember that the data itself is not passed, but the location or address in memory
of that data is. The data is located in the called program by using what is known as the
Linkage Section. The Linkage Section appears immediately before the Procedure
Division of the called program. Under the Linkage Section, the data description of the
same information that is passed is coded. Each item passed, however, must have a Group
Level definition in the Linkage Section. Each item must match exactly what is passed
in the Call statement of the calling program. The simplest way to meet this requirement
is to ensure that the items defined in Working-Storage of the calling program and passed
to the called program are used exactly the same way in the Linkage Section of the
called program. The Linkage Section of Chapt23e (Listing 23.5) is coded as follows:

```
000023 Linkage Section.
000024 01  Passed-Date.
000025     03  Date-To-Validate      Pic 9(8).
000026     03  Date-To-Validate-X Redefines Date-To-Validate.
000027         05  Date-MM           Pic 99.
000028         05  Date-DD           Pic 99.
000029         05  Date-YYYY         Pic 9(4).
000030 01  Valid-Status              Pic X(40).
```

The Procedure Division of the Called Program

In addition to the Linkage Section, the called program must identify the data items
being passed to it on the Procedure Division line. This step is accomplished in a
method that is very similar to the Call statement in the calling program. The Procedure
Division is coded with a Using clause, which references the Call parameters as named
in the Linkage Section. This combination of Linkage Section and Procedure
Division setup allows the called program to reference the passed data in its exact memory location. The called program may modify this data, and when control is passed back
to the calling program, the modified data will be available. The Procedure Division
line for Chapt23e (Listing 23.5) is coded as follows:

```
Procedure Division Using Passed-Date Valid-Status.
```

The full version of Chapt23e, which validates the passed date appears in Listing 23.5.

LISTING 23.5 DATE VALIDATION SUBPROGRAM

```
000001 Identification Division.
000002 Program-Id.  Chapt23e Is Initial.
000003* Validate A Date
000004 Environment Division.
```

```
000005 Configuration Section.
000006 Source-Computer.  IBM-PC.
000007 Object-Computer.  IBM-PC.
000008 Data Division.
000009 Working-Storage Section.
000010 01  Work-Number            Pic 9(5) Value Zeros.
000011 01  Work-Remainder         Pic 9(5) Value Zeros.
000012 01  Work-Remainder-100     Pic 9(5) Value Zeros.
000013 01  Work-Remainder-400     Pic 9(5) Value Zeros.
000014 01  Today-Date             Pic 9(8) Value Zeros.
000015 01  Today-Integer          Pic 9(7) Value Zeros.
000016 01  Test-Integer           Pic 9(7) Value Zeros.
000017 01  Test-Range             Pic 9(7) Value Zeros.
000018 01  Day-Table-Area.
000019     03  Day-Table-Values     Pic X(24) Value
000020         "312831303130313130313031".
000021     03  Day-Table Redefines Day-Table-Values.
000022         05  Days-In-Month    Pic 99   Occurs 12 Times.
000023 Linkage Section.
000024 01  Passed-Date.
000025     03  Date-To-Validate      Pic 9(8).
000026     03  Date-To-Validate-X Redefines Date-To-Validate.
000027         05  Date-MM           Pic 99.
000028         05  Date-DD           Pic 99.
000029         05  Date-YYYY         Pic 9(4).
000030 01  Valid-Status              Pic X(40).
000031 Procedure Division Using Passed-Date Valid-Status.
000032 Chapt23e-Start.
000033     Divide Date-YYYY Of Date-To-Validate-X By 4
000034         Giving Work-Number Remainder
000035             Work-Remainder
000036     Divide Date-YYYY Of Date-To-Validate-X By 100
000037         Giving Work-Number Remainder
000038             Work-Remainder-100
000039     Divide Date-YYYY Of Date-To-Validate-X By 400
000040         Giving Work-Number Remainder
000041             Work-Remainder-400
000042     If Work-Remainder = Zeros And
000043     (Work-Remainder-100 Not = Zeros Or
000044      Work-Remainder-400 = Zeros)
000045         Move 29 To Days-In-Month (2)
000046     Else
000047         Move 28 To Days-In-Month (2)
000048     End-If
000049     If Date-MM Of Date-To-Validate-X  > 12 Or
000050        Date-MM Of Date-To-Validate-X  < 01 Or
000051        Date-YYYY Of Date-To-Validate-X < 1601 Or
000052        Date-DD Of Date-To-Validate-X Not > Zero Or
000053        Date-DD Of Date-To-Validate-X >
```

continues

LISTING 23.5   CONTINUED

```
000054         Days-In-Month (Date-MM Of Date-To-Validate-X)
000055         Move "Invalid Date" To Valid-Status
000056     Else
000057         Move "Valid Date" To Valid-Status
000058     End-If
000059     Exit Program
000060     .
```

The program is coded with the `Is Initial` clause on the `Program-Id` line. This clause allows you to use the routine multiple times, without worrying about leftover values in the `Working-Storage` fields.

Create a new Project named Chapt23d.Prj. Use Chapt23d.cob as your Main program and Chapt23e.cob as the subprogram. Build the project and run the program. Notice how the date-validation functions seamlessly?

> The COBOL standard provides no method for a COBOL program to `Call` itself or another program that calls a program that in turn issues a `Call` to the original program. This type of operation is defined as *recursion*. Standard COBOL does not support recursion; however, many COBOL vendors provide a method for accomplishing recursion. Check your COBOL documentation if you want to use recursion.

Call By Reference and By Content

The method of calling demonstrated thus far, where data values may be changed in the called program, is referred to as calling `By Reference`. When a parameter is passed `By Reference`, its address is passed to the called program. Another option is to call the subprogram specifying `By Content` before the data item being passed. You may mix `By Reference` and `By Content` items in the same `Call` statement. Calling `By Content` causes the program to copy the data being passed to a temporary area, passing the address of that temporary area to the called program instead of the address of the actual data item. This method allows the called program to modify this data, but upon return to the calling program, the original data is left intact, thus protecting it.

Modify Chapt23d.Cob (refer to Listing 23.4) to call the date-validation program `By Content`. The `Call` statement becomes

```
000028     Call "Chapt23e" Using By Content Passed-Date Valid-Status
```

Rebuild the project and run the program. Notice that the message about the validity of the date is not returned! This is because By Content is specified. If you need a value returned, you must always issue the call using By Reference or by not specifying By Content or By Reference and thus defaulting to By Reference.

Under certain circumstances, such as calling a program that needs to manipulate the input field as part of the validation process, you should specify By Content. This step allows the called program to manipulate the passed data as necessary without disturbing the original data. In this case, you still need to be able to return a value. You now have Call parameters that require different methods of being passed—some By Reference and some By Content. Modify the Call statement in Chapt23d.Cob (Listing 23.4) once again, this time adding By Reference before the Valid-Status data item.

```
000028     Call "Chapt23e" Using By Content Passed-Date
000029                           By Reference Valid-Status
```

Rebuild the project and run the program again. Notice that it has started working properly again. The Valid-Status field is being properly passed both to and from the called program.

Dynamic Versus Static Calls

The programs called so far in these examples have been static calls. These programs are actually linked into and become part of the program that issues the Call. If the subprogram is changed, then the calling program must be recompiled or at least relinked so that the new called program can be linked with the calling program.

Most compilers also support a feature called dynamic calls. Dynamically called programs are loaded into memory when the Call is issued. Therefore, these programs can be changed and recompiled independently of the calling program. The use of dynamic calls is specified mainly by the method in which the programs are linked.

> When using dynamic calls, you can very easily change the name of the program being called. Instead of coding the Call statement using a literal for the program to be called, refer to a data item defined in Working-Storage. For example, you can define an item in Working-Storage as 01   Program-To-Call Pic X(8) Value "CHAPT23E". Coding Call Program-To-Call, issues a dynamic call for CHAPT23E. To call a different program, simply move its name into the Program-To-Call field and issue the Call.

Dynamically called programs can be removed from memory and reinitialized upon the next Call by coding a Cancel statement. The Cancel statement is followed by the name of the program being canceled or the data field containing the name of the program to be canceled. For example:

```
000103    Cancel Program-To-Call
```

When a Cancel statement is encountered, all files opened by the program are closed as if a Close statement were issued for each one. No Declaratives that might be coded for the file are performed with this implied Close.

If for some reason the Call is not successful, either because of a memory problem or because the called program is not found, an exception occurs. You may capture this exception by coding the On Exception clause with the Call statement. Similarly, the Not On Exception clause is also supported. If you choose to use On Exception or Not On Exception, I suggest that you use the End-Call explicit scope terminator.

```
000104    Call Program-To-Call
000105        On Exception Display "The Call Failed"
000106        Not On Exception Display "The Call was Successful"
000107    End-Call
```

Copy the programs Chapt23d.Cob (refer to Listing 23.4) and Chapt23e.Cob (refer to Listing 23.5). Change their names to Chapt23f and Chapt23g. Modify Chapt23f to Call Chapt23g with a dynamic call. The modified program follows.

```
000001 @OPTIONS MAIN,TEST
000002 Identification Division.
000003 Program-Id.  Chapt23f.
000004* Enter a date for Validation - Dynamic Call
000005 Environment Division.
000006 Configuration Section.
000007 Source-Computer.  IBM-PC.
000008 Object-Computer.  IBM-PC.
000009 Data Division.
000010 Working-Storage Section.
000011 01  Passed-Date.
000012     03  Date-To-Validate      Pic 9(8).
000013     03  Date-To-Validate-X redefines Date-To-Validate.
000014         05  Date-MM           Pic 99.
000015         05  Date-DD           Pic 99.
000016         05  Date-YYYY         Pic 9(4).
000017 01  Valid-Status          Pic X(40) Value Spaces.
000018 01  Program-To-Call       Pic X(8)  Value "CHAPT23G".
000019 Screen Section.
000020 01  Date-Entry Blank Screen Auto.
000021     03  Line 01 Column 01 Value "Enter Date: ".
000022     03  Line 01 Column 13 Pic 99/99/9999 Using Date-To-Validate.
000023     03  Line 01 Column 24 Pic X(40) From Valid-Status.
000024 Procedure Division.
000025 Chapt23f-Start.
```

```
000026        Initialize Date-To-Validate
000027        Display Date-Entry
000028        Accept Date-Entry
000029        Call Program-To-Call Using Passed-Date Valid-Status
000030        Display Date-Entry
000031        .
```

Fujitsu COBOL handles dynamic calls by creating DLL files, or dynamic link libraries, for the programs being called. To do so, some new options must be set within the project file.

23

The calling and called `Program-Id` are critical. This name is contained internally within the DLL that is the called program. Fujitsu COBOL creates this program name in all uppercase when the DLL is compiled and linked. If you are issuing a dynamic `Call` and you do not specify the program name being called in all uppercase, an error message tells you that the program is unable to make the `Call`. You can correct this problem by using all uppercase letters when you code the called program name in the calling program.

Use the previously discussed steps to create a new project for Chapt23f and then do the following:

1. Add Chapt23f.Exe.
2. Before proceeding to the Dependencies selection, change the filename displayed from Chapt23f.Exe to **Chapt23g.Dll** and click Add.
3. Click OK to proceed to the Dependencies selection. The first target is Chapt23f.Exe. Add **Chapt23f.Cob** as a dependent file.
4. Select the program and click the Main button to make it a main program.
5. Click the field down arrow in the target field and select Chapt23g.Dll.
6. Under the Dependent File, type the name **Chapt23g.Cob** and then click Add.
7. Click OK to proceed to the Project Manager. Click Build to compile and link the programs that are part of the project.

If you fail to change the `Program-Id` in Chapt23g.Cob from Chapt23e to Chapt23g, the build issues an `Unresolved External` message. In this case, the build routine cannot find the program that you are attempting to `Call`. The `Program-Id` is *very* important.

Using Copybooks

Another common problem relating to calling subprograms is failure to ensure that the parameters specified for the Call in the calling program match the parameters coded in the Linkage Section of the called program.

You can alleviate this problem by ensuring that source code that is included in the calling program is exactly the same as that coded in the Linkage Section of the called program. COBOL provides a simple method of handling this situation. It uses the Copy statement.

The Copy statement simply inserts another file containing source code into your program. When compiled, the compiler assembles the full program by *expanding* the copy members into the source of the program. These copy members are referred to as Copybooks. The following Copybook (see Listing 23.6) and modification of the called program, Chapt23g, (see Listing 23.7) illustrate the concept.

LISTING 23.6   DATEVAL.CPY, DATE VALIDATION COPYBOOK

```
000001 01  Passed-Date.
000002     03  Date-To-Validate      Pic 9(8).
000003     03  Date-To-Validate-X Redefines Date-To-Validate.
000004         05  Date-MM           Pic 99.
000005         05  Date-DD           Pic 99.
000006         05  Date-YYYY         Pic 9(4).
000007 01  Valid-Status             Pic X(40).
```

LISTING 23.7   DATE VALIDATION PROGRAM USING DATEVAL.CPY COPYBOOK

```
000001 Identification Division.
000002 Program-Id.  Chapt23h.
000003* Validate A Date
000004 Environment Division.
000005 Configuration Section.
000006 Source-Computer.   IBM-PC.
000007 Object-Computer.   IBM-PC.
000008 Data Division.
000009 Working-Storage Section.
000010 01  Work-Number           Pic 9(5) Value Zeros.
000011 01  Work-Remainder        Pic 9(5) Value Zeros.
000012 01  Work-Remainder-100    Pic 9(5) Value Zeros.
000013 01  Work-Remainder-400    Pic 9(5) Value Zeros.
000014 01  Today-Date            Pic 9(8) Value Zeros.
000015 01  Today-Integer         Pic 9(7) Value Zeros.
000016 01  Test-Integer          Pic 9(7) Value Zeros.
000017 01  Test-Range            Pic 9(7) Value Zeros.
```

```
000018 01  Day-Table-Area.
000019     03  Day-Table-Values        Pic X(24) Value
000020         "312831303130313130313031".
000021     03  Day-Table Redefines Day-Table-Values.
000022         05  Days-In-Month       Pic 99   Occurs 12 Times.
000023 Linkage Section.
000024 Copy "Dateval.Cpy".
000025 Procedure Division Using Passed-Date Valid-Status.
000026 Chapt23h-Start.
000027     Divide Date-YYYY Of Date-To-Validate-X By 4
000028          Giving Work-Number Remainder
000029               Work-Remainder
000030     Divide Date-YYYY Of Date-To-Validate-X By 100
000031          Giving Work-Number Remainder
000032               Work-Remainder-100
000033     Divide Date-YYYY Of Date-To-Validate-X By 400
000034          Giving Work-Number Remainder
000035               Work-Remainder-400
000036     If Work-Remainder = Zeros And
000037       (Work-Remainder-100 Not = Zeros Or
000038       Work-Remainder-400 = Zeros)
000039          Move 29 To Days-In-Month (2)
000040     Else
000041          Move 28 To Days-In-Month (2)
000042     End-If
000043     If Date-MM Of Date-To-Validate-X  > 12 Or
000044        Date-MM Of Date-To-Validate-X  < 01 Or
000045        Date-YYYY Of Date-To-Validate-X < 1601 Or
000046        Date-DD Of Date-To-Validate-X Not > Zero Or
000047        Date-DD Of Date-To-Validate-X >
000048        Days-In-Month (Date-MM Of Date-To-Validate-X)
000049        Move "Invalid Date" To Valid-Status
000050     Else
000051        Move "Valid Date" To Valid-Status
000052     End-If
000053     Exit Program
000054     .
```

The use of the Copy statement is not limited to the Linkage Section. You can use the Copy statement anywhere in a program except within Copybooks.

Summary

In this hour, you learned the following:

- The Call statement executes other programs from within your program.
- The term that describes these called programs is *subprogram*.

- The Is Initial clause of the Program Id reinitializes any Working-Storage entries with a Value clause every time the subprogram is called.

- Programs can be called statically or dynamically.

- Dynamically called programs may be canceled, thus unloading them from memory and resetting their values for the next Call. The Cancel statement accomplishes this job.

- The On Exception clause captures errors that occur while making a Call.

- You can use the Copy statement to include other files containing source code within your COBOL programs.

Q&A

Q Can the Call statement be used to Call programs written in a language other than COBOL?

A Yes. The various COBOL vendors might use a different syntax for the Call statement to accomplish the task. Check your compiler documentation to be sure.

Q What is one advantage of using a dynamic Call over a static Call?

A If you need to change the called program, you can and you don't have to recompile the calling program.

Q Why would I want to ever Cancel a called program?

A One reason is good housekeeping. At the end of your program, you should Cancel any dynamically called programs. Another reason to Cancel a program is to initialize its Working-Storage to a fresh state upon the next Call of the program. Remember that the Cancel statement closes any open files that the called program was using.

Q Can I use the Copy statement to include FD information for a file?

A Yes. This popular use of the Copy statement ensures consistency of file definitions.

Workshop

To help reinforce your understanding of the material presented in this hour, refer to the section "Quiz and Exercise Questions and Answers" that can be found on the CD. This section contains quiz questions and exercises for you to complete, as well as the corresponding answers.

The Graphical User Interface

Most modern computer users are very familiar with the graphical user interface, or GUI. This method of interfacing with the user is very different from the historical approach of the text mode screen. Some argue that the GUI is not well suited to the tasks of business, and there may be some truth to that criticism. Business demands streamlined, fast, accurate, and simple-to-operate applications to minimize training costs and ease user operation.

Unlike a text mode screen, where every field is displayed, the GUI relies on user action to open specific areas of the application. Text mode applications guide the user through the process, but the GUI allows the user to control the process. This type of process is often referred to as *event driven*. Event-driven logic, relating to a GUI, can be very difficult to handle and code. However, COBOL is more than adequate to handle the business logic required behind the scenes in a GUI type of application.

In this hour, you learn about the GUI, concentrating on such items as

- Different methods of achieving a GUI in COBOL

- Using COBOL sp2 to generate a complete GUI program
- What a panel is, and how to define one using sp2
- Using the COBOL Call interface to communicate with the GUI

Different Methods of Achieving the Graphical User Interface

The Graphical User Interface (GUI) has been used on multiple platforms, from UNIX to the PC. COBOL itself has no built-in GUI. The multiple platforms and operating systems that support COBOL make a standard GUI nearly impossible. However, each compiler vendor supports some form of GUI.

One way to produce a GUI for your application is to use one of these vendor-provided solutions. However, they may not be portable to another vendor's compiler and may not be available on all platforms.

Many of these products use a special scripting language to control the user interface, requiring the programmer to learn another set of rules and language elements to create the desired user interface. Some use enhanced Accept and Display statements to actually create a GUI. Still others use COBOL statements to handle the manipulation of data from the GUI.

One method that has some following is using a language other than COBOL to create the interface. Languages such as Visual Basic and Visual C++ handle the user interface, making calls to COBOL programs to carry out the file access and business processing.

Another method that is very popular is to use a third-party tool designed to work with COBOL for the user interface. These tools support multiple compilers and platforms. If at some point you require a different COBOL compiler or are running on a different platform, you do not need to change your COBOL programs. Simply change the version of the third-party tool in use.

One such third-party tool that supports virtually every COBOL compiler available on the PC is COBOL sp2 from Flexus International.

In this hour, you use the COBOL sp2 product to create a GUI program.

Using sp2 to Create a Graphical User Interface

sp2 uses panels to represent each window displayed to the user. Call statements are issued in your COBOL program to manipulate these panels. sp2 creates a Copybook, containing all of data fields that are passed to and from the panel for the user to modify, for use with your program. Additionally, sp2 generates a skeleton COBOL program for you to use with your application. For the demonstration in this hour, you create a GUI interface for the Chapt15d program in Listing 15.3. The program covers dynamic access to an Indexed file.

The first step is to install the COBOL sp2 evaluation version onto your PC. The file is located on the CD-ROM that came with this book. To install the Windows 95, 98, and NT version, run the following, where D: is the drive letter of your CD-ROM drive: **D:\3rdparty\SPFJ3224.EXE**. Follow the prompts to install the programs. To install the Windows 3.1 version, run **D:\3rdparty\SPFJ1624.EXE**. If you are using a compiler other than the provided Fujitsu compiler, you may download the version of sp2 that works with your compiler from the Flexus Web site at http://www.flexus.com.

After installing the software, you should become familiar with the sp2 panel editor. Start the editor by clicking Start, Programs, Fujitsu 32 Bit Version-COBOL sp2, and COBOL sp2 60 Day Evaluation. The window shown in Figure 24.1 should be displayed.

Familiarize yourself with the icons available on the toolbar. Their descriptions are shown in the figure. These buttons are used throughout this hour.

Designing Your Panel

The first step in designing the panel for your GUI is to title the panel and choose a window border style. To do so, select the Panel menu option and click Display. The display shown in Figure 24.2 appears.

For the title, type **Tenant Display Program** and enter the same for the description. Select the radio button next to Main to use a Main Window style display. Click the OK button to accept the selections.

The next step is to add the various fields to the screen display. The first field to add is the dealer number. Some text should be added to describe the field. Click the Text button on the sp2 toolbar. Next, position your mouse at the location on the screen where you want this text to appear. Start near the upper-left corner of the screen but leave some room at the edges. Click the location you desire, and the word Text appears.

24

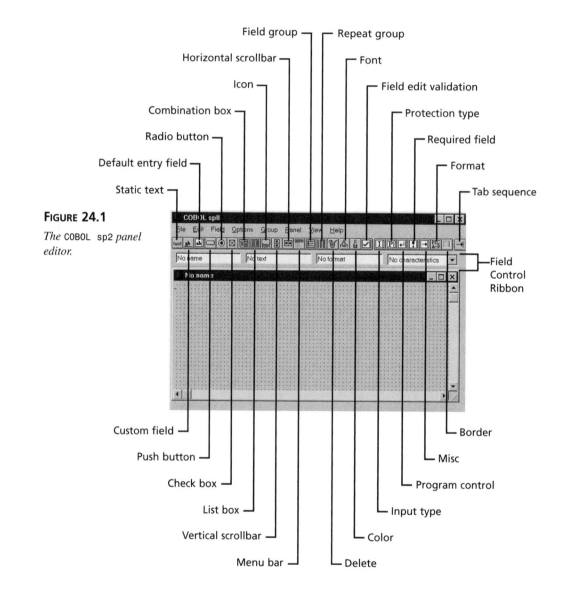

FIGURE 24.1

The COBOL *sp2 panel editor.*

Field group — ┌ Repeat group

Horizontal scrollbar — ┌ Font

Icon — ┌ Field edit validation

Combination box — ┌ Protection type

Radio button — ┌ Required field

Default entry field — ┌ Format

Static text — ┌ Tab sequence

—Field Control Ribbon

Custom field — └ Border

Push button — └ Misc

Check box — └ Program control

List box — └ Input type

Vertical scrollbar — └ Color

Menu bar — └ Delete

In the second field of the *Field Control Ribbon*, you will see the word Text. This field is where you modify the text being displayed on the panel. Click on the field, change the text to **Number:**, and press Enter. The text in the panel changes from the word Text to the word Number:.

Next, you need to add the field for entering the dealer number. Select the System Default Entry Field icon from the sp2 toolbar. Position the mouse so that the pointer is immediately after the text added for Number: and click to position the field. If you do not like the position of the field, double-click the field to select it, drag the field to a new location, and click to accept the position.

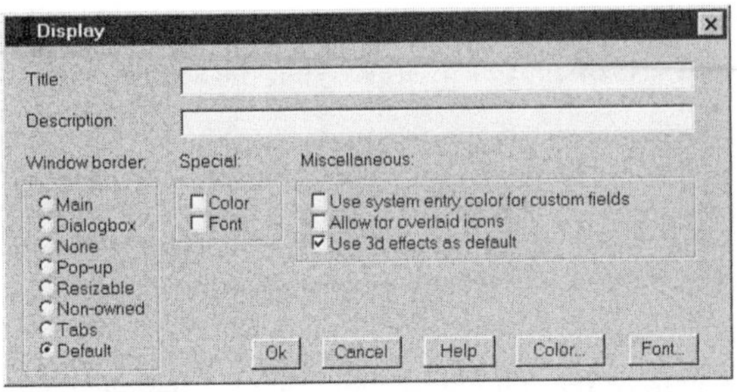

FIGURE 24.2

Selecting panel display options.

The new field is not long enough to display the entire number, so you need to extend the field to the right. Double-click the field to select it, position the mouse over the right border, and drag the edge of the field to the right. This step expands the displayed size of the input field. Make the field approximately the size shown in Figure 24.3.

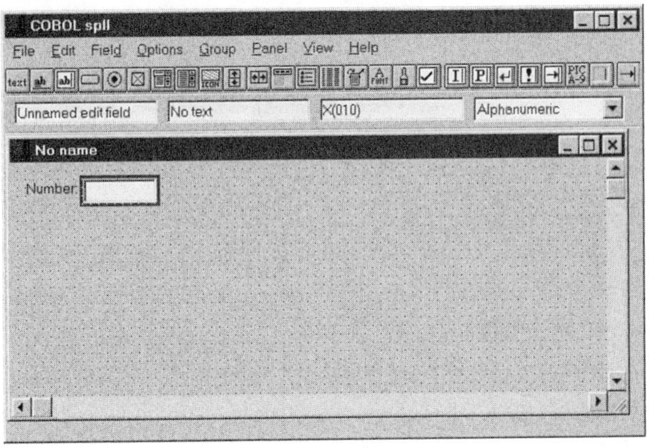

24

FIGURE 24.3

Adding a system default entry field.

The size of the data to be placed in the field is defined by entering a Picture clause definition into the third field of the *Field Control Ribbon*. Select the field again by double-clicking it. The dealer number is a Pic X(8) field, so in the third field of the *Field Control Ribbon*, where the default value of X(10) is displayed, type **X(8)** and press Enter.

The field must have a name attached to it for use in the Copybook generated by sp2. In addition, your program uses that name to fill in the panel with data. To name the Number field, type the name **Number** into the first field of the *Field Control Ribbon*.

Follow the same steps to set up the other entry fields on the screen. These fields are for the dealer name (Last, First, and Middle). The panel should now resemble Figure 24.4. Remember that Last name is 25 characters, First is 15, and Middle is 10.

1. Click the Text icon and position the field description on the panel.

2. Change the text displayed by modifying the second field of the *Field Control Ribbon*.

3. Click the System Default Entry Field icon and position the field where desired, clicking to place the field.

4. Expand the field to a reasonable length by double-clicking to select it and then dragging the mouse from the right border of the field.

5. Set the length of the field by selecting it and then changing the value as appropriate in the third field of the Field Control Ribbon.

6. Name the field by selecting it and then enter the name of the field in the first field of the Field Control Ribbon.

FIGURE 24.4

Panel editor after adding the first few fields.

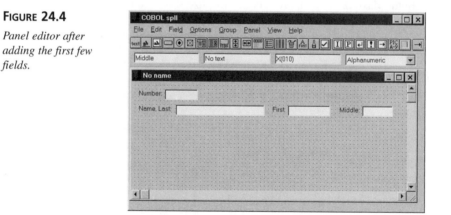

The next set of fields is for display only, and no data may be keyed into them. These fields are added to the screen in the same manner as those described earlier except now you must set a field attribute to indicate that the data is display only. This setting prevents the user from keying any data into the field. The field names and lengths follow:

Address-Line-1	X(50)
Address-Line-2	X(50)
City	X(40)
State-Or-Country	X(20)

```
Postal-Code          X(15)
Home-Phone           X(20)
Work-Phone           X(20)
Other-Phone          X(20)
```

Add the fields to the panel as described in the earlier steps. After specifying the name of each field, click the Protection Type icon. The fourth field of the field control ribbon is a drop-down box. Select the down arrow in the field and then choose the Display Only option for the field. You do not want users to tab into or key anything in these fields. Your panel should now resemble Figure 24.5.

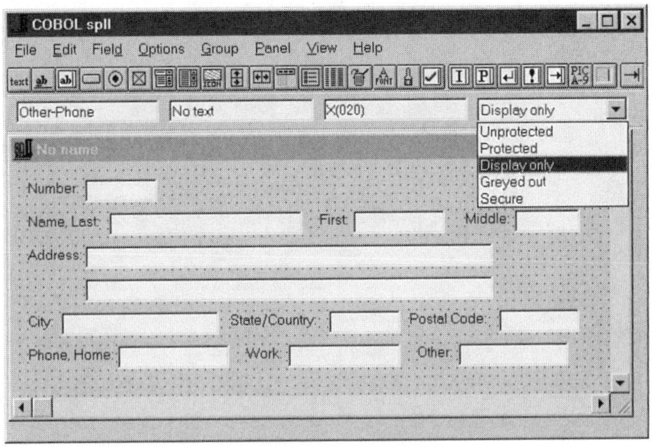

FIGURE 24.5

Panel editor after adding display-only fields.

24

Scroll the display window down a bit so that you can add the remaining display fields. The three date fields are next. Add them in the manner described above. sp2 knows about date fields and date formatting. Place MM/DD/YYYY where the Picture clause would normally go, in the third field of the Field Control Ribbon. Click the Input Type icon and use the fourth field of the Field Control Ribbon to select Date as the field type.

Name the fields as follows: Start-Date, Last-Rent-Paid-Date, and Next-Rent-Due-Date. Don't neglect to set the protection type on these fields to Display Only. The panel should now resemble Figure 24.6.

The final two display-only entry fields to add are the Rent-Amount and Consignment-Percent fields. Use the same method to add these two fields. However, in the Picture field for the Rent-Amount, enter **Z,ZZZ.99**, and for Consignment-Percent enter **ZZ9**. Click the Input Type icon and select Numeric as the input type. The panel should now resemble Figure 24.7. Don't forget to enter the field names.

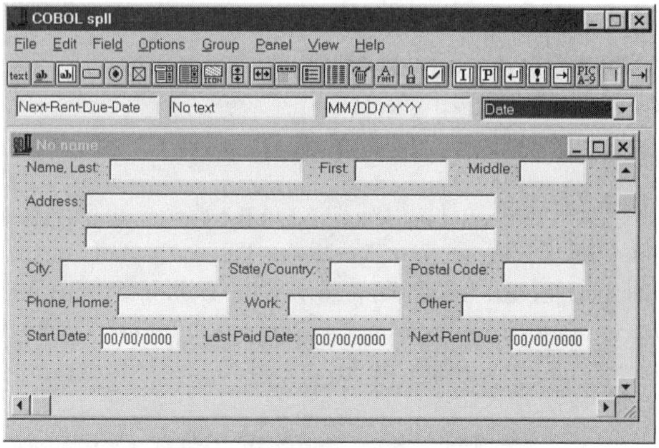

FIGURE 24.6

Panel editor after adding dates.

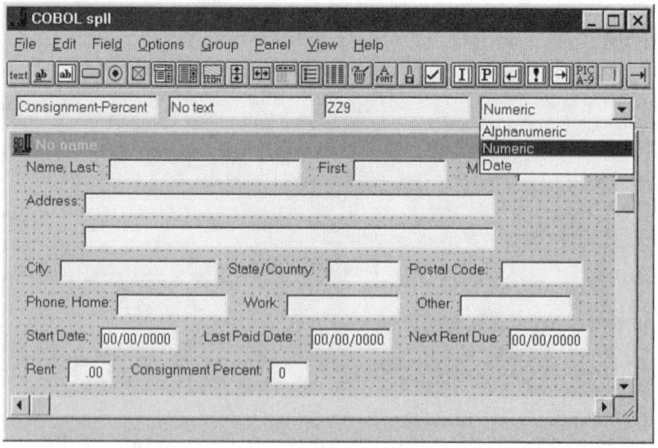

FIGURE 24.7

Panel editor—panel nearly complete.

Finally, it is time to add some push buttons. This program can perform several operations: Read Random Number, Read Random Name, Read Next Number, and Read Next Name. In addition, Clear or Exit are valid operations. Rather than add a button for each read function, add a drop-down box that allows the user to select the desired function.

Scroll the panel down a little so that you can add a drop-down box. Follow these steps to add the field.

1. Click the Combination Box icon.

2. Position the field immediately under Rent: by clicking once to place the field.

3. Type in the field name **Operation-Type** in the first field of the Field Control Ribbon.

4. Change the Picture clause to **X(18)**.

5. The second field of the `Field Control Ribbon` contains the text that is to appear in the drop-down list. Use a comma to separate the items. The first item is repeated because it is to appear by default, and the following items are all of the items that may appear. Change the text to read as follows: **Read Random Number, Read Random Number, Read Random Name, Read Next Number, Read Next Name**.

> You must be very careful in your spelling. If an entry is not spelled properly, it may not show up in the display. Also, make sure you change the `Picture` clause to `X(18)` before entering the text; otherwise, it will be truncated.

Your panel now should resemble Figure 24.8.

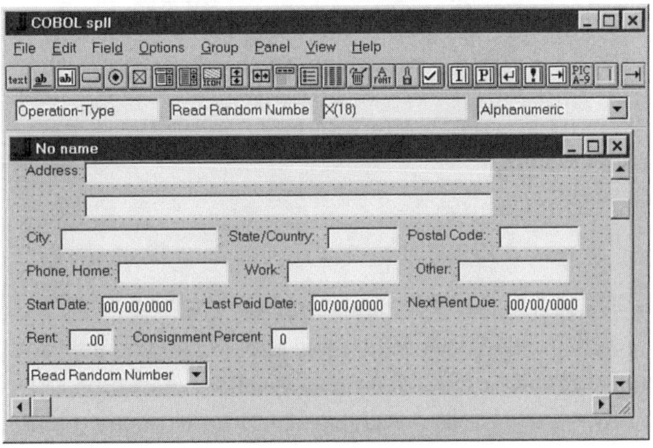

24

FIGURE 24.8

Panel editor after adding the drop-down list.

![Panel editor screenshot showing COBOL spll window with menu bar (File Edit Field Options Group Panel View Help), toolbar, Operation-Type field with "Read Random Numbe" and X(18) Alphanumeric, and a "No name" panel with Address, City, State/Country, Postal Code, Phone Home, Work, Other, Start Date, Last Paid Date, Next Rent Due, Rent, Consignment Percent fields, and a Read Random Number drop-down.]

To complete the panel definition, you need to add three push buttons to the panel. One is Read, the next is Clear, and the final one is Exit. Follow these steps to add the buttons to your panel. You complete panel should resemble Figure 24.9.

1. Click the Push Button icon.

2. Place the button next to the drop-down box that you just added by positioning the mouse and clicking.

3. Change the text that appears on the button by typing **Read** in the second field of the `Field Control Ribbon`, where OK appears by default. Press Enter to accept the change.

4. sp2 detects push buttons as if they were function keys or other special keys. To assign a value to a button that can be detected in your program, click in the third field of the `Field Control Ribbon`. Then press F2 to activate a feature called

Easy Key. The code for the next keystroke you make is entered into the field for you. When you press the F3 key, 317 appears in the field.

5. Change the name of the push button to Read, by typing **Read** into the first field of the Field Control Ribbon.

6. Repeat these steps to add push buttons for Clear and Exit to the right of the Read button. Use the F4 key as the Easy Key value for Clear and F5 for Exit. Name the buttons **Clear** and **Exit**.

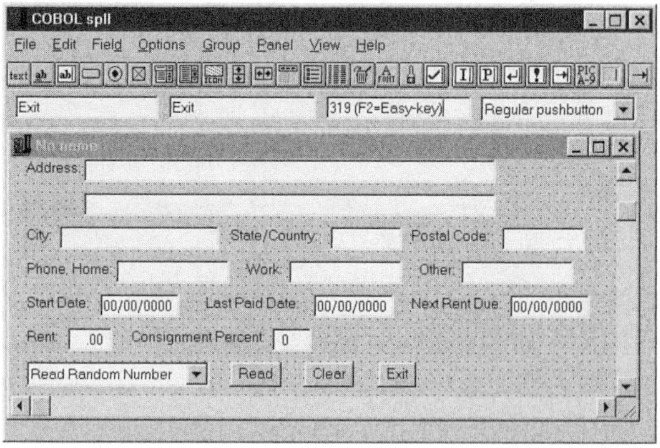

FIGURE 24.9

Panel editor—completed panel.

To save your work, select File and then Save. Panels are saved into panel files that may contain more than one panel. When you click Save, you are prompted for a filename. Enter **Chapt24.Pan** for the panel filename. Then click Open. (Under Windows 3.1, click OK.) Choose Yes when asked whether you want to create the file. Type in **Chapt24a** as the panel name and then click OK.

COBOL sp2 needs to generate a Copybook for use in your program and, in fact, generates a skeleton program for your use as a starting point. This skeleton contains the bare basics required for the interface with sp2 to function. This program is generated in the directory where sp2 was installed, which is SPFJ3224 under Windows 95, 98, and NT and SPFJ1624 under Windows 3.1.

To generate these files, select File and then click Generate.

You may now close the sp2 panel editor window. When asked whether you want to save your work, click Yes.

Modifying the Generated Program

Before changing the program, become familiar with it. The generated program has a file extension of CBL rather than COB. The Fujitsu COBOL compiler recognizes either extension as a COBOL source file. Review Listing 24.1.

LISTING 24.1   SP2 GENERATED PROGRAM

```
000001 IDENTIFICATION DIVISION.
000002 PROGRAM-ID. chapt24a.
000003
000004* TITLE - Tenant Display Program
000005* DESCRIPTION - Tenant Display Program
000006
000007 ENVIRONMENT DIVISION.
000008 CONFIGURATION SECTION.
000009 SOURCE-COMPUTER. IBM-PC.
000010 OBJECT-COMPUTER. IBM-PC.
000011
000012 DATA DIVISION.
000013 WORKING-STORAGE SECTION.
000014
000015 COPY "sp2.cpy".
000016
000017 COPY "chapt24a.cpy".
000018
000019 PROCEDURE DIVISION.
000020 MAINLINE.
000021******************
000022* MAINLINE LOGIC *
000023******************
000024     PERFORM PROC-OPEN-FILE
000025     MOVE LOW-VALUES TO chapt24a-DATA
000026     MOVE "chapt24a" TO chapt24a-NEXT-PANEL
000027     MOVE "y" TO chapt24a-NEW-WINDOW
000028     MOVE LOW-VALUES TO chapt24a-FIELDS
000029     MOVE LOW-VALUES TO chapt24a-COLRS
000030     MOVE LOW-VALUES TO chapt24a-TYPES
000031     PERFORM PROC-CON-chapt24a
000032     PERFORM PROC-CLOSE-WINDOW
000033     PERFORM PROC-CLOSE-FILE
000034     PERFORM PROC-END-SESSION
000035     STOP RUN
000036     .
000037
000038 PROC-OPEN-FILE.
000039******************
000040* OPEN SP2 FILE *
```

continues

LISTING 24.1 CONTINUED

```
000041******************
000042      MOVE LOW-VALUES TO SP2-FI-DATA
000043      MOVE "C:\SPFJ3224\chapt24.pan" TO SP2-FI-NAME
000044      CALL "SP2" USING SP2-OPEN-FILE SP2-FILE-DEF
000045      .
000046
000047 PROC-CON-chapt24a.
000048******************
000049* CONVERSE PANEL *
000050******************
000051      CALL "SP2" USING SP2-CONVERSE-PANEL chapt24a-CONVERSE-DATA
000052      MOVE LOW-VALUE TO chapt24a-NEW-WINDOW
000053      .
000054
000055 PROC-CLOSE-WINDOW.
000056************************
000057* CLOSE CURRENT WINDOW *
000058************************
000059      CALL "SP2" USING SP2-CLOSE-WINDOW SP2-NULL-PARM
000060      .
000061
000062 PROC-CLOSE-FILE.
000063*********************
000064* CLOSE CURRENT FILE *
000065*********************
000066      CALL "SP2" USING SP2-CLOSE-FILE SP2-NULL-PARM
000067      .
000068
000069 PROC-END-SESSION.
000070******************
000071* END SP2 SESSION *
000072******************
000073      CALL "SP2" USING SP2-END-SESSION SP2-NULL-PARM
000074      .
```

The case (upper versus lower) used for the COBOL statements and variable names in the generated code is not quite what you are used to seeing in these lessons. Remember that for the COBOL statements themselves, COBOL is not case sensitive, and it does not matter whether the letters are in upper- or lowercase.

The Proc-Open-File Paragraph makes a call to sp2 to open the panel file that is used by the program.

Proc-Con-Chapt24a is used to "converse" with the panel and thus the user. When the Converse-Panel call is made to sp2, sp2 handles the interaction between the user and the panel. When the user clicks one of the buttons or closes the window, control returns to your program. Based on the values of the fields returned, the program can take appropriate action.

The first time a panel is conversed, it must be displayed in a new window. Use the following code:

```
000027     MOVE "y" TO chapt24a-NEW-WINDOW
```

The value "y" is lowercase and is case sensitive when passed to sp2. Notice in line 52 that Low-Values is moved to this field. This step prevents a new window from being created the next time the panel is displayed.

When exiting the program, sp2 must be called for three purposes: first to close the window that is currently open, handled by the PROC-CLOSE-WINDOW Paragraph; second to close the panel file, handled by the PROC-CLOSE-FILE Paragraph; and last to perform any necessary housekeeping and unload the sp2 program from memory, handled by the PROC-END-SESSION Paragraph.

Working-Storage contains two Copybooks. The first, sp2.Cpy, holds fields and values that sp2 uses. The second is generated by sp2 (Listing 24.2) and includes data to manipulate the fields that your panel uses.

> The sp2 generated Copybook contains many items that are used internally by sp2, but are not directly referenced in the program. The Copybook in Listing 24.2 is an abbreviated version showing only fields with which you are concerned.

LISTING 24.2 sp2 GENERATED COPYBOOK

```
000001*******************************
000002* parameter for CONVERSE-PANEL *
000003* parameter for GET-INPUT      *
000004*******************************
000005 01  chapt24a-CONVERSE-DATA.
000006     05  chapt24a-RET-CODE
000007                                PIC S9(4) COMP-5.
000029     05  chapt24a-DATA.
000030******** chapt24a-IP-NUM-DATA ********
000031          10  chapt24a-KEY
```

continues

LISTING 24.2   CONTINUED

```
000032                                      PIC S9(4) COMP-5.
000033           88  chapt24a-Read-HIT
000034                                      VALUE 317.
000035           88  chapt24a-Clear-HIT
000036                                      VALUE 318.
000037           88  chapt24a-Exit-HIT
000038                                      VALUE 319.

000114******** chapt24a-OP-VAR-DATA ********
000115      05  chapt24a-FIELDS.
000116          10  chapt24a-Number
000117                                      PIC X(0008).
000118          10  chapt24a-Last
000119                                      PIC X(0025).
000120          10  chapt24a-First
000121                                      PIC X(0015).
000122          10  chapt24a-Middle
000123                                      PIC X(0010).
000124          10  chapt24a-Address-Line-1
000125                                      PIC X(0050).
000126          10  chapt24a-Address-Line-2
000127                                      PIC X(0050).
000128          10  chapt24a-City
000129                                      PIC X(0040).
000130          10  chapt24a-State-Or-Country
000131                                      PIC X(0020).
000132          10  chapt24a-Postal-Code
000133                                      PIC X(0015).
000134          10  chapt24a-Home-Phone
000135                                      PIC X(0020).
000136          10  chapt24a-Work-Phone
000137                                      PIC X(0020).
000138          10  chapt24a-Other-Phone
000139                                      PIC X(0020).
000140          10  chapt24a-Start-Date
000141                                      PIC 9(0008).
000142          10  chapt24a-Last-Rent-Paid-Date
000143                                      PIC 9(0008).
000144          10  chapt24a-Next-Rent-Due-Date
000145                                      PIC 9(0008).
000146          10  chapt24a-Rent-Amount
000147                                      PIC 9(04)V9(02).
000148          10  chapt24a-Consignment-Percent
000149                                      PIC 9(003).
000150          10  chapt24a-Operation-Type
000151                                      PIC X(0018).
```

When you examine this listing, start by noticing the 88 levels defined in lines 33 through 38. The program checks these conditional fields to determine which button the user selected.

The second set of important fields starts at line 115. These fields display the user data and are the fields by which you communicate with the user.

The next step in creating your program is to add the specific logic you need to perform the functions. Start by adding the Select and FD for the dealer file. In the Select, because the program is not in the \TYCOBOL directory, specify the full filename of the dealer file. Add Select, FD, Open, and Close statements for the file.

When you open the file \SPFJ3224\Chapt24a.Cbl with Programming Staff, you receive a warning message about line numbers being invalid. This message appears because the generated code has no line numbers. Answer Yes to the question and let the COBOL editor assign the line numbers in the program.

Make sure to specify the whole path to the dealer file in the Select statement. Because the program does not run from the \Tycobol directory, you need to provide the full path information.

```
000013 Select Dealer-File Assign to "\Tycobol\Dealer.Dat"
000014          Organization Indexed
000015          Access Dynamic
000016          Record Key Dealer-Number
000017          Alternate Record Key Dealer-Name
000018          File Status Dealer-Status.
```

When inserting the code for the file access, you will find several places where error messages should be displayed. You should not use the Display statement within a GUI program. Instead, use the facility provided to display a message box. COBOL sp2 accomplishes this by using a special Call to display the message box:

```
000064          MOVE LOW-VALUES TO SP2-MS-DATA
000065          MOVE "b" TO SP2-MS-ICON
000066          MOVE "File Error"              TO SP2-MS-TITLE
000067          MOVE "o"                       TO SP2-MS-BUTTON
000068          MOVE 1                         TO SP2-MS-LINE-CNT
000069          String "Error Opening Dealer File "
000070                 Dealer-Status
000071                 Delimited by Size
000072                 Into Sp2-Ms-Text
000073          End-String
000074          Call "SP2" Using Sp2-Display-Message Sp2-Message-Data
```

The SP2-MS-ICON field contains a value that corresponds to the value of the icon to appear in the message box. Valid values are "b" for bang, (the Exclamation point), "s" for the Stop sign, "i" for Information, and "q" for Question. The SP2-MS-TITLE field

contains the title for the message box. SP2-MS-BUTTON indicates the type of push button
or buttons to be displayed for termination of the message box. "o" is OK, "y" is Yes/No,
"n" is No/Yes, and "r" is Retry. The SP2-MS-LINE-CNT is the number of lines into which
your message is split. For the purposes of this book, you always use 1. SP2-MS-TEXT is
the error message text. The Call to sp2 using the parameters shown will display a message box, warning the user of the error.

After inserting the Select, FD, file Open, and file Close statements, it's time to code the
steps necessary to perform the functions. You need to set up a repeating processing loop.
This loop will converse the panel, return to the program, and take appropriate action
based on the values returned by sp2. Then the loop is repeated. Two conditions terminate
the loop. First, the user clicks the Exit button. Second, the user selects the Close option
by clicking the X in the upper-right corner under Windows 95/98 or NT, or the user dou-
ble-clicks in the upper-left corner under Windows 3.1. One of these conditions is
checked by testing the conditional item, Chapt24a-Exit-Hit. This condition is coded
under a data value named Chapt24a-Key. This field has the value associated with the reason that sp2 returned to your program. The SP2.Cpy Copybook includes a set of fields
that assist you in detecting which key or activity occurred that caused sp2 to return to
your program. The key value associated with closing the window is SP2-KEY-CLOSE.

The main logic in the program revolves around the Proc-Con-Chapt24a Paragraph. It is
the one modified to handle the testing and performing of the various conditions. Walk
through the entire program, examining each area and the steps required to perform the
operations. The full listing of the program is shown in Listing 24.3.

LISTING 24.3   FINAL DEALER DISPLAY PROGRAM

```
000001 @OPTIONS MAIN,TEST
000002 IDENTIFICATION DIVISION.
000003 PROGRAM-ID. chapt24a.
000004
000005* TITLE - Tenant Display Program
000006* DESCRIPTION - Tenant Display Program
000007
000008 ENVIRONMENT DIVISION.
000009 CONFIGURATION SECTION.
000010 SOURCE-COMPUTER. IBM-PC.
000011 OBJECT-COMPUTER. IBM-PC.
000012 Input-Output Section.
000013 File-Control.
000014     Select Dealer-File Assign to "\Tycobol\Dealer.Dat"
000015            Organization Indexed
000016            Access Dynamic
000017            Record Key Dealer-Number
000018            Alternate Record Key Dealer-Name
000019            File Status Dealer-Status.
```

Notice the use of the full path to the Dealer.Dat file. Because this program will not be executed from that directory, specifying the full path allows the program to find the data file.

```
000020 DATA DIVISION.
000021 File Section.
000022 FD   Dealer-File.
000023 01   Dealer-Record.
000024      03  Dealer-Number        Pic X(8).
000025      03  Dealer-Name.
000026          05  Last-Name    Pic X(25).
000027          05  First-Name   Pic X(15).
000028          05  Middle-Name  Pic X(10).
000029      03  Address-Line-1       Pic X(50).
000030      03  Address-Line-2       Pic X(50).
000031      03  City                 Pic X(40).
000032      03  State-or-Country     Pic X(20).
000033      03  Postal-Code          Pic X(15).
000034      03  Home-Phone           Pic X(20).
000035      03  Work-Phone           Pic X(20).
000036      03  Other-Phone          Pic X(20).
000037      03  Start-Date           Pic 9(8).
000038      03  Last-Rent-Paid-Date  Pic 9(8).
000039      03  Next-Rent-Due-Date   Pic 9(8).
000040      03  Rent-Amount          Pic 9(4)V99.
000041      03  Consignment-Percent  Pic 9(3).
000042      03  Filler               Pic X(50).
000043 WORKING-STORAGE SECTION.
000044 01   Dealer-Status     Pic X(2) Value Spaces.
000045      88  Dealer-Success Value "00" Thru "09".
000046 01   Error-Message     Pic X(60) Value Spaces.
000047 COPY "sp2.cpy".
000048
000049 COPY "chapt24a.cpy".
000050 01  Date-Reverse-Area.
000051     03  Date-YYYYMMDD        Pic 9(8).
000052     03  Date-YYYYMMDD-X Redefines Date-YYYYMMDD.
000053         05  Date-YYYY    Pic 9(4).
000054         05  Date-MM      Pic 9(2).
000055         05  Date-DD      Pic 9(2).
000056     03  Date-MMDDYYYY        Pic 9(8).
000057     03  Date-MMDDYYYY-X Redefines Date-MMDDYYYY.
000058         05  Date-MM      Pic 9(2).
000059         05  Date-DD      Pic 9(2).
000060         05  Date-YYYY    Pic 9(4).
000061 PROCEDURE DIVISION.
000062 MAINLINE.
000063******************
000064* MAINLINE LOGIC *
000065******************
000066     PERFORM PROC-OPEN-FILE
```

24

```
000067          MOVE LOW-VALUES TO chapt24a-DATA
000068          MOVE "chapt24a" TO chapt24a-NEXT-PANEL
000069          MOVE "y" TO chapt24a-NEW-WINDOW
000070          MOVE LOW-VALUES TO chapt24a-FIELDS
000071          MOVE LOW-VALUES TO chapt24a-COLRS
000072          MOVE LOW-VALUES TO chapt24a-TYPES
000073          Perform Open-File
000074          If not Dealer-Success
000075* message box display!
000076            MOVE LOW-VALUES TO SP2-MS-DATA
000077            MOVE "b" TO SP2-MS-ICON
000078            MOVE "File Error"                     TO SP2-MS-TITLE
000079            MOVE "o"                              TO SP2-MS-BUTTON
000080            MOVE 1                     TO SP2-MS-LINE-CNT
000081            String "Error Opening Dealer File "
000082                   Dealer-Status
000083                   Delimited by Size
000084                   Into Sp2-Ms-Text
000085            End-String
000086            Call "SP2" Using Sp2-Display-Message Sp2-Message-Data
```

A message box is shown instead of a Display statement.

```
000087          Else
000088* there is no reason to perform these if the open fails
000089            PERFORM PROC-CON-chapt24a
000090            PERFORM PROC-CLOSE-WINDOW
000091            Perform Close-File
000092          End-if
000093          PERFORM PROC-CLOSE-FILE
000094          PERFORM PROC-END-SESSION
000095          STOP RUN
000096          .
000097 Open-File.
000098          Open Input Dealer-File
000099          .
000100 Close-File.
000101          Close Dealer-File
000102          .
000103 PROC-OPEN-FILE.
000104*****************
000105* OPEN SP2 FILE *
000106*****************
000107          MOVE LOW-VALUES TO SP2-FI-DATA
000108          MOVE "C:\SPFJ3224\chapt24.pan" TO SP2-FI-NAME
000109          CALL "SP2" USING SP2-OPEN-FILE SP2-FILE-DEF
000110          .
000111
000112 PROC-CON-chapt24a.
000113*****************
000114* CONVERSE PANEL *
```

```
000115******************
000116     Perform With Test After Until
000117          Chapt24a-Key = Sp2-Key-Close or
000118          Chapt24a-Exit-Hit
000119       CALL "SP2" USING SP2-CONVERSE-PANEL chapt24a-CONVERSE-DATA
000120       MOVE LOW-VALUE TO chapt24a-NEW-WINDOW
000121       Perform Determine-Action
000122     End-Perform
000123     .
```

The Determine-Action Paragraph checks the return fields from the Call to sp2 and performs the appropriate action based on those values.

```
000124 Determine-Action.
000125     Evaluate True
000126        When Chapt24a-Exit-Hit
000127        When Chapt24a-Key = Sp2-Key-Close
000128           Continue
```

The Continue coded here works because the Perform statement is checking for these values after performing this routine. These two conditions cause the processing loop to terminate.

```
000129        When Chapt24a-Read-Hit
000130           Evaluate Chapt24a-Operation-Type
000131              When "Read Random Number"
000132                 Perform Read-Random-Number
000133              When "Read Random Name"
000134                 Perform Read-Random-Name
000135              When "Read Next Number"
000136                 Perform Read-Next-Number
000137              When "Read Next Name"
000138                 Perform Read-Next-Name
000139           End-Evaluate
```

If the user presses the Read button, the program evaluates the value selected in the drop-down list box to determine which type of Read is desired. The appropriate action is performed based on the value of the field.

```
000140        When Chapt24a-Clear-Hit
000141           Initialize Chapt24a-Fields
000142           Move "Read Random Number" To Chapt24a-Operation-Type
```

The Clear button causes the fields controlled by sp2 to be initialized. The reason for moving Read Random Number back into the Chapt24a-Operation-Type is that the act of initializing the field erases its value and prevents the field from functioning properly.

```
000143        When Other
000144           Continue
000145     End-Evaluate
000146     .
```

```
000147 Read-Random-Number.
000148     Move Chapt24a-Number to Dealer-Number
000149     Read Dealer-File
000150       Invalid Key
000151         String "Error on Random Read Number "
000152             Dealer-Status
000153             Delimited by Size
000154             Into Error-Message
000155         End-String
000156         Perform Show-Error-Message
```

Show-Error-Message is a common routine that displays the text in Error-Message in a Windows message box.

```
000157           Not Invalid Key
000158             Perform Fill-Panel-Data
000159     End-Read
000160     .
000161 Read-Random-Name.
000162     Move Chapt24a-Last To Last-Name
000163     Move Chapt24a-First To First-Name
000164     Move Chapt24a-Middle To Middle-Name
000165     Read Dealer-File Key Dealer-Name
000166       Invalid Key
000167         String "Error on Random Read Name "
000168             Dealer-Status
000169             Delimited by Size
000170             Into Sp2-Ms-Text
000171         End-String
000172         Perform Show-Error-Message
000173       Not Invalid Key
000174           Perform Fill-Panel-Data
000175     End-Read
000176     .
000177 Read-Next-Number.
000178     Move Chapt24a-Number to Dealer-Number
000179     Start Dealer-File Key > Dealer-Number
000180      Invalid Key
000181         String "Start Error Number "
000182             Dealer-Status
000183             Delimited by Size
000184             Into Error-Message
000185         End-String
000186         Perform Show-Error-Message
000187     End-Start
000188     If Dealer-Success
000189       Read Dealer-File Next
000190         At End
000191           Move "End of File, Read by Number" To Error-Message
000192           Perform Show-Error-Message
000193         Not At End
```

```
000194              Perform Fill-Panel-Data
000195         End-Read
000196       End-if
000197       .
000198 Read-Next-Name.
000199       Move Chapt24a-Last To Last-Name
000200       Move Chapt24a-First To First-Name
000201       Move Chapt24a-Middle To Middle-Name
000202       Start Dealer-File Key > Dealer-Name
000203        Invalid Key
000204           String "Start Error Name "
000205                  Dealer-Status
000206                  Delimited by Size
000207                  Into Error-Message
000208           End-String
000209           Perform Show-Error-Message
000210       End-Start
000211       If Dealer-Success
000212         Read Dealer-File Next
000213           At End
000214              Move "End of File, Read by Name" To Error-Message
000215              Perform Show-Error-Message
000216           Not At End
000217              Perform Fill-Panel-Data
000218         End-Read
000219       End-if
000220       .
```

Fill-Panel-Data moves the data from the record that was just retrieved to the fields that are passed to sp2 for displaying the data on the panel.

```
000221 Fill-Panel-Data.
000222       Move Dealer-Number       To Chapt24a-Number
000223       Move Last-Name           To Chapt24a-Last
000224       Move First-Name          To Chapt24a-First
000225       Move Middle-Name         To Chapt24a-Middle
000226       Move Address-Line-1      To Chapt24a-Address-Line-1
000227       Move Address-Line-2      To Chapt24a-Address-Line-2
000228       Move City                To Chapt24a-City
000229       Move State-or-Country    To Chapt24a-State-or-Country
000230       Move Postal-Code         To Chapt24a-Postal-Code
000231       Move Home-Phone          To Chapt24a-Home-Phone
000232       Move Work-Phone          To Chapt24a-Work-Phone
000233       Move Other-Phone         To Chapt24a-Other-Phone
000234       Move Start-Date          To Date-MMDDYYYY
000235       Move Corresponding Date-MMDDYYYY-X To Date-YYYYMMDD-X
000236       Move Date-YYYYMMDD       To Chapt24a-Start-Date
000237       Move Last-Rent-Paid-Date To Date-MMDDYYYY
000238       Move Corresponding Date-MMDDYYYY-X To Date-YYYYMMDD-X
000239       Move Date-YYYYMMDD       To Chapt24a-Last-Rent-Paid-Date
000240       Move Next-Rent-Due-Date To Date-MMDDYYYY
```

24

```
000241      Move Corresponding Date-MMDDYYYY-X To Date-YYYYMMDD-X
000242      Move Date-YYYYMMDD        To Chapt24a-Next-Rent-Due-Date
```

When a field is defined to sp2 as a date field, the assumed format is YYYYMMDD, or Year, Month, Day. Because the data in the Dealer.Dat file is stored in MMDDYYYY format, the date must be rearranged before being moved to the display fields.

```
000243      Move Rent-Amount          To Chapt24a-Rent-Amount
000244      Move Consignment-Percent To Chapt24a-Consignment-Percent
000245      .
000246 Show-Error-Message.
000247      MOVE LOW-VALUES TO SP2-MS-DATA
000248      MOVE "b" TO SP2-MS-ICON
000249      MOVE "File Error"                  TO SP2-MS-TITLE
000250      MOVE "o"                           TO SP2-MS-BUTTON
000251      MOVE 1                   TO SP2-MS-LINE-CNT
000252      Move Error-Message To Sp2-Ms-Text
000253      Move Spaces To Error-Message
000254* Spaces Are Moved into Error-Message is preparation of the next
000255* String statement that will occur using the field.
000256      Call "SP2" Using Sp2-Display-Message Sp2-Message-Data
000257      .
000258 PROC-CLOSE-WINDOW.
000259***********************
000260* CLOSE CURRENT WINDOW *
000261***********************
000262      CALL "SP2" USING SP2-CLOSE-WINDOW SP2-NULL-PARM
000263      .
000264
000265 PROC-CLOSE-FILE.
000266*********************
000267* CLOSE CURRENT FILE *
000268*********************
000269      CALL "SP2" USING SP2-CLOSE-FILE SP2-NULL-PARM
000270      .
000271
000272 PROC-END-SESSION.
000273******************
000274* END SP2 SESSION *
000275******************
000276      CALL "SP2" USING SP2-END-SESSION SP2-NULL-PARM
000277      .
```

The program compiles normally. However, to link the program you need to include the Sp2.Lib file provided with COBOL sp2. Perform the following steps to link Chapt24a.

1. In the WINLINK window, for the first link file enter **\SPFJ3224\Chapt24a.Obj**. (Under Windows 3.1, use **\SPFJ1624\Chapt24a.Obj**). Click Add.

Add with Corresponding statement, 357
add-on tools, user interface, 61
Advancing statement, printers, 341
After clause, 330-331
After Initial clause, 100-103
After Zero clause, 336
alert sounds, screen items, 66
aligned numeric fields, 49
alphanumeric fields, 41
  blank characters, 51
  comparing, 127-128
  edited, 51-52, 55, 92
  Initialize statement, 99
  justification, 46
  literals, 47-48
  moving, 90, 131
  numeric fields, 94
  Picture clause, 46
  reference modification, 103, 109
  slash (/), 51
  truncating, 68
  Value clause, 46
    greater, 130
    less than, 129-130
    relative, 129
    zeros, 98
Alternate Key, 232
  beginning-of-file, 255
  File Status values, 244
  Random access, 257
  Select statement, 234
  Start statement, 255
American National Standards Institute (ANSI), 11, 62
And statement, 39, 132

Animate option (debugging utility), 183
Annuity Intrinsic Function, 395-396
ANSI (American National Standards Institute), 11, 62
Any clause, 153
Arccosine Intrinsic Function, 390-391
Arcsin Intrinsic Function, 390-391
Arctangent Intrinsic Function, 390-391
arguments (functions)
  average values, 393
  integers, 392
  Intrinsic Functions, 371
  multiple, 380
  numeric literals, 391
  square root, 392
  standard deviation, 394
  values, 393
arithmetic statements
  add, 83-86
  compute, 89-90
  divide, 88-89
  improvements, 449
  multiply, 87-88
  reference modification, 104
  subtract, 86-87
arrays, see tables
Ascending sorts, 290
Assign clause
  data values, 189
  numeric fields, 42
  Select statement, 212
asterisk (*) in numeric fields, 49

At End clause, 299
  Full-Name field, 225
  Read statement, 257
  Sequential files, 251
audit editing fields, 317
Auto clause, 64, 67

B

B (Blank fill), 49
Background Color clause, 64-67
batch processes, 62
Before clause, 330-331
Before Initial clause, 100-103
beginning-of-file, 255
Bell clause, 66-67
binary search
  Search All statement, 198
  Usage clause, 45
blank characters
  alphanumeric fields, 51
  numeric fields, 49
Blank Erase clause, 65
Blank Line clause, 65, 67, 349, 358
Blank Screen clause, 63, 65, 67
Blank When Zero clause, 67
Blink clause, 66-67
bold printing, 337
bonds, calculating, 397
boundary violations, 193, 204-205
breakpoint (debugging utility), 183
brightening screens, 66
bugs, see debugging

2. Then for the next link file, in the same place that you just entered the program object name, enter **\SPFJ3224\SP2.Lib**. (Use the appropriate directory if using Windows 3.1.) Click Add.

3. Then click OK to link the program. Under Windows 3.1, click Build.

When you run the program, it should display a window that looks like Figure 24.10. Experiment with the operation of the program.

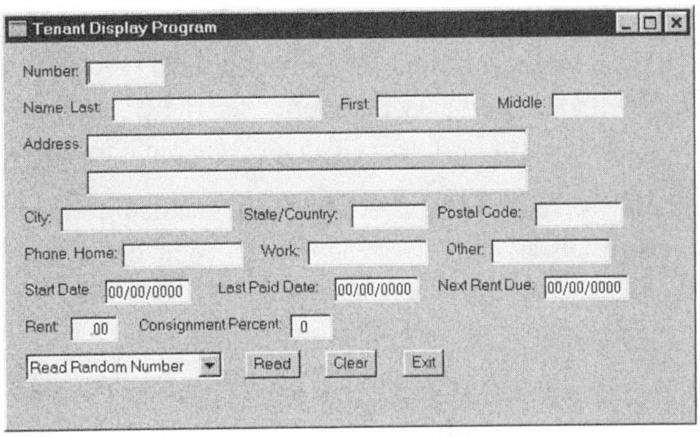

FIGURE 24.10

Chapt24a—display when the program is run.

This small demonstration only begins to touch on the features of COBOL sp2 and a GUI with COBOL. If you are interested in further GUI programming, please read the help file—COBOL sp2 Online Users Guide—that comes with COBOL sp2. It is the complete user's manual.

The Future of COBOL

COBOL has a vibrant present and a bright future. The COBOL standards committee is actively working on the next version of COBOL. This new version promises to build on the present strengths of COBOL to make the language that has been used since the dawn of business computing, robust, stable, and useable well into the twenty-first century.

One expected feature is built-in validations using a new verb, Validate, which will simplify the coding of date validations and the like. Another new feature will specify a standard for COBOL program recursion. File and record locking, used in multiuser environments, are being standardized. Currently, COBOL vendors provide different methods of handling these situations. Numeric fields are being expanded from 18 digits to 31 digits, which should eliminate any need to use imprecise floating-point math.

One of COBOL's strengths has always been its capability to accurately handle financial transactions without relying on the inaccuracies inherent in floating-point arithmetic.

Several changes in the COBOL language will yield even greater portability. Some complex mathematical operations produce different results on different compilers. In the next COBOL standard, the programmer will be able to specify the use of a set of arithmetic rules that will provide predictable and identical results across the different compilers. The capability to read backward through an Indexed or Relative file is being standardized. Most compiler vendors already have a method to accomplish the read, but each differs slightly from the others.

One of the largest changes evident in the next COBOL standard is object orientation. The new COBOL standard will provide COBOL with this very powerful programming method, designed to support easy reuse of code. The COBOL version of object-oriented programming promises to be a very clean and reliable implementation.

Although it may be several years yet before the standard is approved and implemented by the different COBOL compiler vendors, the language remains in wide use today with a rich feature set that makes development a joy. COBOL has been and continues to be a strong performer in business-related programming.

What should your next COBOL programming book be? For a more advanced view of COBOL, try *COBOL: Unleashed!* (ISBN: 0-672-31254-9; Jon Wessler *et al.*).

Summary

I would like to thank you for taking the time and energy to work your way through *Sams Teach Yourself COBOL in 24 Hours*. I hope that you join me in finding COBOL to be a strong, rich, and interesting programming language. No matter what your interest in COBOL, I sincerely hope that this book is your first step in a strong relationship with this historically colorful language and its very bright future. Welcome to the world of computer programming, fellow COBOL programmer!

INDEX

Symbols

$ (currency symbol), **49, 51**

( ) (parentheses), **132**

* (asterisk), **49**

+ (positive), **49**

, (comma character), **49, 65**

- (negative), **49**

. (decimal point), **49**

/ (slash), **49, 51**

0 (zero character), **49, 51, 89**

21 File Status error, **270, 272**

24 File Status error, **284**

39 File Status error, **284**

43 File Status error, **272**

48 File Status error, **270**

88 level items (condition names), **136-140**

A

A-0 programming language, 11

abbreviating complex conditional statements, 133

Accept statement, 62-63, 96-98

attributes, 64

date, 108

Day clause, 368

Exit Program clause, 413

From Date clause, 368

Gregorian calendar, 97

Julian calendar, 97

screen descriptions, 69

Special-Names paragraph, 97

terminating, 70

values, 71-72

accessing

Dynamic, 234, 270

Indexed files, 232

Random, 234, 270

Relative files, 275-283

Sequential, 234, 270, 284

Accumulator statement, control break program, subtotals, 351

Add statement, 83-86, 93

compiler options to programs, 181

data items, 85

end-of-file, 219, 230

files, 270

group-level items, 85

Random access, 270

records, 220

Relative file, 280

Sequential access, 270

subtotals, 345

built-in validations, 449
business processing
  client/server, 9
  computing needs, 8
  data, 8
By Content, 420-421
By Reference, 420-421
bytes, 45

C

calculating
  bonds, 397
  Easter dates, 383-386
  fields, 123
calendars
  COBOL, 387
  dates, 368-369
  Gregorian, 382-383
  Julian, 382-383
Call statement
  By Content, 420-421
  By Reference, 420-421
  canceling, 426
  COBOL sp2, 429
  dynamic, 421-423, 426
  Not On Exception clause, 422
  On Exception clause, 422
  programming languages, 426
  static, 421-423, 426
  subprograms, 417
  Using clause, 417
called programs, *see* **subprograms**
Cancel statement
  programs, 422
  Call statement, 426

capturing
  errors, 277, 294
  function keys, 70
  transaction data, 306-309
Carriage Return/Line Feed (CRLF), 210-211
case sensitivity, 24
central processing unit (CPU), 7
Char Intrinsic Function, 399
characters
  converting, 103
  counting, 100-101
  replacing, 101-102
checking control break sequence, 356
CICS (Customer Information Control System), 62
clauses
  After Initial, 100-101
  And, 132, 199
  Any, 153
  Assign, 212
  At End, 299
  Auto, 64, 67
  Background Color, 63, 65, 67
  Before Initial, 100-101
  Bell, 66-67
  Blank Erase, 65
  Blank Line, 65, 67
  Blank Screen, 63, 65, 67
  Blank When Zero, 67
  Blink, 66-67
  Count In, 119-120
  Currency-Sign is, 25
  Decimal-point is Comma, 25

  decimal position, 43
  Delimited By, 122
  Delimited By Size, 112
  Delimiter In, 120
  Depending On, 203
  Else, 131
  Erase, 67
  File Status, 212
  Foreground Color, 63, 65, 67
  Full, 64, 67
  Giving, 287, 290
  Highlight, 66-67
  Indexed By, 195
  Invalid Key, 244-245, 277
  Justified, 67
  Justified Right, 68, 70
  Leading, 102
  Line, 65-66
  Lowlight, 66-67
  Not, 133
  numeric fields, 44-46
  Occurs, 188
  On Overflow, 120
  Or, 132
  Other, 148
  Picture, 40-41, 46-47, 59, 67
  Pointer, 117, 123
  Redefines, 189-193, 195
  Relative Key, 275
  Renames, 40
  Replacing, 99, 102
  Required, 64-65, 67
  Reverse-Video, 66
  Secure, 64-65, 67
  Sign, 67
  Sign Separate, 43
  Tallying In, 102, 119, 123

To, 69-70
Underline, 66-67
Until, 162
Upon, 28
Usage, 67
Using, 70, 287
Value, 42, 98
Varying, 197
When, 145, 199
Clear push button, 435-436
Clear Screen statement, 281
clearing
    Full-Name field, 225
    lines, 66
    screens, 64, 265
    target fields, 122
client/server processing, 9
Close statement
    COBOL sp2 panels, 441
    files, 313
        Dynamic access, 265
        Sequential access, 215
        Status values, 215
**COBOL (Common Business
    Oriented Language), 7**
    calendar, 387
    Data division, 38
    ease-of-use, 19
    Environment division, 38
    future versions, 449
    Identification division, 38
    industry standards, 11-12
    intrinsic functions, 12
    Procedure division, 38
    recursion, 420
    structured programming,
        12

COBOL sp2, 428
    Call statement, 429
    Clear push button,
        435-436
    Close statement, 441
    conversing, 439
    designing, 429-436
    drop-down boxes, 434-435
    editing, 429, 437-449
    error message, 441
    evaluation version, 429
    Exit push button, 435-436,
        439
    FD statement, 441
    fields, 429, 431-433
    generated program, 436-
        438
    icons, 441
    line numbers, 441-442
    linking, 448
    lowercase, 438
    Open statement, 438, 441
    panels, 429
    Picture clause, 435
    processing loops, 442
    Read push button, 434-
        436, 441
    saving, 436
    Select statement, 441
    text display, 430
    titles, 429, 441
    uppercase, 438
CODASYL committee, 11
coding
    If statement, 142
    Screen_Section program,
        77-78
collating sequence, 25

color
    screens, 64, 76
    toggling, 66
**comma character (,) in
    numeric fields, 49, 65**
command-line arguments
    data, 108
    retrieving, 96
    special names, 108
comment lines, 22, 105
**Common Business Oriented
    Language, see COBOL**
**Communications Section
    (Data Division), 26**
COMP data items, 210
**Comp value (Usage clause),
    45**
comparing
    alphanumeric fields,
        127-130
    Call statement, 421-423
    data items, 126, 128
    date, 319
    Line Sequential, 210, 229
    literals, 127-128
    master files, 319
    numeric fields, 127-129
    Perform statement with
        Go To statement, 163
**compatibility platforms,
    GUI, 428**
compilers
    16-bit version, 32
    collating sequence, 25
    compute statement, 90
    computers, 24
    debugging utilities, 181
    diagnostic messages,
        36-37

directives, 29
division headers, 37
Fujitsu, 71-72
Editing window, 33
error messages, 57
executing, 17-19
hardware requirements, 13
installation, 12-19
object modules, 34
options
    adding, 181
    configuration, 16, 18
    linking, 181
    TEST, 185
output devices, 28
Programming Staff, 30,
    33-34, 415
recompiling, 37
reporting, 31
software requirements, 13
Special-Names paragraph,
    71
statements, 62
syntax errors, 33, 38
text mode, 63
troubleshooting, 36-37
user interface, 62
validating, 15-19
VMS COBOL, 71
Windows 3.1, 14-15
**complex conditional state-
ments, 134-135, 139**
    abbreviating, 133
    isolating, 132
**compute statement, 89, 90,
93, 156**
computers
    bugs, 11
    compilers, 24

condition names, 136
conditional statements
    abbreviating, 133
    And clause, 132
    comparing data items,
        126, 128
    complex, 132-135, 139
    Continue, 133
    Else clause, 131
    equal, 127
    Evaluate statement,
        141, 143
    executing, 128
    false, 137, 143-144
    If, 126-131
    isolating, 132
    less than values, 129
    literals, 131
    multiple, 139
    names, 137-138
    nesting, 135
    Not clause, 133
    Or clause, 132
    Perform statement, 160
    resetting, 137
    Set, 136-137
    Size Error phrase, 126
    terminating, 128
    testing, 136, 139, 150
    Then phrase, 129
    true, 126, 128, 140,
        143-144, 148-149
    unequal, 128
    values, 129
    variable names, 137
Configuration Section
    Fujitsu compilers, 16, 18
    Object-Computer para-
        graph, 24

Source-Computer para-
    graph, 24
Special-Names paragraph,
    25, 70, 72
statements, 72
Console reserved word, 28
Continue statement, 133
**control break programs
(reports)**
    blank lines, 349
    checking order, 356
    creating, 363
    date format, 350
    dealer totals, 345, 359
    Declaratives statement,
        353
    end-of-file, 353
    errors, 357, 364
    grand totals, 345, 360
    headings, 362
    hierarchy, 345
    Initialize statement, 351
    Input Procedure, 348
    layout, 344
    line count, 360-362
    master files, 347
    Random access, 347
    resetting values, 346, 357
    save fields, 351, 357
    Sort sequence, 345-346,
        348, 353-354
    String statement, 350
    subtotals, 344
        Accumulator state-
            ment, 351
        Add statement, 345
        total lines, 350
    transaction date, 345-348,
        358
    usage, 364
    walk through, 346-363

conversing COBOL sp2
  panels, 439
converting
    characters, 103
    Gregorian to/from Julian,
      382-383
Copy statement, file definitions (FD), 426
Copybooks statement,
  source code, 424-425
correcting errors, 76
corresponding fields, 86, 295
corrupting Perform state-
  ment, 167
Cosine Intrinsic Function,
  390
Count In clause, 119
counting
    characters, 100-101, 119
    print lines, 332
    records, 298
    target fields, 119
CPU (central processing
  unit), 7
CR (credit balance), 49
creating
    control break programs,
      363
    folders, 29-30
    Indexed files, 290-292
    input fields, 69-70
    Perform logic, 159-163
    processing loops, 30-31
    records, 281
    Relative file, 277
    Sequential files, 210, 215-
      217, 235-238
    user input, 239-244
    variable-length tables,
      203-204
    see also writing

credit balance (CR), numer-
  ic fields, 49
CRLF (Carriage
  Return/Line Feed), 211
cross-platforming, 10
Crt Status data item, 71-72
currency symbol ($), 49, 51
Currency-Sign is clause, 25
current date/time, 12, 97,
  369-371, 380
Cursor statement, 261
    capturing, 70
    length, 71
    positioning, 64, 70, 76, 79
Customer Information
  Control System (CICS), 62

D

data
    entering in programs,
      32-33
    moving between fields,
      90-93
    passing, 27, 410
    on-screen, 63
    returning, 410
Data Division, 27, 32, 38
    Occurs clause, 188
    Redefines clause, 189-193
    sections, 26
data items
    88 levels, 136
    accepting, 96
    adding, 85
    COMP, 210
    condition names, 136
    Crt Status, 72

decimal limit, 59
defining, 54, 59
elementary-level, 40-41,
  53-54
Evaluate statement, 112,
  141-143, 146, 154
Filler, 54
formatting, 117
group-level, 40, 53-54, 59,
  188
If statements, 126, 128
incrementing, 197
index values, 200
initializing, 197
level numbers, 40-41
moving, 55
numeric, 59
Read statement, 351
Redefine clause, 189-193
reference modification,
  103-104
sizing limitations, 190
storing, 85
subprograms, 416-417
tables, 187
testing, 154
validation, 310-313
Value clause, 52, 144-145,
  172-173, 189
see also fields
data processing, 8
date
    Accept statement, 108
    comparing, 319
    converting from seconds,
      380
    Current, 97
    fields, 78
    format, 98, 317

Gregorian, 97
Julian, 97
validations, 449
Date-Of-Integer Intrinsic Function, 371, 387
dates
COBOL calendar, 387
current days, 369
days, 371-373, 376, 413-414
Easter, 384-386
epact, 384
errors, 379
field values, 376
format, 350, 354
Gregorian calendar, 368, 382-383
headings, 352
history, 368
integers, 372, 377
Intrinsic Functions, 368, 387
Julian calendar, 368-369, 382-383
leap years, 369, 376, 378
months, 376
printing, 337-338
ranges, 377
Sort statement, 348, 350
subprograms, 418-420
two-digit, 368
validation, 376-382
Day clause, 368
Day-Of-Integer Intrinsic Function, 383
days
between dates, 371-375, 413-414
format, 317

values, 376
weekdays, 374-375
DB (debit balance), 49
dealer totals (reports), 345, 359
debit balance (DB), 49
debugging utility, 11
Animate option, 183
breakpoint, 183
compilers, 181
programs, 37
TEST compiler option, 185
troubleshooting, 185
Windows 3.1, 181-182
decimal limit, numeric fields, 41, 43, 59
decimal point (.) position
implied, 43
numeric fields, 49, 58
Decimal-point is Comma clause, 25
Declaratives statement, 248
errors, 245-246, 298
reports, 353
Sections headers, 245
transaction data, 323
default
output devices, 28
sequential files, 210
defining
condition names, 136
data items, 54, 59
fields, 40-41, 55
screens, 79
tables, 188
Delete statement
records, 274, 280
Sort Work File, 300

Delimited By clause, 112, 122
Delimiter In clause, 120
delimiters
Carriage Return, 210-211
Count In clause, 120
length, 122
Line Feed, 210-211
multiple, 119
spaces, 114, 118, 120
String statement, 116
Unstring statement, 118
Depending On statement, 203, 228, 395
Descending sorts, 290
designing
COBOL sp2 panels, 429-436
fields, 73
layout, 328
programs, 338-339
records, 329
reports, 328-330
Screen_Section program, 72
detail lines (reports), 331, 333-336
diagnostic messages, compilers, 36-37
dimming screens, 66
disabling Fujitsu compiler messages, 220
Display statement, 57, 62-63
attributes, 64
edited numeric fields, 67
field contents, 69
on-screen, 63, 69, 263, 265
Upon clause, 28
Usage clause, 45

Display-And-Accept statement, 281

Divide statement
case sensitivity, 24
Data, 26-27, 32, 38
Environment, 24-26, 32, 38
formats, 88-89
headers, 37
Identification, 23-24, 32, 38
Procedure, 27-28, 32, 38, 106
required, 23
sections, 24, 26
statements, 88-89
zero, 89

DLLs (dynamic link libraries), 423

dollar sign ($), 49, 51

drop-down boxes, COBOL sp2 panels, 434-435

Duplicate Key (Indexed files), 248
File Status values, 244
Select statement, 234
Sort Keys sequence, 299

Dynamic access, 270
Indexed files, 234, 258-266, 272, 274
Close statement, 265
error messages, 263
File Status values, 261
Open statement, 259, 262-263, 265
Random Read, 258
Read statement, 264
Relative file, 279
retrieving records, 250

Select statement, 258
Sequential Read, 259
Start statement, 259, 264-265

dynamic Call statement, 421-423, 426

dynamic link libraries (DLLs), 423

E

Easter, 383-386

edit fields
alphanumeric, 51-52, 55, 92
audit, 317
date, 317
day, 317
displaying as spaces, 67
month, 317
numeric, 48-51, 91-92
zero suppression, 49-50

editing
COBOL sp2 panels, 437-449
fields, 55-58
Fujitsu compiler, 33
index values, 196
Line Sequential files, 210
primary Key, 272
screens, 76
subprograms, 412

elementary-level items, 40-41, 53-54
condition names, 136
reference modification, 104, 189

Else clause, 131

End-Compute explicit scope terminator, 89

End-Evaluate scope terminator, 144

End-If explicit scope terminator, 184

end-of-file condition
adding, 230
Output Procedure, 296
records, 219
report control breaks, 353
Rewrite statement, 228
Sequential files, 222
status, 251
transaction data, 323

End-Read explicit scope terminator, 257

End-Return explicit scope terminator, 298

End-Search explicit scope terminator, 197

End-Unstring explicit scope terminator, 118

entering data in programs, 32-33

Environment Division, 24-26, 32, 38

epact (dates), 384

equal conditions, 127

Erase clause, 66-67

errors
Alternate Key, 244
capturing, 277
COBOL sp2 panels, 441
compiler, 57
control break programs, 364
correcting, 76

date validation, 379
File Status, 270, 284
Indexed files, 263, 298
Input Procedure, 294
Primary Key, 244
Procedure Division,
  245-246
Sequential files, 216
subtotals, 357
syntax, 31
transaction data, 309
Write statement, 244-245
Evaluate statement, 143, 154
conditions, 141, 143
data items, 143
executing, 154
false, 143-144
format, 143
group-level items, 146
If logic, 151
literals, 143
multiple, 147-148
nesting, 147, 154
numeric, 144-145
Other clause, 148
rearranging, 153
scope terminators, 144
selection objects/subjects,
  143, 145, 147-148
sequence, 145
source code, 142, 150,
  152-153
stacking, 146
testing, 150
true, 143-145, 148-149
values, 141-143, 154
When clause, 152-153
event-driven logic, 427
executing

conditional statements,
  128
Evaluate statement, 154
Fujitsu compilers, 17-19
Input/Output Procedure,
  296, 301
multiple, 132, 145
Perform statement, 160
programs, 35-36
selection objects, 148-149
statements, 175, 301
Exit Program statement
Accept clause, 413
COBOL sp2 panels,
  435-436, 439
subprograms, 412
explicit scope terminators,
84
End-Compute, 89
End-Evaluate, 144
End-If, 184
End-Read, 257
End-Return, 298
End-Search, 197
End-Unstring, 118
exponents, 89

F

Factorial Intrinsic Function,
391
false conditions
Evaluate statement,
  143-144
setting to false, 137
FD (File Description) state-
ment, 213

fields, 39
aligned, 49
alphanumeric, 41, 46, 99,
  127-128
calculating, 123
characters, 51, 100-101
COBOL sp2 panels, 429,
  431-433
comparing, 127-128
contents, 69
corresponding, 295
counting, 119
creating, 69-70
cursor, 79
data, 90-93
date, 78, 376
decimal positions, 41, 43,
  58
defining, 40-41, 55
delimiters, 122
editing, 48-52, 55-58, 67,
  91-92
filling, 64
formatting, 42
From, 79
initializing, 118
input/output, 79, 105
Inspect statement, 400
justification, 42, 46
length, 398-400
literals, 41, 47-48
moving, 90-91
multiple, 112, 122
name entries, 137-138
numeric, 40-41, 94
Output Procedure, 296
overflowing, 120
packing, 45
quotation marks, 47

receiving, 58
reference modification, 103, 109, 112
Relative-Key, 276
required, 65, 73, 78
resetting, 119
Screen Section program, 71, 73, 76
separating, 118-121
signed, 43-44, 87
slash (/), 51
Sort, 300
source, 118
storage, 44-45
stringing, 117
target, 112
To, 79
troubleshooting, 84
truncating, 90-91
unique, 99
Unstring statement, 138
update, 79
Using, 79
validation, 310, 312
Value clause, 42, 46, 98-99, 129-130
zeros, 49-50, 98
see also data items
File Description (FD) statement, 213
　COBOL sp2 panels, 441
　Copy statement, 426
File Section (Data Division), 26-27
File Status clause, 270, 284
　Alternate Key, 244
　capturing, 277
　Close statement, 215
　Duplicate Key, 244

Dynamic access, 261
Indexed files, 248
Open statement, 214
　in Extend, 219
　in Output, 216, 219
Random access, 244, 256
Read statement, 222, 259
reports, 335
Rewrite statement, 225
Select statement, 212
Sequential access, 221
Start statement, 254
transaction data, 317, 323
Write statement, 216-217, 219, 238
filenames
　physical, 212
　Sequential files, 216
　symbolic, 212
files
　adding, 270
　closing, 313
　Copy statement, 426
　data items, 209
　extensions, 77
　fields, 209
　Indexed files, 231, 292
　Line Sequential, 210, 229
　opening, 313
　reading, 270
　Record Sequential, 210
　retrieving, 270
　saving, 77
　Sequential, 214-217, 225-228
　sorting, 286-291
　Write statement, 210, 219, 270-271, 340
Filler data item, 54, 64
financial functions, 395-396

flags, condition names, 136
Flexus web site, 429
FLOW-MATIC language, 11
folders, 29-30
fonts, 338
Foreground Color clause, 63-67
format
　COBOL programs, 21
　data items, 117
　date, 98
　Evaluate statement, 143
　numeric fields, 42
free-form source code, 23
From Date clause, 368
From statement, 67, 79
Fujitsu compiler, 71-72
　Editing window, 33
　executing, 17-19
　hardware requirements, 13
　installation, 12-19
　messages, 220
　options, 16, 18
　output devices, 28
　Programming Staff, 30
　software requirements, 13
　Sort Work Files, 286
　validating, 15-19
　Windows 3.1, 14-15
Full clause, 64, 67
Full-Name field, 225
functions
　arguments, 380
　capturing keys, 70
　Factorial, 391
　financial
　　Annuity, 395-396
　　Present-Value, 396

integer
    Integer-Of-Date,
        371-372, 374, 387
    Integer-Part, 392
Intrinsic
    Current-Date, 12,
        370-371, 380
    Rem, 379, 392
logarithm, 391
miscellaneous
    Mod, 392
    Random, 403-404
    When-Compiled,
        403-404
    Sqrt, 392
statistical
    Max, 393
    Mean, 393
    Median, 394
    Midrange, 393
    Min, 393
    Ord-Max, 393
    Ord-Min, 393
    Range, 394
    Standard-Deviation,
        394
    Sum, 394
    Variance, 394
string
    Char, 399
    Length, 398
    Lower-Case, 400
    Max, 399
    Min, 399
    Numval, 402
    Numval-C, 402
    Ord, 400
    Ord-Max, 399
    Ord-Min, 399

Random, 397
Reverse, 400
Upper-Case, 400
trigonometric
    Arccosine, 390-391
    Arcsin, 390-391
    Arctangent, 390-391
    Cosine, 390
    Sin, 390-391
    Tangent, 390-391

G

generating COBOL sp2
    panels, 436
Giving clause, 287, 290
GMT (Greenwich Mean
    Time), 380-382
Go To statement
    infinite loops, 168
    Paragraph title, 163-169
    Perform statement,
        163-164, 168, 184
    processing loops, 163, 170
    Section header, 163-169
    unconditional branch, 163
government use of COBOL,
    9
grand totals (control break
    programs), 345, 360
Graphical User Interface,
    see GUI
greater than values, 130
Greenwich Mean Time
    (GMT), 380-382

Gregorian calendar
    converting from Julian,
        382-383
    dates, 97, 368
group-level items, 40, 53-54,
    59
    adding, 85
    Evaluate statement, 146
    Initialize statement, 99
    moving, 92
    paragraphs, 82, 169
    records, 210
    reference modification,
        104, 109
    stringing, 112
    tables, 188
    Value clause, 52
GUI (Graphical User
    Interface)
    add-on tools, 61
    COBOL sp2 panels,
        428-429
    event-driven logic, 427
    platform compatibility,
        428
    third-party tools, 428
    Visual Basic, 428
    Visual C++, 428
    see also user interface

H

hardware requirements for
    Fujitsu compiler, 13
headings (reports)
    control breaks, 362
    dates, 352

reports, printing, 331,
    333-337
times, 352
**hierarchy in control break
    programs, 345**
High-Value (literals), 48
Highlight clause, 66-67
history of
    dates, 368
**Hopper, Grace (Admiral),
    11**
    A-0 language, 11
    CODASYL committee, 11
    computer bug, 11
    FLOW-MATIC, 11
    influence, 10

I

I-O (Open in Input) mode
    Dyanmic access, 270
    Random access, 270
    Sequential access, 214,
        221, 270
    updating, 221
IBM mainframes, 28, 62
**icons in COBOL sp2 panels,
    441**
**Identification Division,
    223-224, 32, 38**
**If conditional statement,
    139, 142, 154**
    abbreviating, 133
    coding, 142
    complex, 132-135
    condition names, 137-138
    data items, 126, 128

Else clause, 131
equal conditions, 127
literals, 131
nesting, 135, 139, 151
terminating, 128
Then phrase, 129
true conditions, 126, 128
values, 129
**implied decimal position,
    43, 58**
**increasing Sort statement
    speed, 295**
incrementing
    data items, 197
    values, 172-173
Index values
    contents, 195
    editing, 196
    element numbers, 195
    referencing, 200
    Search statement
    starting, 196
    tables, 200
    Usage clause, 45
Indexed By clause, 195
Indexed files
    Alternate Key, 232, 234,
        244, 257
    At End condition, 251
    Close statement, 265
    creating, 235-244,
        290-292
    Declaratives, 248
    definitions, 232
    deleting, 274
    Duplicate Key, 234, 248
    Dynamic access, 234,
        258-266, 272, 274
    efficiency, 320
    error messages, 244, 263,
        298

File Status values, 248,
    256, 261
Input/Output, 235-238,
    250
Invalid Key, 248
Key field, 231-233, 235
Move statement, 256
Open statement, 244, 259,
    262-263, 283
Primary Key, 232-233,
    244, 272
Random access, 234, 244,
    256-257, 272, 274
Read statement, 237, 251,
    257-258, 264, 273,
    324-325, 450
records, 232-233,
    250-253, 270-271
rewriting, 271-272
Select statement, 233-235,
    256, 258
Sequential access,
    234-239, 247, 250, 259
sorting, 292
Start statement, 254-256,
    259, 264-265
storing, 234
structures, 232
updating, 233, 271-273,
    283, 320-325
user input, 239-244
validating, 232
Write statement, 238, 244
industry standards
    COBOL, 11-12
    future improvements,
        449-450
infinite loops, 168

Initialize statement, 108
  alphanumeric fields, 99
  data items, 197
  group-level items, 99
  Output Procedure fields, 296
  Redefines clause, 191
  Replacing clause, 100
  reports, 98, 351
  target fields, 113, 118
  Varying statement, 184
inline Perform statement, 171, 174-177
  Go To clause, 184
  inline If statement, 178-180
  left-justification routine, 180
  nesting, 177, 184
  Paragraph, 184
Input Procedure
  control breaks, 348
  data, 105
  errors, 294
  fields, 69-70, 79
  Justified Right clause, 70
  processing loop, 292
  records, 292
  screens, 261
  size, 299
  Sort statement, 293-296, 301
  text file, 235-237
Input-Output Section (Environment Division), 24
Input-Output, *see* **I-O mode**
Inspect statement
  characters, 103, 108
  clause, 100-102

  counting, 100-101
  fields, 400
  leading character phrases, 103
  replacing, 101-102
installation
  COBOL sp2 evaluation version, 429
  Fujitsu compilers, 12-19
  validating, 15-19
  Windows 3.1, 14-15
integer functions
  Integer, 392
  Integer-Part, 392
  Mod, 392
  date validation, 377
  positive numbers, 392
interactive debugging utility, *see* **debugging utliity**
interactive processing, 62
interface, *see* **GUI; user interface**
Intrinsic Functions, 12, 369
  arguments, 317
  Current Date, 12, 370-371, 380
  Date-Of-Integer, 371-372, 374, 387
  Day-Of-Integer, 383
  dates, 368, 387
  Factorial, 391
  financial, 395-396
  Integer, 392
  Integer-Part, 392
  logarithm, 391
  mathematical, 392
  miscellaneous
    Random, 403-404
    When-Compiled, 403-404
  Mod, 392

  multiple, 380
  numerical, 387
  Present-Value, 396
  Rem, 379
  Sqrt, 392
  statistical
    Max, 393
    Mean, 393
    Median, 394
    Midrange, 393
    Min, 393
    Ord-Max, 393
    Ord-Min, 393
    Range, 394
    Standard-Deviation, 394
    Sum, 394
    Variance, 394
  string
    Char, 399
    Length, 398
    Lower-Case, 400
    Max, 399
    Min, 399
    Numval, 402
    Numval-C, 402
    Ord, 400
    Ord-Max, 399
    Ord-Min, 399
    Output-Field, 400
    Random, 397
    Reverse, 400
    Upper-Case, 400
  trigonometric
    Arccosine, 390-391
    Arcsin, 390-391
    Arctangent, 390-391
    Cosine, 390
    Sin, 390-391
    Tangent, 390-391
Invalid Key clause, 248, 277

errors, 244-245
Read statement, 257
Start statement, 254
**Is Initial clause subpro-
grams, 416**
**isolating complex condition-
al statements, 132**

J

**Job Control Language
(JCL), 212**
Julian calendar, 97
converting from
Gregorian, 382-383
dates, 368-369
Intrinsic Functions
Day-Of-Integer, 383
justification
alphanumeric fields, 46
left, 106
numeric fields, 42
Justified clause, 67
Justified Right clause, 68, 70

K

Key fields, *see* **Indexed files**
Keyboard-Status field, 261
keys
master files, 314
transaction data, 314

L

layouts
description, 210
records, 293
Leading clause, 102
counting, 101
level numbers, 41
numeric fields, 42
leap years, 369, 376-378
left-justification, 106, 180
**Length Intrinsic Function,
122, 398**
less than values, 129-130
level numbers
data items, 40-41
elementary, 41, 53-54
fields, 40
group, 52-54
leading digits, 41
Renames clause, 40
Line clause, 65-66
line count
control break, 360-362
printing, 332, 334,
336-337
Line Feed delimiter, 210
line numbers
COBOL sp2 panels,
441-442
programs, 22
Line Sequential files, 229
delimiters, 211
editing, 210
master files, 315-316
records, 230
updating, 225-228,
315-316

lines, clearing, 66
**Linkage Section (Data
Division), 26-27**
called programs, 418
COBOL sp2
panels, 448
compiler options, 181
object modules, 34
programs, 35
listings
3.1 Demonstrate
Group/Elementary
Levels, 53-54
3.2 Demonstrate Edited
Fields, 55-58
4.1 Screen_Section with
Justified Right, 68
4.2 Screen_Section
Demonstration, 74-76
7.1 String Example,
114-115
7.2 Unstring Example, 120
8.1 Intelligent Telephone
Number Format, 134
8.2 Intelligent Name
Separation, 137-138
10.1 Perform logic,
157-158
10.2 Processing Loop,
160-161
10.3 Go To with Perform,
164
10.4 Perform with Go To,
168
11.1 Count to 10, 172
11.2 Count to 10, Revised,
173
11.3 Inline Perform
Example, 176-177

11.4 Inline Perform with Inline If, 178-180

12.1 Month/Date Name Display, 191-192

12.2 State Name Lookup, 193-195

12.4 Search Multidimensional Table, 201-203

13.1 File Creation Example, 217-218

13.2 Read statement, 223-224

13.3 Update Sequential files, 226-227

14.1 Dealer File Creation, 235-237

14.2 Dealer Data Entry, 239-243

15.1 Indexed File/Sequential Access, 251-253

15.3 Dynamic Access Example, 260

16.1 Relative file access, 275-282

17.1 Sort statement, 287

17.2 Creating Indexed File Using Sort, 290-292

17.3 Sort with Input Procedure, 293-296

17.4 Sort with Output Procedure, 297-299

18.2 Sequential File Update, 315

18.3 Indexed File Update, 321-323

21.1 Current-Date Intrinsic Function, 370-371

21.2 Integer-Of-Date, 372

21.3 Days Between Dates, 372-373

21.4 Days between Dates/Weekday, 374-375

21.5 Date Validation, 377

21.6 Convert Local Time to GMT, 381-382

21.7 Easter Date Calculation, 384-386

22.1 Annuity Function, 395-396

22.2 Center a Field, 398-399

22.3 Assemble Full Name, 401-402

22.4 Random Function, 404

23.1 Menu Program, 411

23.2 Called Phone Number Format, 412-413

23.3 Called Days Between Dates, 413-414

23.4 Date Entry, Calling Validation, 417

23.5 Date Validation Subprogram, 418-420

23.6 Date Validation Copybook, 424

23.7 Date Validation Copybook, 424-425

24.1 sp2 Generated Program, 437-438

24.3 Final Dealer Display, 442-448

literals
  alphanumeric, 47-48
  comparing, 127-128
  Evaluate statement, 143
  fields, 41
  If conditional statements, 131
  numeric, 47-48, 391
  quotation marks, 47
  screen, 79
  values, 47-48

loading tables, 189-193, 195, 211

local time, 380

location of Sequential files, 211

logarithm functions391

lookups in tables, 193-195

Low-Value (literals), 47

Lower-Case Intrinsic Function, 400

Lowlight clause, 66-67

M

machine language, 8

main programs, 410, 415

mainframes (IBM)
  CICS, 62
  output devices, 28

master files
  comparing, 319
  control breaks, 347
  Indexed
    efficiency, 320
    Read statement, 324-325
    updating, 320-325
  keys, 314
  Sequential files
    Line Sequential, 315-316
    updating, 313-320
  transaction data, 314

Matchcase of Keyword
  check box, 32
mathematical functions, 89,
  392
Max Intrinsic Function,
  393, 399
Mean Intrinsic Function,
  393
Median Intrinsic Function,
  394
menu programs, 410-411
merging, *see* String statement
messages, Fujitsu compiler,
  disabling, 220
Midrange Intrinsic
  Function, 393
Min Intrinsic Function, 393,
  399
miscellaneous functions,
  403-404
Mod Intrinsic Function, 392
modifying Sort fields, 300
month
    dates, 376
    format, 317
Move statement, 55, 90-93
    alphanumeric fields to
      numeric, 131
    Indexed files, 256
    data items, 55, 90-93
    fields, 295
    group-level items, 92
    spaces, 98
    zeros, 98
multidimensional tables,
  200-203
Multiply statement, 87-89

N

name entries
    unstringing, 137-138
    reports, 337
naming programs, 421
negative (-), 43, 49
nesting
    Evaluate statements, 147,
      154
    If statements, 135, 139,
      151
    inline Perform statement,
      177, 184
Next clause
    Read statement, 258
    File Status values, 259
nibbles (bytes), 45
Not clause, 133
Not On Exception clause,
  422
numeric fields, 41
    alphanumeric fields, 94
    aligned, 49
    arguments, 391
    asterisk (*), 49
    Blank fill (B), 49
    comma character (,), 49
    comparing, 127-128
    credit balances (CR), 49
    currency symbol ($), 49
    debit balance (DB), 49
    decimal point positions,
      41, 43, 49, 58
    defining, 41
    edited, 48-51, 67, 91-92
    literals, 47-48
    moving, 91
    negative (-), 49

packing, 45
Perform statement, 174
positive (+), 49
reference modification,
  103, 109
Relative-Key, 276
right justification, 42
signed, 43-44
slash (/), 49
storage, 44-45
saving, 44
tables, 189
Usage clause, 44-46
values, 42, 129, 144-145,
  172-173
zero suppression, 42,
  49-50, 98
numeric Intrinsic
  Functions, 387, 402
Numval-C Intrinsic
  Function, 402

O

object modules, 34
Object-Computer para-
  graph (Configuration
  section), 24
object-oriented program-
  ming, 450
Occurs clause, 188, 203, 228
On Exception clause, 422
On Overflow clause, 120
On Size Error phrase, 86
Open in Extend mode
    File Status clause, 219
    Indexed files, 244
    Sequential files, 214
    transaction data, 308

Open in Input, *see* **I-O mode**

Open in Output mode
errors, 216
File Status values, 215, 219
Indexed files, 235-238
Sequential, 214-215, 247

Open statement
COBOL sp2 panels, 438, 441
Dynamic access, 262-263
File Status values, 214, 313
Indexed files, 259, 265, 283
Record Sequential file, 284
Relative file, 284
reports, 334-335
Sequential files, 214, 283

Optional clause
Select statement, 229

options, Fujitsu compilers configuration, 16, 18

Or clause, 132, 139

Ord Intrinsic Function, 400

Ord-Max/Ord-Min Intrinsic Function, 393, 399

Other clause, 148

Output Procedure
clauses, 67
data, 105
default, 28
end-of-file detection, 296
executing, 296
fields, 79, 296
processing loop, 296, 298
records, 296

size, 299
reports, 296
Sort statement, 297-299, 301
see also target fields

Output-Field Intrinsic Function, 400

overflowing target fields, 113-114, 120

P

Packed-Decimal value (Usage clause), 45

page breaks (reports)
line counters, 334
printing, 331-339

panels (COBOL sp2)
Clear push button, 435-436
Close statement, 441
conversing, 439
designing, 429-436
drop-down boxes, 434-435
editing, 429, 437-449
error messages, 441
Exit push button, 435-436, 439
FD statement, 441
fields, 429, 431-433
generating, 436
icons, 441
line numbers, 441-442
linking, 448
Open statement, 441
opening, 438
Picture clause, 435

processing loops, 442
push buttons, 434, 441
Read push button, 435-436
saving, 436
Select statement, 441
text display, 430
titles, 429, 441
window display, 429

Paragraph title, 27-28, 157-158
case sensitivity, 24
Go To statement, 163-169
grouping, 82, 169
Perform statement, 159, 167, 184
periods, 82
Procedure Division, 82, 93
Special-Names, 162
Thru clause, 158

passing data, 410

Perform

Perform logic, 157-158

Perform statement, 156
corrupting, 167
executing, 160
Go To statement, 164, 168
comparing, 163
inline, 171, 174-177
left-justification, 180
nesting, 184
Paragraph, 184
nesting, 177
numeric data items, 174
numeric literal items, 174
Paragraph title, 158, 167
multiple, 159
processing loops, 159-161, 169
creating, 159-163

Section headers, 157
Stop Run statement, 159
terminating, 169, 172
testing, 173
Thru clause, 158
Until clause, 162, 172
Varying clause, 172-173
With Test After clause,
    173-174
phrases
After Initial, 103
Before Initial, 103
Size Error, 126
Then, 129
physical filenames, 212
Picture clause, 40, 59, 67
alphanumeric fields, 46
COBOL sp2
decimal position, 43
edited, 49-50
fields, 40-45
panels, 435
platforms, GUI, 428
Pointer clause
data, 117
positioning, 121
Unstring statement, 123
positioning
Auto clause, 64
cursor, 70, 76, 79
Pointer clause, 121
Relative file, 279
positive (+), 43, 49
Present-Value Intrinsic
Function, 396
preserving on-screen data,
63
Primary Key, 231-233, 244,
272

printing
Advancing statement, 341
bold, 337
dates, 337-338
dealer totals, 359
detail records, 335-336
File Status values, 335
fonts, 338
grand totals, 360
headings, 331, 333-337
lines, 331, 333-334
multiple records, 338
name formatting, 337
opening, 334-335
Output Procedure, 296
page breaks, 332
requirements, 332-333
sorting records, 339
time, 337-338
transaction date, 358
underlining, 339
Write statement, 340
Proc-Open-File Paragraph
sp2 program, 438
Procedure Division, 28, 32,
38, 81, 106
batch, 62
called programs, 418-420
Declaratives, 245-246
divide statement, 88-89
Input, 292-296
Paragraphs, 27-28, 82, 93,
    157-158
Output, 296
Sections, 27-28, 82,
    157-158
statements
    add, 83-86, 93
    compute, 89-90, 93
    move, 90-93

multiple, 87-88
Start statement, 255
subtract, 86-87
Process-Files Paragraph,
318
processing
client/server, 9
interactive, 62
processing loop
Input Procedure, 292
Output Procedure, 296,
    298
Relative file, 278
transaction data, 324
processing loops, 156
COBOL sp2 panels, 442
creating, 159-163
Go To statement, 163, 170
Perform statement,
    160-161, 169
terminating, 445
Program-Id paragraph
(Identification Division),
23, 38
programming languages
A-0, 11
business needs, 8
Call statement, 426
files, 77
FLOW-MATIC, 11
object-oriented, 450
sentences, 82
structured, 12, 20
tutorials, 127
Programming Staff (Fujitsu
compiler), 30
programs
called, 410-415
Cancel statement, 422
collating sequence, 25

comment lines, 22, 105
compilers, 33-34, 181
directives, 29
division headers, 26-27,
    36-37
control breaks, 362
creating, 30-31
data
    entering, 32-33
    passing, 27, 410
    returning, 410
debugging, 37
designing, 338-339
Environment, 32
executing, 35-36
formats, 21
Fujitsu compilers, 16-19
line numbers, 22
linking, 34-35
menus, 410-411
naming, 421
object modules, 34
Procedure Division,
    418-420
recompiling, 37
recursion, 420, 449
reinitializing, 421
removing, 421
reserved words, 28
saving, 33
source code, 23
statements, 32
terminating, 29, 107
walk through, 346-363
Project method, 415
projects, subprograms, 416
push buttons, COBOL sp2
    panels, 434, 441

Q-R

Quote value (literals), 47

radians, 391
Random access, 270
    Alternate Key, 257
    control breaks, 347
    Dynamic access, 258
    File Status values, 244,
        256
    Indexed files, 234, 244,
        256-257, 272, 274,
        320-325
    Move statement, 256
    Read statement, 257-258,
        450
    records, 270
    Select statement, 256
    update procedures, 313,
        326
Random Intrinsic Function,
    397, 403-404
Range Intrinsic Function,
    394
ranges, dates, 377
Read statement, 221,
    223-224
    At End clause, 257
    clearing, 225
    COBOL sp2 panels,
        435-436
    Dynamic access, 264
    File Status values, 259
    Full-Name field, 237, 251
    Indexed files, 250-253,
        273, 450
    Invalid Key clause, 257
    master Indexed files,
        324-325

Next clause, 258
Output Procedure, 296
records, 254-258, 270, 314
Relative file, 279
reports, 351
Random access, 257
Sequential files, 222
transaction data, 318
see also retrieving
rearranging selection
    objects, 153
rebuilding subprogram pro-
    jects, 416
receiving fields, 58
recompiling programs, 37
Record Sequential
    opening, 284
    Line Sequential files, 210
    trailing spaces, 211
records
    accessing, 232, 283-284
    adding, 220, 230, 270
    counting, 298
    creating, 281
    deleting, 274, 280
    description, 213
    Dynamic Access, 250
    end-of-file, 219, 230, 270,
        280
    first, 351
    identifiers, 216, 329
    Indexed files, 232,
        250-253
    Input/Output Procedure,
        296, 299
    last, 351
    layout, 210, 293
    opening, 283
    Random access, 250

Read statement, 254-258, 270, 273, 314, 351
Relative file, 282
reports, 338
restricting, 292
retrieving, 220-221, 260, 270
Rewrite statement, 228, 271-272, 281
Sequential access, 210, 219, 250
size limitations, 228
Sort statement, 299, 339
storing, 219
terminating, 210
underlining, 341
updating, 271-273
variable-length, 228
writing in files, 270-271, 292
recursion, 420, 420, 449
Redefines clause, 195
boundary violations, 193
Initialize statement, 191
tables, 189-193
reducing source code, 142, 150, 152-153
reference modification, 103-104
arithmetic expressions, 104
elementary-level items, 104
fields, 103-104, 109
statements, 103
target fields, 112, 117
referencing
called programs, 418-420
elements, 189
index values, 200
Sequential files, 219

reinitializing programs, 421
rejecting transaction data, 314
Relative file, 129
accessing, 275-282, 284
creating, 277
Dynamic access, 279
field size, 275
opening, 284
positioning, 279
processing loop, 278
reading, 279
records, 283
adding, 280
creating, 281
deleting, 280
end-of-file, 282
Select statement, 275, 279
Sequential access, 275
storing, 275
Release statement, 292
Rem Intrinsic Function, 379, 392
removing programs, 421
Renames clause, 40
Replacing clause, 99
characters, 101-102
Initialize statement, 100
Report Section (Data Division), 26
reports
control break programs, 363-364
blank lines, 349
checking order, 356
layout, 344
dates, 337-338, 350-352
dealer totals, 359
Declaratives statement, 353

designing, 328-330, 338-339
detail records, 335-336
end-of-file, 353
File Status values, 335
first, 351
fonts, 338
formats, 354
grand totals, 360
headings, 335-337, 352, 362-363
hierarchy, 345
Initialize statement, 351
last, 351
layout, 328
master files, 347
maximum line count, 360-362
multiple records, 338
name formatting, 337
opening, 334-335
Output Procedure, 296
printing, 331-334
Random access, 347
requirements, 332-333
save fields, 339, 351
Sort statement, 339, 345-348, 353-354
String statement, 350
subtotals, 344-346, 357
syntax errors, 31
time, 337-338, 352
total lines, 350
transaction date, 358
underlining, 339
Write statement, 330-331
Required clause, 23, 64-65, 67, 78
reserved words, 28

resetting
  numeric fields, 119
  subtotal values, 346, 357
restricting records, 292
retrieving
  command-line arguments,
    96
  Indexed files, 233
  records, 220-221, 250, 260
  Sequential access, 250,
    270
  see also Read statement
returning data, 410
**Reverse Intrinsic Function,
400**
Reverse-Video clause, 66
Rewrite statement, 281
  File Status values, 225
  records, 228
  Sequential access, 225,
    271-272
Rounded phrase, 86
rounding, 89

S

save fields (reports)
  Initialize statement, 351
  subtotal values, 357
saving
  COBOL sp2 panels, 33,
    77, 436
  reports to files, 314, 339
  storage space, 44
scope terminators
  End-Compute, 89
  End-Evaluate, 144

End-If, 184
End-Read, 257
End-Return, 298
End-Search, 197
End-Unstring, 118
screens
  background/foreground
    toggle, 66
  brightening, 66
  clearing, 64, 265
  color, 64, 76
  definition, 79, 105
    Accept statement, 69-
      70
    alert sounds, 66
    blinking, 66
    cursor, 70
    erasing, 66
    fields, 76, 79
    literals, 63, 65-66, 79
    underlining, 66
  dimming, 66
  displaying, 69, 263, 265
  editor, 76
  input, 261
  user interface, 27, 65
**Screen Section (Data
Division), 26-27, 63, 70, 307**
  clauses, 65-66
  coding, 77-79
  cursor, 70
  data
    displaying, 63
    preserving, 63
    Justified Right clause,
      68
    screen literals, 65
  designing, 72
  example, 74-76

fields, 73, 78
literals, 63
multiple, 79
Special-Names, 71-72
statements
  accept, 63
  attributes, 64
  display, 63
SD (Sort Description), 286
Search All statement, 205
  And clause, 199
  binary search, 198
  When clause, 198-199
Search statement
  End-Search explicit scope
    terminator, 197
  Indexed By clause,
    195-198
  multidimensional, 200-203
  speed, 205
  tables, 205
  Varying clause, 197
**seconds, converting to con-
ventional date and time,
380**
**Section (Procedure
Division), 82**
**Section headers (Procedure
Division), 27-28**
  Declaratives, 245
  Go To statement, 163-169
  headers, 157-159
  Paragraph title, 157-158,
    169
  Perform statement, 157
Secure clause, 64-65, 67
Select statement
  Alternate Key, 234
  Assign clause, 212

COBOL sp2 panels, 441
Duplicate Key, 234
File Status clause, 212
Indexed files, 233-235,
    258
Optional clause, 229
Primary Key, 233
Random access, 256
Relative file, 275, 279
Sequential files, 211
storing, 234
selection objects/subjects
Evaluate statement, 143,
    145, 147
multiple, 147-148
Other clause, 148
executing, 148-149
multiple, 147-148
Other clause, 148
rearranging, 153
sentences, 82
sequence, 145
stacking, 146, 154
True, 145
When, 143
separating fields, 118-121
Sequential access, 234, 270
adding, 219-220
At End condition, 251
Close statement, 215
creating, 215-217
Depending On statement,
    228
delimiters, 211
errors, 216
end-of-file condition, 222
File Description (FD)
    statement, 213
File Status values,
    215-217, 219, 225

filenames, 216
I-O (Open in Input mode),
    214, 221
Indexed files, 234-239,
    247, 250, 283
Line Sequential, 210-211,
    225-230, 314-320
Occurs statement, 228
Open for
    Input/Output/Extend,
    214-215, 219, 225, 238
Read statement, 222, 237
Record Sequential, 210-
    211
records, 250-253, 270
    description, 213
    identifiers, 216
    referencing, 219
    retrieving, 220-221
    size limitations, 228
    storing, 219
    variable-length, 228
Relative file, 275, 284
Rewrite statement, 225,
    272
Select statement, 145, 211
Start statement, 254-256
tables, 211
update procedure, 313,
    326
Write statement, 210, 216-
    217
Set conditional statement,
136
conditions, 137
to false, 137
fields, 98-99
index values, 196

Sign clause, 64, 67
Sign Separate clause, 43
signed fields
subtract statement, 87
numeric, 43-44
Sin Intrinsic Function, 390-
391
single characters
converting, 103
Inspect statement, 108
sizing
data items, 190
fonts, 338
records in Sequential files,
    228
slash (/), 49, 51
software requirements
Fujitsu compiler, 13
Sort Description (SD), 286
Sort statement, 287
Ascending field, 290
control breaks, 345-348,
    353-354
data, 292
dates, 348-350
Descending field, 290
duplication, 300
executing, 301
files, 286-291
Giving clause, 287, 290
Indexed files, 290-292
Input/Output Procedure,
    287, 291, 293-299
records, 298, 339
restricting, 292
sequence, 299
speed, 295
Using clause, 287
Sort Work File, 346
deleting, 300
Fujitsu COBOL, 286

records, 299
sorting, 301
writing, 292
source code, 8, 118
  characters, 119
  delimiters, 118
  free-form, 23
  reducing, 142, 150, 152-153
  separating, 119, 121
  storing, 29-30
  subprograms, 424-425
Source-Computer paragraph (Configuration section), 24
sp2 program, 437-438
spaces
  delimiters, 114
  moving, 98
  source fields, 118
  using as delimiters, 120
Spaces value (literals), 47
special names in command lines, 108
Special-Names Paragraph, 25, 70, 162
  Accept statement, 97
  Crt Status, 71-72
  cursor, 70-71
  function keys, 70
  statements, 72
speed
  Sort statement, 295
  tables, 205
Sqrt Intrinsic Function, 392
square root of argument, 392
stacking selection objects, 146, 154

Standard-Deviation Intrinsic Function, 394
standards
  improvements, 449-450
  industry, 11-12
Start statement
  Alternate Key field, 255
  beginning-of-file, 255
  Dynamic access, 259, 264
  File Status values, 254
  Indexed files, 259, 264
  Invalid Key clause, 254
  Key fields, 265-266
  Search statement, 196
  Sequential access, 254-256
  String statement, 117
  Unstring statement operations, 120-121
statements
  add, 83-86, 93
  case sensitivity, 24
  complex, 132-135
  compute, 89-90, 93
  conditional, 126
  delimiters, 118
  divide, 88-89
  entering, 32
  executing, 128, 132, 145, 175
  fields, 87, 122
  format, 88-89, 143
  multiple, 87-88, 139
  phrases, 126
  reference modification, 103
  starting, 117, 120-121
  subtract, 86-87
  terminating, 84
  see also specific statements

static Call statement, 421-423, 426
statistical functions
  Max, 393
  Mean, 393
  Median, 394
  Midrange, 393
  Min, 393
  Ord-Max, 393
  Ord-Min, 393
  Range, 394
  Standard-Deviation, 394
  Sum, 394
  Variance, 394
Stop Run statement, 29, 166
  Perform statement, 159
  subprograms, 412
storing
  bytes, 44
  data items, 85
  Indexed files, 234
  numeric fields, 45
  records, 219
  Relative Key clause, 275
  source code, 29-30
string functions
  Char, 399
  Length, 398
  Lower-Case, 400
  Max, 399
  Min, 399
  Numval, 402
  Numval-C, 402
  Ord, 400
  Ord-Max, 399
  Ord-Min, 399
  Output-Field, 400
  Random, 397
  Revers, 400
  Upper-Case, 400

String statement
  clearing, 122
  control breaks, 350
  delimiters, 114-116
  space, 114
  fields, 115, 118-121
    multiple, 122
    group-level data items,
      112
    Pointer clause, 117
  formatting data, 117
  initializing, 113
  overflowing, 113-114
  reference modification,
    112, 117
  starting, 117
  target fields, 112
**structured programming,
  12, 20**
called programs, 410-415
subprograms, 410-414
  Call statement, 417
  Call By Reference,
    420-421
  date validation, 418-420
  editing, 412
  Exit Program statement,
    412
  Is Initial clause, 416
  Linkage Section, 418
  main programs, 415
  projects, 416
  source code, 424-425
  Stop Run statement, 412
subscripts, tables, 187
subtotals (reports)
  Add with Corresponding
    statement, 357
  control break programs,
    344-346, 351

  dealer, 345
  errors, 357
  grand, 345
  resetting values, 357
  save fields, 357
  transaction date totals, 345
subtract statement, 86-87
Sum Intrinsic Function, 394
symbolic filenames, 212
syntax errors, 38
  in compilers, 33
  reporting, 31

T

tables, 187
  assigning values, 189
  binary search, 198
  boundary violations, 193,
    204-205
  creating, 203-204
  data items, 191-192
  defining, 188
  editing, 196
  elements, 189, 195
  Group Level elementary
    items, 188
  incrementing, 197
  index values, 195-198, 200
  initializing, 197
  loading, 189-193, 195,
    211
  lookups, 193-195
  multidimensional, 200-204
  numeric data items, 189,
    195
  occurrences, 203
  Redefine clause, 191-192

  referencing, 200
  Search statement, 195-
    198, 200-203, 205
  speed, 205
  subscripts, 187, 189
  values, 399
  variable-length, 395, 399
**Tallying clause, 102, 119,
  123**
**Tangent Intrinsic Function,
  390-391**
target fields
  clearing, 122
  initializing, 113, 118
  overflowing, 113-114, 120
  reference modification,
    112, 117
terminating
  Accept, 70
  If conditional statements,
    128
  Line Sequential files, 210
  Perform statement, 169,
    172
  processing loops, 445
  programs, 29, 107
  records, 210
  statements, 84
  update procedures, 317
**TEST compiler option,
  debugging screen, 185**
testing
  conditions, 127, 136, 139
  Evaluate statement, 150
  numeric fields, 129
  Perform statement, 173
  values, 129-130
text display
  COBOL sp2
  Input, 235-237
  panels, 430

text mode user interface, 63
Then phrase, 129
Thru clause, 158
time
    converting from seconds,
        380
    current, 380
    GMT, 380-382
    headings, 352
    local, 380-382
    printing, 337-338
titles in COBOL sp2 panels,
    429, 441
To clause, 69-70, 79
total lines (control breaks),
    350
transaction data (reports)
    capturing, 306-309
    control break programs,
        345-348
    end-of-file field, 323
    errors, 309
    File Status values, 317,
        323
    keys, 314
    Open with Extend, 308
    printing, 358
    processing loop, 324
    reading, 318
    rejecting, 314
    saving, 314
    updating, 321
    validation, 310-313, 326
trigonometric functions
    Arccosine, 390-391
    Arcsin, 390-391
    Arctangent, 390-391
    Cosine, 390
    Sin, 390-391
    Tangent, 390-391

troubleshooting
    compilers, 36-37
    debugging screen, 185
    field length, 84
true conditions, 145
    Evaluate statement, 143-
        144
    executing, 128
    If statements, 126, 128
truncating, 68, 90-91
tutorials for programming
    courses, 127
two-digit dates, 368

U

unaligned numeric fields, 49
unconditional branch, 163
Underline clause, 67
    records, 341
    reports, 339
    screens, 66
unedited numeric fields, 48
unequal conditional state-
    ments, 128
UNIX
    compatibilty, 63
    Line Sequential files, 210
    user interface, 63
Unstring statement, 118,
    138
    Count In clause, 119-120
    Delimiter In clause, 118,
        120
    fields, 119, 123
    initializing, 118
    multiple, 119

name entries, 137-138
On Overflow clause, 120
Pointer clause, 123
positioning, 121
spaces, 118
source fields, 118
separating, 121
starting, 120-121
Tallying In clause, 123
target fields, 119-120
Until clause, 162, 172
update items, 70
update procedures
    I-O mode, 221
    Indexed files, 233, 283
    Line Sequential files,
        225-228
    master, 320-325
    Process-Files Paragraph,
        318
    Random, 313, 326
    records, 271-273
    Sequence, 313-320, 326
    terminating, 317
    transaction data, 321
    see also Write statement
Upon clause, 28
Upper-Case Intrinsic
    Function, 400
Usage clause, 44, 64, 67
    numeric fields, 44-46
    storage of bytes, 44
    values, 44-45
user interface
    add-on tools, 61
    ANSI COBOL standard,
        62
    compilers, 62
    Indexed files, 239-244

Screen_Section, 27, 63, 65
text mode, 63
see also GUI
Using clause, 70, 79, 287, 417
utilities, debugging, 181-183

V

Validate statement, 449
data subprograms, 416-417
dates, 376-382
days, 376
errors, 379
fields, 310, 312, 376
Fujitsu compiler installation, 15-19
integers, 377
leap years, 376, 378
months, 376
ranges, 377
records, 232
subprograms, 418-420
transaction data, 310-313, 326
Value clause
accept statement, 71-72
alphanumeric fields, 46
characters, 103
data items, 144-145
dates, 376
Evaluate statement, 141-143, 154
fields, 98-99, 376

greater than, 130
group-level items, 52
incrementing, 172-173
less than, 129-130
literals, 47-48
leading digits, 42
numeric fields, 42
ranges, 129, 136
subtotals, 346, 357
tables, 399
testing, 154
Usage clause, 44-45
variable-length records in Sequential files, 228, 399
creating, 203-204
multidimensional, 204
variables, 137
Variance Intrinsic Function, 394
Varying clause, 197
initializing values, 184
Perform statement, 172-173
verbs, *see* **statements**
versions of COBOL, 449
Visual Basic, 428
Visual C++, 428
VMS COBOL compiler, 71

W

walk through (programs), 346-363
Web sites, 429

weekdays, 374-375
When clause, 143, 145, 152-153
When-Compiled Intrinsic Function, 403-404
Windows 3.1
debugging utility, 181-182
Fujitsu compilers, 14-15, 17
Matchcase of Keyword check box, 32
With Test After clause, 173-174
Working Storage Section (Data Division), 26-27, 55
Read statement, 222
records, 219
tables, 189, 195
Write statement, 270-271
files, 270-271
buffers, 219
Status values, 219, 238
Indexed files errors, 244
Invalid Key errors, 244-245
opened I-O, 225
printers, 340
records
adding, 219
identifiers, 216
reports, 330-331
Sequential, 210, 216-217
Sort Work File, 292
see also **creating; updating**

X-Y-Z

Y2K (Year 2000), 368

zero (0)
    alphanumeric fields, 98
    division, 89
    insertion, 51
    moving, 98
    numeric fields, 49, 98
    suppression (Z), 49-50
Zeros value (literals), 47

What's on the CD-ROM

The companion CD-ROM contains all of the author's source code and samples from the book and many third-party software products.

Windows 3.1 and Windows NT 3.5.1 Installation Instructions

1. Insert the CD-ROM disc into your CD-ROM drive.
2. From File Manager or Program Manager, choose Run from the File menu.
3. Type `<drive>\README.TXT` and press Enter, where `<drive>` corresponds to the drive letter of your CD-ROM. For example, if your CD-ROM is drive D:, type `D:\README.TXT`, and press Enter.
4. The README.TXT file contains information concerning installing the author's source code and third-party programs.

Windows 95/98/NT4 Installation Instructions

1. Insert the CD-ROM disc into your CD-ROM drive.
2. From the Windows 95 desktop, double-click the My Computer icon.
3. Double-click the icon representing your CD-ROM drive.
4. Double-click the icon titled SETUP.EXE to run the installation program.

If Windows 95 is installed on your computer, and you have the AutoPlay feature enabled, the SETUP.EXE program starts automatically when you insert the disc into your CD-ROM drive.